Children's Chances

Children's Chances

How Countries Can Move from Surviving to Thriving

Jody Heymann

with Kristen McNeill

HARVARD UNIVERSITY PRESS

Cambridge, Massachusetts

London, England 2013

Library of Congress Cataloging-in-Publication Data
Heymann, Jody, 1959–
    Children's chances : how countries can move from
surviving to thriving / Jody Heymann, with Kristen McNeill.
        p.   cm.
    Includes bibliographical references and index.
    ISBN 978-0-674-06681-6 (alk. paper)
    1. Child welfare.   2. Children—Government policy.
    3. Children—Social conditions.   4. Children—Services for.
    I. McNeill, Kristen.   II. Title.
    HV713.H49   2013
    362.7—dc23   2012030829

To children and youth, and what they teach us;
To everyone who takes the time to engage with them
and the challenges and opportunities they face;
and
To our family members of every generation,
who continue to help us learn.

Contents

Maps and Tables

Tables

Abbreviations

CRPD   Convention on the Rights of Persons with Disabilities

DTP3   diphtheria-tetanus-pertussis vaccine

ECCE   early childhood care and education

GDP   gross domestic product

ILO   International Labour Organization

OECD   Organisation for Economic Co-operation and Development

PPP   purchasing power parity

UN   United Nations

UNESCO   United Nations Educational, Scientific and Cultural Organization

UNICEF   United Nations Children's Fund

WHO   World Health Organization

Chapter 1

Within Our Reach

If we were to care as much about the world's children as we care about our own, we would measure success not only by child mortality rates, primary-school enrollment, and the prevalence of hazardous child labor, but also by success in school, access to advanced education, comprehensive measures of physical health and development, and social and emotional well-being. For millions of the world's children, we are failing at the basics, well before children have a chance at anything close to opportunity. Too many children are dying before their fifth birthday, do not have enough to eat, are living without access to clean water, do not have the chance to go to school, or are doing hazardous work. These tend to be the maximum boundaries of the world's attention. But even more children fall ill with preventable diseases, do not have the chance to get the kind of education that would allow them to exit poverty, work for too many hours to be able to study, or experience discrimination that limits their options. We need to address both the most basic threats to children's lives and those that decimate opportunities. Part of what has kept the world from setting more than child survival and primary school as global goals have been doubts about what is realistic.

Transforming Children's Lives

Is significant change possible? The simple answer to this question is yes. When there has been sufficient commitment, substantial progress has been made in basic areas critical to children, although much remains to be done. The marked decline in infant and child mortality over the past four decades, a result of action taken around the world, is one example. In 1970, nearly 1 in 10 children died before reaching their first birthday—95 out of every 1,000—and 141 children per 1,000 died before their fifth birthday. By 2010, the number of deaths among children under age 1 had plummeted to 41 per 1,000 and among children under age 5 to 58 per 1,000.[1] These figures simultaneously illustrate the degree of success that is possible on problems that once seemed intractable and reveal the millions of avoidable deaths that still occur. Another example is literacy, the most basic outcome of education. In 1990, more than a quarter of youth aged 15 to 24 in the Arab States, a third in sub-Saharan Africa, and 40 percent in South and West Asia were illiterate. By 2008, these figures had changed dramatically: 87 percent of youth in the Arab States, 80 percent in South and West Asia, and over 70 percent in sub-Saharan Africa were able to read and write. In some regions, such as East Asia and Latin America, over 95 percent of youth are literate.[2] Although much more action on children's chances is necessary, the fact that we have been able to move so far in less than two decades is a reason for substantial optimism and holds lessons for us as we continue to target problems that are challenging but surmountable.

In general, we spend far more of our time considering the role of parents and other caregivers in children's lives than the role of public- and private-sector policy. Indeed, paying attention to parents makes sense: families raise children, not governments or corporations. Yet it is equally essential to care about the policies that frame what even the most loving families are able to provide for their children. The overwhelming majority of parents and caregivers are deeply committed to the quality of their children's lives. If that were enough, we would not see the inequalities we currently do in children's survival, health, education, labor, and other domains.

Countries shape children's chances and the inequalities they experience in important ways. When working parents are not able to earn enough to feed their children, they cannot spend money on fees to send them to school. When adults from a minority group face discrimination and are limited in the job opportunities they can access, they are not able to provide their children with everything that they need, and their children are likely to face this same discrimination at school or when they are receiving health care. When it comes to infant and child mortality, fewer children die as infants or toddlers in countries where births are attended by skilled personnel, where children are fully immunized, where households have access to clean piped water and sanitation facilities, and where girls are better educated.[3] In these areas and others, the steps taken by governments make a difference. When government investments in health care make pregnancy care and preventive pediatric care more affordable and accessible, more women receive care during childbirth and more children are immunized. When education is free, poverty puts fewer limits on all children's, and particularly girls', chance to attend school. When child labor is prohibited and the minimum wage is set high enough that working parents can support their families, children from the poorest families are more likely to go to school instead of work. When laws guarantee equal rights regardless of ethnicity, religion, gender, or disability, families have more tools with which to fight the barriers erected by discrimination.

The impact of national action on children's chances can be immense. The reduction of infant mortality in Chile is one example. In 1950, with an infant mortality rate of 136 per 1,000 live births, more than 1 in 10 newborn girls and boys in Chile died before they were a year old. Chile succeeded in cutting this rate nearly in half to 82 per 1,000 by 1970, and in half again between 1970 and 1980 to 33 per 1,000. By 2000, Chile had managed to ensure that over 90 percent of the children who would have died in 1950 were able to survive, with an infant mortality rate of 9 per 1,000, and vaccine-preventable deaths were nearly eliminated.[4] These improvements did not happen magically. Chile created a national health service to provide care to all children and families. Investments were made in primary care, preventive interventions like immunizations, and specialized care before and during childbirth. At the same time, public health measures that lowered the rate of infectious diseases were implemented, including active promotion of breastfeeding. These actions led to a massive drop in the odds that a child born in Chile would die young.[5]

Country action has also yielded dramatic results in other areas. Eliminating school fees in Malawi in the 1990s, for instance, led primary-school enrollment to jump from under 50 percent in 1991 to

99 percent in 1999. The number of girls and boys completing primary school increased, and the disparity between the proportion of girls and boys completing this level disappeared.[6] When school fees forced parents to choose which of their children would be sent to school, they had sent their sons; when the elimination of school fees made it affordable to educate all their children, they did so.

Child labor is an issue that can seem unsolvable, but Brazil's experience has shown that change is possible. Through the combination of a powerful legislative and constitutional framework on child labor regulation and compulsory education with a financial assistance program conditional on school attendance targeting working children in rural areas, the number of hours worked by children in the program was reduced, the amount of time spent in school increased substantially, academic success improved, and fewer children did hazardous work.[7] Brazil managed to more than halve the proportion of working children in the country, from 16 percent in 1992 to 7 percent in 2008.[8]

International commitment to national change can also make a difference. Children's right to education was recognized in some of the earliest UN agreements, but the emergence of the Education for All movement in 1990 supported major efforts by countries worldwide to universalize primary education by making it free, compulsory, and accessible.[9] As a result of these efforts, since 1990 the number of children attending primary school has climbed dramatically, as have rates of primary-school completion and secondary-school enrollment. As one would expect, far more children have been able to become literate.

The Power of Public Information

Tracking progress and pitfalls was an essential component of making change occur in each of these areas. This is not to say that measurement alone led to progress; the relationship is clearly more complex than that. But measurement matters for progress in a number of ways.

There is little doubt that publicly airing figures about the magnitude of a problem increases the pressure to do something about it. Invisible problems rarely get the attention and resources needed for change. Awareness raising about the extent of the problem and the viability of solutions is an important way for initiatives to gain momentum.

Accurate knowledge about an issue is also critical if we are to address it effectively. If we do not know how many children are out of school and whether school is available and affordable where they live, how can policies and programs even begin to give them a chance at education? Expanded immunization programs are responsible for averting tens of millions of cases of serious disease; key to planning and implementing these programs is knowledge of how many children have not been immunized and where they are located. The cliché "If you can't measure it, you can't manage it" may be an overstatement, but it is hard to name many large successes in either the public or the private sector, from infrastructure construction to the fight against AIDS, that did not rely on the tool of measuring the problem and the progress.

Is there a measurement problem when it comes to children's chances? The global community has begun to measure certain outcomes at a world level that are vitally important but represent only the barest minimum—whether children die, not whether they are spending too many of their early years sick; whether they have been vaccinated, but not whether they can access affordable health care; whether they en-roll in school, but not how often their teachers are in the classroom. The information available on children's outcomes is sparse, but even rarer and less systematic is information on what is being done to meet children's needs. There has been next to no readily comparable infor-mation on what laws, policies, and programs countries have in place to address each of the areas vital to children's healthy development: access to quality education, protection from child labor and early marriage, good health care, working conditions for adults that enable parents to care for their children, freedom from discrimination, and access to resources to meet basic family needs. In the absence of readily comparable information on countries, our ability to support national progress and to hold countries accountable has been limited.

This lack of information on policy solutions is particularly critical because it is easier to consider infant and child deaths, extreme pov-erty, child labor, child marriage, and other experiences that erode children's life chances to be inevitable when one cannot identify feasi-ble and effective approaches to address them. Information alone does not change power structures within or among countries, but it is easier for countries to claim that it is impossible to move forward when one cannot readily point to other countries in similar circumstances that have been able to make progress.

Children's Chances: Mapping Leaders and Laggards

The goal of *Children's Chances* is to demonstrate a way in which we might begin to measure what every country is doing to give all children a chance at healthy development and to begin to provide the tools and visibility needed to move forward. Before the World Policy Analysis Centre, whose data informs this book, began, there were few global maps of what rights children have in countries around the world, no images that rapidly told the story of educational policies on access and quality, no way to readily and reliably compare child labor or child marriage laws around the world. This book seeks to provide a global picture of where we stand in terms of policy tools that governments can use to make a difference in children's life chances.

In Chapters 2 through 8, we begin by reviewing relevant research evidence on what governments can do that makes a difference to children's outcomes; we include references for those who want to look more deeply into the methodology behind each study. When there are important debates about the best ways to frame policies, we raise them. We wish that there were global studies available on all the topics covered in this book. When we have been able to find global studies, we present them. We also give priority to evidence from studies that cover entire regions or a significant number of countries around the world. For many of the topics, neither global nor large multicountry studies were available. When this was the case, we sought relevant studies on countries from a range of geographic areas and economic conditions. To prevent readers from being overwhelmed by a lengthy list of quantitative findings from many countries and at the same time to ensure that readers who want more detail can access it, we have tried to balance summarizing findings in the text and in endnotes.

To the greatest extent possible, we focus on the issues and policies for which the evidence of their importance to children is substantial. From economics to education, from epidemiology to management, every discipline takes a different approach to evidence. In medicine, the gold standard for determining causality is a double-blind randomized clinical trial. Patients are asked to participate in a study and are randomly assigned to a group receiving a new drug or a placebo; neither the patient nor the researcher knows which group the patient is in. Outcomes are measured, and significant differences between the groups are considered the effects of the drug. But randomized clinical trials, with their strengths and limitations, can rarely be tried on national government policies. Countries will not agree to one country providing free education for students and another in similar economic circumstances being randomly selected to pay fees. Even within a country, communities would be up in arms if the decision about whether to make education free or health-care coverage comprehensive was made by a roll of the dice. So, in studies to see which social policies work, different approaches are usually taken. Some studies examine the impact of changing policies over time—for example, how do children's outcomes differ in the decade before and after education was made free? Although these before-and-after designs are highly suggestive of impact, it can be hard to control for other factors that could have affected observed changes. Other studies use multivariate analysis to control for national economic conditions, family income, and other social and political conditions to try to isolate the effects of the policy itself on child outcomes. Multilevel models allow researchers to separate the effect of the circumstances in which a child may live—his or her individual, family, and community characteristics—from the public policy. Each of these tools brings different strengths and limitations.

After a chapter reviews the research evidence for policies, we go on to present original findings on what countries around the world are doing in the particular policy area. The book maps evidence from our global study of where countries stand in terms of laws and policies critical to ensuring an equal start for all children. For example, which countries provide tuition-free primary and secondary education? Where is full-time child labor prohibited? In which nations are children and youth protected against hazardous work? How do different constitutions protect against discrimination? Each chapter concludes with recommendations on how countries can move forward and make progress on the issues discussed.

The majority of the book is dedicated to looking at policy areas central to the lives of all children. The first chapters examine laws and policies that shape what children and youth do in their daily lives.

Chapter 2 looks in detail at education policy—many would argue that learning is the central task of childhood. Chapter 3 examines the laws regulating child labor and child marriage, which shape whether children and youth have a chance at a childhood free of adult responsibilities. The following two chapters examine policies that color the nature of children's daily lives. Chapter 4 examines what countries can do to prevent illness and injury, as well as to limit the consequences when they occur. Chapter 5 looks at how workplace policies affect the ability of parents to meet their children's health and developmental needs.

The following two chapters examine policies that determine whether all children have equal chances across class, gender, ethnicity, and religion. Chapter 6 examines policies that shape the likelihood that children will be raised in poverty and that families will fall into poverty from the middle class. Because poverty shapes children's educational chances, health, and likelihood of laboring and marrying young, as well as the likelihood that parents can spend time with them, the chapter takes a comprehensive look at what countries are doing to address it. Likewise, preventing discrimination and ensuring equal treatment have profound effects on children's education, health, and quality of life during childhood through their effects on both children and their parents. Chapter 7 examines constitutional guarantees of equity across gender, race, ethnicity, and religion.

Chapter 8 examines a question that cuts across all the policy areas of Chapters 2 through 7: what is required to ensure that children with disabilities have an equal chance at healthy development and a life free of poverty and discrimination? Children with disabilities are one of the groups that across social class and country borders we have failed most frequently in the past, but for whom the world may be on the verge of transformational change.

Chapter 9 concludes the book with strategic and concrete steps needed to move forward on making equal chances for children a reality. It examines what policymakers, interested citizens, organizations, the private sector, and researchers can do to effect change in key areas.

This book is broad in scope. We believe that its breadth matters both to people concerned with children's outcomes across spheres and to people focused on individual fields. People primarily interested in children's education recognize that it is not enough to focus only on

tuition, textbooks, and teachers; a child's chance of attending and succeeding in school is affected by whether his parents can earn enough
income to get by without the child's earnings in the labor market,
whether she is well fed enough to be able to concentrate in class, whether
he faces discrimination from teachers and peers, and whether her parents can be available to help with homework and meet with teachers.
The book addresses how social policy across these diverse areas lays
the foundation for education. For those interested in children's health,
medical services do not tell the whole story—health is deeply affected
by whether children are involved in hazardous work, whether they
marry at a young age, and whether they experience discrimination in
their daily lives. This book examines the wide range of social policy
areas shaping children's healthy development and adult lives. It will
not answer all questions, but we hope that it is an important first step
in a new direction.

When we were selecting the policy data that we would present in
this book, there was inevitable interaction between what we would
have liked to examine and what data were available. We worked hard
to ensure that our priorities were set by children's needs, not merely by
ease of data acquisition. However, the dearth of globally comparable
data in some fields has meant that there are topics we have not yet
been able to address. It is important to know where children have
universal access to health care, but at the time we began this work,
these data were simply not available. Likewise, it is important to examine laws protecting children from violence. We were unable to find
systematic global sources of comparable data on this topic. Telling
the whole story of policies around the world that matter to children
will necessarily be an iterative process. Our goal here is to begin to
tell the story—to move the issues forward by providing substantially
more information than was previously available. Our hope is that others will join us in ensuring that remaining key information gaps get
filled.

The selection of the topics discussed in this book has a strong
foundation in global agreements. All are contained in the United
Nations' Convention on the Rights of the Child, ratified by every country except the United States and Somalia. These areas have also been
recognized and widely accepted for decades through other key agreements from international bodies. However, at a global level, there is no

government, little governance, and next to no enforcement mechanism for commitments like the Convention on the Rights of the Child. For any international agreements to have substantial impact on the daily lives of people around the world, nations must take action within their borders.

One of the central goals of *Children's Chances* is to demonstrate an approach that would facilitate far greater accountability for these national actions or lack thereof. We examined what all countries around the world are doing on behalf of children so that this information can be easily accessible to citizens, whether with a click of a computer mouse or in brief print, radio, video, or other formats. Citizens can now find out what their country's policies and laws are doing for children and families and how they compare with other countries around the world, in their own region, or in similar economic situations. Key facts that would otherwise take thousands of hours to learn become knowable in seconds and minutes. What has the potential to be transformative is not our discussion of the literature on these agreed-on areas, but rather the potential for countries to readily be held publicly and visibly accountable for whether they are taking steps to make their commitments real in practice.

A Global Policy Center at Its Foundation

All the original findings in this book come from the World Policy Analysis Centre, a global data initiative that I have been extraordinarily fortunate to develop together with an exceptional team of committed researchers. Its goal is to facilitate the spread of knowledge about what countries around the world are doing to improve social and economic conditions, to make it easier for nations to learn what is feasible and effective from other countries, and to make it more practical for citizens to hold their own countries accountable. We have examined thousands of aspects of public policy in 193 countries. Throughout this book, I will speak about our work and what we have done together. The plural is used to credit how many people's talents and efforts went into every aspect of this book and the data behind it, not to infer a single viewpoint. One of the richest parts of this experience has been debating and analyzing what we are learning from a wide variety of experiences and perspectives.

This initiative began when we went looking for data that we assumed already existed. You could say that the research initiative that this book draws on began in a closet—UNESCO's closet. Over a decade ago, colleagues and I wanted to know where around the world early childhood care and education programs were provided. There was no simple online way to find out, no easily accessible global report on the topic at that time. However, UNESCO received regular reports from nations around the world reporting on the state of their education system and invited us to Paris to examine them. When a member of my research staff arrived, he found stacks of cardboard boxes full of paper reports stowed away. The UNESCO staff that greeted him were welcoming, committed to education around the world, and eager to share the information. However, there was clearly no way in which this wealth of information could be widely used in its then-existing form.

UNESCO was not alone. We also wanted to know what labor protections were available to allow families to support the healthy development of their children. We contacted the International Labour Organization (ILO) about whether it had a straightforward way to answer questions like the following: How many countries in the world provide paid paternity leave and for how long? Where do parents have the right to take leave from work to care for their sick children without losing their jobs? We were referred to NATLEX, an online database of legislation. The ILO had collected labor, social security, and other legislation from countries around the world and had produced a tremendous resource of original legislation in the country's own language or in translation. But as valuable as NATLEX was, it did not facilitate ready comparisons of laws and policies across countries. Labor codes and other laws are lengthy; for the average person to find out what countries around the world were doing would require thousands of hours of heavy reading in multiple languages, as well as making in-depth comparisons across countries.

Out of these closets packed full of information—a physical one with paper reports and an online one with legislation—the World Policy Analysis Centre was born, and it grew as we sought to systematically analyze global progress in a wide range of social policy areas for which we learned that this had not been done. We undertook to find out what countries around the world were doing in terms of law and policy to improve the conditions under which children and adults studied, worked, and lived and to make this information readily accessible, visible, and comparable. I assembled a team with fluency in the official UN languages, as well as additional languages as needed, to systematically analyze legislation, constitutions, policies, and programs from every country.

After a decade of work, the World Policy Analysis Centre includes, among others, the Education Database, the Poverty Database, the Child Labour Database, the Child Marriage Database, the Adult Labour Database, and the Constitutions Database. Each of these has yielded information critical to this book and to the assessment of children's chances worldwide; for additional information on each database, see Appendix 1. The World Policy Analysis Centre focuses on national laws and policies. Clearly in federal systems, being able to examine all state and provincial policies makes an enormous difference. Ultimately, we hope that individual country initiatives will also examine what subnational governments do. As a first step, we examine what every person in a country is guaranteed on a national level.

While it also includes information on policies, much of the World Policy Analysis Centre deals with laws. There are several reasons for this. In countries with effective governance, national laws are the best long-term guarantees of protections, supports, and rights that can less rapidly be removed when a new government takes office. Legal guarantees allow children and families to claim their rights when they are not enforced. At the same time, reasonable questions can be raised about enforcement. Over the course of this initiative, we have been asked whether laws really make a difference in many settings. While we recognize the limitations of legal protections and the importance of the factors that affect whether they are enforced, we believe that legal guarantees do have a profound impact on what nations do and on the ability of citizens to advocate effectively for improvements.

Laws regulating tangible conditions can have profound impacts under a wide range of national conditions. An examination of nations' experiences provides insight into how laws with a clear intent to support children and families can make a difference even when they are imperfectly implemented (as is the case for many countries). The Mexican Institute of Social Security guarantees both paid leave and access to formal child care for the private-sector workers whom it covers.[10] Our study of working parents in two cities in Mexico showed that despite the fact that the implementation of these policies was not complete, they did have an impact: while 75 percent of formal-sector workers were able to take paid leave when necessary, less than a quarter of parents working in the informal economy had any access to paid leave.[11] Beyond the direct impact of laws, legal protections are tools that citizens can use to realize their rights, improve service delivery, and protect children from abuses. When children have legal rights, it greatly strengthens the hand of individual citizens, families, and organizations working for change, because these legal rights can be used to challenge actions harmful to children. For example, Nepal's Labour Act precluded children under the age of 16 from working in hazardous settings and children under 14 from working at all. At the same time, the Nepalese army permitted the recruitment of children aged 15 to 18, and the police force permitted boys to be hired as young as 13. Although the government argued that recruited boys were used as tea boys and cooks, these children were nevertheless required to take an oath stating that they would lay down their lives should the need arise, and they were not permitted to leave until the age of retirement (50). In a David and Goliath matchup, a Nepalese nongovernmental organization went to court to challenge these recruitment policies on the grounds that they contravened the country's child labor laws, as well as international conventions. The Supreme Court ruled against the government, and both regulations were overturned.[12] These examples do not change the fact that implementation of laws is key, and that issues like corruption and the nature of the judiciary have a strong impact on their effectiveness. However, these and other examples repeatedly demonstrate the impact that laws and constitutions can have under a wide range of conditions.

While we have worked hard to ensure that our databases are as comprehensive, accurate, and up to date as possible, errors are nearly inevitable. New legislative amendments may not be made available online promptly; any errors or omissions in national reports would also be reflected in our data. Finally, even if preventive measures are taken, errors can be made by the research team. These challenges are common in any data-collection effort. They do not negate the importance of undertaking these efforts but rather point to the value of an iterative process through which findings are continually reviewed and updated. Much research and discovery—as well as many business processes—have relied on an iterative process through which results become increasingly accurate (in the case of research) and the quality of the product markedly improves (in the case of business). It is easy to see that our databases too would benefit from a similar method.

We imagine that the steps taken by the World Policy Analysis Centre will be just the beginning of this iterative process in several respects. As we hear from experts around the world with additional information on laws and policies, we look forward to updating our databases with new and more complete information. Additionally, our data currently focus on legal rights and national policies. We hope that future efforts will also include findings on the extent to which they are implemented. This will require resources we did not have for the first iteration, but there are many ways this could be feasible for a range of actors moving forward.

Over the course of this project, we have often been asked why this information has not been made available before. There may be many reasons; one is certainly the amount of work required. The sheer quantity of information that needs to be searched for and reviewed is enormous and requires fluency in a series of UN and other languages. Countries take quite varied approaches to drafting policies and laws governing hazardous child labor, teacher-training requirements, and each of the policy areas treated in the databases. Substantial time and thought are required to create a policy analysis framework that works for any given policy area across 193 countries. As just one example, it appears at first glance that minimum wage could be captured by a yes–no answer about whether it has been established and a currency figure to show the level. But there is an enormous amount of salient variation across countries in everything from how the minimum wage is set to who is covered and exempted and how increases in the wage level are determined.

The magnitude and challenges of this type of initiative may in part explain why it has not been undertaken before, but so too may the transparency and power of the results. When countries' choices are buried in thousands of pages of text, few will sort through them, and countries that have failed to support their children have little to fear in terms of public scrutiny. When single maps can capture and highlight which countries provide strong support for children's development and which are failing to do so, the likelihood that pressure will be placed on the laggards is far greater.

This book is a call for action. It acknowledges the questions and unknowns that still remain, but focuses on the many areas where we do know what works and what needs to be done. This book is intended to increase the knowledge that we have available, to highlight areas where we need to know more, but most important, to inspire action to make equal chances for children around the world a reality.

Chapter 2

Beyond Basic Education

Crista Robles lived with her parents and six siblings in San Cristóbal, Mexico. Her father was a bricklayer, and her mother made and sold tortillas; their earnings were barely enough to meet the needs of their children. From a young age, Crista was working any time she was not in school to supplement the family's income. When she got home from school, instead of studying, she would get to work making tortillas to sell. After Crista completed the fifth grade, she dropped out of school. Her parents could no longer afford to send her. She explained, "Because my parents were poor, they couldn't give us our studies. So I just studied till [fifth grade], and then I stopped . . . and that was it." Her description of her feelings about being pulled out of school was to the point: she felt "sad, because I wanted to keep studying, but my parents couldn't afford it." From that time onward, Crista worked full-time.

Crista grew up and got married. At age 25, she and her husband had their first child, a girl named Sofía. She stopped working to take care of the baby; she and her husband had nowhere to leave the child if she were to go to work. Four years later, they had another daughter. Crista's husband was a mechanic; he worked 12-hour days 6 days a week and made 1,000 pesos per month, about US$165 at the time of the interview.[1]

Shortly after their second daughter was born, it became clear that Crista's husband's earnings were not sufficient; to give her elder daughter, Sofia, a chance to go to school, Crista went back to work. "I told her, 'Look, I'm going to work. I'll help you.'" She was well aware of the importance of education for her children, and of the restrictions her own lack of education placed on her life. Crista took a job as a domestic servant, despite health problems that sometimes made her work painful, "because that's all I know how to do. Like I said, my father couldn't send me to school so I never learned how to get ahead. And to work in a store you need to have studied more than I had. I went to fifth year of primary school but that isn't good for anything but working as a servant." Working close to 40 hours per week, she made 400 pesos per month.

Sofia wanted to stay in school, but she was struggling. At age 10, she had already failed a year and was often kept late in the classroom. Her teacher frequently wanted to meet with her parents about her progress, but coming in during the day to meet with the teacher would mean missing work and losing income that was needed to keep Sofia and her sister in school. Although both parents were committed to her education, they had completed little education themselves and so could do little to help her with her homework. Moreover, when someone was needed to care for her 2-year-old brother, either Sofia or her sister was kept home from school for the day.[2]

The question is, can we do enough for children like Sofia? Can we ensure that all children are enrolled in school irrespective of family income? Can we provide a high-enough quality of education to ensure that all children learn even if their parents cannot teach them academic material?

Although significant progress has been made in getting children enrolled in school over the past decade, the shortfall remains staggering. Seventy-two million primary-school-age children around the world are not in school; 31 million of these children are unlikely ever to enroll.[3] Beyond basic education, the gaps are even greater, in spite of the fact that the global economy is a skills-based one where adults need more than a primary education in order to have any real chance at exiting poverty. In 32 countries, fewer than three-quarters of students make the transition from primary to secondary school, and in countries such as Burundi, Cameroon, the Central African Republic, Niger, and Suriname, less than 50 percent of students do so. Overall, gross enrollment in secondary education is 89 percent in Latin America and the Caribbean, 88 percent in Central and Eastern Europe, 78 percent in East Asia and the Pacific, 65 percent in the Arab States, 52 percent in South and West Asia, and just 34 percent in sub-Saharan Africa.[4]

Both boys and girls from poor families face particular disadvantages when it comes to their education. In 30 countries accounting for over 30 million of the world's out-of-school children, children from the poorest fifth of households are four times more likely to be out of school than children from the richest families.[5] In India, more than three times as many children in the poorest quintile are out of school as those in the richest quintile.[6] In Pakistan, 49 percent of the poorest children and just 5 percent of the richest are not in school.[7] In Burkina Faso, children from the most affluent fifth of households are ten times more likely to complete primary school than children from the poorest fifth.[8] These disparities also exist in high-income countries. In the United States, secondary-school-age children from low-income households are three times more likely to be out of school than children from wealthier families (17 percent versus 5 percent).[9] In Canada, half of children from poor families end their schooling at high school compared with a quarter of those from affluent families.[10]

As a girl from a poor family, Sofia's odds of attending school were doubly disadvantaged. The recent global commitment to giving both boys and girls an equal chance at education has been effective to some extent, but gender-based disparities in education nonetheless continue to affect millions of children. Globally, 96 girls are enrolled in primary school for every 100 boys; if gender parity in school enrollment were achieved, 6 million more girls would be in school.[11] Inequalities are greatest in sub-Saharan Africa and the Arab states, where 90 girls per 100 boys are enrolled in primary school. Fewer than 75 girls per 100 boys are enrolled in primary school in some of these nations, such as Afghanistan, the Central African Republic, Chad, and Yemen. Moreover, girls who are not in school are less likely than out-of-school boys ever to enroll. In Yemen, for example, while 64 percent of boys currently out of school are expected to enroll at some point in their childhood, just 20 percent of out-of-school girls are expected to do so; in Pakistan, 73 percent of boys and 38 percent of girls currently out of school are expected to enroll.[12]

In secondary school, gender parity has also not yet been achieved in most regions; disparities still exist in the Arab states, Central and Eastern Europe, Central Asia, South and West Asia, and sub-Saharan Africa.[13] In addition to enrollment gaps, girls face barriers to continuing and completing secondary education. In Bangladesh, for example, although girls tend to enroll initially in secondary school at rates equal to those for boys, they are five times more likely to drop out before age 16.[14]

While in a number of nations the percentage of women at university surpasses that of men, female disadvantage persists in the regions where girls lag behind boys substantially in primary and secondary school. In sub-Saharan Africa, only 66 women attend university for every 100 men, and in South and West Asia, 77 women attend per 100 men.[15] While statistics show that more women than men are enrolled in tertiary education in the Arab states, this is largely because in many countries in the region, daughters are usually kept in schools close to home if they are sent to university, whereas sons are commonly sent to study abroad.[16] Additionally, although gender parity in tertiary education has largely been achieved in North America and Europe, women are still overrepresented in fields that lead to lower-paying jobs and underrepresented in fields leading to higher-paying jobs.[17]

A Right to Education

Children's right to education has been recognized at an international level for decades in documents such as the Universal Declaration of Human Rights (1948), accepted by all UN member states; the International Covenant on Economic, Social and Cultural Rights (1966), ratified by 160 countries; and the Convention on the Rights of the Child (1989), ratified by all but two UN member states.[18] The right to education free from discrimination has also been recognized in documents such as the Convention against Discrimination in Education (1960), the International Convention on the Elimination of All Forms of Racial Discrimination (1965), the Convention on the Elimination of All Forms of Discrimination against Women (1979), and the Convention on the Rights of Persons with Disabilities (2006).

The right to education is firmly rooted in treaties at the international level, but which countries guarantee all children the right to education? For which countries is this right so fundamental that it is included in their constitution? In order to answer this question, we systematically analyzed all constitutional texts and amendments from 191 countries to create a comparative database on what kinds of educational rights, protections, and guarantees are contained in constitutions around the world; for details on this and other databases discussed in this chapter, see Appendix 1.

Around the world, the constitutions of 109 countries specifically guarantee the right to primary education to their citizens. In 60 of these 109 countries, citizens are guaranteed free and compulsory primary education, and in an additional 46, they are guaranteed either free or compulsory primary education (see Map 2.1). In some cases, this right is discussed in the constitution but is expressed in aspirational rather than categorical terms: the nation will endeavor to provide this right or intends to do so, but the constitution does not use language strong enough to be considered a guarantee. Twelve countries include an aspirational right to primary education.[19]

Fewer countries guarantee secondary and higher levels of education to their citizens (see Map 2.2). In 120 countries, the right to secondary education is not explicitly guaranteed in the constitution in either categorical or aspirational terms, and 124 do not guarantee or aspire to the right to higher education. Some countries discuss a general right to education—124 countries guarantee a right to education without specifying the level.*

These guarantees are strongly linked to the date when the constitution was originally passed; few have been amended to guarantee education. Universal primary education spread throughout Western Europe and North America in the nineteenth century, while public availability of university education did not become widespread until the second half of the twentieth century. As a result, constitutions in these regions, which tend to be among the earliest written, are far more likely to guarantee only primary education or an unspecified amount of education, whereas more recent constitutions have increasingly discussed higher levels of education. Two-thirds of the constitutions written before 1960 include either general or primary education;

---

*World Policy Analysis Centre, Constitutions Database. Number of countries for which we have data: 191 (rights in education).

Map 2.1. Do citizens have a general right to education or a specific right to primary education?

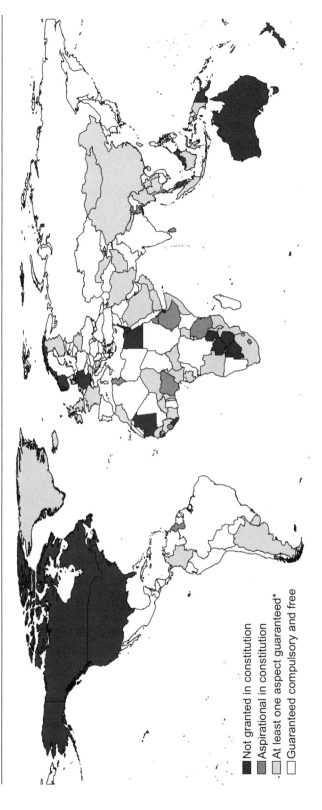

- ■ Not granted in constitution
- ▨ Aspirational in constitution
- ▧ At least one aspect guaranteed*
- □ Guaranteed compulsory and free

At least one aspect guaranteed includes cases where a general right to education or primary education is guaranteed, as well as when education is guaranteed to be either free or compulsory.

Source: World Policy Analysis Centre, Constitutions Database

Map 2.2. Do citizens have a specific right to secondary education?

- ■ Not granted in constitution
- ■ Aspirational in constitution
- ▨ At least one aspect guaranteed*
- □ Guaranteed compulsory and free

*At least one aspect guaranteed includes cases where a general right to secondary education is guaranteed, as well as when secondary education is guaranteed to be either free or compulsory.

Source: *World Policy Analysis Centre, Constitutions Database*

all but one constitution written since 2000 include a guaranteed or aspirational right to education at this level. Among those constitutions written before 1960, 4 out of 5 do not mention secondary or higher education. There was a gradual shift in the prevalence of these rights, so that among constitutions written since 2000, almost half have addressed secondary education, and nearly 40 percent have either aspired to or guaranteed higher education.

Some constitutions address the greater barriers faced by low-income children by promising to provide them with financial or other additional resources—the constitutions of 11 countries contain provisions for this type of support. For example, the Philippines commits to supporting the education of underprivileged children by "establish[ing] and maintain[ing] a system of scholarship grants, student loan programs, subsidies, and other incentives," while Greece promises that "the State shall provide financial assistance to those who distinguish themselves, as well as to students in need of assistance or special protection, in accordance with their abilities." Some countries promise a broader range of support for low-income students. Paraguay's constitution states that the country "will implement programs to provide nutritional supplements and school supplies to low-income students [and] will provide for the allocation of funds for scholarships and other types of aid." In Bolivia, the constitution promises to provide economically disadvantaged students with "economic resources, meal programs, clothing, transportation, school materials, and student residences." An additional 2 countries, Serbia and Peru, support the education of low-income children by providing them with access to free tertiary education. Peru's constitution, for example, states that "in State universities, the government guarantees free education to those students who maintain an adequate standard but lack the economic means to defray the cost of education." Beyond the 11 countries providing financial support to low-income children, 9 countries discuss educational access for the poor without specifying financial support.

Additional provisions are made in some constitutions for groups speaking a different language from the majority of students. In 36 countries, education in an alternative language for at least some linguistic minority groups is guaranteed, including 18 countries in Europe and Central Asia, 10 in the Americas, 3 in each of South Asia and sub-Saharan Africa, and 1 in each of East Asia and the Pacific and the Middle East and North Africa.

This type of guarantee can be formulated in different ways; some constitutions contain more than one formulation. In 5 countries, everyone is guaranteed education in one of the country's official languages, or in one of a given selection of languages.[20] Nine countries guarantee education to all in the language of their choosing.[21] Interestingly, guarantees of education to indigenous peoples in an indigenous language appear in the constitutions of only 7 countries, all located in Latin America.[22] The most common type of guarantee, present in the constitutions of 19 countries, is of education for national or linguistic minorities in their own language.[23]

Taking a closer look at constitutional text, it is important to recognize that these guarantees of the right to education in a particular language are not equivalent to guarantees that the State will provide this education. For example, Estonia's constitution guarantees that "the state and local governments shall maintain the requisite number of educational institutions. Other educational institutions, including private schools, may also be established and maintained pursuant to law. . . . Everyone has the right to receive instruction in Estonian. The language of instruction in national minority educational institutions shall be chosen by the educational institution."

Making Schooling Free

A constitutionally guaranteed right to education can be used as a tool by citizens to hold their governments accountable for providing educational opportunities. At the same time, simply having a right in place does not automatically guarantee its realization. Indeed, the constitutions of a number of the countries that are performing poorly on education indicators do guarantee a right to education. Government policies beyond constitutional rights can make a big difference in determining whether children have access to good-quality schools in practice.

Ndalama was leading a teachers' association in Malawi and believed in the power of free education to give all children, but particularly girls, an equal chance at attending school. He explained the commonly held belief that "girls are not as economically viable as boys, so they are not worth the investment." As a result, parents were less willing to pay for their daughters to attend.[24] School fees were abolished in Malawi in 1994, and this led to a dramatic increase in primary-school enrollment. While the net enrollment rate in primary education was less than 50 percent in 1991, meaning that less than half of primary-school-age children went to school, it grew rapidly to 99 percent by 1999.[25] Although this inevitably brought challenges with regard to adequate supplies of teachers, classrooms, and textbooks, enormous improvements in outcomes were made both overall and in terms of gender equality. In 1991, 36 percent of boys and 21 percent of girls completed primary school, but 55 percent of both boys and girls completed primary school by 2006.[26]

Eliminating tuition fees has been promoted internationally as one of the most important policies for making access to education universal. At the same time, however, it has been argued that tuition fees are not what is keeping children out of school. In some countries where primary schooling is nominally free, low-income families still cite insufficient financial resources as the reason that their children are out of school.[27] Even if there is no tuition, fees may be charged for school necessities like textbooks or uniforms; in addition, indirect costs for transportation and food can be substantial and may be prohibitive for the poorest families. In Sierra Leone, the cost of uniforms doubles the cost of attending school.[28] In Bangladesh, the average slum-dwelling household spends 10 percent of its income on education per child in school including both tuition and non-tuition costs, and among the poorest fifth of families, the figure approaches 20 percent.[29] Beyond the money that families must pay to send their children to school, the opportunity costs of education can be significant enough to keep children out of school. When children are in class, they cannot be earning income to supplement their family's resources, performing household chores such as collecting water or firewood, or caring for younger siblings. In some settings, families may simply not value formal education; if schooling is of poor quality, if what is taught is not relevant or useful to children or their families, or if job opportunities are scarce with or without a diploma, sending a child to school may not be seen as an optimal investment of their time. To the extent that tuition fees are not what is keeping children out of school, making schooling free will not be effective.

What is the empiric evidence? When school fees are eliminated, the impact on the number of children able to attend school can be immense, as was the case in Malawi. Burundi eliminated school fees in 2006, and primary school enrollment skyrocketed. While in 2005 the gross enrollment ratio in primary education was 88, in 2006 it jumped to 107, and in 2010 this figure further increased to 155. Net enrollment, which takes into account only children of primary-school-going age and not older children who are enrolled, immediately increased from 63 percent in 2005 to 81 percent in 2006 and 90 percent one year later.[30] These dramatic results can be explained by the vastly greater accessibility of primary education in the absence of tuition. Shortly after the abolition of school fees, over 40 percent of the poorest families sending their children to school reported that if these fees had not been eliminated, some of their children would not be enrolled, consistent with pre-2006 estimates that one-third of the poorest children were out of school because their families could not afford to pay the costs of education.[31]

Uganda provides another striking example. In 1997, the country sought to eliminate primary-school fees for up to four children in every household, at least two of whom had to be girls. At the same time, a media campaign was launched to encourage girls' school attendance and discourage early marriage. Disparities in attendance between the richest and poorest children decreased, as did gender-based differences. In 1992, when school fees existed, only 46 percent of children aged 6 to 12 years in the poorest income quintile attended primary school, compared with 82 percent of children in the richest quintile; by 1999, 75 percent of the poorest children and 89 percent of the wealthiest attended school. The gap between girls and boys also narrowed, especially among children in the lowest income quintile: in 1992, 40 percent of girls and 51 percent of boys in the poorest families attended primary school, compared with 74 percent and 77 percent, respectively, in 1999.[32]

The converse is also true—introducing or increasing fees tends to reduce school enrollment. One of the most costly examples of this occurred in the 1980s, when World Bank structural adjustment programs pressed for greater household financing for education and other public services in much of the world, leading to a rise in tuition costs and other expenses such as textbooks and uniforms.[33] Education fees, alone or combined with the fees introduced for other public services, began to severely hinder low-income families from educating their children. For example, in one Nigerian state, enrollment in primary school dropped to 60 percent in 1984 from the 90 percent it had been just before fees were instated less than two years previously. In Viet Nam, 1 year of primary education cost families in the lowest income quintile a quarter of their income in the 1980s. The results of studies showing the detrimental impact of user fees on access to education gradually fueled a global movement to eradicate fees for education, at least at the primary level.[34]

Although tuition is certainly not the only barrier to schooling, it is an important one. With this in mind, we investigated how many countries have taken steps to make all levels of schooling financially accessible to children by eliminating tuition fees. To do so, we primarily reviewed the wealth of qualitative information available in reports produced by and submitted to UNESCO's International Bureau of Education to create a database of systematic and easily comparable information on education policy around the world. These reports draw on national governments' reports to the UN. Although country reports may overestimate the extent of educational access because nations may seek to make their conditions look more favorable, these findings still document serious barriers to secondary and higher education.

In terms of affordability, the world has made the greatest strides at the primary-school level. Primary education is tuition-free in 166 of the 174 countries around the world for which we have data. Just 8 countries are reported to charge tuition fees for primary education: Comoros, Fiji, Guinea, Papua New Guinea, Samoa, South Africa, Zambia, and Zimbabwe.*

For secondary education, a minimum requirement for most jobs that provide a decent income, the situation starts to deteriorate. Students can begin secondary school tuition-free in 142 countries (Map 2.3); in 120 countries, students can complete secondary school without

---

*World Policy Analysis Centre, Education Database. Number of countries for which we have data: 174 (tuition in primary education).

Map 2.3. Is beginning secondary education tuition-free?

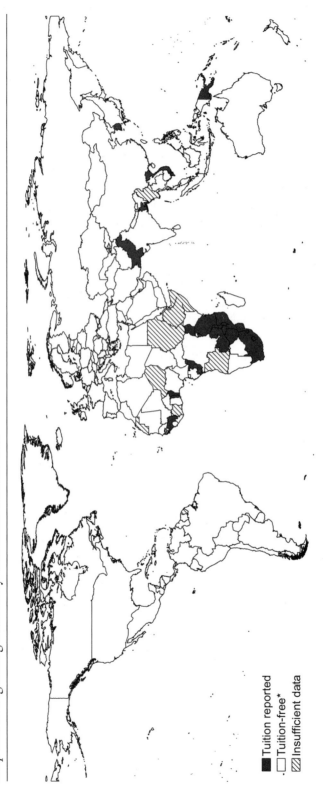

■ Tuition reported
□ Tuition-free*
▨ Insufficient data

*Tuition-free includes cases where no tuition is charged, but there may be other fees. Adequate information for systematic assessment of other fees is not available.

Source: World Policy Analysis Centre, Education Database

paying tuition (Map 2.4). The majority of countries stating that they charge tuition at this level (23 at the beginning of secondary school and 38 by the end) are low-income or middle-income countries, but 2 high-income countries charge fees upon beginning secondary school, and 3 report charging at least some tuition by the end of secondary schooling.*

Higher education is even less accessible in most of the world. Of the 79 countries that report that they provide tuition-free higher education, 28 are in Europe and Central Asia. While more common in higher-income countries, countries at all income levels and in all regions show that this can be feasible. Twenty countries in sub-Saharan Africa, 16 in the Americas, 11 in the Middle East and North Africa, 2 in East Asia and the Pacific, and 2 in South Asia provide tertiary education without tuition.†

All nations need to ensure that financial barriers do not prevent any child from receiving a comprehensive education. To do so effectively requires eliminating all school fees. However, this inevitably removes an important source of revenue from school systems while also increasing demand, which can present significant challenges. Many more school spaces need to be made available, more teachers need to be hired and trained, and more materials are required, to name just a few. For example, when all primary-school fees were eliminated simultaneously in Malawi in 1994 and attendance dramatically increased, at first only 1 textbook was available for every 7 primary school students. By 1997, this had improved to 1 book for every 3 students, and by 2004, there was 1 book for every 1.5 students. In contrast to Malawi's approach, Ghana implemented reductions in school fees more gradually. Tuition fees were abolished in 1996, but user fees for textbooks and uniforms were not eliminated until 2005. As a result, Ghana was able to maintain a higher number of textbooks and teachers per student throughout the early years of the transition to free education. However, Ghana did not increase attendance as rapidly or experience

---

*World Policy Analysis Centre, Education Database. Number of countries for which we have data: 165 (tuition in lower secondary education), 158 (tuition in upper secondary education).

†World Policy Analysis Centre, Education Database. Number of countries for which we have data: 146 (tuition in tertiary education).

Map 2.4. Is completing secondary education tuition-free?

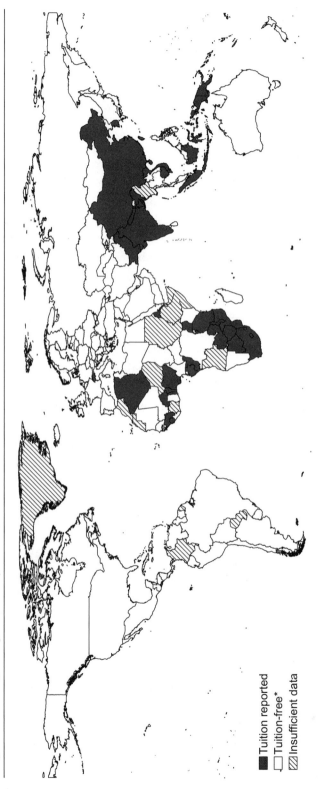

■ Tuition reported
☐ Tuition-free*
▨ Insufficient data

Tuition-free includes cases where no tuition is charged, but there may be other fees. Adequate information for systematic assessment of other fees is not available.

Source: World Policy Analysis Centre, Education Database

the same degree of reduction in income-based and rural-urban inequalities as Malawi.[35] Although the ideal pace for abolishing school fees can be debated, it is clear that in the long run, many more children have access to school in the absence of fees.

Making Schooling Compulsory

Is making public education available and affordable sufficient, or does it need to be compulsory as well? On the one hand, shouldn't children have a chance to attend school even if their parents prefer that they work at home, on a farm, or elsewhere in the labor force? Laws mandating school attendance mean that parents or guardians cannot legally decide to keep children out of school in order to benefit from their labor or for any other reason. Youth may also underestimate the long-term benefits of education; compulsory schooling means that they cannot choose not to attend. On the other hand, some contend that if parents are not sending their children to school, it must be because they cannot (e.g., because of insufficient financial resources) or because they do not see formal schooling as the best option for their child. Simply making education compulsory would not change these realities.

What is the empirical evidence on compulsory education? Compelling evidence from around the world documents the effectiveness of compulsory education in a wide range of settings. In Canada, data from 1920 to 1990 show that educational attainment and adult income both rose as a result of increases in the duration of compulsory schooling.[36] Great Britain increased the age for leaving school and expanded funding for teachers and school buildings shortly after World War II; this led to a decline in the number of 14-year-olds dropping out of school from 57 percent to 10 percent over a 3-year period.[37] Similarly, studies across Europe demonstrate that compulsory-education laws are associated with increased educational attainment.[38] In Turkey, compulsory-schooling laws are linked to higher school enrollment rates.[39] In the United States, where compulsory education is linked to age, students born at the beginning of the calendar year (and who thus tend to be among the older students in a grade) leave school after attaining less education on average than students born at the end of the calendar year, who have reached a higher grade level by the time they reach the legal school-leaving age.[40] An assessment of compulsory-schooling legislation in China found that it contributed to enrollment increases, lower dropout rates, reduced inequalities, and more years of schooling among the rural population.[41]

From a national perspective, compulsory-education laws imply that the government has a responsibility to provide educational opportunities for all children and ensure that children and their families are able to take advantage of them; countries that make education compulsory recognize the implication that education is "a public service and a public responsibility."[42] Despite its clear educational and economic advantages, the natural link between families' obligation to send their children to school and nations' obligation to provide educational opportunities is a reason that some governments, hesitant to take on this responsibility, have resisted making school attendance compulsory.

To examine the extent to which governments have been ready to commit themselves to keeping children in school, we drew on our original comparative database of education policy around the world. By thoroughly analyzing the information available in thousands of pages of reports, we found that this commitment varies greatly around the world. Globally, 15 countries do not require that children receive any education, including 7 countries in sub-Saharan Africa, 3 in South Asia, 2 in the Middle East and North Africa, 2 in East Asia and the Pacific, and 1 in the Americas.*

We found that 126 countries mandate that children begin secondary education, but only 27 require that they complete this level. Among the few countries that make it mandatory to complete secondary education are 12 countries in Europe and Central Asia, 10 in the Americas, 3 in East Asia and the Pacific, 1 in the Middle East and North Africa, and 1 in sub-Saharan Africa.†

When schooling is compulsory, it is particularly crucial that it also be free since poor families will often be unable to comply with compulsory-education laws if schooling requires expenditures be-

---

*World Policy Analysis Centre, Education Database. Number of countries for which we have data: 174 (compulsory education in primary schooling).

† World Policy Analysis Centre, Education Database. Number of countries for which we have data: 173 (compulsory education at beginning of secondary schooling), 172 (compulsory education at end of secondary schooling).

yond their financial means. Additionally, combining the free provision of education with compulsory attendance is a more powerful way of increasing children's chances than adopting free education alone. Making schooling compulsory means that states have a greater obligation to provide sufficient spaces, and families cannot legally withhold children to do unpaid or paid work in its stead.

By combining our data on free and compulsory education, we see how many countries are fully committed to access. The news is encouraging for primary education: our findings show that most of the world (153 countries) has legislated compulsory, tuition-free education at this level. When the world makes a commitment, as it has to universal primary education in Millennium Development Goal 2, it is possible to make significant advances.

At the secondary level, the situation begins to deteriorate. The beginning of secondary education is compulsory and tuition-free in 119 countries, but there are relatively few countries where completing secondary education is compulsory and tuition-free: these 26 countries include 10 high-income, 14 middle-income, and 2 low-income countries. We desperately need a global commitment, similar to that for primary education, ensuring that all children can achieve a secondary-school education.

The Quality Imperative

Ndalama described the transformation in access to education that had occurred when tuition was eliminated in Malawi. Although the massive increase in students was a resounding success, the challenges it presented were equally large. With the spike in the number of children attending primary schools, class sizes increased drastically; some classrooms had as many as 100 to 200 children per teacher. In order to meet the massive increase in demand, many primary schools in Malawi had to hire teachers who had little education and training, and many of these teachers were failing to provide an adequate education in the classroom.

By the year 2000, the bubble of increased primary-school enrollment had begun to hit secondary schools. However, too few Malawians had completed university to supply sufficient secondary-school teachers. In an attempt to solve this problem, the government began selecting the best-educated primary-school instructors and offering them short training courses to become secondary-school teachers. In Ndalama's view, this was a disastrous policy. Primary schools were hemorrhaging their best instructors, and secondary schools were being flooded with teachers who had not been educated beyond the secondary level themselves.[43]

The challenges that Malawi faced are common to many countries when they rapidly increase their school enrollment levels. By 2008, Victoria had been a teacher and school inspector in Tanzania for years. She felt that the poor quality of the public school system was epitomized by the fact that on the national exams required for university entry, the best students from government schools, where teachers are only required to have a secondary education, performed worse than the average students from private schools. Free primary education was introduced in Tanzania in 2001,[44] *resulting in an influx of students into the public education system and a shortage of teachers to educate them. She observed, "It's not easy. Is it better to have a partially qualified teacher, someone with no qualifications at all, or no teacher? How do you train people in the first place? It's a chicken and egg kind of thing." As in Malawi, ballooning class sizes were another problem.*[45]

The challenges that Victoria and Ndalama witnessed on a daily basis are common around the world. Teacher shortages, inadequate training, and high student-to-teacher ratios imperil the learning opportunities of hundreds of millions of children around the world, and marginalized children are almost always the most severely affected. Although educational access is critical, the goal is not simply for children to enroll in school, but for them to attend and complete school and ultimately to benefit from the education they receive. Educational quality is as essential as access in order to give each child a true chance. If a child is enrolled in school but has not been taught to read, repeats the second grade three times because of ineffective instruction, or is taught in a classroom with too many students for one teacher to handle, he or she is barely benefiting from education.

Troubling educational outcomes reveal the gravity of this challenge in many nations. In at least 12 sub-Saharan African countries, young adults have a 40 percent probability of illiteracy after having completed 6 years of schooling.[46] Less than half of third-grade students in the Dominican Republic, Ecuador, and Guatemala have more than very basic reading capabilities.[47] In rural Pakistan, just two-thirds of third-grade students are able to perform simple subtraction with numbers under 10.[48] Average students in some nations, such as Ghana, Indonesia, and Morocco, score below the lowest-performing students in other nations, such as Japan and the Republic of Korea, on international math and science assessments.[49] Although learning outcomes can be affected by outside factors, such as family income and parental education levels, the goal of the education system must be to overcome these obstacles and ensure that all children are acquiring the knowledge and skills that they require.

Class size is often discussed in relation to educational quality, as it was by Ndalama and Victoria, but how much does it really matter? When teachers are responsible for many more students than they can teach effectively, reducing class sizes has obvious advantages. Having over 100 or even several dozen students in a classroom reduces the time and attention that a single teacher is able to devote to each student, and makes it more difficult to avoid teaching to one level and to ensure that all children above and below that level are able to reach their full potential. At the same time, investing in smaller class sizes means fewer resources to invest elsewhere; would scarce dollars be better spent on infrastructure, supplies, or teacher training?

That student outcomes improve with smaller class sizes has been documented around the world.[50] A study of data from 13 Latin American countries shows that test scores and repetition rates improved when pupil-to-teacher ratios were smaller.[51] A global study using data from several decades confirms the association between pupil-to-teacher ratios and test scores: smaller ratios are associated with an increase in test scores and lower repetition and dropout rates among students.[52]

On the other hand, when class sizes are relatively small to begin with, does devoting resources to reducing the number of students per teacher make sense? Evidence suggests that even small changes have an impact on student outcomes. For example, Project STAR (Student-Teacher Achievement Ratio) in the U.S. state of Tennessee randomly assigned students to regular-sized classes (22–26 students) or small classes (13–17 students) from kindergarten to the third grade.[53] Compared with their peers in regular-sized classes, by the third grade students in small classes were 4.5 months ahead in reading, 5.5 months ahead in word-study skills, and 2.6 months ahead in math skills. These benefits continued even after students returned to regular-sized classes; students who had been part of the program continued to be several months ahead of their peers in grades 4, 6, and 8.[54] Disadvantaged students experienced even greater benefits than other students.[55] For example, in inner-city schools, 64 percent of minority students in small classes passed reading tests, compared with 45 percent in regular-sized classes; in suburban schools, 75 percent of minority students passed reading tests, compared with 53 percent in regular-sized classes.[56] Other programs aimed at class-size reduction in the United States and the United Kingdom have had similarly positive results.[57]

This does not answer the questions about where the ideal balance lies between investing in smaller class sizes versus other educational inputs nor about the exact number of students in a classroom that is optimal for their performance. Nonetheless, there is little doubt that the ideal is far smaller than the reality observed in many of the world's countries.

UNESCO has collected comprehensive data on student-to-teacher ratios around the world, and these data paint a worrying picture. While pupil-to-teacher ratios are important at all levels, they play a particularly important role with young children. Yet 27 countries have 40 or more pupils for every primary-school teacher, and an additional 27 countries have between 30 and 39 students for every teacher. Children in Africa and South Asia not only face the greatest barriers to educational access but are also likely to face some of the greatest learning challenges even when they are able to attend school. Sub-Saharan African countries tend to have the highest primary-school student-to-teacher ratios: 22 countries have over 40 students per teacher, and of these, 7 countries have between 50 and 60 students per teacher, 2 countries have between 61 and 80, and the Central African Republic has a staggering ratio of 84 students per teacher. These numbers clearly impair teachers' ability to instruct their students effectively. Similarly, half the countries in South Asia, including India, Pakistan, and Bangladesh, have 40 or more students for each teacher in primary school.[58] When the data are disaggregated by national income level, we find that students in the lowest-income countries also have the most limited access to teachers. Sixty-two percent of low-income countries have a student-to-teacher ratio of at least 40:1, whereas no high-income country and only 7 middle-income countries have such a high ratio. Moreover, for many countries these numbers understate the gravity of the situation because they average the class sizes in very congested schools with the smaller numbers in sparsely populated areas.

At the secondary level, class sizes tend to be smaller overall, although the greatest disadvantages continue to follow the same pattern. Once again, countries with high student-to-teacher ratios are concentrated among low-income nations. At the lower secondary level, 26 countries have a pupil-to-teacher ratio of at least 30, and 15 of these countries are low-income. Twelve of the 17 countries with a student-to-teacher ratio of at least 30:1 at the upper secondary level are considered low-income and are concentrated in the South Asian and sub-Saharan African regions.[59]

Why do student-to-teacher ratios at the secondary level tend to be smaller than at the primary level? As we pointed out earlier in this chapter, to date the world has focused far less on ensuring that all children have access to secondary education than it has on access to primary school. As a result, the number of children who do not continue on to secondary school is large in many countries. Fees are far more frequently charged for secondary school, and secondary education is less often compulsory. In addition, secondary-school-age children more commonly have to work instead of attending school. Lower attendance rates by students, combined with the hiring of more teachers to teach specialized subjects with higher pay, contribute to lower student-to-teacher ratios in secondary school than in primary school.[60]

The number of students per teacher clearly matters, but the quality of the teacher in charge of those students is a critical determinant of how much they learn, no matter the class size. How important is teacher training in determining the quality of classroom experience as countries seek to find enough qualified teachers? Intuition suggests that in order to teach a given level of school well, teachers should have received more education than their students, and that additional specialized teacher training that affects instruction techniques would be even more advantageous. Although an advanced level of knowledge about the teaching subject seems desirable, advanced degrees far beyond the teaching level in unrelated subjects seem less directly beneficial.

In general, the research upholds these assumptions. A study of Latin American countries found that the number of years of postsecondary education that a teacher had completed was significantly associated with student performance: students taught by a teacher with 4 years of postsecondary education scored an average of 5 points higher on regional standardized assessments than students taught by a teacher who had completed only 2 years.[61] In francophone sub-Saharan Africa, teachers' education has been shown to be a significant determinant of student achievement in French and math.[62] Studies in the United States have demonstrated that when secondary-school math or science teachers have undergraduate or graduate degrees in related fields, their students perform better in those subjects.[63] However, simply having a teacher with a graduate degree does not affect the outcomes of students in the United States at the primary or secondary level.[64]

In addition to university degrees, pedagogical training for teachers has been demonstrated to affect student outcomes positively across countries. Data from Bangladesh demonstrate that higher levels of general and specialized education among teachers positively affect enrollment, dropout, and failure rates among students.[65] According to UNESCO's review of the evidence, a majority of studies conducted in low- and middle-income countries found that teacher training had a positive and significant effect on student performance.[66] This is likewise true in high-income countries. In middle schools in the United States, for example, teachers with formal pedagogical training were found to be more effective than those without this training: they used positive teaching approaches more often, and these techniques were linked with better student learning.[67]

The systematic review of national reports contained in our education policy database allows us to compare clearly what education and training countries require for their teachers. Our findings reveal that there are marked disparities in teacher-training requirements around the world. In Canada, much of Europe, and Australia, primary-school teachers must have completed a bachelor's degree in addition to teacher training, but in close to half of the world's countries, including 30 countries in sub-Saharan Africa, 17 in Latin America and the Caribbean,

12 in East Asia and the Pacific, 9 in Europe and Central Asia, 6 in the Middle East and North Africa, and 6 in South Asia, primary-school teachers must have completed only secondary school or secondary school and some teacher training.*

Even more striking are lower secondary-school teacher requirements: in 48 countries, teachers need to have completed barely more education than their students, including over 50 percent of sub-Saharan African nations and nearly three-quarters of South Asia (see Map 2.5).†

One hopes that teachers at the upper secondary level would be required to have some postsecondary education. Nearly all high-income countries require at least a bachelor's degree to teach upper secondary school; 11 require a master's degree. However, the numbers are quite different among poor countries. A third of low-income countries require only that upper secondary-level teachers have completed secondary school themselves, along with some teacher training (Map 2.6).‡

Eleven sub-Saharan African countries require only a secondary education with some teacher training in order to teach upper secondary school, as do 8 countries in Latin America and the Caribbean, 4 in East Asia and the Pacific, 2 in South Asia, 1 in the Middle East and North Africa, and 1 in Europe and Central Asia. Additionally, 2 countries in Latin America and 1 in South Asia require only the completion of secondary school.

Although teacher training and education are clearly important for educational quality, many questions remain unanswered. What kind of education and training is the ideal, and how much? Increasing the prerequisites necessary to become a teacher will reduce the number of teachers available in the short term because cohorts will take longer to complete the requirements; is it worth it, especially if class sizes tend to be large to begin with?

---

*World Policy Analysis Centre, Education Database. Number of countries for which we have data: 168 (primary teacher training).

†World Policy Analysis Centre, Education Database. Number of countries for which we have data: 164 (lower secondary teacher training).

‡World Policy Analysis Centre, Education Database. Number of countries for which we have data: 164 (upper secondary teacher training).

Map 2.5. How much education must lower secondary-school teachers complete?

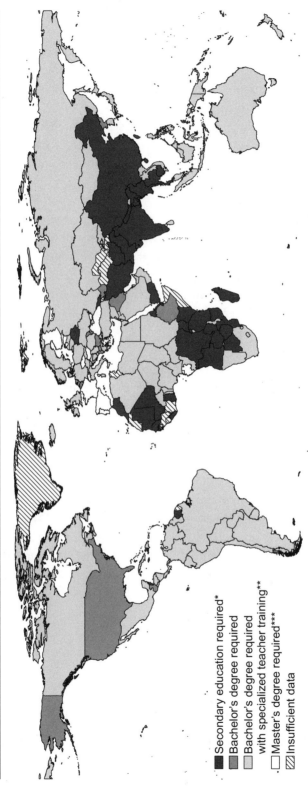

- ■ Secondary education required*
- ▨ Bachelor's degree required
- ▢ Bachelor's degree required
  with specialized teacher training**
- ▢ Master's degree required***
- ▨ Insufficient data

Secondary education required includes countries that require a teacher to have completed no more than a secondary level of education, whether or not they require specialized teacher training.
**Specialized teacher training* includes a bachelor of education or a general bachelor's with additional teacher training.
***Master's degree required* includes countries that require a teacher to have completed a Master's degree, whether or not they require specialized teacher training.
Source: *World Policy Analysis Centre, Education Database*

Map 2.6. How much education must upper secondary-school teachers complete?

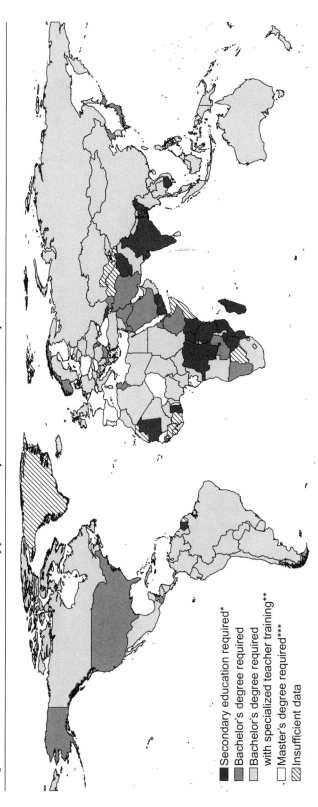

- ■ Secondary education required*
- ■ Bachelor's degree required
- ☐ Bachelor's degree required
    with specialized teacher training**
- ☐ Master's degree required***
- ▨ Insufficient data

*Secondary education required includes countries that require a teacher to have completed no more than a secondary level of education, whether or not they require specialized teacher training.
**Specialized teacher training includes a bachelor of education or a general bachelor's with additional teacher training.
***Master's degree required includes countries that require a teacher to have completed a Master's degree, whether or not they require specialized teacher training.
Source: *World Policy Analysis Centre, Education Database*

This question of trade-offs is key in achieving rapid expansion of access to a decent education. Class-size reductions create a pressing need for more teachers, which can compromise teacher quality in terms of years of experience or training. When instructional time is increased, teacher salaries may also need to be increased. When additional textbooks or other materials are made available, less money can be dedicated to infrastructure unless additional resources are raised.

Countries' Progress

Recent experience has made it clear that we can make a difference in the educational opportunities available in many nations. The substantial progress that has been made since the global community first directed its attention to education demonstrates that disparities in access, quality, and outcomes are not permanent or inevitable if steps are taken to address them. While every child's right to education has been recognized since the earliest UN agreements,[68] this right was more powerfully brought to the world's attention in 1990 by the launch of the Education for All movement and its call to universalize primary education and significantly reduce illiteracy by the new millennium. In 2000, this movement was further strengthened by countries' decision to include universal primary education and gender parity in the Millennium Development Goals.[69]

Since then, countries have acted on the commitments they made to children's educational chances and have taken steps, together with support from the international community, to eliminate financial barriers and improve access. As a result, outcomes have improved and disparities have diminished. Between 1990 and 2007, the most recent year for which data were available as of 2011, enrollment in primary education improved in almost every region of the world, most dramatically in the Caribbean, which experienced a rise in net enrollment from 51 to 72 percent, and in sub-Saharan Africa, where it rose from 53 to 73 percent. Literacy rates among youth aged 15–24, many of whom benefited from the changes inspired by Education for All commitments, are higher than adult literacy rates in every region, indicating that improvements in access to education are yielding results.[70]

Gender parity has also improved since nations focused on ensuring universal access to education and made giving girls an equal chance a priority. At least 29 of the countries that had fallen short of gender parity in primary-school enrollment in 1999 had achieved it by 2007. In addition, some of the regions with especially marked inequalities have been closing the gap. Between 1991 and 2007, gender parity in primary-school enrollment improved significantly in South and West Asia (from 77 to 95 girls per 100 boys), the Arab states (from 79 to 90 girls per 100 boys), and sub-Saharan Africa (from 84 to 90 girls per 100 boys). In every region, literacy rates among male and female youth differ less than they do among adults.[71]

Although persistent disparities highlight the fact that much work still needs to be done in order to give every child a chance at an education, recent progress underscores what can be achieved when nations commit to education for all. The problem remains that the goals have been set too low—primary schooling is insufficient to prepare youth for labor-market competition.

Net enrollment in secondary education still leaves many adolescents out of school—more than one-third of secondary-school-aged children are not in school in the Arab States, and nearly 30 percent are out of school in East Asia and the Pacific and Latin America and the Caribbean. Of even greater concern are the 54 percent of secondary-school-aged children in South and West Asia and the 73 percent in sub-Saharan Africa who are not enrolled in secondary school.[72] Moreover, when children are enrolled in schools with scarce learning materials and few or inadequately trained teachers, the quality of the education they receive is markedly constrained. Access to quality secondary and postsecondary training and education is crucial to give all children a fair chance.

Tracking the Essentials

To understand the successes and failures and to ensure more rapid progress, we need to track more of the features essential to making education accessible and effective. Reliable and comparable information on school fees, for example, is very important for understanding the reality of educational access. Although some information that we would like to know, such as the quality of teacher performance, may be very difficult to measure, there are other indicators that are readily measurable and yet have not been collected systematically.

Instructional time is one example. The lengths of the school year and of the school day markedly influence the amount of schooling to which children have access. Although an outstanding teacher may accomplish more in fewer days than a bad teacher, it should come as no surprise that all else being equal, children have a greater opportunity to learn when they have more instructional time.[73] Unfortunately, data are not currently available on a globally comparative basis to enable the analysis of even the most straightforward indicator of learning time: the official length of the school year. In addition to the length of the school year, the number of hours per day school is in session and the amount of time spent on educational activities shape learning hours. These data are not available either. Actual teaching time may differ significantly from official instructional hours because of considerable amounts of classroom time not being spent teaching effectively, as well as frequent student or teacher absences from school.[74] Teacher absenteeism is a significant problem in much of the world, and many countries urgently need to monitor teacher attendance.[75] In India, for example, a nationally representative study of teacher absence in primary schools based on unannounced visits showed that 1 in 4 teachers were not present in the school during teaching hours; absence rates differed among states, ranging from under 20 percent to over 40 percent. Similar methods show teacher absence rates of 19 percent in Indonesia and 27 percent in Uganda.[76] It is next to impossible to address teacher absenteeism without first beginning to monitor the extent of the problem.[77]

Teacher-training requirements provide another illustration of the importance of assessing implementation. Although having good standards for teacher training is an important start, these standards must be followed to have any effect. According to data from UNESCO, large proportions of teachers in many countries do not meet the minimum legal requirements. For example, in Benin, Burkina Faso, Cameroon, Republic of the Congo, Guinea-Bissau, Mozambique, and Togo, between 10 and 60 percent of primary-school teachers have not completed the required lower secondary education. In Namibia, Angola, and Chad, where primary-school teachers should have completed upper secondary education, less than 50 percent of them have done so. In South Africa, 60 percent of primary-school teachers have not completed the required tertiary education. On the other hand, in some countries these standards are fulfilled: in Senegal, Zambia, Côte d'Ivoire, Kenya, and Botswana, at least 95 percent of primary-school teachers have met educational requirements.[78] In this area, as in others, it is critical that we track policy implementation.

It is also important to understand the reality of schools on other measures of access and quality. For example, student learning is very much affected by the availability of educational materials and the quality of the physical school environment. In fact, increasing the availability of learning materials has been cited as one of the most cost-effective interventions to improve educational quality.[79] The evidence is clear that having textbooks and other learning tools available to students radically improves their outcomes.[80] Yet there are no comparable global measures of these resources on a country-by-country basis—the type of data needed to target improvements.

Looking before School

Early childhood care and education (ECCE) programs have been shown to benefit children's school achievement in contexts as diverse as Bangladesh, the United Kingdom, Argentina, and the United States. These improvements are apparent upon entry into school, and in many cases these programs continue to have an impact during primary and secondary school.[81] Decreased grade-repetition rates have been documented among preschool participants in Brazil and the United States,[82] and a meta-analytic review of evidence concluded that children who have attended preschool are almost 50 percent less likely to repeat a grade.[83] Some studies have also found that preschool participants are less likely to require remedial or special education.[84] Children who participate in early childhood education complete more years of education on average than children who do not. In Uruguay, for example, a study found that children who had attended preschool were 24 percentage points more likely to have completed primary school than their siblings who had not.[85] Studies of preprimary programs in the United States show that children who have attended these programs are 8.5 percent more likely to graduate from high school[86] and 4 times more likely to attend a 4-year college.[87]

Like primary and secondary school, for early childhood education to be available to children, it must be available to all families irrespective of their ability to pay. As of yet, early childhood education options are extremely limited for families worldwide. Approximately half of the world's countries do not have any formal ECCE programs for children under age 3; when only private programs are available, most parents living in poverty will not be able to afford to send their children. After age 3, ECCE is more commonly provided by the government— government-run preprimary public education programs can go by various names, including preschool education and kindergarten. These programs are provided for children aged 3 and over for between 5 hours and 60 hours per week in the countries for which data are available, with most countries providing between 15 and 40 hours.[88] More information on ECCE programs, including whether they are free, whether they are publicly provided, what kind of educational services they offer, how educators are trained, and other key questions, must be made available to assess children's educational chances early in life.

Are the Costs Affordable?

The data presented in this chapter often show that children living in the poorest countries have the poorest educational opportunities. Although this may not be surprising, it is especially troubling given that one of the surest ways for countries to improve their economic competitiveness is by investing in education. The combination of poverty and poor learning environments is devastatingly costly for nations and children alike.

Once we have pulled together significant policy data on educational access and teacher training, a natural question is whether countries could afford to be spending more on programs that promote access to good-quality education. To examine this, we use data from the UNESCO Institute for Statistics. All nations should be able to achieve a reasonable amount of spending on education when measured in terms of percentage of gross domestic product (GDP). The findings make clear that some low-performing countries could be investing more in education. Thirty-nine countries begin charging tuition before the end of secondary education; 13 of these countries spend less than 4 percent of their GDP on education. These countries could be allocating more resources to eliminating these financial barriers for youth. Many of the countries with large class sizes at the primary level could also be spending more on children's education; given the evidence that smaller class sizes benefit student learning, this would be an important investment. Eight of the 26 countries with 40 students or more for each primary-school teacher for which expenditures are known spend less than 3 percent of their GDP on education, and an additional 4 of these countries spend less than 4 percent (Map 2.7).[89] The Central African Republic and Zambia, for example, are among the countries with the lowest percentage of GDP spent on education, at just 1.2 and 1.3 percent, respectively. At the same time, the Central African Republic has 84 pupils for each primary-school teacher and 52 for each secondary-school teacher—a proportion so high that it is impossible for many students to succeed. In Zambia, primary-school teachers are responsible for an average of 58 students, again an untenably high number. Additional resources could be made available and spent on hiring teachers, providing materials, and other mechanisms for ensuring that children are learning in an appropriate environment. Other low-income countries have shown that more is possible: 5 low-income countries spend at least 6 percent of their GDP on education.[90]

Education expenditures can pay for themselves through their long-term employment and income effects. Around the world, individuals with secondary and tertiary levels of education are more likely to be employed than those with less education. In OECD countries, for example, men who did not complete secondary school are more than twice as likely to be unemployed as men who graduated with a secondary education, and similar results have been documented among women. Employment rates for men and women with a tertiary education are higher still.[91] In low- and middle-income countries, there is a similar positive relationship between education and labor-market outcomes in terms of unemployment and underemployment.[92] For example, in countries as diverse as Malaysia, Paraguay, Brazil, and Tunisia, there is a clear gradient in women's labor-force participation: employment increases along with educational attainment from the primary through the secondary and up to the tertiary level. In Paraguay, 45 percent of women with no schooling and 47 percent of women who did not complete primary school are employed, while 75 percent of women who completed upper secondary school and 92 percent of those who completed tertiary education are employed. Men's employment follows a similar trajectory.[93]

Map 2.7. How much do governments spend on education?

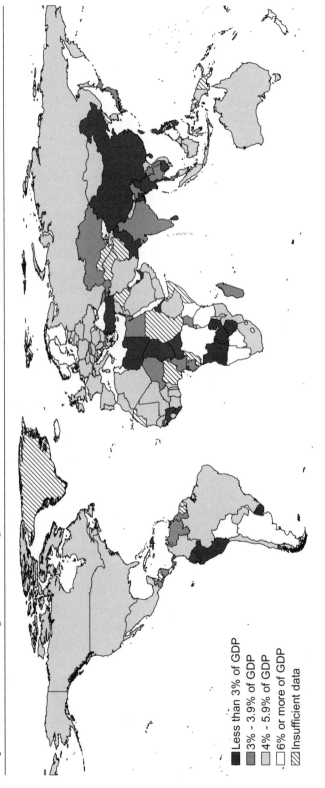

Less than 3% of GDP
3% - 3.9% of GDP
4% - 5.9% of GDP
6% or more of GDP
Insufficient data

Data Source: UNESCO Institute for Statistics, http://stats.uis.unesco.org

Education is also important for narrowing opportunity gaps between men and women. In OECD countries, the probability of employment for males who did not complete secondary school is 23 percentage points higher than for females who did not complete secondary
school, whereas the gender gap in employment shrinks to 10 percentage points between men and women who have attended college or
university.[94] A UNESCO study of 10 low- and middle-income countries showed similar results. While the employment rates of men with
no schooling and men with a primary-level education are approximately 40 percentage points higher than those of women with the
same educational attainment, the gap is reduced to 28 percentage
points between men and women with an upper secondary education.
Among those who have completed a tertiary-level technical, occupational, or practical program, this gap is just 15 percentage points.[95]

As well as leading to better employment outcomes, higher levels of
education improve income. Studies of identical twins raised in the
same households in the United States attempted to isolate the effects
of schooling from other potential influences on labor-market outcomes, such as ability and environment, and found that an additional
year of education increased wages by between 9 and 16 percent.[96] An
analysis of 8 low- and middle-income countries shows a clear relationship between earnings and level of education. For men, the income
increase that can be expected from acquiring tertiary education relative to upper secondary education ranges from 82 percent in Indonesia
to nearly 300 percent in Paraguay. For women, this income advantage
ranges from 55 percent in Indonesia to almost 180 percent in Brazil.[97]
A study of adults in 13 middle- and high-income countries found that
earnings increased by 5 percent for each additional year of schooling.[98]
Similar effects have been documented around the world.[99]

These employment and income effects have an impact on national
economic growth, as well as on individuals, in both high- and low-
income countries.[100] A UNESCO study based on 50 countries estimated that a 1-year increase in average educational attainment could
increase GDP by 0.37 percent per year.[101] A study of 65 low-income,
middle-income, and transition countries found that these nations could
increase their economic growth by $92 billion each year if they were to
educate girls and boys to the same level. This estimate includes only
the effects of increasing girls' upper secondary participation to that of

the current proportion of boys in each country, and not the far greater effects of universal secondary education.[102] A 2010 study projected that if OECD nations increased their average Programme for International Student Assessment scores by 0.25 standard deviations in the next 20 years, a total increase of $115 trillion in the aggregate GDP of OECD countries could be expected over the lifetime of the population born in 2010. If performance were increased to the level of Finland, the best in the OECD, GDP would increase by $260 trillion.[103]

Although many poor performers could afford to spend a higher percentage of GDP on education, there is still likely to be a need for a time-limited global financial commitment to ensure that all children have access to high-quality education. The magnitude of low-income countries' needs and the limited size of their current GDP may mean that the dollar amount available for education, even when a higher proportion of GDP is spent, will be insufficient. International assistance should not be required indefinitely, as the nation's GDP will gradually rise as a result of the return on investment in education, enabling the country to fully fund its own enhanced educational system.

Looking beyond Schools

Although many of the answers to the challenges of educational access and quality may lie within the education system, an equal or greater number of solutions lie outside it. Many of the external factors that prevent children from attending school or reaching their fullest educational potential have been identified, and more important, many of them can be addressed. If the combination of parental income and social supports were sufficient to cover the costs of food, child rearing, and other basic necessities, many families would be less likely to keep children out of school in order to help meet basic needs. Poverty-reduction policy therefore plays an essential role not only in lifting families out of poverty, but also in increasing children's educational opportunities. Likewise, addressing child labor increases the odds that children will attend school, and preventing child marriage removes a fundamental barrier to school attendance for many children around the world. These issues and others are addressed in detail in other chapters of this book.

Table 2.1. Children's rights to education in national constitutions

	Low-Income	Middle-Income	High-Income
General Right to Education in Constitutions			
Constitution does not include relevant provisions on the right to education	2 (6%)	30 (28%)	17 (34%)
Constitution aspires to protect the right to education	6 (17%)	8 (8%)	4 (8%)
Constitution guarantees the right to education	17 (49%)	41 (39%)	15 (30%)
Constitution states that education is compulsory or free	8 (23%)	20 (19%)	8 (16%)
Constitution states that education is compulsory and free	2 (6%)	7 (7%)	6 (12%)
Specific Right to Primary Education in Constitutions			
Constitution does not include relevant provisions on the right to primary education	13 (37%)	34 (32%)	23 (46%)
Constitution aspires to protect the specific right to primary education	4 (11%)	7 (7%)	1 (2%)
Constitution guarantees the specific right to primary education	1 (3%)	1 (1%)	1 (2%)
Constitution states that primary education is compulsory or free	10 (29%)	26 (25%)	10 (20%)
Constitution states that primary education is compulsory and free	7 (20%)	38 (36%)	15 (30%)

(*continued*)

Table 2.1 (*continued*)

Specific Right to Secondary Education in Constitutions			
Constitution does not include relevant provisions on the right to secondary education	25 (71%)	57 (54%)	38 (76%)
Constitution aspires to protect the specific right to secondary education	4 (11%)	12 (11%)	1 (2%)
Constitution guarantees the specific right to secondary education	0 (0%)	7 (7%)	3 (6%)
Constitution states that secondary education is compulsory or free	6 (17%)	21 (20%)	8 (16%)
Constitution states that secondary education is compulsory and free	0 (0%)	9 (8%)	0 (0%)
Specific Right to Higher Education in Constitutions			
Constitution does not include relevant provisions on the right to higher education	25 (71%)	60 (57%)	39 (78%)
Constitution aspires to protect the specific right to higher education	7 (20%)	20 (19%)	3 (6%)
Constitution guarantees the specific right to higher education	3 (9%)	14 (13%)	5 (10%)
Constitution states that higher education is free	0 (0%)	12 (11%)	3 (6%)

Source : World Policy Analysis Centre, Constitutions Database.

Definition : Low-income, middle-income, and high-income refer to World Bank classifications of national income. Here, middle-income countries include those classified as lower-middle and upper-middle income.

Table 2.2. Policies affecting enrollment in primary, secondary, and higher education

	Low-Income	Middle-Income	High-Income
Tuition-Free Education			
Financial Barriers to Accessing Primary Education			
Tuition fees are charged in primary education	3 (9%)	5 (5%)	0 (0%)
Primary education is tuition-free	30 (91%)	91 (95%)	45 (100%)
Financial Barriers to Accessing the Beginning of Secondary Education			
Tuition fees are charged in the first year of secondary education	11 (38%)	10 (11%)	2 (4%)
At least the first year of secondary education is tuition-free	18 (62%)	81 (89%)	43 (96%)
Financial Barriers to the Completion of Secondary Education			
Tuition fees are charged in at least the last year of secondary education	16 (59%)	19 (22%)	3 (7%)
The completion of secondary education is tuition-free	11 (41%)	68 (78%)	41 (93%)
Financial Barriers to Accessing Higher Education			
Tuition fees are charged in higher education	13 (45%)	33 (45%)	21 (49%)
Higher education is tuition-free	16 (55%)	41 (55%)	22 (51%)
Compulsory Education	**Low-Income**	**Middle-Income**	**High-Income**
Compulsory Education at the Primary Level			
Primary education is not compulsory	5 (15%)	8 (8%)	2 (4%)
Primary education is compulsory	29 (85%)	87 (92%)	43 (96%)

(continued)

Table 2.2 (*continued*)

	Low-Income	Middle-Income	High-Income
Compulsory Education at the Beginning of Secondary Education			
Education is not compulsory for at least the first year of secondary education	19 (56%)	28 (29%)	2 (4%)
Education is compulsory for at least the first year of secondary education	15 (44%)	68 (71%)	43 (96%)
Compulsory Education through the Completion of Secondary Education			
Education is not compulsory through the completion of secondary education	32 (94%)	80 (84%)	34 (77%)
Education is compulsory through the completion of secondary education	2 (6%)	15 (16%)	10 (23%)
Tuition-Free and Compulsory Education	**Low-Income**	**Middle-Income**	**High-Income**
Compulsory and Free Education at the Primary and Secondary Levels			
Primary education is compulsory and free	26	84	43
At least the first year of secondary education is compulsory and free	13	65	41
The completion of secondary education is compulsory and free	2	14	10

Source : World Policy Analysis Centre, Education Database.

Definition : Tuition-free includes cases where no tuition is charged, but there may be other fees. Adequate information for systematic assessment of other fees is not available.

Note : When countries split primary education among levels, we consider upper primary as the equivalent of lower secondary to increase comparability across countries.

Table 2.3. Teachers, teacher preparation, and expenditures

Teacher-Training Requirements	Low-Income	Middle-Income	High-Income
Minimum Level of Training Required to Teach at the Primary Level			
Completion of secondary education required	2 (6%)	4 (4%)	1 (2%)
Completion of secondary education and specialized teacher training required	26 (84%)	45 (49%)	2 (4%)
Completion of a bachelor's degree required	0 (0%)	1 (1%)	4 (9%)
Completion of a bachelor of education or a bachelor's degree and specialized teacher training required	3 (10%)	42 (46%)	34 (76%)
Completion of a master's degree required	0 (0%)	0 (0%)	4 (9%)
Minimum Level of Training Required to Teach at the Lower Secondary Level			
Completion of secondary education required	1 (3%)	2 (2%)	1 (2%)
Completion of secondary education and specialized teacher training required	17 (57%)	26 (29%)	1 (2%)
Completion of a bachelor's degree required	2 (7%)	7 (8%)	3 (7%)
Completion of a bachelor of education or a bachelor's degree and specialized teacher training required	10 (33%)	53 (60%)	31 (69%)
Completion of a master's degree required	0 (0%)	1 (1%)	6 (13%)
Completion of a master's degree and specialized teacher training required	0 (0%)	0 (0%)	3 (7%)

(continued)

Table 2.3 *(continued)*

Minimum Level of Training Required to Teach at the Upper Secondary Level

	Low-Income	Middle-Income	High-Income
Completion of secondary education required	1 (3%)	1 (1%)	1 (2%)
Completion of secondary education and specialized teacher training required	10 (33%)	16 (18%)	1 (2%)
Completion of a bachelor's degree required	5 (17%)	13 (15%)	5 (11%)
Completion of a bachelor of education or a bachelor's degree and specialized teacher training required	12 (40%)	57 (64%)	27 (60%)
Completion of a master's degree required	0 (0%)	1 (1%)	6 (13%)
Completion of a master's degree and specialized teacher training required	2 (7%)	1 (1%)	5 (11%)

Pupil-to-Teacher Ratios

	Low-Income	Middle-Income	High-Income
Number of Students per Teacher at the Primary Level			
On average, 50 or more students for every teacher	9 (28%)	1 (1%)	0 (0%)
On average, 40 - 49 students for every teacher	11 (34%)	6 (6%)	0 (0%)
On average, 30 - 39 students for every teacher	7 (22%)	20 (20%)	0 (0%)
On average, 20 - 29 students for every teacher	5 (16%)	29 (28%)	3 (7%)
On average, 10 - 19 students for every teacher	0 (0%)	44 (43%)	35 (76%)
On average, fewer than 10 students for every teacher	0 (0%)	2 (2%)	8 (17%)
Number of Students per Teacher at the Lower Secondary Level			
On average, 50 or more students for every teacher	1 (3%)	0 (0%)	0 (0%)
On average, 40 - 49 students for every teacher	3 (10%)	1 (1%)	0 (0%)
On average, 30 - 39 students for every teacher	11 (37%)	10 (10%)	0 (0%)
On average, 20 - 29 students for every teacher	7 (23%)	24 (24%)	1 (2%)
On average, 10 - 19 students for every teacher	8 (27%)	52 (52%)	27 (60%)
On average, fewer than 10 students for every teacher	0 (0%)	13 (13%)	17 (38%)

Number of Students per Teacher at the Upper Secondary Level

	Low-Income	Middle-Income	High-Income
On average, 50 or more students for every teacher	2 (7%)	0 (0%)	0 (0%)
On average, 40 - 49 students for every teacher	0 (0%)	2 (2%)	0 (0%)
On average, 30 - 39 students for every teacher	10 (34%)	3 (3%)	0 (0%)
On average, 20 - 29 students for every teacher	8 (28%)	23 (23%)	1 (2%)
On average, 10 - 19 students for every teacher	9 (31%)	54 (54%)	32 (68%)
On average, fewer than 10 students for every teacher	0 (0%)	18 (18%)	14 (30%)

Public Expenditure

Amount of Government Spending on Education as a Percentage of GDP	Low-Income	Middle-Income	High-Income
Less than 2% of GDP is spent by the government on education	2 (7%)	4 (4%)	3 (6%)
2% - 2.9% of GDP is spent by the government on education	7 (23%)	11 (12%)	4 (8%)
3% - 3.9% of GDP is spent by the government on education	3 (10%)	21 (23%)	7 (14%)
4% - 5.9% of GDP is spent by the government on education	13 (43%)	37 (40%)	26 (53%)
6% or more of GDP is spent by the government on education	5 (17%)	20 (22%)	9 (18%)

Sources : World Policy Analysis Centre, Education Database and UNESCO Institute for Statistics, http://stats.uis.unesco.org.

Chapter 3

A Chance at Childhood

Phan Thi Chau grew up in Viet Nam, the eighth of nine children. Her father had been a driver before he got too sick to work. In the fourth grade, she had to quit school and work for pay. She explained, "I stopped going to school [when] I was 11 or 12 years old because of my difficult family situation. We didn't have money, so . . . I'd carry things around the neighborhood to sell."

Her need to drop out of school and start working at such a young age had lifelong consequences. As an adult, Chau did not have the education necessary to compete for jobs with a decent wage. As was the case for many people who left school as children to labor, Chau's job as an adult was low skilled and low paid: she sold vegetables at a stand in front of her house. Despite typically working 17-hour days, from 4:00 A.M. to 9:00 P.M., she was unable to earn enough to meet all her needs, let alone those of her 9-year-old son, Thanh. Her earnings varied enormously from day to day; on a good day, she could make 30,000 dong (approximately US$5.75, adjusted for purchasing power parity),[1] while on a bad day she would bring home just 10,000. When business was bad, she could not afford to feed both her son and herself. As she put it, "In the morning, often other people's children could eat a bowl of noodles; my child couldn't, so that makes me sad. I'd refrain from eating so that my child could eat."

Because of their limited resources, Thanh had to work both at home and at the vegetable stand in order for them to subsist.

Although he had not yet dropped out of school, the time he had available to study was severely limited by the labor he performed. At the age of 9, he got up with his mother at 4:00 A.M. to help prepare the vegetable stand, after which he studied until it was time to go to school. After school, from 5:00 P.M. until 8:00 or 9:00 P.M., he took over the stand from his mother, selling vegetables while she went to buy supplies for the following day. As an only child, Thanh also helped out around the house, sweeping and cooking rice. The only unusual aspect of this was that he was a boy doing the household tasks; around the world it is more common for girls to shoulder the burden of unpaid work. [2]

Concern about child labor is not new. As early as 1860, the International Workers' Congress called for an international campaign against child labor. When the International Labour Organization (ILO) was established in 1919, establishing conventions on the minimum working age for various sectors was among its first activities. Interest in and action on the issue of child labor continued throughout the twentieth century; child labor was largely articulated as a violation of children's rights and thus a target for total elimination. However, child labor remained extremely prevalent, and beginning in the 1990s, an explosion of cross-border advocacy and action made child labor once again a truly international concern. Nongovernmental organizations publicized cases of exploitation, pressured corporations to change their practices, and raised public awareness about the issue; international organizations devoted increasing amounts of attention and resources to it through the establishment of programs such as the ILO's International Programme on the Elimination of Child Labour (1992) and the World Bank's Global Child Labor Program (1998). Collectively, these movements transformed child labor into an international cause célèbre. [3]

After all the attention, is there anything left to be done? Campaigns against child labor have led to dramatic declines in some countries; Brazil, for example, more than halved its proportion of working children aged 5 to 15 from 16 percent in 1992 to 7 percent in 2008. [4] Still, child labor continues to radically reduce the life chances of a vast number of children in low- and middle-income nations. According to recent global estimates, there are 215 million child laborers in the world aged 5 to 17. The Asia and Pacific region is home to the greatest

number of these children (113.6 million); sub-Saharan Africa has the
highest incidence of child labor, at 25 percent of children aged 5 to 17.[5]
Not all these child laborers are out of school; many struggle to combine work and education. A study of 16 countries in Latin America,
Eastern Europe, and Asia showed that more than a quarter of working
boys and girls below the age of 15 were employed for at least 28 hours
per week,[6] inevitably reducing the time and energy they had left for
schooling. Not included within the estimated 215 million child laborers are the additional 91 million children involved in so-called light
work, which by definition should not interfere with a child's health or
education.[7] But even paid work labeled "light" can limit children's
chances of an education when it is combined with extensive unpaid
hours. Ninety-two percent of girls and 67 percent of boys involved in
paid employment also perform household labor. The proportion of
children aged 5 to 14 doing unpaid household work for over 28 hours
per week is twice as high for girls as it is for boys, and it is three times
as high for girls between the ages of 15 and 17.[8]

The numbers make clear that eliminating harmful child labor remains an essential priority for those concerned with children's chances,
and many actors, including the ILO, call for further passage and implementation of legislation addressing this issue.[9] However, doubts
have been voiced about the extent to which legislation is effective in
addressing child labor, given that poverty is a widely recognized root
cause of much of the labor that children perform, as well as the difficulty of enforcing child labor laws among the small employers and
households where many children work.

What is the evidence on legislation? Although child labor laws are
not perfectly implemented, and complementary interventions targeting poverty and education are essential (discussed later in this chapter), research supports the importance of child labor legislation. In
1991, Pakistan passed the Employment of Children Act, which prohibited children aged 13 and younger from working in factories, mines,
hazardous employment, and specific occupations and increased the
penalties for employers who violated this law. A study examined the
employment of children aged 10 to 13 (below the minimum age established by the act) in the months before and after the law's enactment
and implementation and compared it with the change in employment
over the same period in a control group that was not affected by the

new law. The law clearly reduced child labor in the sectors that it covered.[10] A study of 16 countries shows that the proportion of boys and girls working at least 28 hours per week tends to double above the minimum legal working age.[11]

What Protections Are Necessary?

Few argue against efforts to eliminate the "worst forms" of child labor (defined by the ILO as hazardous work, sexual exploitation, forced labor, and illegal activities). In 2008, a staggering 115 million children were involved in hazardous work alone, which includes work in dangerous environments (such as underground), with dangerous substances (such as lead), and under other inherently harmful conditions.[12]

However, questions have been raised about the extent to which other forms of labor should be universally regulated. If a child's family lives in poverty and his or her work increases household income, allowing the family to purchase more food, pay the fees necessary to send the child or other children to school, or afford better housing, is labor harmful or beneficial to the child? If part-time work teaches youth the skills and responsibilities that they will need later in life, allowing them to be more successful within their community or workplace, should it be prevented? Is some level of work beneficial because it instills a sense of responsibility?

It is important to answer these questions if we are to examine prohibitions not only of hazardous labor but of other types of work. Although labor can provide the income necessary to permit youth and/or their siblings to attend school,[13] the evidence suggests that more than a small number of hours of work is detrimental across a wide range of economies.

Child labor is associated with lower school enrollment and attendance around the world. Child laborers generally complete fewer years of education than their nonworking counterparts in countries as diverse as Nepal, Bolivia, Venezuela, Ghana, and Brazil.[14] In Viet Nam, research on children who combined work and school showed that the highest grade attained by children who worked was three grades lower than for children who did not work, even after family and regional characteristics were controlled for.[15] As well as affecting the number of years children spend in school, child labor can have an impact on their success in school. In Latin America and the Caribbean, child labor has been shown to detrimentally affect achievement levels in language and mathematics, even when school and household characteristics are controlled for.[16] A study of 11 countries in this region found that third- and fourth-grade students who sometimes or often worked outside the home scored an average of 7.5 percent lower on math exams and 7 percent lower on language exams than students who almost never worked outside the home after factors such as parental and school characteristics and resources are taken into account.[17] A study of math and science test scores in 23 countries also found that employment had a negative impact on achievement among eighth-grade students in most countries, and that it did not have a positive impact in any country.[18] Among 9- to 18-year-olds in Ghana, working outside the home reduced basic reading test scores by the equivalent of 2 years of schooling, basic math scores by 3 years, and advanced math scores by 1 year.[19] Poorer academic achievement from math and science to reading and English among working children compared with non-working children has also been documented in Nigeria, Britain, and Tanzania.[20]

The greater the number of hours of labor, the more substantial the impact. Data from over 60 countries show that as the number of hours that children work increases, their school attendance decreases; this relationship holds true for the total number of hours spent working, as well as hours spent performing market work and hours spent on domestic work.[21] A study drawing on national household-based child labor surveys in 16 countries around the world found that as the number of hours children spent on paid employment or household chores increased, their capacity to attend school decreased.[22] In Ghana, each additional hour of paid work is associated with a decrease of over a year of completed schooling,[23] and in Tanzania, it is estimated that if a girl's working hours were reduced by an hour per day, she would be 8 percentage points more likely to be able to read a newspaper.[24] Early literacy scores in Brazilian children are incrementally reduced with each additional domestic task they perform at home, even when family background is controlled for.[25] Other studies show a threshold effect rather than a consistent relationship, but still confirm that working too many hours per week hurts children's chances at school. In the

United States, negative educational impacts have been documented when high-school-age children worked for over 15 hours per week[26] or over 20 hours per week.[27] In Guatemala, a significant decline in schooling begins at approximately 19 hours per week of market work; in Nepal, this decline occurs at 22 hours per week of market work.[28] In Egypt, working for over 14 hours per week has a large negative impact on school attendance among both boys and girls aged 6 to 14.[29] In Cambodia, work has a negative impact on schooling at 22 hours per week.[30]

Beyond education, what are the implications for children's health? Some studies have documented a positive association between labor and nutrition- and growth-related outcomes.[31] This is thought to result at least partially from the greater nutritional and other resources available to children as a result of the income that they earn for their family, which may not otherwise have sufficient resources to provide adequately for the child. Although it is possible that a child's labor can increase the resources that his or her family has available to invest in nutrition, increasing adult earnings has as strong an impact without child labor's detrimental effects on girls' and boys' health. Children are particularly vulnerable to many occupational hazards, and high rates of work-related injuries have been documented among child laborers around the world.[32] Conditions that may not pose a significant danger to adults can nonetheless interfere with the development of children's bodies. Since child laborers begin working at a young age, overall they are exposed to workplace conditions and hazards for a longer period of time than those who begin working as adults. Children also have more exposed skin per volume, more energy and fluid requirements per unit of body weight, higher metabolism, and a higher rate of oxygen consumption than adults, each of which increases their absorption of toxic substances to which they are exposed. Moreover, since most protective equipment in the workplace is designed for adults, children often work without adequate equipment or protections. Children laboring in industry and agriculture, as well as in the informal economy, are frequently exposed to hazardous substances, such as lead, pesticides, and solvents, that can lead to cognitive problems, including poor memory and attention and reduced hand-eye coordination, in addition to symptoms such as headaches, dizziness, nausea, and coughing.[33] Toxic blood lead levels have been documented in child laborers engaged in work ranging from rag picking in the Philippines to tile making in Ecuador and industrial shops in Lebanon.[34] Domestic child workers are commonly exposed to chemical hazards and heightened risk of injury, as well as chronic sleep deprivation and verbal, physical, or sexual abuse.[35]

The health effects of child labor can plague children for their entire lives and reduce their long-term productivity and quality of life. Child laborers are more likely to experience poor health as adults than adults who did not work as children.[36] In Guatemala, having worked between the ages of 6 and 14 was found to increase the probability of health problems as an adult by over 40 percent.[37] A study of 18- to 65-year-olds conducted in Brazil showed that the younger individuals began working, the higher their probability of poor health as adults: men and women who had begun working before the age of 10 were over 1.5 times more likely to report less than good health than those who had begun working at age 15 or older.[38]

Child Labor Protections Worldwide

In short, the evidence supports efforts to prevent full-time work and work that conflicts with school, as well as all hazardous work. How many countries have taken steps to limit the amount and nature of the work that children do? Although labor laws are publicly available, until now, comparing child labor legislation in countries around the world required sifting through thousands of pages of legislation in many different languages. Our research team undertook this analysis effort for all of the UN's member nations.[39] We examined all labor codes and child-labor-specific legislation located through the ILO and other legal sources (for details, see Appendix 1) and thoroughly reviewed and analyzed their provisions related to hazardous work, general employment, working conditions, time off, and other aspects. What follows is a picture of what countries are doing and where they are falling behind.

Prohibiting Hazardous Labor

In its Convention on the Elimination of the Worst Forms of Child Labor (1999), the ILO defined hazardous labor as "work which, by its nature or the circumstances in which it is carried out, is likely to harm the health, safety or morals of children."[40] Although the specific types of labor banned as too hazardous for children differ across countries, which are expected to define this term according to their contexts, the concept of hazardous labor is universal.

There are two main ways in which nations can protect children of a given age from doing hazardous work. Some countries prohibit all work, thus preventing children from doing hazardous work, and some permit general work but set a higher minimum age for work considered hazardous. When legislation differentiates minimum working ages, some countries define hazardous work explicitly in their legislation, and others single out certain categories of work (such as work in mines) and set a higher working age for these industries. The ILO has laid out standards for types of work considered hazardous: "(a) work which exposes children to physical, psychological or sexual abuse; (b) work underground, under water, at dangerous heights or in confined spaces; (c) work with dangerous machinery, equipment and tools, or which involves the manual handling or transport of heavy loads; (d) work in an unhealthy environment which may, for example, expose children to hazardous substances, agents or processes, or to temperatures, noise levels, or vibrations damaging to their health; (e) work under particularly difficult conditions such as work for long hours or during the night or work where the child is unreasonably confined to the premises of the employer."[41] We consider work hazardous if it is defined as such by the country itself or by the ILO, and when analyzing labor legislation, we give nations credit for protecting children from hazardous work at a given age if they take any of these approaches.

Protections from hazardous work should be universal, but 46 countries do not prohibit children and youth from performing hazardous work before the age of 18. Three high-income countries and 13 middle-income countries allow those aged 15 or younger to do hazardous work. In 3 of these countries, Australia, Tonga, and Micronesia, there is no lower age limit for performing hazardous work; Australia is included in this category because although a number of Australian states have protections in place, not all do. In addition, 30 countries, including 10 high-income countries, fail to protect youth and allow 16- or 17-year-olds to perform hazardous work (Map 3.1).*

---

*World Policy Analysis Centre, Child Labour Database. Number of countries for which we have data: 176 (hazardous work).

Map 3.1. How long are children protected from hazardous work?

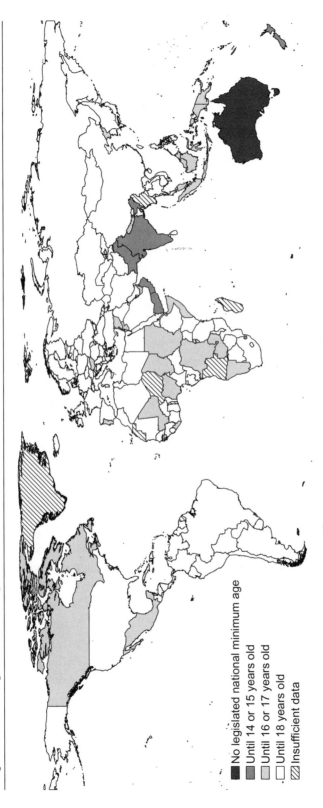

Hazardous work is work that countries themselves or the International Labour Organization define as hazardous. If the country does not specify a separate minimum age for hazardous work, it is assumed that children are protected from hazardous work only for as long as they are protected from general work.

Legend:
- No legislated national minimum age
- Until 14 or 15 years old
- Until 16 or 17 years old
- Until 18 years old
- Insufficient data

Source: World Policy Analysis Centre, Child Labour Database

Even in countries that have set a minimum age for hazardous work, not all children are protected. Many nations include exceptions in their legislation that allow children younger than the official minimum age to do hazardous work.[42] We analyzed what the minimum age is in practice by looking at laws that allow hazardous work for children and youth for particular types of work; upon the request or approval of a government official or body; or for educational, vocational, apprenticeship, volunteer, cultural, or artistic activities. The only exceptions not included in this map are force majeure, which refers to extraordinary circumstances such as war, and when the legislation specifies that work performed under a particular exception must not cause harm to a child (this occurs when a type of work or industry is deemed hazardous in general, but children of a younger age are permitted to do nonhazardous aspects of work in that industry). Map 3.2 shows the minimum age at which a child can perform hazardous work either because legislation routinely allows it or because exceptions to the legislation allow some children to perform such work.

Once exceptions to prohibitions of hazardous work are taken into account, the number of countries permitting this work before age 18 climbs to 83. The most common exceptions allowing children younger than the minimum age to perform hazardous work are for educational, vocational, or training purposes, present in the legislation of 28 countries, or for specific kinds of work, often agricultural, in 20 countries. Twelve countries also allow children to do hazardous work below the minimum age when they are working with family members; however, the presence of relatives does not eliminate children's risk of harm as a result of exposure to hazardous conditions. In 8 countries, children are permitted to do hazardous work if government approval is granted; it is unclear how the criteria for this exception adequately safeguard children.*

Preventing Full-Time Work

As the research evidence discussed earlier in this chapter documents, full-time and extensive part-time work markedly reduce children's

---

*World Policy Analysis Centre, Child Labour Database. Number of countries for which we have data: 176 (hazardous work).

Map 3.2. If exceptions are taken into account, how long are children protected from hazardous work?

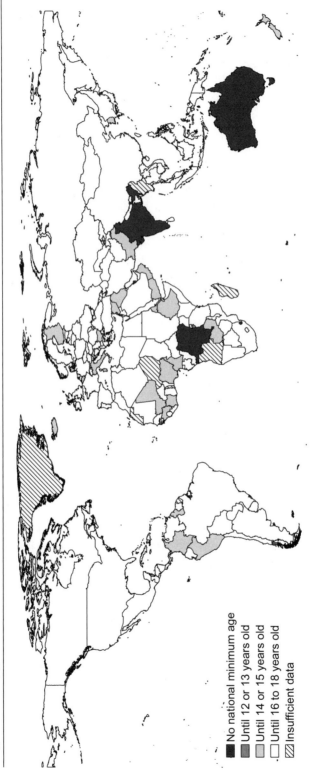

No national minimum age
Until 12 or 13 years old
Until 14 or 15 years old
Until 16 to 18 years old
Insufficient data

Exceptions are cases where the legislation allows children to do hazardous work at younger ages under specific circumstances. For hazardous work, we include any exception to the minimum age for hazardous work except force majeure (extraordinary circumstances such as war).

Source: World Policy Analysis Centre, Child Labour Database

chances at an education and a healthy childhood. Therefore, there has been a large degree of global consensus that children and youth should not have to work extensive hours at a young age. The Convention on the Rights of the Child, which has been ratified by all countries except Somalia and the United States, clearly articulates boys' and girls' right to be free from working long hours during childhood. Article 32 of the convention affirms that "States Parties recognize the right of the child to be protected from economic exploitation and from performing any work that is likely . . . to interfere with the child's education."[43]

We examined labor legislation around the world to determine whether children are protected from working full-time at a young age. We consider 35 or more hours per week full-time work. Many countries specify the number of hours that children are allowed to work per week. In the countries that specify daily rather than weekly hour limits, we combined our data on the minimum working age, the number of hours of work permitted on school days if the child is subject to compulsory schooling, the number of hours permitted on nonschool days, and the number of days of rest guaranteed per week to calculate the maximum number of hours that a child could work at a given age; for more details about this calculation, see Appendix 1. Where a lower working age is permitted with only the requirement of a parent's permission, this lower age is used.

Our results show that in 6 countries, there is no legislated national minimum age for full-time employment.[44] In 5 countries, the minimum age for full-time work is 12 or 13.[45] Countries with no minimum age or with a minimum below 14 clearly contravene the ILO's 1973 Minimum Age Convention, which remains in force and declares that the minimum age of employment should be no less than 15 but that 14 is permitted if a nation's "economy and educational facilities are insufficiently developed."[46]

Many of the countries that meet the 1973 standard still set ages that do not allow youth to complete secondary school, a necessity to compete in the labor market and to exit poverty in a global economy. In 29 countries, the legislated minimum age for full-time employment is 14. These include 16 countries in sub-Saharan Africa, 6 countries in the Americas, 3 countries in East Asia and the Pacific, 3 in South Asia, and 1 in the Middle East and North Africa. In 63 countries, the minimum age for full-time employment is set at 15, which similarly impedes children's ability to finish secondary school. Fifty-nine countries permit full-time work at age 16 or 17, and just 18 countries protect children until the age of 18 (Map 3.3).*

In practice, the number of countries that permit full-time labor by children is likely to be greater than those presented above because of loopholes built into much of the legislation; the hashing on Map 3.3 indicates where these exceptions are present. In 14 countries, there are exceptions to the minimum-age legislation that allow children younger than the minimum age to do specific types of work, such as agricultural work, or to do temporary or seasonal work. However, full-time or high-hour work is as costly for children engaged in agricultural work as in other areas. Twenty-eight countries allow children younger than the minimum age to work if they are working with family members, but working with family members neither ensures that children have a chance at an education nor places expectations on employers to hire adults and pay them an adequate wage so children will not need to supplement family income for survival. Both exceptions are not only costly but may also contribute to the high number of child laborers; two-thirds of child laborers work with family members, and 60 percent of child laborers work in agriculture.[47] Exceptions may also be made when children can work with government approval or when the work is termed essential to the child or family's subsistence, as is the case in 23 countries.

Limiting Labor That Interferes with School

As noted earlier in this chapter, the number of hours children work has a significant effect on the extent to which labor detrimentally affects their life chances. While there is good reason to believe that youth can work a modest number of hours per week without seriously impinging on their education, the scheduling of those hours makes a difference. Youth who work long hours during the school week are unable to take full advantage of their education. In our team's analysis of child labor legislation around the world, we examined the number of hours that nations permit children to work on school days. Some nations

---

*World Policy Analysis Centre, Child Labour Database. Number of countries for which we have data: 180 (full-time work).

Map 3.3. How long are children protected from full-time work?

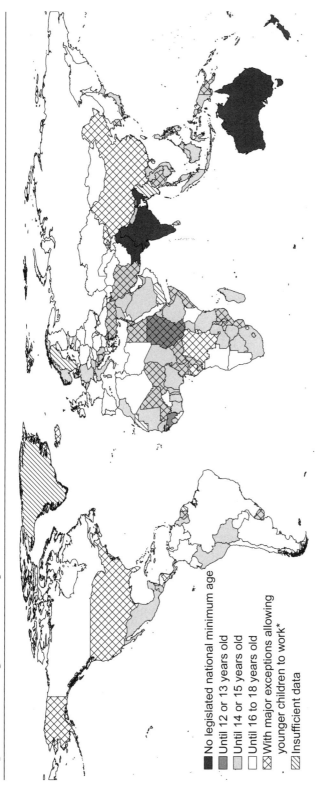

- No legislated national minimum age
- Until 12 or 13 years old
- Until 14 or 15 years old
- Until 16 to 18 years old
- With major exceptions allowing younger children to work*
- Insufficient data

Full-time work is defined as 35 hours of work per week. If a country allows children to work at a younger age subject only to parental permission, the younger age is shown to increase comparability across countries.

Major exceptions include younger ages set for specific types of work, such as agricultural, temporary, or seasonal work; exceptions to allow children to work with family members; and exceptions that require only minister or government approval or when the work is termed indispensable for the child or their family.

Source: World Policy Analysis Centre, Child Labour and Adult Labour Databases

explicitly set a maximum number of hours that children may work on school days.[48] Some countries do not specify the number of hours permitted on school days but do have a general maximum daily number of hours; we assume that these regulations also apply to school days. In some cases, legislation is less explicit about the number of hours that a child can work. Some nations have chosen to protect children by permitting only "light work" on school days, without specifying the number of hours. Light work is defined by the ILO as work for a small number of hours per week that cannot interfere with a child's health, education, or development;[49] we consider that these countries permit fewer than 6 hours of work on school days. Some nations state that work is prohibited during school hours, but do not include additional details. In these cases, to determine whether a child could work for more than 6 hours, we assume that school lasts for 6 hours per day and combine that with our data on the number of hours that children are not permitted to work at night.

Our results show that the majority of countries do not protect secondary-school-age children and youth from having to work for 6 hours or more on school days (Map 3.4). In 12 countries, children can work over 6 hours on school days at age 13 or younger. Thirty-two countries allow children to work for 6 or more hours on school days once they reach the age of 14, and 74 countries permit this once children turn 15, leaving 15-year-olds unprotected from long working hours on school days in a total of 118 countries. In 53 countries, the age at which children can begin working 6 or more hours on school days is 16 or 17. In total, 171 countries permit 6 hours of work or more on school days before a child turns 18.*

Limiting Night Work

Likewise, having to work a night shift impairs anyone's ability to function effectively the next day—schoolchildren and adults alike. Insufficient sleep is associated with a variety of health and behavioral problems; impaired memory, attention, and concentration; and reduced academic performance, including lower grades.[50] When children work

---

*World Policy Analysis Centre, Child Labour Database. Number of countries for which we have data: 180 (work hours on school days).

Map 3.4. How long are children protected from working 6 or more hours on a school day?

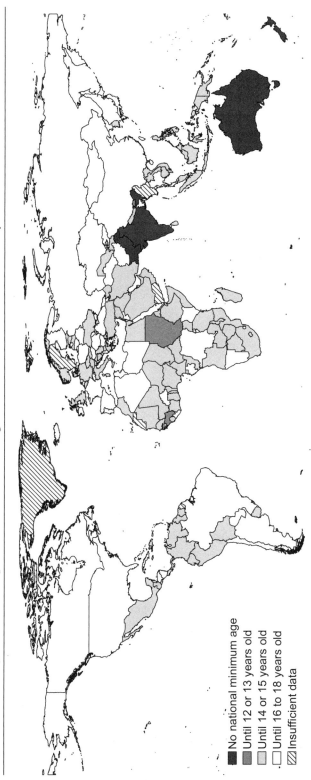

No national minimum age
Until 12 or 13 years old
Until 14 or 15 years old
Until 16 to 18 years old
Insufficient data

If legislation specifies that children can do only light work which by definition should not interfere with schooling, it is assumed that they are protected from working 6 or more hours on a school day.

Source: World Policy Analysis Centre, Child Labour Database

at night, they have an increased risk of work accidents or injuries and a reduced ability to pay attention and learn in the classroom (if they manage to attend school at all). The ILO recommends that legislation guarantee children 12 consecutive hours of night rest.[51]

In far too many countries, children and youth are not guaranteed 12 hours off from work at night until they finish secondary school (Map 3.5). Although these provisions are often termed "night rest," the time it takes to travel from work to home has already cut into these hours. Seventeen-year-olds are not guaranteed 12 hours off at night in a total of 82 countries, 16-year-olds are not guaranteed 12 hours off at night in 58 countries, and 15-year-olds are not guaranteed 12 hours off at night in 25 countries. In 18 countries, children are no longer guaranteed 12 hours off from work at night once they turn 14. Additionally, 7 countries (Australia, New Zealand, Tonga, Micronesia, Dominica, Turkmenistan, and Sudan) do not guarantee 12 hours off at night to children aged 13 or less. In Australia, there are no national provisions for night rest; state-level provisions are inconsistent, and children in some states are unprotected.*

How Long Does Labor Legislation Protect Children and Youth?

Bringing together much of the preceding information, we have evaluated the type of work that children are permitted to do at a given age, taking exceptions into account.[52] Light work is work that does not interfere with a child's health, education, or development; general employment is work that is above this light-work limit but is not hazardous by nature. At age 12, most of the world protects the youngest children from labor. In 106 countries, these children are not allowed to work, and in 26 they are allowed to perform only light work. But general employment is not prohibited for all 12-year-olds in 30 countries, and 15 countries have no work protections or do not protect these children from hazardous work.†

---

*World Policy Analysis Centre, Child Labour Database. Number of countries for which we have data: 180 (night rest).

†World Policy Analysis Centre, Child Labour Database. Number of countries for which we have data: 177 (type of work, age 12).

Map 3.5. How long are children guaranteed 12 hours off from work at night?

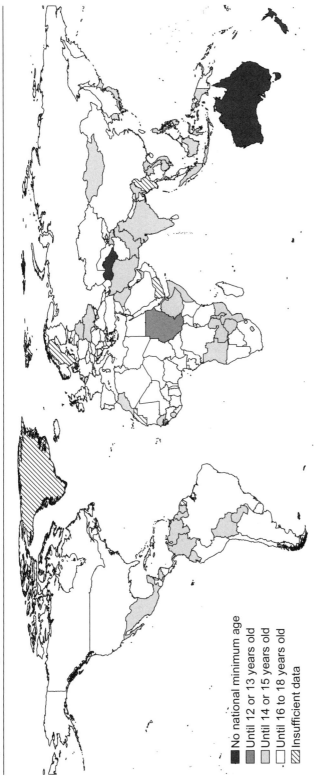

No national minimum age
Until 12 or 13 years old
Until 14 or 15 years old
Until 16 to 18 years old
Insufficient data

If legislation specifies only that a child cannot work at night, it is not assumed that children have at least 12 hours off at night.

Source: World Policy Analysis Centre, Child Labour Database

Map 3.6. If exceptions are taken into account, what work protections do 14-year-olds have?

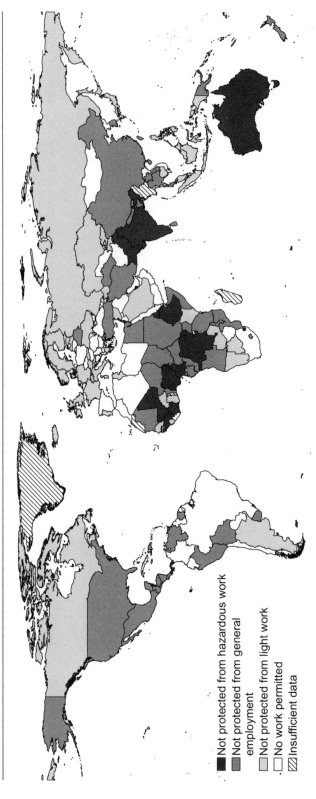

- ■ Not protected from hazardous work
- Not protected from general employment
- Not protected from light work
- □ No work permitted
- ▨ Insufficient data

Exceptions are cases where the legislation allows children to do work at a younger age under specific circumstances. For light work and general employment, exceptions include younger ages set for specific types of work, such as agricultural, temporary, or seasonal work; exceptions to allow children to work with family members; and exceptions that require only minister or government approval or when the work is deemed indispensable for the child or their family. For hazardous work, we include any exception to the minimum age for hazardous work except force majeure (extraordinary circumstances such as war).

Source: *World Policy Analysis Centre, Child Labour Database*

By age 14, fewer children are protected from work that could harm their health, education, or development. In 81 countries, 14-year-olds are not protected from general employment, and in 29 of these countries they could be involved in hazardous work (Map 3.6). By age 16 the majority of children can be working in general employment, many of them in hazardous occupations. Just 5 countries protect 16-year-olds from general employment. In 79 countries these boys and girls can be hired for hazardous work.*

Marrying Young

For many girls, early labor is in the household. This can be work as a paid domestic servant or unpaid labor in their own home. It can also be a consequence of an early marriage that was not their choice. Like child labor, child marriage damages children's chance at an education, jeopardizes their health, and has intergenerational consequences. Although early marriage affects boys as well as girls, it is much less prevalent among boys. The ratio of married girls to married boys aged between 15 and 19 is very high in countries where early marriage is common, such as Mali, where the ratio is 72:1, and is also significant in countries where early marriage is less prevalent, such as the United States (8:1) and El Salvador (6:1).[53]

Forty-six percent of young women in South Asia are married before the age of 18, as are 38 percent in sub-Saharan Africa and 21 percent in Latin America and the Caribbean. Within regions, these rates vary widely by country. The proportion of women who are married before the age of 18 in sub-Saharan African countries ranges from 75 percent in Niger to 6 percent in South Africa.[54] In South Asia, 66 percent of girls in Bangladesh are married before turning 18, compared with 12 percent in Sri Lanka.[55] In countries around the world, girls from low-income families are more likely to be married as children than girls from richer families; this is also true for boys who are married as children.[56]

When girls marry young, they tend to marry men who are significantly older than they are. In Benin, for example, the husbands of girls

---

*World Policy Analysis Centre, Child Labour Database. Number of countries for which we have data: 179 (type of work, age 14), 187 (type of work, age 16).

who married under the age of 18 are an average of 11 years older than their wives, and the husbands of girls who married at age 15 or younger are an average of 12 years older. In India, the husbands of child brides are an average of 7 years older, and in Colombia, they tend to be 6 years older.[57] The age gap between child brides and their husbands tends to be greater than that between men and women who marry as adults.[58] A similar trend has been observed regarding gaps in education between husbands and wives. When a husband and wife have similar levels of education, the wife is less likely to have married as a child.[59]

Detrimental Effects of Early Marriage

When children marry, their education suffers; many girls are forced to drop out of school once they marry.[60] There are a number of reasons for this, including her husband's demands or those of his family; the perception that married girls have no need for education or that they are adults and thus do not belong in school; and, in some cases, married girls' legal exclusion from schools. In a number of African countries, such as Burkina Faso, Cameroon, Côte d'Ivoire, Ghana, Guinea, Nigeria, and Togo, between 12 and 22 percent of school dropouts among girls are attributed to early marriage.[61] In rural Bangladesh, which has one of the world's highest rates of early marriage, a study found that each additional year that marriage was delayed among girls who were enrolled in school at age 9 resulted in a 5.6 percent increase in literacy. The authors estimated that if the average age of marriage among girls was increased to 18 from the current average age of 15, average years of schooling among girls, as well as female literacy rates, would increase by close to 15 percent.[62] Limited education in turn affects subsequent financial independence through employment.

Clearly, early marriage can be detrimental to a child's education, but is it detrimental to health? Many women under the age of 18 have a sexual partner outside marriage. Are the risks higher for those who marry? In fact, evidence shows that early marriage and early childbirth have serious health consequences for both mother and child.

Women who marry as children are less likely to have control over their health decisions and freedom of movement, as well as household expenditures, than women who marry as adults.[63] Early marriage has been linked with lower contraceptive use resulting from a lack of accurate information about options, from the pressure on young married girls to prove their fertility and quickly begin bearing children, and from their limited control over sexual and reproductive decisions.[64] The limited use of contraceptives, the high prevalence of sexual abuse, and the large age and power gaps between spouses all contribute to putting women who married as children at higher risk of contracting HIV and other sexually transmitted diseases than women who married at an older age and unmarried girls who are sexually active.[65] Furthermore, young wives' limited access to information and resources influences their ability to access necessary health care.[66] A study in Bangladesh showed that among women who had been enrolled in school at age 9, delaying marriage by 1 year was linked with an 8.6 percent increase in the likelihood of their receiving prenatal care and a 5.7 percent increase in the average number of prenatal care visits they received. Delaying marriage also affected health decisions among women who had never attended school.[67]

In addition, early marriages commonly result in early childbirth, which can have serious effects on both mothers and babies.[68] In Togo, for example, the maternal mortality rate for women giving birth between the ages of 15 and 19 is 286 per 100,000 live births, compared with 39 for women giving birth between the ages of 20 and 34. Across the ocean in Guatemala, the maternal mortality rate for girls aged 15 to 19 is 35 per 100,000, compared with just 5 for women in their early twenties.[69] Around the world, compared with maternal mortality among women giving birth in their twenties, mortality in childbirth is twice as high among girls aged 15 to 19 years and 5 times as high among girls under age 15.[70] Factors contributing to the high rates of maternal mortality and morbidity among young mothers include eclampsia, anemia, postpartum hemorrhage, and obstructed labor.[71] These higher rates are partially attributable to the physical limitations of younger and smaller bodies.[72]

Even when young mothers survive childbirth, their increased likelihood of obstructed labor markedly increases their chance of experiencing significant morbidity following pregnancy, including the formation of fistulae.[73] Fistulae are caused by the pressure of the baby in the vagina for long periods of time during obstructed labor, which cuts off the blood supply to parts of the tissue, causes the tissue to decompose, and leaves a hole between the vagina and the bladder or rectum, leading to incontinence. Beyond their high degree of morbidity, fistulae can also cause social stigma, ostracism, and isolation.[74]

When a girl becomes a parent young, her child's chance of healthy development suffers just like her own. Infant mortality rates are higher for babies born to young mothers around the world, and their mortality and morbidity rates continue to be higher through age 5.[75] A child born to a teenager has double the chance of dying in the first year of life compared with a child born to a mother in her twenties.[76] Higher rates of preterm delivery, infant low birth weight, and stillbirths have also been documented among young mothers.[77]

Finally, wives who married as children are at higher risk of sexual and physical abuse within their marriage.[78] For example, in Colombia, women who married before the age of 18 were more likely to have experienced emotional, physical, and sexual abuse within their marriage than women who married as adults; women who married at age 15 or younger were the most likely of all to have experienced this abuse, and the prevalence of abuse decreased as their age at marriage increased.[79] In India, women who married as children were nearly three times more likely to have been beaten in the previous year than women who married at age 21 or older.[80]

Minimum-Age Legislation

How much are countries doing to eliminate child marriage? What laws, if any, address the disproportionate impact on girls? To begin to answer these questions, we built a database analyzing the minimum age of marriage for girls and boys around the world.[81] We drew on country reports submitted to the monitoring committees of the UN Convention on the Rights of the Child and the UN Convention on the Elimination of All Forms of Discrimination against Women between 2005 and 2011, as well as the committees' concluding observations. When data were unavailable or incomplete, we drew on national legislative sources and legal compendiums. The minimum ages presented here represent the youngest age at which a girl or boy can be married with no restrictions, or subject only to parental permission. Because the vast majority of child marriages occur with parental permission and involvement, we do not consider this requirement alone sufficiently protective for at-risk children.

Map 3.7. How long are girls protected from marriage compared with boys?

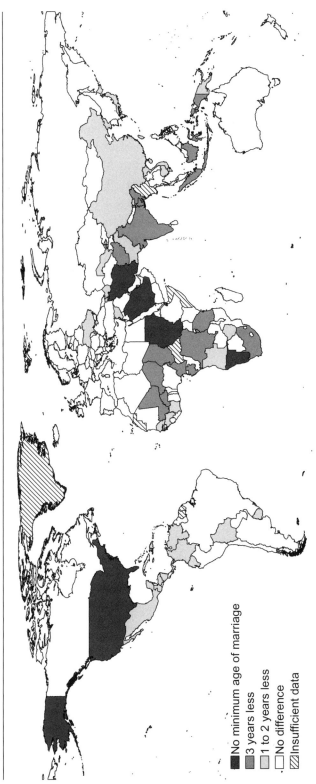

No minimum age of marriage
3 years less
1 to 2 years less
No difference
Insufficient data

If a country allows children to marry at a younger age subject only to parental permission, the younger age is used. There are no cases where the minimum age for boys to marry is younger than the minimum age for girls.

Source: World Policy Analysis Centre, Child Marriage Database

In 7 countries, there is no nationally set minimum legal age of marriage: Djibouti, the Gambia, Iran, Namibia, Saudi Arabia, Sudan, and the United States. Twelve countries allow girls to be married at age 13 or younger. Although the research evidence is clear about the enormous health and educational consequences of marriage at or below age 15, another 30 countries allow girls to be married at age 14 or 15, including 13 in the Americas, 10 in sub-Saharan Africa, 4 in East Asia and the Pacific, 2 in the Middle East and North Africa, and 1 in South Asia. In 57 countries, girls can be married at age 16 or 17.*

Boys are guaranteed a chance to grow up free from marriage for somewhat longer. Only half as many countries allow boys to marry at age 13 (6 countries) or at age 14 or 15 (15 countries) as allow girls to do so.† Forty-three countries permit boys to marry at age 16 or 17.[82]

We also mapped the disparity in the ages at which girls and boys are protected from early marriage (see Map 3.7). Do these age protections reflect the disproportionate impact of early marriage on girls? While the minimum age of marriage does not differ for boys and girls in 120 countries, girls can be married at an age 3 or more years younger than boys in 17 countries. These include 11 countries in sub-Saharan Africa, 3 in South Asia, 2 in East Asia and the Pacific, and 1 in the Americas. In an additional 37 countries, girls can marry 1 to 2 years earlier than boys. In no country can boys be married at a younger age than girls.‡

Protecting Childhood

In order for children to have a chance at childhood, they should not have to perform the work of adults, should not have to marry or bear children when they are children themselves, and should have the chance to attend school.

We examined what we have termed "protected childhood," which represents a period during which general employment and marriage

---

*World Policy Analysis Centre, Child Marriage Database. Number of countries for which we have data: 183 (age of marriage for girls).

†World Policy Analysis Centre, Child Marriage Database. Number of countries for which we have data: 180 (age of marriage for boys).

‡World Policy Analysis Centre, Child Marriage Database. Number of countries for which we have data: 181 (difference in age of marriage for girls and boys).

are prohibited and education is compulsory. In 104 countries, childhood is protected until age 12. Twelve countries do not make education compulsory at this age, 25 do not prohibit employment, and 6 permit marriage. In 12 countries, two of these areas are not protected. At age 14, 77 countries continue to protect all aspects of childhood, 2 do not protect any of these areas, and 35 lack protection for two of them. By the age of 16, no country prohibits marriage, makes education compulsory, and prohibits employment. Fifty countries do not protect 16-year-olds in any of these areas, and 85 lack protections in two areas.*

Strengthening Legal Solutions

Although it is commonly accepted that legislation is an important first step in addressing both child labor and early marriage, laws alone are often not enough. Clearly there are countries that have high rates of child marriage or child labor despite laws that prohibit these practices. This does not undermine the importance of legal action; instead, it underscores the importance of implementation and multifaceted interventions.

What can countries do to ensure that child labor legislation is effective? First, laws should establish sanctions for child labor violations that are severe enough to deter employers from using child labor. These laws and sanctions need to be strictly enforced. In addition, complementary legislation should reinforce the minimum working age laws. For example, free and compulsory schooling should not end at a younger age than the minimum age for general employment, since this contradiction undermines the effectiveness of the minimum working age. This is especially important in order to reach children working in areas that are difficult to regulate, such as domestic work and the informal

---

*World Policy Analysis Centre, Child Labour Database, Child Marriage Database, and Education Database. Number of countries for which we have data: 159 (protected childhood, age 12), 160 (protected childhood, age 14), 165 (protected childhood, age 16). When the minimum age for marriage differs for girls and boys, the younger age is used. The minimum age for general employment includes major exceptions.

economy, because it is easier to verify that a child is attending school than that he or she is not working.[83]

Similarly, the specifics of child marriage laws shape their efficacy.[84] As our data show, in many cases the law is not gender neutral but reinforces the disparities in disadvantage experienced by girls. Laws need to be changed to treat girls and boys equitably. Additionally, the data we presented take into account only marriage permitted with no restrictions or subject only to parental consent. The minimum ages we present, already problematic in many cases, may not even apply to all children. Many marriage laws have additional exceptions that allow younger children to marry, such as when members of certain ethnic or religious communities are exempt from civil laws and can operate instead under alternative legal systems, or when younger girls or boys are permitted to marry under "special circumstances" that are often so poorly defined that they essentially remove the impact of the law. These loopholes must be closed.

Once an appropriate minimum age has been established by law, sanctions should be defined and imposed on anyone involved in arranging, officiating at, or facilitating a marriage involving a child. As recommended by UNICEF, reporting of child marriage should be made mandatory. The law should allow married children to apply without barriers to make such marriages void. Once a marriage is declared void, protection must be the paramount concern. It is crucial that child marriage laws exist in a legal framework that is not discriminatory toward women and girls. A woman's right to property, to joint custody of her children, and to protection from harm must be recognized. It must be ensured that she has a place to go and adequate resources to support herself.[85]

Knowing a child's age is essential to the efficacy of both child labor and child marriage legislation. Efforts to universalize birth registration are an important foundation. The absence of birth registration is a significant problem in many countries; unregistered children are less likely to get protection from legislation covering child labor and early marriage because their exact ages, and in some cases their existence, are not officially known. Children from poor families are less likely to have their birth officially registered and are more likely to experience child labor and early marriage. In South Asia, which has the world's greatest number of child laborers, just 21 percent of children from the poorest quintile are registered at birth; even among the richest families, only 60 percent of births are registered. In sub-Saharan Africa, which has the highest proportion of working children, only one-fifth of the poorest children are registered, compared with over half of the richest. These disparities exist in every region.[86]

In addition to the importance of civil laws, the contexts in which these laws operate are fundamental to their impact. In many countries, civil law exists alongside parallel legal systems such as customary or religious law. Although civil law may prohibit child marriage, customary law may allow it, weakening the civil law prohibitions.[87] In Liberia, for example, while the civil law set the minimum age for marriage at 18, or 16 with parental consent, customary law governing some populations permitted girls to marry as young as 15.[88]

Critical Complementary Interventions

There are compelling arguments that poverty and education have a powerful impact on child labor and child marriage, and substantial evidence supports the importance of related interventions to complement legal solutions.

The power of poverty and education has been revealed by the success of approaches to child labor reduction that combine legislative bans on child labor with income- and education-focused supports. Brazil markedly reduced child labor and increased school attendance through this combination. It established a powerful legislative framework around children's rights and protections in its new constitution and in its Child and Adolescent Statute (1990). Specifically, this statute addresses access to education in detail, sets the minimum age for employment at 14, includes protections for employed adolescents, and establishes enforcement and complaint mechanisms for children's rights. These reforms, combined with the 8 years of compulsory education mandated by the new constitution (later increased to 9 years), gave Brazil a highly lauded foundation for child protection.[89] In 1996, Brazil supplemented this legislation with the Programa de Erradicação do Trabalho Infantil (Program for the Eradication of Child Labor), a government-funded conditional cash transfer program targeting child laborers in rural areas, particularly those involved in the worst forms of child labor.[90] The program mandates school attendance and provides an income transfer to families to compensate for the income lost because of increased school attendance. The program was largely successful: among participating children, the average number of hours per week spent in school rose by between 11 and 17 hours, the hours spent at work were cut nearly in half, and academic success improved. Moreover, the program reduced children's participation in hazardous occupations.[91]

Other nations, such as Bangladesh, Mexico, and Ecuador, have similarly increased school attendance and decreased child labor by supplementing legal restrictions on child labor with provisions for compulsory schooling and conditional cash transfers.[92] In order for this strategy to be successful, educational facilities must be equipped to deal with the increased demand for schooling, and cash transfers must be sufficient to lift families above the subsistence level without depending on income from child labor. Brazil's program, for instance, was less successful in reducing the work hours of children who worked longer hours per week before the program began,[93] perhaps because of the greater income contribution needed by their families. Additionally, although cash transfers may reduce children's work hours in ordinary circumstances, they may not be sufficient to protect children from the need to work as a response to economic shocks.[94] Nonetheless, combining poverty- and education-related programs with legislation can be an effective option for nations seeking to address child labor.

Income-replacement programs and the provision of educational alternatives to child labor require immediate government expenditures, but there are substantial economic returns to these investments. The economic benefits of eliminating child labor are expected to exceed the costs by 6.7 to 1 over a 20-year time span, according to a global study by the ILO.[95]

How much of a role does poverty play in early marriage? Although the extent to which early marriage is driven by social norms versus social constraints may be difficult to determine, there is little doubt that poverty plays a strong role.[96] Poverty may encourage early marriage where families' economic costs are reduced or gains are increased by early marriage. The bride-price a husband pays to a wife's family can encourage a girl's family to marry her young to meet financial needs. Where dowries are the norm, the dowry that a wife's family must pay to the husband's family may be lower when a girl marries at a younger age. Even in the absence of both payments, families may hope to provide daughters with more economic security through marriage than they are able to give her. Child marriage rates are most common in the poorest 20 percent of households in all 48 of the countries analyzed by UNICEF.[97]

Programs combining financial incentives with initiatives aimed at other factors that influence child marriage have enjoyed considerable success. Social norms regarding gender roles, marriageable age, and marital relationships often have a large impact on child marriage,[98] and programs have successfully addressed these factors directly and indirectly by addressing economic factors that often undergird them. For example, a program in rural Ethiopia aiming to reduce the prevalence of early marriage combined support for girls' schooling, including financial incentives and provision of school materials, with community discussions of key issues. An assessment of the program 2 years later, based on a quasi-experimental research design comparing the program's participants with girls in a control area, found that 10- to 14-year-old girls exposed to the program were 10 times less likely to have gotten married than their counterparts. Although marriage during older adolescence remained common, the program seems to have delayed marriage among younger girls.[99]

Can educational opportunities make a difference as well? On the one hand, although child marriage often creates a barrier to attending school, being a student might do little to protect girls from familial and social pressures to marry. On the other hand, if secondary school were available and affordable, it could change the economic equation;[100] parents might be less likely to seek out marriage opportunities right away, and girls might be less likely to choose to marry right away. Furthermore, education can increase girls' sense of autonomy, make girls less susceptible to pressure to marry, and give them greater influence over whom they marry and when. In nations as diverse as Ghana, Indonesia, Mexico, Sri Lanka, Taiwan, and Thailand, increased education has been linked to increased age at marriage.[101] It is estimated that in the majority of sub-Saharan African countries, increased education accounts for at least half of the observed declines in early marriage rates.[102] Moreover, the daughters of women with more education are more likely to be sent to school and are less likely to be married early.[103]

In order to promote girls' education, it is important to ensure that schools are in practice accessible to them. Expanding free and compulsory education beyond primary school to the secondary level is vital.[104] Providing parents with financial incentives to offset the costs of sending children, especially girls, to school can help improve educational attainment and reduce early marriage.[105] Improving employment opportunities for women once they are educated is also important.[106] In Bangladesh and Taiwan, both parents and girls viewed delaying marriage more positively when job opportunities were available for young women.[107]

Child labor, marriage, and education policies are fundamentally intertwined. When children marry young, they are less likely to continue going to school; when they are prohibited from working, they can stay longer in school. When the laws targeting each of these areas are complementary, their power increases exponentially; when they are contradictory, their impact is severely limited.

Clearly, we need to ensure that child labor and marriage laws protect children and youth in all countries. We also need to close the loopholes. Child labor laws must explicitly apply to work areas that are often excluded from labor legislation. Although the majority of child laborers work in the agricultural sector, often under potentially dangerous conditions, to date this area has received inadequate attention, as has domestic labor. Marriage laws offer inadequate protection if they make exceptions for young children with family permission and reinforce gender inequities.

At the same time, we will succeed at reducing both child labor and child marriage only by addressing the underlying social and economic drivers. Neither child labor nor child marriage exists alone. Child labor laws can affect and are influenced by poverty policy. When children are not allowed to work full-time and when there are no exceptions to the legislation, employers cannot use lower child wages to undercut adult wages, and governments need to ensure that adult minimum wages are sufficient to support a family; thus family incomes increase in the long term through adult earnings instead of relying on children's. More immediately, when poverty is addressed, as discussed in Chapter 6, pressures for child labor and marriage are reduced.

Table 3.1. Legal protections against hazardous work for children

	Low-Income	Middle-Income	High-Income
Age Until Which Children are Protected from Hazardous Work			
No legislated national minimum age for hazardous work	0 (0%)	2 (2%)	1 (2%)
Protected from hazardous work until age 14	0 (0%)	4 (4%)	0 (0%)
Protected from hazardous work until age 15	0 (0%)	7 (7%)	2 (4%)
Protected from hazardous work until age 16	7 (23%)	11 (11%)	8 (17%)
Protected from hazardous work until age 17	0 (0%)	2 (2%)	2 (4%)
Protected from hazardous work until age 18	23 (77%)	73 (74%)	34 (72%)
Age Until Which Children are Protected from Hazardous Work when Exceptions to Minimum-Age Protections are Considered			
No legislated national minimum age for hazardous work	0 (0%)	7 (7%)	4 (9%)
Protected from hazardous work only until age 12 or 13	1 (3%)	4 (4%)	0 (0%)
Protected from hazardous work until age 14	4 (13%)	6 (6%)	3 (6%)
Protected from hazardous work until age 15	0 (0%)	11 (11%)	9 (19%)
Protected from hazardous work until age 16	6 (20%)	13 (13%)	11 (23%)
Protected from hazardous work until age 17	0 (0%)	2 (2%)	2 (4%)
Protected from hazardous work until age 18	19 (63%)	56 (57%)	18 (38%)

(continued)

Table 3.1 (continued)

Examples of Exceptions to Minimum-Age Protections for Hazardous Work (Countries may have several)			
Minimum-age protection excludes children engaged in specific types of work, including agricultural	2 (7%)	11 (11%)	7 (15%)
Minimum-age protection excludes children engaged in work with family members	0 (0%)	8 (8%)	4 (9%)
Minimum-age protection excludes cases where children can work with government approval	1 (3%)	6 (6%)	1 (2%)
Minimum-age protection excludes children engaged in vocational work	3 (10%)	14 (14%)	11 (24%)

Source : World Policy Analysis Centre, Child Labour Database.

Definitions: Hazardous work is work that countries themselves or the International Labour Organization define as hazardous.

Exceptions are cases where the legislation allows children to do hazardous work at younger ages under specific circumstances. For hazardous work, we include any exception to the minimum age for hazardous work except force majeure (extraordinary circumstances such as war).

Low-income, middle-income, and *high-income* refer to World Bank classifications of national income. Here, middle-income countries include those classified as lower-middle and upper-middle income.

Notes: If the country does not specify a separate minimum age for hazardous work, it is assumed that children are protected from hazardous work only for as long as they are protected from general work.

Table 3.2. Legal protections regulating children's hours of work

	Low-Income	Middle-Income	High-Income
Age Until Which Children are Protected from Working 6 or More Hours on a School Day			
No legislated national minimum age for work and no protection	0 (0%)	4 (4%)	2 (4%)
Protected only until age 12 or 13	1 (3%)	5 (5%)	0 (0%)
Protected until age 14	10 (30%)	20 (20%)	2 (4%)
Protected until age 15	13 (39%)	39 (39%)	22 (47%)
Protected until age 16	7 (21%)	28 (28%)	15 (32%)
Protected until age 17	0 (0%)	1 (1%)	2 (4%)
Protected until age 18	2 (6%)	3 (3%)	4 (9%)
Age Until Which Children are Guaranteed 12 Hours Off from Work at Night			
No legislated national minimum age for work and no guarantee	0 (0%)	3 (3%)	2 (4%)
Guaranteed only until age 12 or 13	0 (0%)	2 (2%)	0 (0%)
Guaranteed until age 14	3 (9%)	14 (14%)	1 (2%)
Guaranteed until age 15	7 (21%)	20 (20%)	6 (13%)
Guaranteed until age 16	3 (9%)	14 (14%)	5 (11%)
Guaranteed until age 17	0 (0%)	1 (1%)	1 (2%)
Guaranteed until age 18	20 (61%)	46 (46%)	32 (68%)
Minimum Age Protection for Full-Time Work			
No legislated national minimum age for full-time work	0 (0%)	4 (4%)	2 (4%)
Minimum age for full-time work is 12 or 13	1 (3%)	4 (4%)	0 (0%)
Minimum age for full-time work is 14	11 (33%)	16 (16%)	2 (4%)

(continued)

Table 3.2 (*continued*)

Minimum age for full-time work is 15	11 (33%)	34 (34%)	18 (38%)
Minimum age for full-time work is 16	8 (24%)	31 (31%)	16 (34%)
Minimum age for full-time work is 17	0 (0%)	2 (2%)	2 (4%)
Minimum age for full-time work is 18	2 (6%)	9 (9%)	7 (15%)
Examples of Exceptions to Minimum-Age Protections for General Employment (Countries may have several)			
Minimum-age protection excludes children engaged in specific types of work, including agricultural, temporary, or seasonal work	1 (3%)	11 (11%)	2 (4%)
Minimum-age protection excludes children engaged in work with family members	5 (15%)	16 (17%)	7 (16%)
Minimum-age protection excludes cases where children can work with government approval or when the work is termed indispensable for the child or their family	7 (21%)	13 (14%)	3 (7%)
Minimum-age protection excludes children engaged in vocational work	9 (27%)	32 (33%)	19 (42%)

Source: World Policy Analysis Centre, Child Labour Database.

Definition: *Full-time work* is defined as 35 hours of work per week. If a country allows children to work at a younger age subject only to parental permission, the younger age is shown to increase comparability across countries.

Notes: If legislation specifies that children can do only light work, it is assumed that they are protected from working 6 or more hours on a school day.

If legislation specifies only that a child cannot work at night, it is not assumed that children have at least 12 hours off at night.

Table 3.3. Legal protections against child marriage

	Low-Income	Middle-Income	High-Income
Minimum Legal Age of Marriage for Girls			
No minimum age of marriage	1 (3%)	4 (4%)	2 (4%)
Girls are protected only until age 13 or younger	0 (0%)	4 (4%)	1 (2%)
Girls are protected until age 14	0 (0%)	6 (6%)	1 (2%)
Girls are protected until age 15	7 (21%)	12 (12%)	4 (8%)
Girls are protected until age 16	6 (18%)	27 (26%)	11 (23%)
Girls are protected until age 17	4 (12%)	8 (8%)	1 (2%)
Girls are protected until age 18 or older	15 (45%)	41 (40%)	28 (58%)
Minimum Legal Age of Marriage for Boys			
No minimum age of marriage	1 (3%)	4 (4%)	1 (2%)
Boys are protected until age 14	0 (0%)	4 (4%)	2 (4%)
Boys are protected until age 15	1 (3%)	5 (5%)	3 (6%)
Boys are protected until age 16	4 (13%)	25 (25%)	8 (17%)
Boys are protected until age 17	1 (3%)	3 (3%)	2 (4%)
Boys are protected until age 18 or older	25 (78%)	60 (59%)	31 (66%)

(continued)

Table 3.3 *(continued)*

Difference in Legal Age of Marriage between Girls and Boys			
The law does not establish a minimum age of marriage	1 (3%)	4 (4%)	2 (4%)
Minimum legal age for girls is 3 or more years lower than for boys	9 (28%)	8 (8%)	0 (0%)
Minimum legal age for girls is 2 years lower than for boys	2 (6%)	20 (20%)	5 (10%)
Minimum legal age for girls is 1 year lower than for boys	2 (6%)	8 (8%)	0 (0%)
Minimum legal age to marry is the same for girls and boys	18 (56%)	61 (60%)	41 (85%)

Source : World Policy Analysis Centre, Child Marriage Database.

Definition: Minimum legal age is the age at which a child is permitted to marry subject to no conditions or subject only to parental consent.

Note: There are no cases where the minimum age for boys to marry is younger than the minimum age for girls.

Table 3.4. Legal protections from work for children at ages 12, 14, and 16

	Age 12	Age 14	Age 16
Legal Protections Against Working on a School Day			
Children are legally protected from performing any work on a school day	137 (75%)	65 (36%)	2 (1%)
Children are legally protected from working more than 1 - 2.9 hours on a school day	5 (3%)	20 (11%)	1 (1%)
Children are legally protected from working more than 3 - 5.9 hours on a school day	3 (2%)	12 (7%)	4 (2%)
Children are legally protected from working more than 6 - 7.9 hours on a school day	3 (2%)	18 (10%)	49 (27%)
Children are not legally protected from working 8 hours or more on a school day	7 (4%)	28 (15%)	120 (66%)
Children are legally protected from performing anything other than light work on a school day	28 (15%)	40 (22%)	5 (3%)
Legal Guarantees of Time Off From Work at Night for Children			
Children are protected from working at any time	169 (94%)	128 (71%)	6 (3%)
Children are guaranteed at least 12 hours off from work at night	4 (2%)	27 (15%)	94 (52%)
Children are guaranteed only 10 - 11.9 hours off from work at night	2 (1%)	11 (6%)	23 (13%)
Children are guaranteed fewer than 10 hours off from work at night	2 (1%)	6 (3%)	22 (12%)

(continued)

Table 3.4 (*continued*)

Children may not work at night but are not protected for a specified length of time	0 (0%)	2 (1%)	7 (4%)
Children are not guaranteed a period of time off from work at night	3 (2%)	6 (3%)	28 (16%)
Work Protections for Children When Legal Exceptions are Considered			
Children are protected from engaging in work	106 (60%)	44 (25%)	2 (1%)
Children are not protected from engaging in light work	26 (15%)	54 (30%)	3 (2%)
Children are not protected from engaging in general employment	30 (17%)	52 (29%)	103 (55%)
Children are not protected from engaging in hazardous work, or there are no protections for children's work	15 (8%)	29 (16%)	79 (42%)

Source : World Policy Analysis Centre, Child Labour Database.

Definition : Legal exceptions are cases where the legislation allows children to do work at a younger age under specific circumstances. For light work and general employment, exceptions incorporated include younger ages set for specific types of work, such as agricultural, temporary, or seasonal work; exceptions to allow children to work with family members; and exceptions that require only minister or government approval or when the work is termed indispensable for the child or their family. For hazardous work, we include any exception to the minimum age for hazardous work except force majeure (extraordinary circumstances such as war).

Table 3.5. Overall protection of children in work, marriage, and education at ages 12, 14, and 16

	Age 12	Age 14	Age 16
Three Protections:			
Children are protected from labor and marriage, and education is compulsory	104 (65%)	77 (48%)	0 (0%)
Two Protections:			
Children are protected from labor and marriage, but education is not compulsory	12 (8%)	10 (6%)	1 (1%)
Children are protected from marriage and education is compulsory, but labor is permitted	25 (16%)	33 (21%)	27 (16%)
Children are protected from labor and education is compulsory, but marriage is permitted	6 (4%)	3 (2%)	2 (1%)
One Protection:			
Children are protected from marriage, but labor is permitted and education is not compulsory	6 (4%)	21 (13%)	64 (39%)
Children are protected from labor, but marriage is permitted and education is not compulsory	2 (1%)	3 (2%)	2 (1%)
Education is compulsory, but labor and marriage are permitted	4 (3%)	11 (7%)	19 (12%)
No Protections:			
Labor is permitted, marriage is permitted, and education is not compulsory	0 (0%)	2 (1%)	50 (30%)

Sources: World Policy Analysis Centre, Child Labour Database, Child Marriage Database, and Education Database.

Chapter 4

Beyond Survival to Health

Limited access to health care left a deep scar on the life of Iris García Flores. When she was less than 2 months old, she got sick; her mother could barely afford health care and so did not immediately seek the help of a physician. Moreover, services were limited in the small town in which she lived. Her mother explained, "The girl wasn't even 40 days old when she started to get a fever. What happened is that my husband was living in [another town for work], and I was here without money, without anything." When Iris did receive care, it was inadequate. Her mother continued, "The doctor said it was a stomach infection. We had her at the hospital for two days and on the third day they said that she wasn't—that she was going to die. Then I left, desperate, and I looked for another doctor. . . . I took her to an infants' hospital in Tuxtla Gutiérrez [a larger city] and there they told me that it was meningitis . . . and that she was going to have problems."

Although meningitis is inevitably acutely serious, had Iris had access to adequate health care sooner, the long-term consequences of her illness could have been reduced. By the time she received specialized care, Iris's illness was so advanced that little could be done to mitigate its effects. Iris survived, but she lost her hearing and had seizures for months as she recovered. No specialized care was available near her home, and her mother could not often afford to take Iris to Mexico City to see doctors with expertise in acquired hearing loss or epilepsy.

> *While she was fortunate to have survived, the consequences of her illness and insufficient medical care were severe. In a context with few supports for the deaf, the inadequate treatment she had received drastically limited her chances at education. At the age of 13, Iris had never learned to speak; she made guttural sounds to communicate with her mother and sister. Her cognitive capacity was unaffected by her illness, but the school she had attended was of such poor quality that she had not been taught enough sign language or lip reading to communicate fluently. These communication difficulties also meant that she was never left alone or given the chance at an independent life.[1]*

Like Iris, the lives of millions of children are shaped by whether their families have adequate access to public health services and medical care. Each year, 4 million children do not live even 1 month;[2] they most commonly die as a result of preterm birth, asphyxia, and infection, including pneumonia, diarrhea, tetanus, and sepsis.[3] Three-quarters of these infants die within a week after birth.[4] If all children under the age of 5 are considered, the number of deaths more than doubles. Together, over 40 percent of child deaths are caused by pneumonia, diarrhea, and malaria;[5] many of these deaths could be prevented through known and affordable interventions, from providing safe water sources and insecticide-treated mosquito nets to making medical care available to treat children before their pneumonia becomes life threatening. Even when they do not lead to loss of life, preventable and readily treatable conditions take a large toll on children's daily lives and can have long-term effects.[6]

Although children may become ill or injured during middle childhood, the highest risks are in the first few years of life and then again during adolescence. During youth, among the most prevalent risks are accidents, tobacco, alcohol, and sexual exposures.[7]

Who Gets Sick and Injured?

If all children are to be given an equal opportunity to reach their full potential, the first step must be making sure that they survive and that avoidable poor health and disability do not limit their options. Disease and injury are often seen as biological or random risks, but in fact the risks of dying as a young child, becoming ill frequently or chronically,

being injured, and not receiving adequate health care are not distrib-
uted evenly either around the globe or within nations. They are determined far more by the conditions under which children live than by
chance or their genetic endowment.

A look at the statistics makes the pattern of socioeconomic disparities devastatingly clear. At a regional level, children in industrialized
countries fare relatively well, with less than 1 percent of children, or
6 per 1,000 live births, dying before the age of 5. In Latin America and
the Caribbean, nearly 4 times as many children die before this young
age; the same is true in Eastern Europe and Central Asia. In South
Asia, children are more than 12 times as likely to die before reaching
age 5 as children in industrialized countries; in sub-Saharan Africa,
they are 24 times as likely to die.[8] Over 95 percent of child deaths resulting from injury occur in low- and middle-income countries.[9] At
the same time, within high-income countries, the odds of dying young
are higher for poor children. In the United States, children living in
poor counties are more than 50 percent more likely to die than those
living in affluent ones,[10] and in New Zealand, low-income children living in poor areas are more than twice as likely to die as their higher-
income counterparts.[11]

Poverty and equity are fundamental determinants of the likelihood
of any child becoming sick or injured and need to be addressed directly; this book discusses these key social determinants of health in
Chapters 6 and 7. While policies that affect social conditions form a
critical foundation for child health, access to health care shapes children's outcomes when they become sick or injured, and public health
measures play an essential role in reducing leading causes of morbidity
and mortality.

Children from poor families are disadvantaged here as well; within
high- and low-income countries alike, poor children are less likely to
be immunized, to have a skilled attendant present at their birth, and to
receive prenatal care.[12] The disparities hold true even for simple therapeutic and preventive measures.[13] As just one example, in sub-Saharan
Africa, children from high-income families are 60 percent more likely
than the lowest-income children to sleep with the protection of
insecticide-treated nets, a key intervention for malaria prevention, and
70 percent more likely to receive appropriate medication when malaria
is suspected.[14] A study in the United States showed that women from

the poorest income group were 8 times more likely to lack prenatal care than women from the most affluent group.[15]

Beyond socioeconomic disparities, other aspects of equity can affect children's access to prevention and treatment, particularly when families bear part of the cost. In northern India, for example, parents are more likely to have their sons immunized than their daughters, and this contributes to the excess girl child mortality documented in this region.[16] Rural Chinese parents are more likely to seek medical care for their sons than for their daughters when they are ill.[17] In Pakistan, young boys tend to be favored in health-care allocation compared with their sisters.[18] In Nepal, a study found that although polio affects boys and girls at equal rates, the survival rate for boys with polio was double that of girls, a disparity attributed to a combination of girls not receiving adequate medical care and being given less access to nutrition and other resources.[19]

In this chapter, we address the public health and medical-care side of child health.

Prevention during Early Childhood

Although some children will inevitably become ill and require medical care, the majority of early childhood illnesses that currently occur are preventable. Simple steps such as breastfeeding, immunization, and access to safe water and sanitation facilities have long been known to tip the balance dramatically toward child survival and healthy development. It has been estimated that nearly two-thirds of the child deaths occurring each year could be prevented by known and affordable interventions. These include preventive interventions, such as immunizations, breastfeeding, and vitamin A supplementation, as well as treatment interventions, including oral rehydration therapy and antibiotics.[20] As with other topics covered in this volume, an entire book could be dedicated solely to the subject of measuring how well a country is preventing diseases and injuries and promoting the health of its children; here we look at just a few affordable interventions that have proved to play essential roles.

Although the limited comparative data on medical-care policy prevent us from fully examining countries' approaches around the world, there are existing data sources for access to certain public health and medical interventions. In this chapter, we present data primarily from the World Health Organization's Global Health Observatory.

Immunization is central to child survival and health. Each year, the deaths of an estimated 2.5 million children under age 5 are prevented because of immunizations.[21] Yet comprehensive global coverage has not yet been achieved. As of 2009, 22 million infants were still not protected by routine immunizations.[22]

In this section, we examine immunization coverage for the combined diphtheria, tetanus, and pertussis vaccine (DTP3) as an indicator of childhood immunization status. Each year, pertussis kills 254,000 people around the world, diphtheria kills 5,000 children under age 5, and 144,000 children under 5 die of tetanus.[23] The DTP3 vaccine can protect children against these diseases. Receiving vaccinations protects not only the children vaccinated but those around them as well; when girls and boys are less likely to become sick with contagious diseases themselves, they are also less likely to spread them to others.

Although it is not necessary that every single child receive an immunization in order for the risk of a contagious disease to drop dramatically, it is necessary that the majority receive it. The necessary vaccination coverage for herd immunity from diphtheria is estimated at 85 percent, and for pertussis this figure is between 92 and 94 percent.[24] DTP3 coverage among 1-year-olds is less than 85 percent in 27 countries in sub-Saharan Africa, 7 countries in East Asia and the Pacific, 4 countries in the Americas, and 3 countries in each of Europe and Central Asia, South Asia, and the Middle East and North Africa, including countries with very large populations, such as India, Indonesia, South Africa, and Nigeria.[25]

Another intervention that could radically reduce disease and death is improving access to clean drinking water and adequate sanitation facilities. Diarrhea is one of the most prevalent diseases in early childhood. It kills 1.5 million children under age 5 each year and is the second-leading cause of death among young children and the second most common cause of lost disability-adjusted life years in children under 5; an estimated 2.5 billion cases of diarrhea annually occur among young children.[26] It has been estimated that over 85 percent of diarrheal deaths around the world are due to poor-quality water, inadequate sanitation facilities, and poor hygiene.[27] A review of the evidence concludes that interventions to improve water and sanitation in areas where conditions were poor to begin with can be expected to reduce the incidence of diarrhea by one-third to nearly two-thirds. The reduction of diarrheal disease also has other health benefits. Frequent diarrhea is linked to malnutrition. Persistent or severe malnutrition makes children more likely to suffer from and die from other diseases, including pneumonia, and can markedly impair physical and cognitive development, limiting children's chances throughout childhood and adulthood.[28]

Yet, preventive measures in this area similarly remain incomplete, with critical consequences. In 6 sub-Saharan African countries, as well as 1 country in East Asia and the Pacific, at least half the population lacks access to improved drinking-water sources; between 16 and 50 percent of the population lacks this critical access in an additional 43 countries around the world.[29] In the majority of countries in sub-Saharan Africa and South Asia, as well as 3 countries in East Asia and the Pacific and 2 in the Americas, less than half the population is using improved sanitation facilities.[30]

When we combine these three preventive interventions and examine how many countries have reached 85 percent coverage of DTP3 immunization, improved water sources, and improved sanitation facilities, we see that much of the world is leaving its children unprotected from preventable illness (Map 4.1). Thirty countries do not meet any of these standards; just 69 have met all three, the majority in Europe and Central Asia.

Prevention: A Focus on Youth

As children get older, injuries become the most prevalent health threat. Among children aged 10 to 19, unintentional injuries are the leading cause of death. These injuries account for the deaths of over 850,000 children under the age of 18 each year. Millions of others experience nonfatal injuries, the consequences of which can be severe. A study of 2.25 million people in South and East Asia showed that for each child death that resulted from injury, 12 children had injuries severe enough to require hospitalization or to cause a permanent disability, and 34 had injuries that required either medical care or missing school or work. The majority of child injuries are from five causes: road traffic

Map 4.1. Do countries have strong coverage of preventive health measures in early childhood?

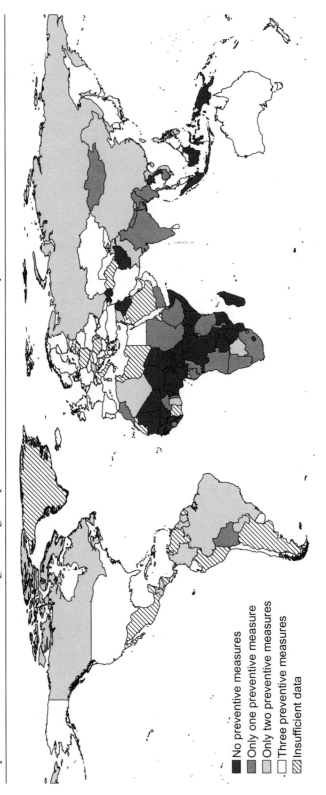

No preventive measures
Only one preventive measure
Only two preventive measures
Three preventive measures
Insufficient data

Preventive health measures are at least 85 percent DTP3 immunization coverage for 1-year-olds, at least 85 percent of the population with access to improved water sources, and at least 85 percent of the population with access to improved sanitation facilities.

Data Source: World Health Organization, Global Health Observatory Data Repository, http://apps.who.int/ghodata/

injuries, drowning, burns, falls, and poisoning. Although the majority of child deaths from injury occur in low- and middle-income countries, even in high-income countries, injuries account for 40 percent of deaths of children under the age of 18.[31]

One of the single largest causes of injuries is road traffic accidents. Each year, an estimated 10 million children are injured or disabled because of road traffic accidents. A study of Colombia, Bangladesh, Egypt, and Pakistan showed that 63 percent of road traffic injuries lead to some form of disability; 20 percent of these injuries lead to a long-term or permanent disability.[32]

Wearing a seatbelt in a car or other motor vehicle can protect children and youth from serious injury or death in the event of an accident. However, in far too many countries—88 worldwide—there are no laws mandating restraints for children in motor vehicles. In much of the world, motorcycles are the most common way to travel; a child on the back of a motorcycle has very little protection in case of an accident. Although most countries have laws mandating helmets on motorcycles at a national or subnational level, 14 countries have no such regulations. Thirty-two countries have no road safety strategy on a national or subnational level.[33]

Throughout their early years, children and youth are exposed to tobacco smoke. This exposure is harmful both because of its direct effects and because of its impact on the odds of children and youth becoming smokers themselves. Around the world, an estimated 40 percent of all children and youth, approximately 700 million, are regularly exposed to secondhand tobacco smoke. Exposed children and youth have a higher risk of acute respiratory illness, ear infections, developmental disabilities, and behavioral problems; they are also more likely to become tobacco users themselves. Approximately 200,000 children die each year as a result of exposure to secondhand smoke. Enacting legislation that makes public places smoke-free both reduces children's exposure to secondhand smoke in places where they spend a lot of time and has been shown to encourage parents to make their homes smoke-free as well, which further reduces child and youth exposure as well as the chance that they will begin smoking themselves.[34] Despite this, few countries have made key public places, even those commonly frequented by children and youth, smoke-free. Seventy-seven countries have no legislation making health-care facilities smoke-free, and 79 have not mandated that education facilities be free of secondhand smoke. Even more countries (108) lack legislation making public transportation smoke-free. Just 74 countries have legislation making all three of these areas free of secondhand smoke.[35]

In adolescence, youth often begin practices that lay the foundation for adult health. Initiating smoking in particular has devastating health consequences through adulthood. Each year, tobacco use kills more than 5 million individuals globally, and this figure is rising; it is the world's leading cause of preventable death.[36] The need for tobacco control has reached a high level of international consensus, and the World Health Organization's key convention on tobacco control calls for mandating bans on tobacco advertising and increasing the price of tobacco products through taxes.[37]

Most tobacco users begin using this substance before the age of 18; nearly a quarter of users begin before the age of 10.[38] Research shows that exposure to tobacco advertising increases the chances that youth will smoke; bans on advertising are met with strong resistance by tobacco companies because of their effectiveness in reducing demand for these products.[39] Data from the World Health Organization (WHO) show that the majority of countries have banned direct advertising of tobacco products on national television and radio (139 countries), billboard and outdoor advertising (123), and local magazines and newspapers (121). However, just 55 countries ban this advertising at point of sale, the same number on the Internet, 33 in international television and radio, and 30 in international magazines and newspapers. Just 11 countries have banned direct tobacco advertising in all these areas; this is a serious gap in global legislation coverage because tobacco companies will simply redirect their marketing efforts and budgets toward permitted media when some are banned.[40]

Another way to reduce the prevalence of tobacco use among youth is to increase the prices of tobacco products; youth are particularly responsive to price changes.[41] Taxes as a proportion of the price of the most sold brand of cigarettes vary widely among countries. In 25 countries, less than 20 percent of this price consists of taxes; in 47 countries, taxes are between 20 and 39.9 percent of the price; in 45 countries, taxes are between 40 and 59.9 percent of the price; in 65 countries, they make up 60 to 79.9 percent; and in 9 countries, taxes make up 80 percent or more of the price of the most sold cigarette brand. In general, higher-income countries tend to place higher levels of taxes on cigarettes than lower-income countries.[42]

Alcohol use similarly affects youth because of health effects when parents and others around them are heavy users and when youth begin early use themselves. Alcohol use increases the odds of risky behavior and violence and is a significant risk factor for injury. Alcohol can lead directly to death in adolescence and young adulthood (an estimated 320,000 youth between the ages of 15 and 29 die each year due to alcohol-related causes),[43] can affect the developing brain during adolescence, and has long-term health consequences. Alcohol is the largest cause of lost disability-adjusted life years throughout the life course in high-income countries and the third-largest cause in low- and middle-income countries. Initiating alcohol consumption at an older age can reduce the developmental, short-, and long-term health effects; the establishment of a minimum drinking age as a component of alcohol policy has been found to be effective.[44]

Over half of the world—112 countries—has established the minimum age to purchase alcohol legally at 18 or older. However, 15 countries set this age at 15, 16, or 17, and 24 countries have no minimum age for the purchase of alcohol, including 10 low-income countries, 10 middle-income countries, and 4 high-income countries.[45]

While risks and exposures related to sexual activity are also a major concern for youth health, we were unable to find comprehensive global sources of data on relevant indicators. General indicators of country action taken to promote youth health in this area, such as quality of, access to, and nature of sexual health education, are unavailable. On indicators that could be relevant, such as the unmet need for family planning among girls aged 15–19 or youth with comprehensive knowledge of HIV/AIDS, data are available on less than a third of the world's countries. Additional global data collection on this topic is urgently needed.[46]

Availability of Medical Care

Although public health and preventive measures can dramatically reduce rates of illness and accidents, some children and youth will still become sick or injured and need medical care. For these children and youth, the availability of medical care can have a powerful impact on the extent of their recovery and the long-term complications they face. Ideally, we would like to present data on the availability of health facilities serving children and youth, their accessibility and proximity to family homes, and the affordability, nature, and quality of services, among other features. In reality, the measures of health-care availability are currently quite crude. However, even these measures show gross disparities. Using data available through the WHO, we mapped the availability of physician, nursing, and midwifery personnel around the world (Map 4.2).

The WHO considers 23 health professionals per 10,000 people the minimum necessary for delivery of essential services.[47] However, 65 countries do not meet even this basic level of personnel. The majority of countries in sub-Saharan Africa and South Asia, as well as half of Southeast Asia, do not meet this minimum standard; a number of countries in Central and South America and the Middle East and North Africa also lack sufficient health personnel. Thirty-nine countries are in especially poor condition, with less than half the recommended number of health professionals per 10,000 people.[48]

This dearth of health professionals and health-care services has severe consequences for children in need of care. Therapeutic interventions require the availability and affordability of sufficient numbers of health-care professionals. Just 43 percent of children in rural areas and 56 percent in urban areas are brought to a health-care provider when they have pneumonia. Pneumonia is responsible for the deaths of more young children than any other illness; if appropriate prevention and treatment interventions were universally available, its death toll could be reduced by 1 million annually.[49] A study of 64 countries showed that many children suffering from diarrhea are also not receiving the treatment they need. The proportion of children receiving oral rehydration therapy for diarrhea ranged from over 75 percent in the Philippines to just 10 percent in Somalia and Botswana, with a median of 42 percent.[50]

Although the global importance of dentistry professionals is less widely recognized, their availability is critical. Poor oral health can have serious consequences for quality of life and overall health status.[51] Far rarer than physicians, nurses, and midwives, in nearly all of sub-Saharan Africa the number of dentistry personnel per 20,000 people is less than 1 (Map 4.3). In much of South and East Asia, there is a

Map 4.2. How many physicians, nurses, and midwives are available?

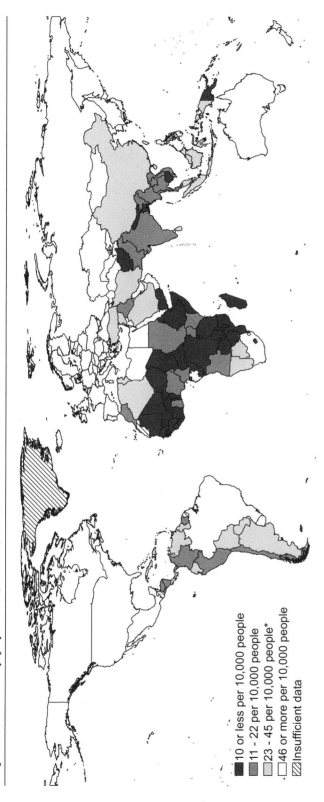

■ 10 or less per 10,000 people
▨ 11 - 22 per 10,000 people
▨ 23 - 45 per 10,000 people*
☐ 46 or more per 10,000 people
▨ Insufficient data

These totals are the sum of the number of physicians, nurses, and midwives available.
*The number 23 is used as a cutoff because the World Health Organization has identified it as a critical threshold for the delivery of essential health services.

Data Source: World Health Organization, World Health Statistics 2011 (Geneva: WHO, 2011).

Map 4.3. How many dentistry personnel are available?

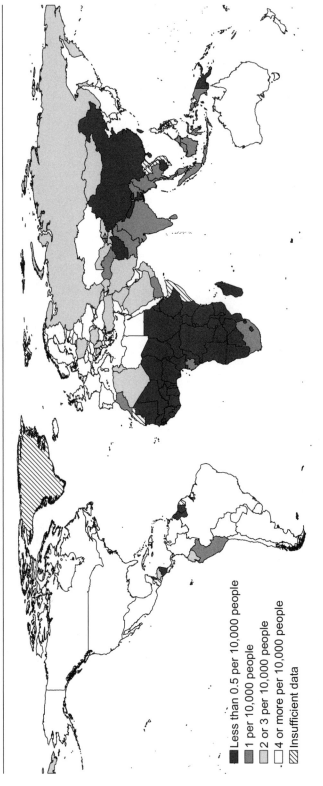

Less than 0.5 per 10,000 people
1 per 10,000 people
2 or 3 per 10,000 people
4 or more per 10,000 people
Insufficient data

Data Source: World Health Organization, World Health Statistics 2011 (Geneva: WHO, 2011)

maximum of 1 dentistry professional per 10,000 people, clearly indicating that the majority of the population has no access.[52]

The availability of health professionals is critical for children throughout childhood. However, there are periods when children are especially
vulnerable to health threats and when the presence of health-care providers is particularly essential. One of these times is at birth. The presence of a health-care professional during childbirth is critical for both
mother and child. Each year, over 280,000 women die during pregnancy
or childbirth,[53] and roughly 3 million babies die during their first week
of life.[54] For every newborn death, it has been estimated that an additional 20 babies experience birth injury, infection, or other neonatal
complications.[55] Maternal mortality is highest in sub-Saharan Africa,
at 500 per 100,000 live births, and South Asia, with 220.[56] Sixty percent
of maternal deaths are a result of hemorrhage, obstructed labor, sepsis,
or eclampsia.[57]

Making adequate care available to women during and after childbirth can markedly reduce the incidence of the worst complications
of labor and delivery (including decreasing maternal death, severe
illness, and injury) by 95 percent, and can reduce newborn deaths
due to asphyxia by 40 percent.[58] Additionally, reducing the odds of
maternal mortality increases the odds of child survival; upon the
death of their mother, surviving children are between 3 and 10 times
more likely to die within 2 years than children with two living
parents.[59]

The data on the proportion of births that are attended by skilled
health personnel show that parts of the world have nearly complete
coverage for all children. At the same time, in 9 countries, at least 70
percent of births are not attended by skilled health personnel—3 countries in sub-Saharan Africa, 3 in South Asia, 2 in East Asia and the
Pacific, and 1 in the Americas. In an additional 20 countries, 15 of
which are in sub-Saharan Africa, between 50 and 69 percent of births
are not attended by skilled personnel, leaving many mothers and babies at risk of preventable morbidity and death.[60]

Medical-care availability reflects a strong income gradient. All high-
income countries, with the exception of Equatorial Guinea, discussed
below, have surpassed the WHO minimum for number of health providers, most have at least 4 dentistry personnel per 10,000 people, and
over 90 percent of births in these countries are attended by skilled

Map 4.4. What proportion of the population is covered by publicly funded health insurance in OECD countries?

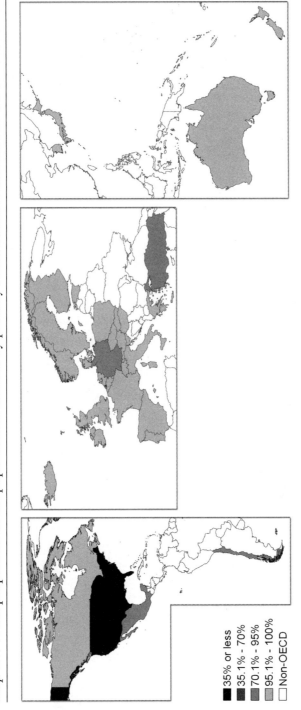

35% or less
35.1% - 70%
70.1% - 95%
95.1% - 100%
Non-OECD

Data Source: Organisation for Economic Co-operation and Development, OECD Health Data 2011, http://stats.oecd.org

health personnel. Do high-income countries have anything left to do when it comes to child health?

Although comparative data on the availability of public health insurance are not available globally, this information is available for high-income countries. An examination of the OECD, a group of 34 mostly high-income countries, makes clear that gaps remain (Map 4.4). Although most countries cover the majority of their population with public health insurance, the United States is a striking outlier— less than 30 percent of its population is covered by public health insurance.[61] The combination of inadequate population health and health-care services investments has led to much worse health outcomes in the United States than in comparable countries. For example, the U.S. maternal mortality rate of 24 per 100,000 is on a par with that of countries with fewer economic resources, like Fiji, Lebanon, Oman, Saudi Arabia, and Turkey, and many times higher than that of such European countries as Ireland (3 per 100,000), Sweden (5 per 100,000), and Germany (7 per 100,000).[62] The United States' infant mortality rate (7 per 1,000 live births) is more than double that of countries like the Czech Republic, Finland, France, Japan, and Singapore.[63]

A notable exception to the trend of good health-care access indicators in high-income countries is Equatorial Guinea. A spike in revenue generated by the country's oil industry has led its gross domestic product (GDP) to skyrocket in recent years; its per capita GDP has more than quadrupled since 2000 and more than doubled since 2003. The nation's GDP per capita is higher than the OECD average and compares to that of France, Iceland, and the United Kingdom. However, the country's wealth distribution is staggeringly unequal—more than three-quarters of the population lives below the poverty line.[64] Unsurprisingly, Equatorial Guinea's health-care access indicators are poor and have not caught up with national income. The country has 3 physicians, 5 nurses or midwives, and 0.3 dentistry professionals per 10,000 people, and just 65 percent of births are attended by skilled personnel.[65]

A Commitment to Health

Much is known about how to prevent and address serious illnesses and injuries from infancy through adolescence, but doing so will require commitment and resources on the part of countries. Political parties can change policy priorities and parliaments can frequently amend or rewrite legislation, but constitutions contain national commitments that are harder to undo. While constitutional promises are clearly not enough without implementation, available evidence suggests that constitutional guarantees of health-related rights are associated with higher levels of medical service delivery.[66] We examined the world's constitutions to see how many have made a commitment to health; our research team reviewed and analyzed constitutional text and amendments through June 2011 for 191 countries (Map 4.5). For detailed information on this database, see Appendix 1.

We found that constitutions address the broad protection of health in three main ways. Some have general language guaranteeing an overall right to health. Others make a more specific guarantee of a right to medical services, using language such as treatment of diseases, medical aid, health-care services, or curative services, among others. Countries can also address a right to public health, using terms such as preventive care, disease prevention, or public health protection, or by outlining specific measures, including access to immunizations or health education. Some countries include more than one approach to health rights. In some cases, these rights are discussed in the constitution but are expressed in aspirational rather than guaranteed terms.[67]

Around the world, 68 countries guarantee a right to health for all citizens, 25 countries aspire to this protection, and 8 countries protect the right to health for specific groups but not universally. The right to medical services is guaranteed in 74 countries and is aspirational in an additional 26 countries. The right to public health is the least commonly addressed—just 28 countries guarantee it and 21 aspire to it.

Around the world, 105 countries guarantee either a right to health, public health, or medical services, and among these, 19 countries guarantee all three types of protection. An additional 32 countries aspire to protect at least one type of health right. However, 54 countries neither guarantee nor aspire to any of these rights in their constitutions.*

The frequency of commitment has increased over time. Before 1970, more than three-quarters of constitutions did not mention a right to

---

*World Policy Analysis Centre, Constitutions Database. Number of countries for which we have data: 191 (rights to health or health care).

Map 4.5. Does the constitution take any approach to health?

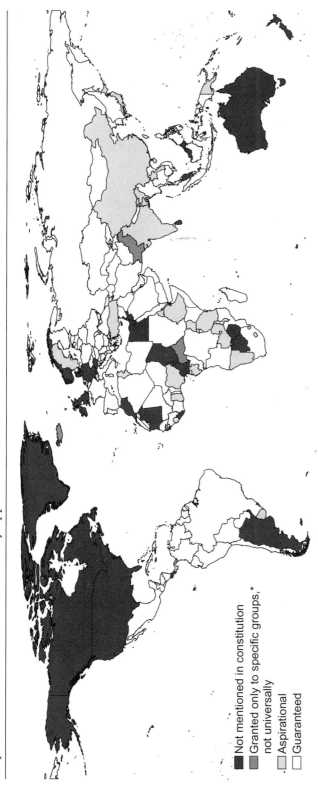

■ Not mentioned in constitution
■ Granted only to specific groups, *
   not universally
▨ Aspirational
□ Guaranteed

Approaches to health include the right to health, public health, or medical services.
Specific groups include families, children, prisoners, and individuals unable to earn an income.

Source: World Policy Analysis Centre, Constitutions Database

health or medical services, but 70 percent of constitutions written after 1980 did. While the right to public health is much less frequently mentioned than other health rights, it follows a similar pattern. Less than 10 percent of constitutions written before 1970 mentioned public health, compared to 30 percent written after 1980. The majority of constitutions from high-income countries were written before those from low-income countries. As a result, it is more common that constitutions in low-income countries mention health rights.

It is worth highlighting that in some countries, the constitution specifically discusses the nation's responsibility for ensuring that all can access care regardless of income. For example, Poland states that "equal access to health care services, financed from public funds, shall be ensured by public authorities to citizens, irrespective of their material situation." Thailand declares that "a person shall enjoy equal rights to receive quality public health services and the deprived shall enjoy the rights to receive medical treatment from State public health facilities free of charge." In Cambodia, "Poor citizens shall receive free medical consultation in public hospitals, infirmaries and maternities." Panama obliges the state to establish "centers which provide comprehensive health care services, and supply medicines to all the people. These services and medicines shall be given free to those who lack economic means to purchase them." Some countries, such as Ecuador, declare health-care services to be cost-free for all ("Public state health services shall be universal and free of charge at all levels of care"), a provision that disproportionately benefits low-income citizens.

Resources for Child Health

As this chapter's findings show, many governments could be doing more in terms of both prevention and care to improve children's life chances. Is the problem that some countries simply cannot afford it? Financial investments are clearly required in order to make health-care and prevention services available. Given that the highest rates of infant and child mortality are in countries with few resources, it is reasonable to wonder whether these countries are doing the best they can, and it is just not enough to reach all children.

A look at the facts makes clear that this is not the full story. Some of those countries that are performing especially poorly on indicators of health-care access could be doing more to make these services available to their populations. Although there are advanced medical treatments that will inevitably be more difficult for low-income countries to make widely available, such as treatments for a child with cancer, the majority of illnesses and injuries that are threatening children worldwide are less complex and costly to avert and treat.

Most of the countries that lack sufficient health-care providers invest little in health care. In fact, 52 of the 64 countries that do not meet the WHO minimum of 23 health professionals per 10,000 people spend 4 percent or less of their GDP on health, and 22 of these countries spend 2 percent or less (Map 4.6). In the 28 countries where 50 percent or less of births are attended by skilled health personnel and for which data on expenditures are available, 24 spend 4 percent or less of GDP on health; the same is true of 37 of the 46 countries with a DTP3 immunization rate of less than 85 percent and for which expenditures are known. Although disparities in national incomes clearly play a role in the dollar amount that countries can spend on their health services, countries could be devoting more of their resources to this key area.[68]

However, spending a reasonable portion of GDP on health will not always be enough for low-income countries to provide adequate coverage; a global commitment will still be essential. Although costs of critical interventions are often low and the return on investment is high, some of the poorest countries are likely to need assistance to provide their populations with adequate preventive and curative care. These nations can be expected to apply a reasonable proportion of their GDP to improving population health, but their GDP is low enough that the dollars generated may still be inadequate in the short term. The international community should step in to fill the funding gaps. In the long term, growing productivity linked to improved population health, as well as to investments in education, should make it feasible for countries to increasingly cover their full health-care costs. Here too, with political will and commitment to child and youth health, more resources could readily be made available. The world's leading economies committed to giving 0.7 percent of their gross national product internationally first in 1970 and again in 2002,[69] but most countries are falling short of this standard. Overseas development assistance accounts for 0.5 percent in the United Kingdom, 0.4

Map 4.6. How much do governments spend on health care?

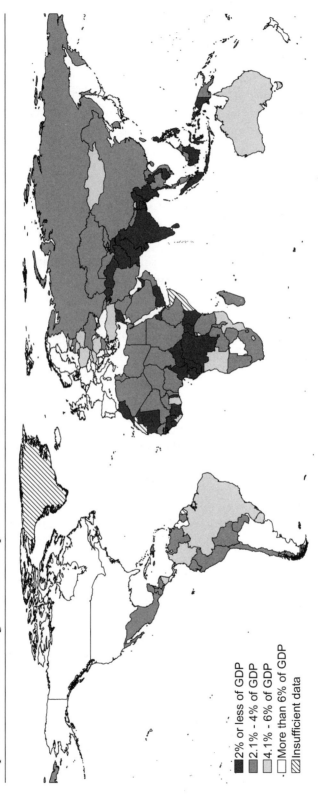

2% or less of GDP
2.1% - 4% of GDP
4.1% - 6% of GDP
More than 6% of GDP
Insufficient data

Data Source: World Health Organization, Global Health Observatory Data Repository, http://apps.who.int/gho/data/

percent in Germany, 0.3 percent in Australia and Canada, and 0.2 percent in the United States.[70] International funding sources, such as the Global Fund to Fight AIDS, Tuberculosis and Malaria, have shown how financial assistance can be made available to nations to mitigate health threats effectively; programs supported by the Global Fund are estimated to have provided 3.3 million people with anti-retroviral treatment, 8.2 million people with treatment for tuberculosis, and 230 million people with insecticide-treated bed nets.[71]

The costs of many of the essential preventive interventions are far from prohibitive. Even the resources required to ensure that all girls, boys, men, and women live in houses with adequate access to water and sanitation are modest by global standards. Providing access to improved water supply and sanitation facilities for all would cost an estimated $22.6 billion per year;[72] this is only 0.04 percent of global GDP. The benefits of these investments are significant financially, as well as in terms of children's lives. For every dollar spent on improving access to proper water and sanitation, between $5 and $46 can be expected in economic returns. This estimate is based on acute illness and mortality; if the long-term effects of chronic diarrhea were taken into account, these figures would be even higher.[73]

Relying on international sources of funding to supplement national health expenditures does not have to create long-term dependence on external funds. The evidence is strong that nations' economies are detrimentally affected by poor population health. Improving the health of individuals increases their ability to work productively and reduces their need for health-care services and associated public expenditures.[74] As the health of citizens improves, national economies strengthen, and low-income nations will be in a better position to fund health-care and prevention services on their own.

Although having sufficient funding available is critical, not only how much money is available matters, but also how this money is being spent. No matter how affluent they are, it is impossible for nations to afford high-quality health-care services for all citizens who need them without paying attention to prevention. This includes public health measures to prevent infectious diseases, population health approaches to lower rates of noncommunicable diseases from diabetes to heart disease and stroke, and preventive medical interventions. Providing new mothers with treatment to prevent mother-to-child transmission of HIV, for example, is vastly less expensive than treating an HIV-positive child for the rest of his or her life. Every dollar spent on measles, mumps, and rubella immunizations leads to at least $21 in savings on direct medical-care costs; each dollar spent on the diphtheria, tetanus, and acellular pertussis vaccine saves an estimated $24.[75] Encouraging good nutrition and physical exercise is a relatively low-cost way to promote population health and reduce the prevalence of high-cost obesity and type 2 diabetes; diabetes prevalence nearly tripled in the United States between 1980 and 2010,[76] doubled in Canada in only a decade,[77] and has risen rapidly in a wide range of countries from Saudi Arabia to China.

If the world were to take steps to show that we cared equally about all children, it would be unimaginable to continue to allow millions of children to die each year, the majority from preventable causes, nor could we allow even greater numbers of children to suffer from preventable diseases and live without appropriate treatment for them. The action steps required are not difficult to imagine, nor are the barriers to implementation insurmountable. Many of the tools we need to ensure that most children and youth have a chance at healthy development are well known and readily within our reach.

Table 4.1. Prevention policies in early childhood

	Low-Income	Middle-Income	High-Income
Diphtheria, Tetanus and Pertussis (DTP3) Immunization Coverage Among 1-Year-Olds			
Less than 50% of 1-year-olds are fully immunized against DTP3	1 (3%)	2 (2%)	1 (2%)
50% - 84% of 1-year-olds are fully immunized against DTP3	19 (54%)	21 (20%)	3 (6%)
85% - 91% of 1-year-olds are fully immunized against DTP3	4 (11%)	25 (23%)	3 (6%)
92% - 94% of 1-year-olds are fully immunized against DTP3	5 (14%)	13 (12%)	9 (18%)
95% or more of 1-year-olds are fully immunized against DTP3	6 (17%)	46 (43%)	33 (67%)
Proportion of Population With Access to Safe Drinking Water Sources			
Less than 50% of the population has access to safe drinking water	6 (18%)	1 (1%)	0 (0%)
50% - 84% of the population has access to safe drinking water	23 (68%)	20 (22%)	0 (0%)
85% - 94% of the population has access to safe drinking water	3 (9%)	32 (35%)	2 (5%)
95% - 100% of the population has access to safe drinking water	2 (6%)	38 (42%)	40 (95%)

(continued)

Table 4.1 *(continued)*

Proportion of Population With Access to Improved Sanitation Services			
Less than 50% of the population has access to improved sanitation services	26 (76%)	18 (20%)	0 (0%)
50% - 84% of the population has access to improved sanitation services	6 (18%)	34 (37%)	0 (0%)
85% - 94% of the population has access to improved sanitation services	2 (6%)	17 (18%)	1 (2%)
95% - 100% of the population has access to improved sanitation services	0 (0%)	23 (25%)	40 (98%)

Source: World Health Organization, Global Health Observatory Data Repository, http://apps.who.int/ghodata/.

Definition: Low-income, middle-income, and high-income refer to World Bank classifications of national income. Here, middle-income countries include those classified as lower-middle and upper-middle income.

Notes: The herd immunity level for diphtheria is 85%. The herd immunity level for pertussis is 92% - 94%.

Table 4.2. Prevention policies in youth

Prevention Policies in Youth	Low-Income	Middle-Income	High-Income
Protection of Youth through Motor Vehicle Restraints Law			
The country does not have a restraints law	23 (77%)	60 (61%)	5 (11%)
A restraints law exists at the subnational level	2 (7%)	1 (1%)	3 (7%)
The country has a national restraints law	5 (17%)	37 (38%)	36 (82%)
Protection of Youth Through Motorcycle Helmet Law			
The country does not have a motorcycle helmet law	7 (23%)	7 (7%)	0 (0%)
A motorcycle helmet law exists at the subnational level	1 (3%)	3 (3%)	3 (7%)
The country has a national motorcycle helmet law	23 (74%)	89 (90%)	41 (93%)
Protection of Youth Through Road Safety Strategy			
The country does not have a road safety strategy	11 (35%)	18 (19%)	3 (7%)
A road safety strategy exists at the subnational level	0 (0%)	5 (5%)	0 (0%)
Multiple ministries have road safety strategies	6 (19%)	18 (19%)	7 (16%)
The country has a national road safety strategy	14 (45%)	55 (57%)	34 (77%)
Protection of Youth From Smoke in Public Places			
Smoking is banned in health-care facilities	16 (46%)	69 (64%)	29 (59%)
Smoking is banned in schools	16 (46%)	62 (58%)	34 (69%)
Smoking is banned on public transportation	11 (31%)	50 (47%)	22 (45%)

(continued)

123

Table 4.2 *(continued)*

Potential Penalties for Breaking Non-Smoking Laws

There are no laws against smoking in health-care facilities, schools, and on public transportation	19 (54%)	30 (28%)	12 (24%)
There are no fines for breaking non-smoking laws	3 (9%)	17 (16%)	2 (4%)
Either the individual who breaks the law or the establishment where the violation occurs receives a fine	7 (20%)	23 (22%)	7 (14%)
Both the individual who breaks the law and the establishment where the violation occurs receive a fine	6 (17%)	36 (34%)	28 (57%)
Protection of Youth from Direct Tobacco Products Advertising			
Banned on domestic television and radio networks	21 (60%)	75 (71%)	43 (90%)
Banned on international television and radio networks	5 (14%)	21 (20%)	7 (15%)
Banned in local magazines and newspapers	21 (60%)	64 (60%)	36 (75%)
Banned in international magazines and newspapers	5 (14%)	22 (21%)	3 (6%)
Banned on billboards and other outdoor advertising	20 (57%)	67 (63%)	36 (75%)
Banned in locations where tobacco products are sold	10 (29%)	29 (27%)	16 (33%)
Banned on the Internet	8 (23%)	26 (25%)	21 (44%)

Prevention of Youth Smoking Through Taxes on the Most Widely Sold Brand of Cigarettes

Less than 20% of the price is the total tax on cigarettes	6 (17%)	17 (16%)	2 (4%)
20% – 39.9% of the price is the total tax on cigarettes	12 (34%)	27 (25%)	8 (16%)
40% – 59.9% of the price is the total tax on cigarettes	10 (29%)	31 (29%)	4 (8%)
60% – 79.9% of the price is the total tax on cigarettes	7 (20%)	29 (27%)	29 (59%)
80% or more of the price is the total tax on cigarettes	0 (0%)	3 (3%)	6 (12%)
Minimum Age to Purchase Alcohol Legally			
No minimum age limit to purchase alcohol legally	10 (34%)	10 (12%)	4 (10%)
15, 16, or 17 is the minimum age to purchase alcohol legally	1 (3%)	4 (5%)	10 (25%)
18 is the minimum age to purchase alcohol legally	17 (59%)	57 (70%)	22 (55%)
19 or 20 is the minimum age to purchase alcohol legally	0 (0%)	4 (5%)	2 (5%)
21 or older is the minimum age to purchase alcohol legally	1 (3%)	7 (9%)	2 (5%)

Source : World Health Organization, Global Health Observatory Data Repository, http://apps.who.int/ghodata/.

Table 4.3. Access to public health and medical-care services

	Low-Income	Middle-Income	High-Income
Number of Doctors, Nurses and Midwives per 10,000 People			
10 or fewer health professionals on average per 10,000 people	28 (82%)	10 (10%)	1 (2%)
11 - 22 health professionals on average per 10,000 people	3 (9%)	23 (22%)	0 (0%)
23 - 45 health professionals on average per 10,000 people	0 (0%)	31 (30%)	3 (7%)
46 or more health professionals on average per 10,000 people	3 (9%)	39 (38%)	42 (91%)
Number of Dentistry Personnel per 10,000 People			
Fewer than 0.5 dentistry personnel on average per 10,000 people	29 (88%)	27 (27%)	1 (2%)
1 dentistry personnel on average per 10,000 people	1 (3%)	22 (22%)	0 (0%)
2 or 3 dentistry personnel on average per 10,000 people	2 (6%)	19 (19%)	6 (13%)
4 or more dentistry personnel on average per 10,000 people	1 (3%)	33 (33%)	39 (85%)
Percentage of Births Attended by Skilled Health Personnel			
30% of births or less are attended by skilled health personnel	7 (20%)	2 (2%)	0 (0%)
31% - 50% of births are attended by skilled health personnel	13 (37%)	7 (7%)	0 (0%)

51% - 90% of births are attended by skilled health personnel	13 (37%)	34 (32%)	1 (3%)
91% - 99% of births are attended by skilled health personnel	2 (6%)	43 (41%)	7 (20%)
100% of births are attended by skilled health personnel	0 (0%)	20 (19%)	27 (77%)
Amount of Government Spending on Health Care as a Percentage of GDP			
Less than 2% of GDP is spent by the government on health care	15 (45%)	16 (15%)	3 (6%)
2.1% - 4% of GDP is spent by the government on health care	15 (45%)	52 (49%)	11 (22%)
4.1% - 6% of GDP is spent by the government on health care	2 (6%)	21 (20%)	10 (20%)
More than 6% of GDP is spent by the government on health care	1 (3%)	18 (17%)	25 (51%)

Sources : World Health Organization, World Health Statistics 2011 (Geneva: World Health Organization, 2011) and Global Health Observatory Data Repository, http://apps.who.int/ghodata/.

Definition : *Health professionals* is the sum of the number of physicians, nurses, and midwives available.

Note : The number 23 is used as a cutoff for the number of doctors, nurses, and midwives per 10,000 people because the World Health Organization has identified it as a critical threshold for delivery of essential health services.

127

Table 4.4. Constitutional protections of health rights

	Low-Income	Middle-Income	High-Income
Constitutional Right to Public Health for Citizens			
Constitution does not include relevant provisions on right to public health	27 (77%)	75 (71%)	40 (80%)
Constitution protects the right to public health for specific groups, but not for all citizens	0 (0%)	0 (0%)	0 (0%)
Constitution aspires to protect right to public health for all citizens	5 (14%)	11 (10%)	5 (10%)
Constitution guarantees right to public health for all citizens	3 (9%)	20 (19%)	5 (10%)
Constitutional Right to Medical Services for Citizens			
Constitution does not include relevant provisions on right to medical services	16 (46%)	38 (36%)	30 (60%)
Constitution protects the right to medical services for specific groups, but not for all citizens	1 (3%)	5 (5%)	1 (2%)
Constitution aspires to protect right to medical services for all citizens	8 (23%)	16 (15%)	2 (4%)
Constitution guarantees right to medical services for all citizens	10 (29%)	47 (44%)	17 (34%)
Constitutional Right to Health for Citizens			
Constitution does not include relevant provisions on right to health	10 (29%)	49 (46%)	31 (62%)

Constitution protects the right to health for specific groups, but not for all citizens	5 (14%)	2 (2%)	1 (2%)
Constitution aspires to protect right to health for all citizens	5 (14%)	16 (15%)	4 (8%)
Constitution guarantees right to health for all citizens	15 (43%)	39 (37%)	14 (28%)
At Least One Constitutional Health Right for Citizens			
Constitution does not include relevant provisions on right to public health, medical services, or health for all citizens	4 (11%)	28 (26%)	22 (44%)
Constitution aspires to protect right to public health, medical services, or health for all citizens	9 (26%)	18 (17%)	5 (10%)
Constitution guarantees right to public health, medical services, or health for all citizens	22 (63%)	60 (57%)	23 (46%)
Constitutional Right to Public Health, Medical Services, and Health for Citizens			
Constitution does not guarantee the right to public health, medical services, and health for all citizens	32 (91%)	82 (77%)	47 (94%)
Constitution at least aspires to the right to public health, medical services, and health for all citizens	2 (6%)	8 (8%)	1 (2%)
Constitution guarantees the right to public health, medical services, and health for all citizens	1 (3%)	16 (15%)	2 (4%)

Source : World Policy Analysis Centre, Constitutions Database.

Definition : *Specific groups* named include children, the elderly, the poor, the disabled, pregnant women, mothers, and/or indigenous people.

Chapter 5

Parents and Children

*Martin Thomas and Leah Loredo were young parents living in the
United States with one child, a daughter named Hannah Marie. There
were no state or national laws where they lived guaranteeing any paid
leave from work for family reasons, including the birth of a child.
Martin took just one day off on the day that his daughter was born,
and he had to provide his employer with a doctor's note justifying his
absence.*

*As an infant, Hannah Marie began to get frequent ear infections.
She often experienced high fevers and vomiting and was on an antibi-
otic nearly every other month. During one episode, when she was only
2 months old, she was hospitalized for a week because doctors worried
that the infection might have become systemic. In the absence of legal
guarantees, whether or not to provide employees with leave to care for a
sick child was up to each employer. Leah worked part-time at an office;
while she was initially given time off to care for her daughter when she
was seriously sick, her employer's resistance grew with the frequency of
the illnesses. Martin worked as a truck driver, and his employer was
even less ready to give him any time off. When Hannah was 7 months
old, she was running a high fever and needed an urgent trip to the
pediatrician's office. Leah and Hannah needed Martin to drive them if
they were going to make it in time for their 7:00 A.M. emergency
appointment; they only had one car. Martin was scheduled to start*

*work at 7:00 a.m. that day; an hour earlier, as soon as he knew that he
would be late, he let his employer know about his daughter's health
emergency. Martin was written up for having given such late notice.
Leah added, "And they told him next time it happened, he would lose
his job."*[1]

This chapter examines the role of parental care for children and the
policies that make this care possible.

Children's Care, Parents' Work

Throughout history and around the world, it has rarely been the case
that children were raised in homes with one parent as a full-time caregiver. Fathers and mothers have long engaged in economically productive labor, whether it be work on a farm, in home production, or for an
employer. That the majority of parents do paid work in addition to the
work of childrearing is not new. What have changed in important
ways are the nature and location of parents' paid work. For centuries,
most families had at least one parent working from home, in work-
shops near their homes, or on their lands. Today, these circumstances
are true only for the minority in many countries. This began to change
in some nations over the past two centuries, and has occurred in more
and more countries around the world over the past 60 years, resulting
in increasing numbers of parents working away from their homes.

Over the course of the nineteenth century, many of today's high-
income countries transitioned from largely agricultural economies to
largely industrialized ones. The United States' experience is one example. In 1830, 70 percent of children lived in farming families with
both of their parents; by 1930, just 30 percent of children did so.[2] A
similar transition is now occurring throughout much of the world.
Young adults are increasingly moving away from agricultural work in
rural areas to industrial and service work in urban areas. The percentage of the world's population living in urban areas increased from less
than 30 percent in 1950 to over 50 percent in 2010, and it is expected to
increase to 70 percent by 2050.[3]

By and large, this change is driven by men and women seeking better jobs, higher incomes, and more reliable ways to sustain their families. They often leave behind work on the farm or in the home that had

allowed their children to be present, even if under precarious circumstances, and trade it for workplaces where their sons and daughters cannot accompany them. At the same time, as they move to cities, young adults often move away from the extended family members who traditionally provided support by caring for children. In our interviews with working parents in countries ranging from Russia to Mexico, from Botswana to Viet Nam, parents spoke of how geographic distance from extended family, grandparents' need to work, and grandparents' declining health limited their ability to get assistance with child care. This had implications for their children, who were much less likely to be left at home alone when extended family members were available than when they were not.[4]

Numerically, the transformations in the nature and location of economically productive work is captured by the rising proportion of women in the paid labor force. According to World Bank figures, the female proportion of the labor force increased between 1960 and 2009 from 32 percent to 46 percent in the United States, from 25 percent to 47 percent in Canada, and from 21 percent to 41 percent in Latin America and the Caribbean. In East Asia and the Pacific, Europe and Central Asia, and sub-Saharan Africa, this proportion began at 40 percent or more in 1960 and maintained that level or slightly increased. The Middle East and North Africa saw a small increase from 21 percent in 1960 to 25 percent in 2009. Only South Asia saw a decline in the female proportion of the labor force during this period, from 34 percent to 29 percent.[5]

This has led to advances in gender equity, as well as improvements in children's lives, as women and families have gained access to greater economic resources, particularly given the evidence that mothers tend to spend more of their income on children than fathers.[6] At the same time, in the absence of significant changes in workplace policies, the transformation of women's and men's work has brought new challenges for children and for public policy.

Conservative estimates are that 340 million children under the age of 6 and 590 million children between the ages of 6 and 14 live in households where all adults work for pay outside the home.[7] Reaping the full potential rewards of these labor-force transitions without compromising children's needs requires that workplaces adapt to this transformation. Working conditions originally formulated with the assumption that employees were not caring for children or other family members need to be redesigned so that adults can succeed at work while fulfilling their caregiving responsibilities.

Care during the Early Years

Much is debated about how best to support families in the evolving context of work. Especially intense debate surrounds the question of who should provide care during the early years. Some contend that only parents or other primary caregivers can provide adequate care for infants and toddlers, and that parents should therefore be provided with several years of job-protected parental leave. Others argue that parental leave is not necessary for more than short periods—high-quality care provided by formal child care centers benefits children and families alike, and gender equity for men and women at home and at work can only be achieved in the absence of long periods of parental leave, which tend to be taken mostly by mothers. They contend that businesses cannot be expected to provide job-protected leave for more than a few weeks or a few months.

The research evidence sheds light on several aspects of the debate. First, the early period of life is critical to healthy development. In many countries, the greatest risks for morbidity and mortality come during the first year of life; globally, 8.8 million children die before they are 1 year old.[8] Moreover, much of the most rapid brain and nervous system development occurs during the early years. Synapses are developed quickly during these years; this process slows down and some synapses are eliminated as children get older.[9] The newborn period is also a crucial time for the development of attachment and bonding between a parent and a new child.[10]

Second, maternal leave matters for children. Evidence confirms that maternal leave significantly improves infant and child health. Our global study of paid leave for new mothers showed that an increase in this leave by 10 paid full-time-equivalent weeks was associated with 9 to 10 percent lower neonatal mortality, infant mortality, and under-5 mortality rates.[11] These global findings are consistent with studies done in high-income countries showing a positive impact of combined maternity and parental leave, which is overwhelmingly taken by women, on child health. A study of 30 years of data from 18 OECD countries showed that paid maternity and parental leave reduced infant and child mortality;[12] these findings are confirmed by a study of 16 European countries.[13]

While many factors contribute to this decrease in mortality, breast-feeding is an important contributor. The benefits of breastfeeding for the health of mothers and infants are well documented.[14] For infants, being breastfed reduces the leading infectious risks, including diarrheal disease, respiratory illness, and meningitis, among others; markedly reduces the risk of malnutrition; and promotes neurocognitive development.[15] Infants who are not breastfed are between 4 and 14 times more likely to die from diarrheal disease than breastfed infants,[16] and 5 times more likely to die from pneumonia.[17] Maternal leave increases the odds that a child will be breastfed—in Australia, for example, a study showed that taking paid maternity leave for 6 weeks or more significantly increased the likelihood that infants were breastfed, and children's health outcomes also improved.[18]

Third, leave for fathers as well as mothers matters to infants. Fathers have a substantial role, even if a different one, in children's health, nutrition, and developmental outcomes. Paternal leave builds fathers' relationships with their children and shapes the home environment. When fathers take leave from work, they are more involved with their infants, and child-care responsibilities are more equally shared.[19] While most fathers take little or no leave in the United States because they receive no paid leave, children benefit when fathers do take leave. Fathers who took at least 2 weeks of leave when their child was born were more likely to be regularly involved in child care 9 months later, even after preexisting commitment to child care was controlled for.[20] Similarly, in the United Kingdom, fathers who took leave after the birth of a child were 19 percent more likely to participate in feeding and get up with the baby at night 8 to 12 months later than fathers who did not take leave.[21] Furthermore, evidence shows that when fathers are more involved in the home, the occurrence of maternal depression is lower; this has important benefits for children because maternal depression is a strong predictor of poor outcomes for children.[22]

For both mothers and fathers, it is critical that leave from work be paid as well as job-protected. When only unpaid leave is available to new parents, many families cannot afford to use it. In the United

States, for instance, where the only guaranteed leave for family or medical needs (including parental leave) is unpaid, 1 in 10 of those who needed leave could not afford to take any.[23] Lack of pay inevitably affects the duration of leave taken as well. The limited benefits of unpaid leave are reflected in many of the studies showing links between parental leave and child health. In the previously mentioned study of the OECD, unpaid leave and leave that was not job protected were unrelated to all five of the measures of infant and child mortality.[24] In Europe, unpaid leave had no effect on infant mortality,[25] and in Australia, it was unrelated to children's health status.[26]

A question that has no easy answers when it comes to parental leave is for how long leave should be provided. Evidence from several European countries with long periods of parental leave shows that this can contribute to greater gender inequality in the workforce and more limited career trajectories for women.[27] There is also less evidence on the benefits of very long periods of leave from a child's perspective.

Finally, the research evidence shows that early childhood care and education (ECCE) programs lay invaluable foundations for children. Around the world, good-quality ECCE has been shown to benefit children's health and development in terms of school achievement, grade-repetition, and completion rates.[28] As well as being independently beneficial for children, the availability of affordable ECCE supports parents' ability to succeed in the paid labor force. In summary, the research evidence makes a strong case for the benefits to children and families of guaranteeing paid maternal and paternal leave, ensuring that mothers in the labor force can breastfeed, and providing quality ECCE for young children.

Where does the world stand on addressing these areas through policy? Before our study, there was no easy way to compare the parental-leave provisions guaranteed by the world's countries. There were some good, comprehensive sources on maternity leave; databases from the International Labour Organization, the United Nations, and Social Security Policies throughout the World had information on maternity-leave provisions for a large number of countries. However, quantitatively comparable information on paternity and parental leave was far less available. To find information on paternity leave around the world, one had to identify relevant provisions country by country in labor codes and social security regulations. Our database on adult

labor policy pulled together for the first time detailed and comparable information on new mothers' and fathers' entitlement to leave
from work, drawing on primary sources of legislation as well as supplemental secondary sources, such as government informational pam-
phlets, regional information centers, and international organizations.
For detailed information on the construction of this database, see
Appendix 1.

Leave can be provided to new parents in two ways—through leave
specifically available to a mother or a father, or leave that is available to
either parent; this leave may be shared between them or taken entirely
by one parent. When we look at leave for new mothers and fathers, we
take both of these kinds of leave into account.[29] The number of weeks
of leave presented in this chapter includes only paid leave. The amount
of money received by a parent while on leave differs by country. The
vast majority of countries provide a portion of the individual's wages
while she or he is on leave; this portion can even differ within countries when a higher wage-replacement rate is offered for a given amount
of time and a lower rate afterward.

Our data show that in most of the world, providing paid leave for
new mothers is the norm across regions and income groups (see Map
5.1). Just 8 countries do not provide this leave: Liberia, Nauru, Palau,
Papua New Guinea, Samoa, Suriname, Tonga, and the United States.
When both paid maternity and paid parental leave that is available to
women are taken into account, 45 countries, the majority of which are
in Europe, provide this leave for at least 6 months; an additional 52
countries provide between 14 and 25 weeks of paid leave.* The majority of countries providing paid leave, 149, replace new mothers' wages
at a rate of 75 percent to 100 percent for at least part of their leave; 24
countries replace between 50 and 74 percent of wages.† Four countries
replace less than half of women's wages during leave, and 1 country
provides a flat-rate payment.[30]

Although the world has made great progress in ensuring paid maternity leave, far less progress has been made in guaranteeing paid pa-

---

*World Policy Analysis Centre, Adult Labour Database. Number of countries
for which we have data: 188 (maternal leave).

†World Policy Analysis Centre, Adult Labour Database. Number of countries
for which we have data: 186 (maternal-leave wage replacement).

Map 5.1. Is paid leave available for mothers of infants?

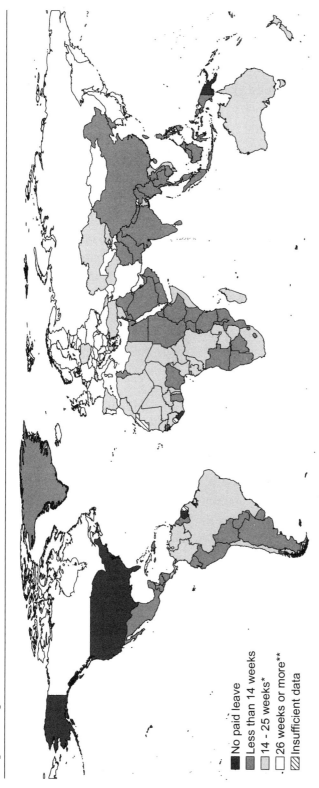

No paid leave
Less than 14 weeks
14 - 25 weeks*
26 weeks or more**
Insufficient data

*International Labour Organization standards state that women should be guaranteed at least 14 weeks of paid maternity leave.
**The World Health Organization recommends at least 6 months of breastfeeding, which is facilitated by paid leave.

Source: World Policy Analysis Centre, Adult Labour Database

ternity leave. While some differential may be appropriate to address pregnancy and breastfeeding, the extreme differences in access to parental leave for women and men are both based on and perpetuate historical biases. The International Labour Organization adopted its first Maternity Protection Convention in 1919 and revised it in 1952 and 2000. Although the recommendation accompanying the 2000 convention mentions parental leave available to either parent, it does not discuss paternity leave at all, and to date, a convention on paternity leave has not been signed.[31]

Globally, only a minority of countries, 81, provide paid leave that can be taken by new fathers (Map 5.2). Forty of these countries provide less than 3 weeks of paid leave. In only 37 countries do fathers have access to 14 weeks or more of paid leave; in most cases, this is through parental leave that is available to either mothers or fathers.* Sixty of the countries that provide leave pay at least 75 percent of men's wages for at least part of their leave; 5 replace between 50 and 74 percent of wages. Four countries provide less than 50 percent of men's wages during parental leave, and 10 have a flat-rate payment during this time.†

These numbers include countries that provide leave for fathers through father-specific paternity leave, gender-neutral parental leave, or a combination of both. Although parental leave was designed to be gender neutral, it has proved to be less open to men than intended. Many employers expect mothers to be the ones to take parental leave, and due to societal expectations, parental leave is overwhelmingly used by women. Fathers are more likely to take leave when it is specifically allocated paternity leave. For example, in Portugal, Denmark, Iceland, Sweden, and Norway, when a portion of gender-neutral parental leave was replaced with leave that could be taken only by fathers, more men took leave after the birth of a child.[32] In 2001, Iceland implemented a policy allocating 3 months of nontransferable paid leave to each parent, plus an additional 3 months that could be taken by either parent. While only 3.3 percent of total leave days taken by

---

*World Policy Analysis Centre, Adult Labour Database. Number of countries for which we have data: 189 (paternal leave).

†World Policy Analysis Centre, Adult Labour Database. Number of countries for which we have data: 187 (paternal-leave wage replacement).

Map 5.2. Is paid leave available for fathers of infants?

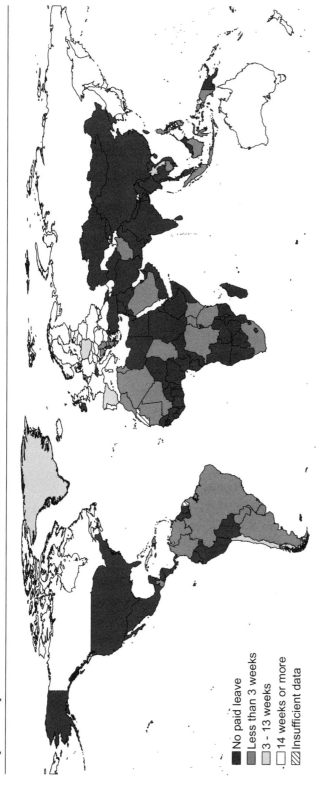

No paid leave
Less than 3 weeks
3 - 13 weeks
14 weeks or more
Insufficient data

Source: World Policy Analysis Centre, Adult Labour Database

new parents were used by fathers in 2000, by 2004 this had climbed to 35 percent.[33]

When just father-specific paid paternity leave is considered, the number of countries providing leave drops to 67. Of the 65 countries for which we were able to determine the duration of paternity leave, 58 offer 3 weeks or less. Just five countries provide more than 4 weeks of father-specific paid leave: Iceland, Laos, Norway, Slovenia, and Sweden guarantee between 2 and 3 months.*

There are additional challenges when it comes to the design of leave for new parents. Policies should be structured so that caregivers in all family types are able to take adequate leave to care for their children. Maternity and paternity leave work well for families with a mother and a father as primary caregivers, but they need to be designed carefully to ensure that all children receive adequate care. In single-parent households, when the available duration of leave is per parent rather than per child, a parent may not be able to take all of the leave himself or herself so that the infant can benefit from the same duration of parental care as a child living with two parents. Where two mothers or two fathers are the child's primary caregivers, what is the coverage? When a primary caregiver is someone other than a parent, for example, a grandparent, is he or she able to take advantage of leave from his or her job to care for the new child? The guiding principle should be ensuring that children have access to adequate care, and that primary caregivers are able to forge a relationship with a new child, while supporting equity.

It is also important to consider what policies are needed beyond parental leave for the healthy development of infants. The importance of breastfeeding for children's health was discussed above; is the provision of maternal leave sufficient to ensure that mothers are able to breastfeed their infant? Looking at the reality of leave duration around the world, the majority of countries (143) currently provide maternal leave for less than 6 months, which in the absence of breastfeeding breaks at work would make it nearly impossible for mothers to breastfeed exclusively for the 6 months recommended by the World Health Organization. Even in countries where working women are entitled to

---

*World Policy Analysis Centre, Adult Labour Database. Number of countries for which we have data: 189 (paternal leave).

six months of leave, some will choose or need to return to work earlier. Evidence shows that in the absence of sufficient support, work can be a significant barrier to breastfeeding. In most settings where data are available, a majority of women who reenter the paid labor force after childbirth express a desire to breastfeed. Although work does not change women's intention or physical capacity to breastfeed, a mother's working conditions can markedly limit an infant's chance of being breastfed.[34] Workplace support for breastfeeding through the provision of breaks can facilitate the continuation of breastfeeding for working women who choose to do so. This key intervention costs countries and companies very little. Any business that can afford to provide workers with even unpaid breaks for meals can afford to provide breaks so that a nursing mother can continue breastfeeding her child.

Can women around the world count on being able to take breaks to breastfeed once they return to work? Our global data show that 136 countries guarantee women the right to breastfeed while they are at work, requiring workplaces to provide at least unpaid time for a mother to feed her infant or express milk; 112 of these countries guarantee these breaks for at least a year (Map 5.3). However, a significant minority of nations do not yet guarantee working mothers the chance to take advantage of this inexpensive way of preventing infant illness, malnutrition, and death. Among countries with high infant mortality rates, where the option to breastfeed is particularly crucial, Kenya, Uganda, Zambia, Myanmar, and Pakistan are a few that do not currently guarantee breastfeeding breaks. Although infant mortality is far lower in affluent nations, breastfeeding still reduces morbidity and mortality. Yet breastfeeding breaks are not guaranteed in Canada, Australia, and the United Kingdom, among other countries.*

Once mothers and fathers return to work, their young children need affordable and good-quality care, especially during the early years before they enter school. As of yet, early childhood care options are extremely limited for families worldwide. Information compiled by UNESCO shows that approximately half of the world's countries do not have any formal ECCE programs for children under age 3. After

---

*World Policy Analysis Centre: Adult Labour Database. Number of countries for which we have data: 181 (breastfeeding breaks).

Map 5.3. Are mothers of infants guaranteed breastfeeding breaks at work?

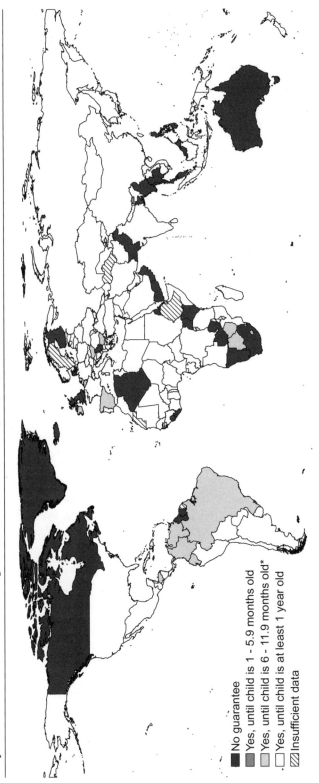

■ No guarantee
■ Yes, until child is 1 - 5.9 months old
■ Yes, until child is 6 - 11.9 months old*
☐ Yes, until child is at least 1 year old
▨ Insufficient data

*The World Health Organization recommends at least 6 months of breastfeeding.

Source: World Policy Analysis Centre, Adult Labour Database

age 3, government provision of ECCE improves; most countries have some kind of government-run preprimary public education program. The number of hours per week that ECCE is provided for children aged 3 and over ranges from 5 hours to 60 hours in the countries for which data are available, with most countries providing between 15 and 40 hours.[35]

In the absence of both lengthy parental leave and full-day ECCE for toddlers and preschoolers, most countries currently leave low-income families poor choices for their children. When ECCE is not publicly provided, the cost of decent-quality programs is prohibitive for most parents living in poverty. When the only option is to leave children at home alone or with the poor-quality caregivers their parents can afford, children's health and development suffer. Although having a program that provides a few hours of ECCE is better than no program, it is not sufficient to meet the needs of children and parents in households in which all adults work.

An important issue in framing all of these policies is how to ensure protections for all working parents, regardless of where they work. Several steps can be taken. First, in many nations, legal guarantees in the formal sector could be improved to reach more people. At present, small employers are exempted from work regulations more often than necessary. Small employers have demonstrated their ability to compete while offering short-term leave, and longer-term leave can be paid through social insurance. If legal guarantees covered employees in small firms, many more working parents would receive needed benefits. The issue of the informal economy is a larger one. Although making work protections available to all those in formal jobs would have an impact on many families, given that at least one member of the household works in the formal sector in a large proportion of households, this would not solve the problem of what to do about parents working in the informal economy. These working parents tend to be among a country's poorest, and they and their children are in need of the same kinds of support as parents working in the formal sector. There are ways to meet the needs of families who have all members earning a living in the informal economy. When income replacement for parental leave is provided through publicly supported social insurance systems financed through taxes or a contributory system rather than solely by employers, maternal and paternal leave policies can be designed to reach new parents working in both the informal and formal economies. ECCE can be provided to all families whether they are participating in the formal or informal economy if it is publicly provided either through the national education system or through social security programs that all workers can contribute to. Extending universal education to children of younger ages would require countries to make a substantial investment, but it also yields substantial economic returns in better education and work outcomes as children grow up. Moreover, providing universal ECCE beginning at a young age is an option that contributes to gender- and income-related equity.

Caring for Older Children

The vigorous policy debates that often occur around the care of young children are much less often present when it comes to older children— their needs are largely ignored in policy circles. When the needs of older children do receive some attention, they tend to focus on whether public or private policy really has anything to do with the role of parents. Some argue that once children are in school and when health services are available, it is teachers and health care providers who play the primary role in determining outcomes, not parents. Others believe strongly that parents' roles do matter to their children's education and health outcomes, but see no place for public policy in this relationship.

The research is illuminating both with respect to whether parents' roles matter to educational and health outcomes even when professionals are available, and whether workplace policies, and the public policies that shape them, affect parents' roles. Parental care makes a marked difference to children's health, from access to basic health care to disease and injury outcomes. Sick children are often prohibited from attending day care or school; young children cannot care for themselves when they are sick, and even older children often require additional care when they are sick or injured. When illnesses or injuries require a child to consult a health-care provider, the child commonly needs to be accompanied by an adult. Even once they have received the professional health care they need, parental involvement makes an enormous difference to children's outcomes. Evidence shows that for both outpatient procedures and hospitalization, children's physical and mental health markedly improve when parents are involved in their care.[36] This is also true of children with long-term health conditions, such as asthma, diabetes, or epilepsy.[37] When parents are involved, children are more likely to recover more rapidly from injuries and illnesses, have chronic conditions under better control, and follow medical advice regarding prevention and treatment. Parental involvement also plays an important role in managing mental and emotional health conditions in childhood and adolescence.[38]

Parents are key players in children's access to preventive care and interventions. In countries around the world, parents or other adult caregivers often have to take time off from work in order to bring children to be immunized.[39] As a result, in contexts as diverse as Haiti, Indonesia, and the United States, where leave for children's preventive care is unavailable, work schedules and time-use conflicts have been found to interfere with parents' ability to have their children vaccinated.[40]

Parental involvement also has a large impact on children's educational outcomes.[41] With regard to achievement in primary school, studies from the United States and the United Kingdom have shown that first- and second-grade students whose parents are actively involved in their schooling perform better on reading and math tests than students whose parents are not actively engaged;[42] one U.S. study shows that 25 percent of the variance in students' performance on standardized tests can be attributed to parental involvement in their education.[43] Studies in the United States have also shown that primary-school-age children are between 30 and 50 percent less likely to have repeated a grade if a parent is moderately or highly involved in their school.[44] These effects can be seen around the world. In Sri Lanka, for example, students scored better on tests when their parents interacted more with their teachers,[45] and in Indonesia, parental involvement (including help with homework) had a significant impact on student achievement in math, science, and language.[46]

Older children and youth depend on parental involvement just as younger children do; parents continue to have an impact on academic achievement among secondary-school students.[47] For example, in Albania, children who continued in school were twice as likely to report that their parents helped them with studying as children who had dropped out of school, and they reported five times as many meetings between their parents and teachers.[48] In the United States, secondary-school-age students were between 24 and 43 percent less likely to have been suspended or expelled from school when their mothers were moderately or highly involved with their education, and they were 43 percent more likely to receive very high grades when their fathers were highly involved in their school.[49]

Working conditions play an important role in determining parents' ability to provide health and educational support for their children. Without guaranteed access to paid leave, working parents risk income and job loss when they must take time off to care for a sick child. In Botswana and Viet Nam, which lack guaranteed leave that can be taken for children's health needs, many of the parents we interviewed lost pay, missed out on job promotions, or had difficulty retaining their jobs because of their need to care for sick children—this was true of 28 percent of parents in Botswana and 62 percent in Viet Nam.[50] In the United States, where paid leave is also not mandated, having a child with health problems was associated with a 36 percent increase in job loss among low-income working mothers, even once education, skills, and local work environment were taken into account.[51] Work-related policies also have a powerful impact on parents' ability to meet their children's educational needs. Once children enter the school system, parents need to be able to take occasional leave from work to meet with teachers, specialists, and principals during the day to advocate on behalf of their child, work with the school and the child to find solutions to developmental problems, and provide support and follow-through.

When leave is not nationally guaranteed, those most likely to lack it are those least able to afford it. For example, in the United States, low-income working parents are less likely than middle-income parents to have access to paid leave and flexibility policies that can be used to meet children's needs.[52] This has effects for children: parents with access to paid leave were more than five times as likely to attend to their sick children themselves as parents who lacked access to paid leave.[53]

How many countries ensure that parents can take essential leave to address their children's health and educational needs? Our data reveal that in much of the world, mothers and fathers risk losing their jobs if they take time off from work to care for a sick child or address a child's educational needs. Only 54 countries, half of which are high-income nations, provide parents with paid leave specifically to meet their children's health needs. In poor countries, where parents are least likely to be able to afford to take time off without pay, they are also more likely to lack paid leave; just 5 low-income countries provide paid leave to meet children's health needs. In countries that provide unpaid leave, parents are protected from job loss when they are caring for a sick child, but they still suffer wage loss; 16 countries guarantee only unpaid leave for children's health needs. Even fewer countries, just 3 worldwide, provide either paid or unpaid leave specifically to meet children's educational needs.*

Some countries have legislated leave that can be taken for family needs in general, leave that can be taken at the employee's discretion, or leave that can be taken for emergencies. Map 5.4, on leave for children's health needs, takes all these types of leave into account. When family, discretionary, and emergency leave are included, 76 countries provide paid leave and 21 unpaid leave that can be taken for a child's health needs. Map 5.5, on leave for children's educational needs, includes leave for family needs as well as discretionary leave; it is unlikely that families could use emergency leave to meet most educational needs. Fewer countries provide leave that can be taken to meet a child's educational needs—21 provide paid leave and 9 unpaid leave.†

Allowing parents to take leave to meet a child's health and educational needs—either through paid leave or through job flexibility—is essential and readily affordable.[54] Even small employers could and should be required to ensure that parents will not lose their jobs if they take time off from work to care for a sick child, even if this leave is unpaid. This would mean that many more working parents would have access to these work protections; currently, many countries exempt small employers from similar work regulations.

---

*World Policy Analysis Centre, Adult Labour Database. Number of countries for which we have data: 187 (health needs), 178 (educational needs).

†World Policy Analysis Centre, Adult Labour Database. Number of countries for which we have data: 187 (health needs), 178 (educational needs), 182 (family needs), 181 (discretionary), 181 (emergency). When at least one kind of leave is paid, the country is considered to provide paid leave.

Map 5.4. Can working parents take leave to meet children's health needs?

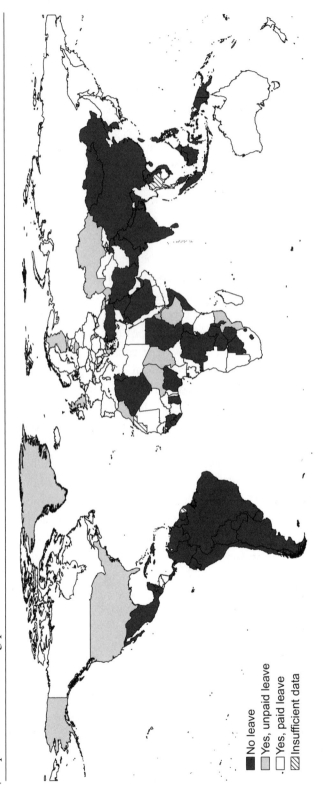

No leave
Yes, unpaid leave
Yes, paid leave
Insufficient data

Leave to meet children's health needs includes leave specifically for children's health needs, as well as discretionary, family needs, and emergency leave which may be used for health needs. It also includes cases where leave is available only for serious illnesses, hospitalization, or urgent health needs.

Source: World Policy Analysis Centre, Adult Labour Database

Map 5.5. Can working parents take leave for children's educational needs?

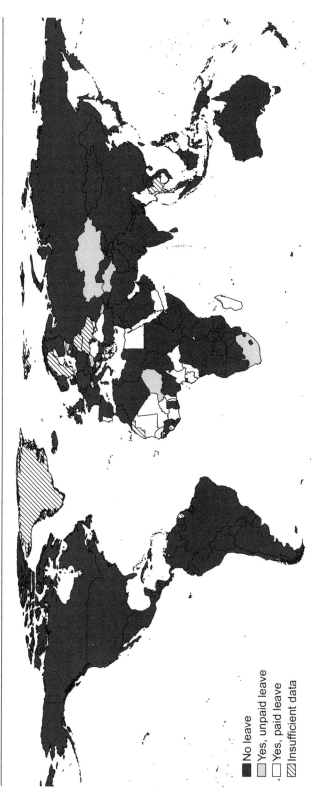

No leave
Yes, unpaid leave
Yes, paid leave
Insufficient data

Leave for children's educational needs includes leave specifically for children's educational needs, as well as discretionary and family needs leave which may be used for educational needs.

Source: World Policy Analysis Centre, Adult Labour Database

Parents need to be available to their children at home on a routine basis as well as during special health and educational circumstances. Once children enter school, the time available for parents and children to spend together is during out-of-school hours: late afternoons, evenings, and weekends. Parents who work daytime shifts during the week are generally able to take advantage of this time. Although working parents must find care for their children for the time between the end of the school day and the end of the work day, there is not a large conflict between parents' ability to work and their ability to spend time regularly with their sons and daughters. However, when parents are required to work evening or night hours, the time they have available to spend with their children suffers; many workplaces mandate night shifts, and working these hours is not always a matter of choice.

Amid globalization, pressure to function around the clock because it is always daytime somewhere in the world has led to an increase in 24-hour factories and business services and a marked rise in the prevalence of evening and night work. In the United States, for example, almost 15 percent of full-time wage and salary workers work nontraditional hours; more than half of these workers do so because the job requires it rather than as a matter of personal choice.[55] In the European Union, 22 percent of men and 18 percent of women work evening shifts, and 9 percent of men and 5 percent of women work night shifts.[56]

When parents regularly work evenings or nights, their children feel the effects of their absence. Our research on working families in the United States showed that nearly one-fifth of the low-income parents we interviewed had little or no time to spend with their children during the work week because of their schedules, and 2 out of every 5 low-income working parents also faced work-related barriers to their involvement in their children's education. Working parents experience these barriers all over the world. Fifty-one percent of the working parents we interviewed in Viet Nam, 66 percent in Mexico, and 82 percent in Botswana had difficulty helping their children with homework, participating in school events, or otherwise being involved in their children's education as a result of work responsibilities and restrictions.[57] The children of mothers and fathers who work nonstandard schedules in the United States, Canada, and Australia, where employers are not discouraged from requiring it, are more likely to experience poorer school performance and engagement, as well as emotional or behavioral problems.[58] Our previous work showed that in the United States, for every hour parents regularly worked in the evening, their children were 17 percent more likely to score in the bottom quartile of math tests.[59] When parents worked at night, their children were close to three times more likely to be suspended from school.[60]

Previously, comparative data were not available on what regulations countries have regarding evening and night work for their employees. Through reviews primarily of original labor legislation, supplemented by secondary sources, we have analyzed details of national policies regarding night-work bans, hour regulations, and wage premiums, among other aspects of workplace policy.

Some countries have chosen to deal with the issue of evening and night work by banning it for particular groups. Our data show that around the world, 47 countries prevent employers from requiring pregnant women, nursing mothers, or women with young children to work nights and evenings, 8 countries permit night work for these women only with their consent, and 14 countries permit these women to request exemption from night shifts. This provides some protection for mothers but does not effectively cover most school-age children. A total of 54 countries ban night work for all women or for women working in industrial settings.* Although this approach covers older children, it, like the others, contains an inherent gender bias. The regulations provide no protection for fathers and could lead to workplace discrimination against women, in spite of the clear evidence that children feel the effects when either parent works evenings and nights. For example, a study using data from the United States shows that the quality of a child's home environment (with regard to its ability to support academic, cognitive, and emotional development) decreases substantially when either a mother or a father works evenings or nights.[61] Information collected by the International Labour Organization shows that some countries have responded to night work with gender-neutral exceptions for parents. In at least 8 countries, parents with children under a given age cannot be required to work at night without the

---

*World Policy Analysis Centre, Adult Labour Database. Number of countries for which we have data: 186 (night-work regulations).

Map 5.6. What is the wage premium for night work?

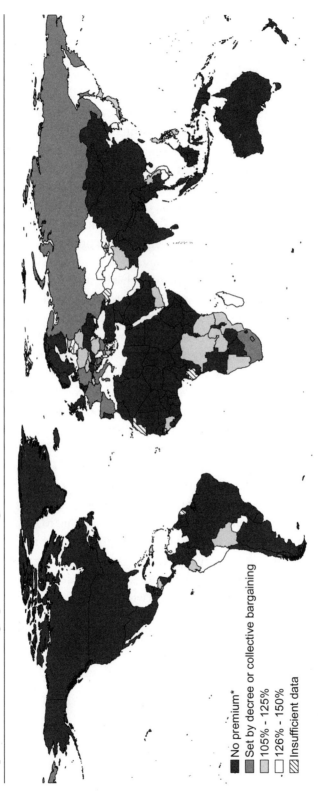

■ No premium*
■ Set by decree or collective bargaining
▦ 105% - 125%
□ 126% - 150%
▨ Insufficient data

*No premium includes countries where there is no premium for night work or where there are premiums only for certain categories of workers (such as shift workers or workers who do not normally work at night). It also includes 2 countries which offer no premium but have a general ban on non-essential night work (Belgium and Norway).

Source: World Policy Analysis Centre, Adult Labour Database

parent's consent; 6 countries have this protection specifically for single parents.[62]

Instead of or as well as banning or restricting evening and night work, some countries have adopted an alternative approach, requiring employers to pay a wage premium to employees who work these hours. Mandating a wage premium has several benefits. When evening and night work is more expensive for employers, they are less likely to require employees to work these hours unless necessary. Higher wages also make evening and night shifts more attractive to employees, thereby increasing the demand for these shifts and reducing the odds that employees—including working parents—will be assigned to them on a mandatory basis. Furthermore, although higher wages do not entirely replace the benefits of parents being able to stay home with their children, they make it easier for parents to afford quality child care when they have to work an evening or night shift, and this helps mitigate the negative effects on their children.

Our data show that a total of 64 nations set a general wage premium for night work (Map 5.6). Thirty-four percent of low-income countries and 36 percent of middle-income countries do so, as do 32 percent of high-income countries. In 13 of these countries, these premiums are set by decree or by collective bargaining. Legislated wage premiums for evening and night work range from 105 to 150 percent of wages; in 30 countries, they are between 105 and 125 percent of wages, and 21 countries mandate premiums between 126 and 150 percent. Additionally, 2 countries ban nonessential night work, and 11 mandate extra pay for night work only for certain categories of workers, such as shift workers or those who do not normally work at night.*

Can Countries and Companies Afford What Is Needed?

Even though the benefits for children's outcomes of the policies discussed in this chapter are clear, some have questioned whether countries and companies can afford to provide them. Will the additional expenditures associated with providing income to parents during leave be detrimental to the country's economic competitiveness? Will em-

---

*World Policy Analysis Centre, Adult Labour Database. Number of countries for which we have data: 184 (night-work wage premiums).

ployers be forced to reduce the number of people they employ to compensate for higher costs? Can low-income countries afford to guarantee these policies, especially when many attract jobs because of lower labor costs?

On the one hand, there is ample evidence that some countries and companies have chosen to compete by having poorer working conditions. In the context of globalization, in both high- and low-income countries, greater pressure is placed on those who produce and sell goods to do so at lower prices. Although there are many ways to achieve lower prices, some producers and vendors have sought to do so by lowering compensation and benefits.[63] On the other hand, although better working conditions for parents have costs, they are investments that pay off in the long run by fostering the development of a healthy and well-educated next generation of workers, and by fully using the capacity of the current generation of workers through facilitating their ability to care for their families while staying in the workforce.

We used unemployment rates reported by the World Bank to investigate the feasibility of providing labor protections while maintaining low unemployment rates. In our global analysis, we examined the availability of paid maternity and paternity leave, breastfeeding breaks at work, paid time off to care for personal or family health needs, and several other protections. We found no evidence of a relationship between any of these protections and higher unemployment rates.

In order to verify this finding further, we took a closer look at the countries of the OECD; at the time of analysis, the OECD was composed of 34 countries totaling over 1.2 billion people.[64] World Bank unemployment figures are nationally reported, but OECD figures are independently verified and are collected according to a single definition.[65] Additionally, most OECD countries have effectively implemented their labor laws, which makes this group a good platform for a more in-depth examination. We analyzed the OECD countries that had the lowest unemployment rates in at least 8 of the 10 years between 2002 and 2011.[66] We examined the work protections guaranteed by these nations and found that low-unemployment countries overwhelmingly provided good work protections. All of the 12 countries with consistently low unemployment rates offer paid leave for new mothers, ranging in duration from 12 weeks to over 1 year. The majority of these countries also guarantee paid leave for new fathers: when paternity and parental leave are combined, fathers have access to paid leave in 11 of the 12 countries, including 1 year or more in 2 countries and at least 6 months in 5 others. Ten of these 12 countries provide paid or unpaid leave to address children's health needs, and 5 have wage premiums or restrictions on evening and night work. Although such analyses cannot demonstrate whether working conditions that benefit families and children have any effect on employment rates, they do document the economic feasibility of countries guaranteeing benefits. It is clear that strong protections for employees and their children do not inevitably lead to high unemployment.

Beyond employment, do these protections hurt national economic competitiveness? To investigate this issue, we combined our data on labor conditions around the world with data collected by the business-led World Economic Forum (WEF). Each year, the WEF publishes the "Global Competitiveness Report," which ranks 131 countries using a series of indicators it deems to be the key drivers of economic growth and competitiveness.[67] For the purposes of this study, we considered countries to be highly economically competitive if they were ranked among the top 20 most economically competitive countries in at least 8 of the 10 years between 2002 and 2011.[68] Again, the answer to our question was clear: countries can be economically competitive while protecting families and children. Paid leave for new mothers is guaranteed in 15 of the 16 most competitive countries. All the countries guaranteeing paid leave offer at least 14 weeks, and many offer much longer leave; 11 countries offer 6 months or more of paid leave for new mothers. Thirteen of the 16 most competitive countries also offer paid leave for new fathers. All 16 countries guarantee either paid or unpaid leave to care for children's health needs. This should not be surprising. For short-term leave, even providing a yearly allocation of 2 weeks for family-related needs, relatively long by current global standards, would cost just 4 percent of wages if all of this leave were taken, and less if employees take fewer than the allocated number of days.[69] In low-income and low-wage countries the absolute dollar amount of providing these policies would be less than in high-income countries. For long-term leave, even in countries where the average family has four children, guaranteeing 26 weeks of paid leave for mothers and fathers would mean providing income for just 2 years out of more than a

40-year working career; most countries provide shorter leaves that cost even less.

Ultimately, the barrier to change is not economic feasibility but the need for a cultural transformation. Just as protecting working adults from hazardous conditions was once contentious but is now taken for granted in operating a business, providing parents with the time they need to care for the next generation of working adults should be as well. The costs to children of insufficient work protections are enormous, particularly when working conditions mean that preschool-age children are left home alone or with poor-quality caregivers, that older children are left to manage serious illnesses alone, and that parents cannot be available to address educational issues. Putting the needed laws and public policies in place can lead to a transformation of our expectations, as has occurred before in regard to workplace hazards or a minimum wage. Removing the needless obstacles parents currently face globally is essential not only to children's healthy development but to the financial solvency of many families.

Table 5.1. Workplace policies before and after childbirth

	Low-Income	Middle-Income	High-Income
Duration of Paid Leave for Mothers			
No guaranteed paid maternal leave	1 (3%)	6 (6%)	1 (2%)
Fewer than 14 weeks of paid maternal leave	16 (47%)	54 (52%)	12 (24%)
14 - 25 weeks of paid maternal leave	15 (44%)	25 (24%)	13 (26%)
26 - 51 weeks of paid maternal leave	1 (3%)	2 (2%)	11 (22%)
52 weeks or more of paid maternal leave	1 (3%)	17 (16%)	13 (26%)
Maximum Wage Replacement Rate of Paid Leave for Mothers			
No guaranteed paid maternal leave	1 (3%)	6 (6%)	1 (2%)
A flat rate paid to mothers	0 (0%)	0 (0%)	1 (2%)
25% - 49% of regular salary paid to mothers	0 (0%)	4 (4%)	0 (0%)
50% - 74% of regular salary paid to mothers	5 (15%)	14 (14%)	5 (10%)
75% - 100% of regular salary paid to mothers	27 (82%)	79 (77%)	43 (86%)
Duration of Paid Leave for Fathers			
No guaranteed paid paternal leave	24 (69%)	67 (64%)	17 (34%)
Fewer than 3 weeks of paid paternal leave	10 (29%)	23 (22%)	7 (14%)
3 - 13 weeks of paid paternal leave	0 (0%)	2 (2%)	2 (4%)
14 weeks or more of paid paternal leave	1 (3%)	12 (12%)	24 (48%)
Maximum Wage Replacement Rate of Paid Leave for Fathers			
No guaranteed paid paternal leave	24 (71%)	67 (65%)	17 (34%)
A flat rate paid to fathers	0 (0%)	5 (5%)	5 (10%)
30% - 49% of regular salary paid to fathers	0 (0%)	2 (2%)	2 (4%)

(continued)

Table 5.1 *(continued)*

50% - 74% of regular salary paid to fathers	0 (0%)	2 (2%)	3 (6%)
75% - 100% of regular salary paid to fathers	10 (29%)	27 (26%)	23 (46%)
Availability of Breastfeeding Breaks at Work			
No guaranteed breastfeeding breaks at work	8 (25%)	24 (24%)	13 (27%)
New mothers are guaranteed breastfeeding breaks until the child is 1 - 5.9 months old	0 (0%)	2 (2%)	1 (2%)
New mothers are guaranteed breastfeeding breaks until the child is 6 - 11.9 months old	2 (6%)	11 (11%)	8 (17%)
New mothers are guaranteed breastfeeding breaks until the child is 1 year old or more	22 (69%)	64 (63%)	26 (54%)

Source: World Policy Analysis Centre, Adult Labour Database.

Definition : Paid leave for mothers includes both paid maternity leave and paid parental leave that can be taken by women.

Paid leave for fathers includes both paid paternity leave and paid parental leave that can be taken by men.

Low-income, middle-income, and *high-income* refer to World Bank classifications of national income. Here, middle-income countries include those classified as lower-middle and upper-middle income.

Notes : International Labour Organization standards state that women should be guaranteed at least 14 weeks of paid maternity leave.

The World Health Organization recommends at least 6 months of breastfeeding, which is facilitated by paid leave and breastfeeding breaks at work.

Table 5.2. Workplace policies to meet the needs of older children

	Low-Income	Middle-Income	High-Income
Leave Specifically for Children's Health Needs			
No guaranteed leave for parents specifically to take care of their children's health needs	27 (77%)	74 (73%)	16 (32%)
Unpaid leave is guaranteed for parents to take care of their children's health needs	3 (9%)	6 (6%)	7 (14%)
Paid leave is guaranteed for parents to take care of their children's health needs	5 (14%)	22 (22%)	27 (54%)
Leave Specifically for Children's Educational Needs			
No guaranteed leave for parents specifically to take care of their children's educational needs	35 (100%)	100 (100%)	46 (94%)
Unpaid leave is guaranteed for parents to take care of their children's educational needs	0 (0%)	0 (0%)	1 (2%)
Paid leave is guaranteed for parents to take care of their children's educational needs	0 (0%)	0 (0%)	2 (4%)

(continued)

159

Table 5.2 (*continued*)

Leave for Family Needs			
No guaranteed leave for employees specifically to take care of family needs	24 (73%)	92 (93%)	47 (94%)
Unpaid leave is guaranteed for employees to take care of family needs	1 (3%)	0 (0%)	2 (4%)
Paid leave is guaranteed for employees to take care of family needs	8 (24%)	7 (7%)	1 (2%)
Discretionary Leave			
No guaranteed leave for employees for discretionary reasons	33 (97%)	89 (92%)	49 (98%)
Unpaid leave is guaranteed for employees for discretionary reasons	0 (0%)	6 (6%)	1 (2%)
Paid leave is guaranteed for employees for discretionary reasons	1 (3%)	2 (2%)	0 (0%)
Leave for Emergencies			
No guaranteed leave for employees specifically for emergencies	30 (91%)	90 (91%)	45 (92%)
Unpaid leave is guaranteed for employees for emergencies	2 (6%)	4 (4%)	1 (2%)
Paid leave is guaranteed for employees for emergencies	1 (3%)	5 (5%)	3 (6%)

Level of Wage Premium for Night Work			
No higher rate of pay guaranteed for night work	21 (60%)	59 (59%)	27 (55%)
General ban on non-essential night work	0 (0%)	0 (0%)	2 (4%)
Higher rate of pay available only to certain types of employees for night work	2 (6%)	5 (5%)	4 (8%)
Higher rate of pay for night work is set by decree or collective bargaining	0 (0%)	7 (7%)	6 (12%)
105% - 125% of regular wage paid to employees for night work	6 (17%)	15 (15%)	9 (18%)
126% - 150% of regular wage paid to employees for night work	6 (17%)	14 (14%)	1 (2%)

Source: World Policy Analysis Centre, Adult Labour Database.

Definitions : *Leave specifically for children's health needs* includes both leave available for any health needs and leave available only for serious illnesses, hospitalization, or urgent health needs.

Family needs leave is leave that employees can take to address family or household issues, which could include health or educational needs.

Discretionary leave is leave that employees can take for personal reasons not covered by other types of leave.

Chapter 6

Meeting Basic Needs

*At 25 years old, Kesego Mpofu was too well versed in the costs of
meeting basic needs on a meager salary. She had a 4-year-old son and
was 9 months pregnant with her second child. She worked as an office
cleaner in Gaborone, Botswana's capital city. She had to leave her
young son with her sister in her home village 50 kilometers away
because she could afford to live only in a one-room dwelling, and even if
she had space for a child, she could not afford to pay anyone to look after
him while she was at work. While her income was barely enough to
support herself, her 4-year-old son, and her younger sister's school fees,
it was more than double what she had earned at her previous job as a
maid in another town. When she got this chance at a higher-paying job,
she took it. Although she would have liked to get a job nearer her
family, she had been unable to find one.*

*Each month, she struggled to make ends meet. She made 590 pula
per month, approximately US$200.[1] Her room cost 100 pula, and she
limited her food expenditures to just 100 pula per month as well. Once
her family's expenses were taken into account, there was nothing left at
the end of the month. Kesego focused on how her struggles affected her
child and the family members who depended on her: "There are times
that we're without food, especially at midmonth. It means I have to ask
for food or borrow money from somewhere, but that means that at the
end of the month, I have to pay back more people than I had budgeted*

for. Some things have to suffer. . . . I can't afford clothing for myself or clothing for my child. . . . These problems, like the lack of food, have a particular effect on [my son and younger sister]. I can see it in their end-of-term reports. The teachers write as comments that many times the children are just sleeping in class. At times they are brought back from school and it is reported that the children are crying they are so hungry. . . . Another thing is that when there is no food, it means that we don't even have firewood. . . . They've all lost weight these days and I think it's because of starvation; they're not eating as they're supposed to be. Most of them are very lean, and to make matters worse, they go to school in bare feet. We can't afford shoes—if we buy them shoes, it means we don't buy food. We prefer to buy food rather than school shoes."[2]

This book is fundamentally about ensuring that all children have an opportunity to develop to their fullest potential, with aspirations for themselves and the chance to achieve them, not just about meeting their most basic daily needs. But we cannot speak about equal life chances for all children without knowing what countries are doing when it comes to the basics.

The scale of the problem of poverty is staggering. In low- and middle-income countries, 1 in 4 people, or 1.4 billion, live on less than $1.25 per day, the World Bank's measure of extreme poverty. Nearly half the population of these countries lives on less than $2.00 per day.[3] Millions of children lack access to essentials such as adequate nutrition, water, and shelter.[4] In OECD countries, more than 1 in 10 children live in poverty, defined as having a household income below half the national median.[5] Approximately 10 percent of households in the OECD are unable to meet at least one of their basic needs, including a sufficiently heated home, an adequate diet, or health care access unimpeded by financial concerns.[6]

The combined effects of poverty mean that young children are more likely to die if they live in a poor household. In low- and middle-income countries, a child from the poorest fifth of the population is more than twice as likely to die before the age of 5 as a child from the wealthiest fifth.[7] The risk of dying as a child is markedly higher for the poor even in high-income countries. In England, for example, infant mortality is over twice as high in the poorest economic quintile as in the more affluent, and a child's risk of accidental death is more than five times higher.[8]

Profound Consequences for Children's Chances

Poverty affects each aspect of children's chances discussed in this volume. Poor children are less likely to attend school and more likely to labor; when they do attend school, they are less likely to succeed because of their multiple responsibilities and financial constraints. Poor girls are more likely to marry and give birth at a young age. From nutrition to immunizations, from infectious diseases to chronic ones, children living in poverty also have worse health outcomes.

Although the global community has made progress on breaking the tight link between poverty and malnutrition, malnutrition and its lifelong consequences still affect tens of millions of children and youth.[9] In the short term, inadequate food leads to weight loss; if this deprivation continues, children's growth becomes permanently stunted. UNICEF has found globally that children in the poorest fifth of families are twice as likely to be stunted and almost three times as likely to be underweight as children from the richest families.[10] Undernutrition in expectant mothers and young children is responsible for 35 percent of child deaths worldwide.[11] However, both national economies and policies affect the extent of the problem. The proportion of underweight children under the age of 5 ranges from 48 percent in South Asia to 6 percent in Latin America and the Caribbean.[12]

Further, deficiencies in protein, fat, calories, and micronutrients have serious health and developmental impacts. Even when poverty-linked malnutrition does not lead to death early in life, the health consequences can be severe: malnutrition has a negative impact on physical, cognitive, behavioral, and emotional development.[13] Food insecurity affects children living in poverty in affluent countries as well. In the United States, even before the global recession, 15 percent of children in low-income families did not always get enough to eat.[14] After the recession that began in 2008, the number of American children in poor families who did not always have enough to eat swelled to nearly 1 in 4.[15]

Although the effects of insufficient food tend to receive more attention, not having enough to eat is not the only nutrition-related risk faced by poor children. Even if families are able to purchase an adequate amount of food with respect to calories, many families lack the income they need to purchase a nutritionally balanced diet for their children.[16] In 24 OECD countries, 11 percent of households report that they are unable to afford a healthy diet, ranging from under 5 percent of households in 11 countries to over 30 percent in 3 countries.[17]

In many contexts, lower-income families are more likely to purchase food that is high in starch and low in nutritional value, which tends to be cheaper and provides the calories needed to quiet hunger but contributes to childhood obesity.[18] In most affluent countries, children in lower-income families are at a higher risk of becoming overweight or obese; obesity is also a rising trend among the urban poor in many less affluent nations. Obesity among children puts them at increased risk of chronic disease, including type 2 diabetes and heart disease, as well as other conditions.[19]

Poverty has health consequences beyond food- and nutrition-related problems; the poorest families are the most likely to lack access to clean drinking water and sanitation facilities.[20] In sub-Saharan Africa, for instance, children in the poorest quintile are five times less likely to have improved sanitation facilities than the wealthiest children.[21] This leaves poor children far more vulnerable to water-related diseases, such as diarrhea, which accounts for 1.5 million deaths among children under 5 each year and is the second-largest single cause of death among these children.[22] Diarrhea is closely linked to nutritional status, and as a result, chronic or frequent episodes can affect long-term growth, cognitive capacity, and school achievement.

Children who are being raised in poverty face greater noninfectious risks as well. Poor neighborhoods have higher risk exposures. For example, poor communities are more likely to be situated near factories and heavily traveled roads and are thus exposed to greater quantities of air pollution. The effects of these and other poverty-linked exposures can be seen in the case of asthma. Rates of diagnosed asthma, one of the most common chronic diseases among children, as well as asthma attacks, are higher among children living in poverty in countries around the world, from the United States and Canada to Brazil and the Republic of Korea.[23]

Poverty has a variety of other health impacts, from higher risks of injury to poorer mental health. In Canada, for example, children in the lowest-income urban areas are 4.5 times more likely to die from injury than those in the highest-income areas, and in New Zealand, children from the poorest households are nearly three times as likely to die from injury as those from the wealthiest.[24] Children living in poverty are also more likely to suffer from depression and mental health problems;[25] this should perhaps not be surprising, given the daily struggles their families face.[26] When individuals are able to exit poverty, these mental health effects are mitigated for both children and parents.[27]

Compounding their disadvantage, from birth and throughout childhood, poor children are less likely to receive the health care they need. In much of Africa, women from the poorest fifth of the population are three times less likely to give birth with a doctor, nurse, or midwife present than women from the richest fifth; in South Asia, they are nearly five times less likely to do so.[28] As these children grow up, they continue to receive limited health care. Most health systems require some payment of fees for clinic visits, laboratory tests, or preventive measures such as immunizations. Even when all these services are free, medications must often be purchased separately at pharmacies. Moreover, even reaching health services requires paying for transportation and taking time off from work, which can be a barrier for the poorest families. When higher-level health-care services are located far away, accessing them can require overnight stays, meals, and other expenditures.

As a result, in high- and low-income countries alike, children in poor households are less likely to receive preventive and curative services, even when it comes to basic care. In West and Central Africa and South Asia, rates of measles immunization for children in the richest quintile are double those for the poorest children. In Pakistan, three times more children from the richest fifth of households have been immunized with the combined diphtheria, tetanus, and pertussis vaccine than children in the poorest fifth. In sub-Saharan Africa, children in the richest fifth of families are 70 percent more likely to receive antimalarial treatment when they have a fever than children in the poorest fifth. In a number of countries, these disparities are even greater.[29] Over 20 percent of households in Greece, Italy, the Slovak Republic, and Turkey face income-based restrictions in access to health care.[30]

The longevity of the health impacts of childhood poverty is striking and has been demonstrated by studies around the world using a variety of techniques. In the United Kingdom, the National Child Development Study followed a cohort of children born in 1958 and took detailed measures of their family income and the circumstances in which they were raised. Family income in childhood predicted health as a middle-aged adult even after many other social factors were taken into account.[31] Study after study has demonstrated the same findings. In New Zealand, a cohort of children was followed regularly from birth into young adulthood. Twenty-six-year-olds who had spent their childhood in poverty were more likely to have poor dental health, poor mental health, and risk factors for long-term cardiovascular disease, including a high body mass index.[32] Similar effects on heart disease, strokes, and premature death have been documented across Europe.[33]

Equally consequential is poverty's impact on children's education. With tragic consistency, the world's poorest children have fewer educational opportunities. When families cannot afford basic necessities of food or health care, they sacrifice school fees. Even when tuition is free, the poorest families must often choose between sustaining their family and paying for the school uniforms or textbooks their children need. Furthermore, for many families, the most significant cost of sending a son or daughter to school is the opportunity cost of the child's time. Poor children are more likely to work outside the home than children from more affluent families, and they are less likely to combine this work with education.[34] When all adults in the household work and family income is barely enough for subsistence, children may also be taken out of school to care for younger siblings because parents cannot afford to pay another adult to provide child care in the absence of publicly provided early childhood care and education.[35] A study of 80 countries from diverse regions showed that children from the poorest quintile are more than three times as likely as children from the richest quintile to be out of school.[36]

Even when children from low-income families are able to attend school, poverty can affect their ability to succeed. Many poor children who attend school must combine attendance with substantial work within or outside the home, and when children combine education with labor, their performance at school tends to suffer. As a result, in every region and in nearly every country around the world, children who are being raised in poverty complete fewer years of education on average.[37] In over 20 lower-income countries studied by UNESCO, the average length of schooling completed by the richest quintile of the population is more than 5 years greater than that of the poorest quintile.[38] However, the gaps in educational attainment between the richest and poorest children, as well as how well the poorest children fare, vary from one country to the next, suggesting that these large educational disparities are not inevitable.

Clearly, there are children who grow up in poverty and receive an excellent education, are in good health, and go on to rewarding work as adults, but the probability of being able to do so is much lower than it is for children who grow up in a household where all their basic needs and more are met. Just as some children who are exposed to violence will experience fewer long-term effects than others, some children exposed to poverty—often considered a form of structural violence—will be less affected than others. Nonetheless, this exposure unnecessarily places their health, education, and development at risk.

Addressing Poverty around the World

Persistent poverty has existed for millennia, leaving many to perceive it as inevitable. Can nations make a dent in the extent of poverty? Can countries improve the life chances of children already affected?

Some of the effects of poverty can be mitigated without addressing poverty directly. For instance, malnutrition can be reduced by distributing food to families in need. Making education free can reduce the barriers that poor children face. Ensuring that all communities have access to adequate water and sanitation facilities can mitigate the risk of waterborne disease. Making health care and essential medicines affordable can improve access to care. All these approaches are important, and many are discussed in other chapters of this book.

However, these steps are not enough to eliminate the poverty-related disadvantages that children experience. Even when schooling is fee-free, the poorest families may not be able to afford the transportation costs of getting children to and from school, the books and paper they need to do their homework, or the loss of income resulting from the child's inability to labor while in class. Insufficient financial resources often keep children from poor families out of school even in countries where primary schooling is nominally free, such as Cambodia, India, Malawi, and Uganda.[39]

Even when health systems do not charge for services, poor children experience worse health outcomes. In Canada, for example, which has a universal health-care system, although the income-based health disparities observed are significantly less than in the United States, where health-care coverage has not been universal, free health-care delivery does not eliminate all disparities. Children who experience intermittent poverty have poorer reported health than nonpoor children, and children from chronically poor households experience asthma attacks more than twice as often as children from nonpoor households.[40]

In order to give all children a truly equal chance, nations must address poverty directly, as well as take steps to increase access to key services. The enormous progress made globally over the past few decades tells an encouraging story about what is possible. The most widely used measure of extreme poverty is the World Bank's cutoff of $1.25 per day (adjusted for purchasing power parity). Between 1981 and 2005, the proportion of the population in low- and middle-income countries living in extreme poverty was cut in half, from 52 percent to 26 percent. Much of this decline can be attributed to China's successful poverty reduction, but even if China is excluded, this proportion declined significantly, from 40 percent to 29 percent. Much of the reduction in China was achieved through addressing extreme rural poverty and productivity in subsistence agriculture. Successfully reducing the number of people worldwide living on between $1.25 and $2.00 per day, currently 1.2 billion, will require addressing the needs of the poor who work for wages as well.[41]

The policy data presented in this chapter are drawn from the database created by our research team on poverty-reduction policy around the world. By analyzing a wealth of legislative text as well as other government and international sources, including the Social Security Programs Throughout the World database (for more details, see Appendix 1), we produced a quantitatively comparable global data source on the minimum wage, family benefits, unemployment protections, and other poverty-related policies.

Increasing Parental Income through Work

Access to decent jobs and decent wages—irrespective of gender, ethnicity, religion, or national origin—is the most likely way for working adults and their children to exit poverty. Evidence shows that programs that increase income from parental employment can improve children's outcomes. A study of 13 programs in the United States and Canada geared toward increasing parental employment shows that the programs that led to an increase in family income had positive effects on young children's school achievement, largely as a result of the increased income and increased use of center-based child care; programs that increased employment but not household income had insignificant effects on school achievement.[42]

A natural mechanism for increasing the amount of income that low-income families have access to has been raising the minimum wage. However, the minimum wage as an income-improving policy has been hotly debated. It has been argued that minimum-wage policies are essentially ineffective—that they are so rarely enforced, especially in low-income-country settings, that their existence is largely irrelevant. Others argue that minimum-wage policies apply to too small a proportion of the labor force to matter, and that the poorest working adults are in the informal economy unaffected by minimum-wage policy. Some of those who do believe that these policies have an impact see their effects as negative. There are concerns that raising the minimum wage would lead companies to lay off workers because they will be unable to afford to pay them all.[43]

Is there empirical evidence on the impact of raising the minimum wage? In the United States, several studies have shown that increasing wages at the bottom of the scale reduces poverty in general and child poverty more specifically.[44] Similarly, studies in Britain demonstrate that minimum-wage increases can reduce poverty among children and working families.[45] Studies from a wide range of economies around the world have found that disemployment effects are very small or nonexistent.[46] Moreover, a number of studies have shown that minimum wages established in formal-sector occupations can have a beneficial effect on the informal economy as well.[47] In Costa Rica, for example, minimum-wage increases positively affected the earnings of workers in the informal economy, despite the fact that the policy was not directly applicable.[48] A study of 19 Latin American countries showed that in 14 of these countries, minimum-wage increases improved wages in the informal economy.[49] Another study affirms that these wage increases do not inadvertently push more people into informal work.[50]

At first blush, our database of poverty-related policies shows that the world is doing well in establishing minimum wages. Out of 189 countries on which we have information, a minimum wage is ensured in 167 countries, with 155 establishing it through legislation and 12 through collective bargaining.[51] Just 22 countries have no minimum wage. Six of these countries have legislation establishing a framework for the minimum wage but have no wage level set, leaving their workers unable to benefit from this legislation.*

However, the world's progress on minimum wages is less convincing when one looks at the details. For those workers receiving the minimum wage, the first question is whether it is high enough to allow employed adults and their dependents to have a decent quality of life. A commonly used global floor of poverty is the figure of $2 per person per day, adjusted for purchasing power parity (PPP). Yet in 40 countries, a working adult earning the minimum wage and one dependent child would be living on $2 or less per person per day, PPP-adjusted. This is particularly true throughout sub-Saharan Africa (Map 6.1).†

Furthermore, data from the International Labour Organization show that in 23 countries, half of which are middle-income, annual growth in the minimum wage lagged behind inflation, meaning that workers effectively had fewer resources over time to support their families. Many countries could be doing better; the failure to provide an adequate minimum wage to all working men and women cannot simply be attributed to the national economy's ability to pay. We used ILO data to examine whether minimum wage kept pace with GDP growth prior to the recession. In 19 of these countries, as well as an additional 26 countries, productivity (measured in gross domestic

---

*World Policy Analysis Centre, Poverty Database. Number of countries for which we have data: 189 (establishment of minimum wage).

†World Policy Analysis Centre, Poverty Database. Number of countries for which we have data: 177 (level of minimum wage).

Map 6.1. At what level are minimum wages set?

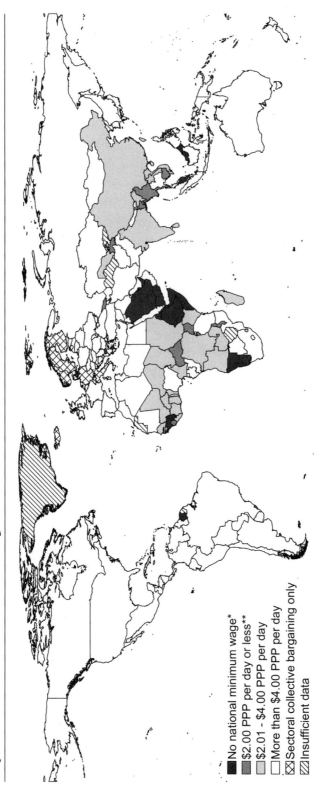

- No national minimum wage*
- $2.00 PPP per day or less**
- $2.01 - $4.00 PPP per day
- More than $4.00 PPP per day
- Sectoral collective bargaining only
- Insufficient data

No national minimum wage includes cases where there is no minimum wage legislation as well as where legislation provides a framework for establishing a minimum wage, but the country has not yet implemented one.
**Buying power of the minimum wage, adjusted for purchasing power parity.

Source: World Policy Analysis Centre, Poverty Database

product per capita) grew at least 5 percent faster than the minimum wage between 2001 and 2007 (Map 6.2).[52]

Moreover, minimum wages vary within countries. The established minimum-wage level varies by region in many cases, which may not detrimentally affect workers when this variation is based on differing costs of living. However, minimum wages can also vary by type of work, which can contribute to particularly poor living conditions for and inadequate attention paid to the worst-paid occupations.

Countries have chosen different ways to enforce their minimum-wage legislation. In 125 countries, workplaces must keep records on wages and/or inspections are mandated; in 39 countries, employees have the right to legal action against their employer. In the case of violations of minimum-wage policy, 128 countries mandate fines, 58 ensure compensation for lost wages, 41 have the potential to imprison employers, and 5 may suspend the business's operations.* It is not self-evident which method is ideal. If fines are so small that they do not deter employers from paying workers less than they are entitled to receive, they will not be effective. At the same time, if penalties are so harsh that they are rarely applied in practice, they have limited power. The data do not currently allow us to make judgments about the relative value of different mechanisms beyond the clear need for effective enforcement.

There are other ways to increase the income earned by working adults. For example, nations can facilitate the ability of working adults to get better-paying jobs by making opportunities available for them to gain skills. Literacy, skill-development, and vocational-training programs have been shown to positively affect earnings, employability, and participation in income-generating activities in contexts as diverse as Bangladesh, Cambodia, Cape Verde, the Philippines, Rwanda, South Africa, Tajikistan, and the United Kingdom.[53] Adult education and training programs simultaneously benefit children; for instance, parental participation in literacy programs has been shown to increase school attendance among their children in Bangladesh, the number of parent-teacher meetings in Nepal, and the frequency of homework checking in Uganda.[54] While adult education is a crucial

---

*World Policy Analysis Centre, Poverty Database. Number of countries for which we have data: 181 (minimum-wage enforcement mechanisms).

Map 6.2. Has minimum-wage growth kept pace with productivity growth?

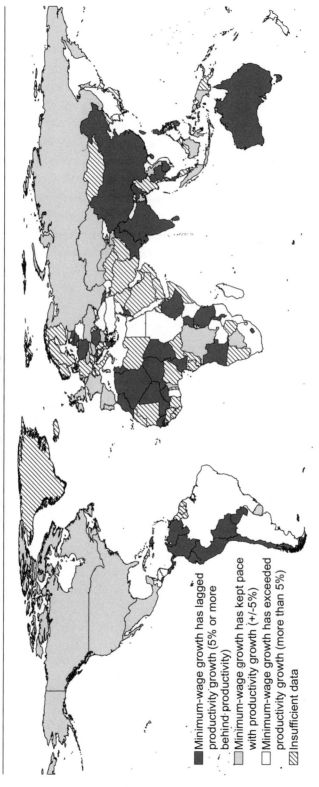

Minimum-wage growth has lagged productivity growth (5% or more behind productivity)

Minimum-wage growth has kept pace with productivity growth (+/-5%)

Minimum-wage growth has exceeded productivity growth (more than 5%)

Insufficient data

Productivity growth is measured as the change in per capita GDP over 6 years

Data Source: International Labour Organization, Global Wage Report 2008/09 (Geneva: ILO, 2008).

component of poverty reduction, data are not currently available to enable us to compare its provision worldwide and are not regularly collected by UNESCO, the World Bank, or other global organizations focused on education and poverty. Comparative information so we can examine best practices and track gaps that can be filled is a pressing need.

Providing Resources during Temporary Unemployment

Although jobs can and should ensure that working adults are not living in poverty, addressing parental earnings alone is not enough to ensure that children are not raised in poverty. A widely recognized feature of many economies at the beginning of the twenty-first century is the extent of job turnover. In the United States, adults aged between 44 and 51 had held an average of 11 jobs over 26 years.[55] Parents with young children and low-income adults are most vulnerable to job transitions and unemployment. In Britain, for example, job mobility for parents is highest among those with a child under the age of 4.[56] When adults experience job turnover, they frequently have gaps between jobs. In the above-mentioned U.S. study, the proportion of time spent in unemployment was higher among those adults with less education, who were thus more likely to be working poorly paying jobs.[57]

The availability of an income safety net during these job gaps is crucial if parents are to avoid falling into poverty. Although low-income families with little savings are more vulnerable to the potentially devastating effects of unemployment, the toll is also high on middle-income families. While overall unemployment is still more likely to affect parents with less than a high-school diploma, across Europe and North America college-educated parents as well lost jobs in the recent recession.[58] In the United States, 40 percent of jobs lost were in higher-wage industries and 36 percent in midwage industries.[59]

To examine the availability of an income safety net during periods of unemployment, we developed a database to compare quantitatively the extent and nature of unemployment insurance and severance pay.[60] We found that most countries around the world recognize the need for income support through unemployment insurance or severance pay. Of the 182 countries for which we have data, just 19 guarantee neither to workers; 10 of these countries are located in East Asia and the Pacific, 4 in sub-Saharan Africa, 2 in South Asia, 2 in the Middle East and North Africa, and 1 in the Americas. Eighty-one countries have government unemployment benefits available; in 82 countries, no benefits are available but workers are guaranteed severance pay (Map 6.3).*

The problem is the limited extent of coverage. Workers employed in the informal economy and those designated self-employed (many of whom in fact have employers who hire them as contract laborers) are often not covered by these protections. Of the 81 countries with national unemployment benefit schemes, only 28 include the self-employed on a compulsory or voluntary basis.[61] Severance pay by definition excludes the truly self-employed; those workers in the informal economy who do have an employer but are treated as self-employed, such as domestic workers, are not covered either.[†] The limited nature of unemployment benefits for the self-employed is especially problematic because of their greater likelihood of experiencing precarious working conditions and their commonly lower income and assets. The informal economy accounts for a substantial share of employment in much of the world: an estimated 72 percent of workers in sub-Saharan Africa work in the informal economy, as do 65 percent in Asia, 51 percent in Latin America, and 48 percent in North Africa.[62]

When we look at the monthly unemployment benefit provided to a worker earning the minimum wage, which we were able to calculate for 64 of the 81 countries providing government unemployment insurance, most countries have ensured that unemployment benefits are high enough that families depending on these benefits for income are not living in extreme poverty.[63] However, in 12 countries, this worker would be earning $4.00 or less per day, adjusted for PPP, an amount that places even a small family of one adult and one child below the World Bank poverty line.[‡]

---

*World Policy Analysis Centre, Poverty Database. Number of countries for which we have data: 182 (unemployment protections).

†World Policy Analysis Centre, Poverty Database. Number of countries for which we have data: 178 (unemployment protections for the self-employed).

‡World Policy Analysis Centre, Poverty Database. Number of countries for which we have data: 169 (amount of unemployment benefits).

Map 6.3. Is income protection during unemployment available?

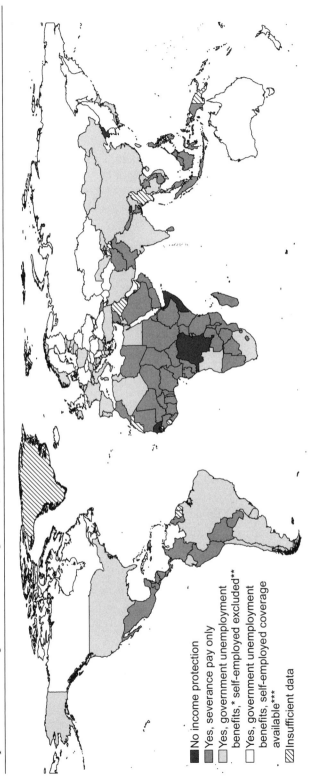

No income protection

Yes, severance pay only

Yes, government unemployment
benefits,* self-employed excluded**

Yes, government unemployment
benefits, self-employed coverage
available***

Insufficient data

Government unemployment benefits applies to countries with unemployment insurance. These countries may or may not also mandate severance pay.
**Self-employed excluded* also includes cases where it is unknown whether self-employed coverage is available.
***Self-employed coverage available* includes both mandatory and voluntary coverage.

Source: World Policy Analysis Centre, Poverty Database

Our database also allows us to compare the maximum length of time during which a worker could receive government unemployment benefits. In 15 countries, these benefits are available for 6 months or less; it is unclear whether this is long enough to cover families during severe economic downturns, when finding work may be particularly difficult and some nations have experienced high unemployment rates for extended periods. In 34 countries, unemployment benefits are available for between 6 months and 1 year; and in 24 countries, workers can receive benefits for over a year.*

Increasing Family Income through Transfers

Until earnings lift all families out of poverty, should governments create an income safety net that is strong enough to ensure that children are not brought up in poverty? Although providing income to poor families may be the most direct way to ensure that basic needs are met, such policies are often quite contentious. Some doubt that these income transfers positively affect children's well-being. At the core of the debate is whether these policies create dependence and work disincentives, as well as uncertainty regarding how the money is spent. When transfers are unconditional, there is no guarantee that the money is being spent on children's needs. As well, transfers may not reach the families who are most in need of them because of a lack of awareness about their existence or the bureaucratic processes necessary to receive them.

Although empirical studies do not answer all unknowns, they do provide an important foundation of insights. The extent to which transfers reduce poverty levels differs according to the type of benefits and the wider social security context of each country, but a wealth of evidence from South Africa to Europe shows that they benefit low-income children and families by reducing the prevalence and intensity of family poverty.[64] In Ecuador, for example, the Bono de Desarollo Humano is given to poor women with children and is not attached to any conditions. During the rollout, eligible families were randomly divided into treatment and control groups, allowing rigorous evaluation of the ef-

---

*World Policy Analysis Centre, Poverty Database. Number of countries for which we have data: 178 (duration of unemployment benefits).

fects of this additional income. This income advanced the development of poor children: disparities in fine motor control, short-term memory, and behavioral problems were eliminated between children in the poorest quartile and children in richer quartiles, and disparities in vocabulary, long-term memory, and visual integration were markedly reduced.[65] Furthermore, even though the transfer was less than what a child could earn in the labor market, child labor declined significantly and school attendance increased in recipient families.[66] A study isolating the effects of income transfers from the effects of other elements of Mexico's Oportunidades program shows that this income improved indicators of physical health and cognitive development, including stunting, underweight, overweight, language development, and memory.[67]

Similar effects of income transfers have been documented in other regions as well. A study of an unconditional cash transfer scheme in Zambia showed that half of all youth aged 7 to 17 in recipient families who were not in school before the transfers had enrolled 1 year later. When family members report being hungry even after meals, it is an important indication that they have too few resources to adequately feed themselves. Among families receiving the transfers, the percentage of households who experienced this type of hunger fell from 56 to 35 percent, fewer household members had to subsist on only one meal per day, and the number of households consuming vegetables, fruits, and protein increased.[68] In Sri Lanka, the Samurdhi National Poverty Alleviation Scheme provided income transfers to poor families, as well as some access to group savings, credit schemes, and an infrastructure-development program, and was conditional only on the recipient adult providing some voluntary labor to the program. These transfers have been shown to improve the nutritional status of children in both the short and long term as measured by weight and height indicators.[69]

Because of the demonstrated positive effect of direct financial assistance, we examined global social policy in this area. Our data on family benefits include only cash benefits; we were unable to examine other types of transfers to families, such as housing assistance or tax credits, because there was no reliable global data source for this information.

Our results show that around the world, 103 countries have legislated some form of family cash allowances. In 18 of these countries, these benefits are provided only in certain circumstances, such as upon the birth of a child, for children with terminally ill parents, or for unemployed single mothers. In 31 countries, benefits are means tested and are provided to families who fall below a given income level. Fifty-four countries provide benefits to families that are not subject to an income test (Map 6.4).*

This support for families is very common in high-income countries; over three-quarters of them provide family allowances, the majority of which are not means tested. Just over half of middle-income countries and about one-third of low-income countries provide some form of family benefits. Nearly all European and Central Asian countries provide these benefits; approximately half of countries in the Americas and sub-Saharan Africa, more than one-third of countries in the Middle East and North Africa, and approximately one-fifth of countries in East Asia and the Pacific provide some family benefits. The prevalence of family benefits tends to increase with rising national income levels, but disparate national responses are not simply due to this factor. While most West African countries provide family allowances (most of which are not means tested), almost no countries in East Africa provide any benefits at all.

The amount of family cash benefits provided varies widely around the world. We calculated the monthly benefits that a low-income family with two preschool-age children would receive.[70] Eighteen countries would provide this family with less than US$20 per month, PPP-adjusted, 13 provide between $20.00 and $59.99, 19 provide between $60.00 and $149.99 monthly, and 21 provide $150 or more. The amount of the benefit is associated with national income levels. Of the 18 countries providing less than $20 per month, 10 are low-income and 8 are middle-income. Sixteen of the 21 countries providing at least $150 per month are high-income countries, and none are low-income. The situation is similar for low-income families supporting two school-age children. For low-income families supporting two teenagers, benefits start to fall away; just 39 countries provide financial assistance to these families.†

---

*World Policy Analysis Centre, Poverty Database. Number of countries for which we have data: 182 (availability of family benefits).

†World Policy Analysis Centre, Poverty Database. Number of countries for which we have data: 168 (benefits for preschool-age children), 167 (benefits for school-age children), 168 (benefits for teenage children).

Map 6.4. Do families receive income support?

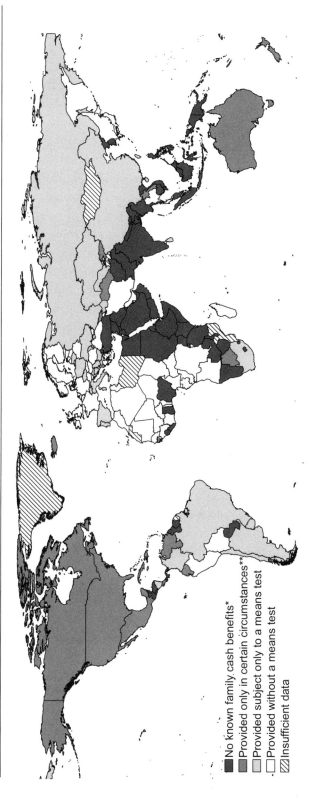

■ No known family cash benefits*
■ Provided only in certain circumstances**
□ Provided subject only to a means test
□ Provided without a means test
▨ Insufficient data

*No known family cash benefits also includes cases where a framework for benefits has been legislatively established, but the benefits themselves have not been established.
**Only in certain circumstances includes cases where benefits are available only to specific subpopulations, such as single parents or orphans, or as benefits to fund specific aspects of life, such as housing allowances, birth grants, and school allowances.

Source: *World Policy Analysis Centre, Poverty Database*

Certain periods are particularly expensive when a family is raising a child. Many families incur large expenses at the birth or adoption of a child for medical care, time away from work, infant care, and supplies. Early childhood care and education can be expensive when not provided free by the government. Schooling, even when free, can entail expenses for books, materials, transport, and clothing or uniforms. Sixty-one countries provide a birth or maternity grant for the first child; in most cases, however, it is less than US$500, PPP-adjusted. Only 23 countries provide benefits for child care or school, and none of these countries are low-income.*

There are many other mechanisms through which resources can be transferred to families. For example, increasing income through tax benefits has been shown to benefit children. In Canada, a study used the differences in child tax benefits across provinces and across time to determine their impact on child well-being. More generous benefits had an impact on raising test scores, decreasing hunger levels, and reducing aggressive behavior among children.[71] A U.S. study used longitudinal data to examine the impact of increased family income resulting from the expansion of the Earned Income Tax Credit on children's outcomes; it showed that reading and math test scores improved among children in poor families receiving the additional income, with greater effects among younger children.[72] Some countries have chosen to make their cash transfers to low-income families conditional, using such criteria as children's school attendance and family preventive-care visits. The advantages, disadvantages, and implications of conditional versus unconditional cash transfers are still debated. Nations can also provide public housing or housing subsidies, food stamps, and many other programs. Global tracking of each of these approaches could dramatically increase our ability to understand and assess what countries are doing to address poverty, what measures have the highest impact, and what would be the most effective way to finish the campaign to eliminate child poverty.

---

*World Policy Analysis Centre, Poverty Database. Number of countries for which we have data: 171 (birth, maternity, child-care, and school grants).

Moving Forward: What Is Missing?

The elimination of poverty is not a simple endeavor, but neither is a dramatic reduction in poverty impossible to achieve. A number of the necessary ingredients are clear. Jobs need to pay a living wage so that those who work full-time are not living in poverty. Adults need a chance to get the education necessary to obtain or upgrade the skills required to improve their income. Mothers and fathers both need to have the opportunity to work at decent jobs and to take time off to provide essential care for their children without fear of being fired. During the periods when individuals are out of work—whether because of the birth or adoption of a new child, a serious illness, or transitions in the labor force—there needs to be a source of temporary income support.

How far has the world come? There appears to be consensus on the need for a minimum wage, and a legislative framework has been established in most countries around the world. Yet far too often the wage is set too low to lift families and their children out of poverty. A great deal of attention has been paid to whether children are educated, but very little global attention has been paid to ensuring that adults who missed out on schooling when they were young can access it once they are grown; this neglect is reflected in the dearth of available data. This gap in opportunities is as costly to children as it is to their parents; children pay a price in the increased likelihood that their family will live in poverty, as well as the reduced ability of their parents to help with their schooling and other needs.

A focus on putting a basic floor in place for working men and women has meant that most of the world provides some kind of unemployment insurance or severance pay during job gaps. However, workers in the informal economy are often unprotected, leaving children whose parents work informally with no safety net when their parents lose their jobs. Although benefits to families provide an important supplement in roughly half of the world's countries, in some countries they are not enough to provide any meaningful assistance in meeting children's basic needs, and many countries do not have these benefits at all.

A commitment to addressing poverty both in the short and the long term is crucial. This commitment to improving the welfare of children and adults presently living in poverty calls for programs and policies that will have an immediate impact on family income; some of these have been discussed in this chapter. When these programs are combined with approaches to improve children's chance at healthy development and full education, which are discussed in other chapters, they also provide a firm foundation for dramatically reducing the chances that future generations of children will be raised in poverty.

Table 6.1. Ensuring an income floor for working parents and their children

Establishment of Minimum Wage	Low-Income	Middle-Income	High-Income
Type of Minimum Wage Protection			
No minimum wage set by law or collective bargaining	4 (12%)	12 (11%)	6 (12%)
Minimum wage set by collective bargaining only	0 (0%)	1 (1%)	11 (22%)
Minimum wage set by law	30 (88%)	93 (88%)	32 (65%)
Buying Power of Minimum Wage, PPP-Adjusted			
No national minimum wage established	4 (13%)	12 (12%)	6 (13%)
Minimum wage set by collective bargaining at the sectoral level	0 (0%)	0 (0%)	8 (17%)
Minimum wage is $2 per day or less	10 (32%)	1 (1%)	0 (0%)
Minimum wage is $2.01 - $4 per day	12 (39%)	17 (17%)	0 (0%)
Minimum wage is $4.01 - $10 per day	5 (16%)	36 (36%)	2 (4%)
Minimum wage is $10.01 - $20 per day	0 (0%)	29 (29%)	7 (15%)
Minimum wage is $20.01 - $30 per day	0 (0%)	4 (4%)	8 (17%)
Minimum wage is more than $30 per day	0 (0%)	1 (1%)	15 (33%)

(continued)

Table 6.1 *(continued)*

Growth of Minimum Wage	Low-Income	Middle-Income	High-Income
Average Yearly Growth in Minimum Wage (2001-2007), Adjusted for Inflation			
Decrease in the value of minimum wage	7 (39%)	12 (20%)	4 (17%)
0% - 2.4% increase in the value of minimum wage	3 (17%)	15 (25%)	9 (39%)
2.5% - 4.9% increase in the value of minimum wage	4 (22%)	7 (12%)	4 (17%)
5% - 7.4% increase in the value of minimum wage	0 (0%)	7 (12%)	2 (9%)
7.5% or more increase in the value of minimum wage	4 (22%)	18 (31%)	4 (17%)
Growth in Minimum Wage Compared with Per Capita GDP Growth (2001 - 2007)			
Minimum wage growth has lagged behind per capita GDP growth by more than 5%	10 (53%)	30 (52%)	5 (22%)
Minimum wage growth has stayed within 5% of per capita GDP growth	4 (21%)	11 (19%)	16 (70%)
Minimum wage growth has outpaced per capita GDP growth by more than 5%	5 (26%)	17 (29%)	2 (9%)

Enforcement of Minimum Wage	Low-Income	Middle-Income	High-Income
Means of Ensuring that Employers Do Not Pay Workers Less Than the Minimum Wage			
Workplaces must keep records on wages and/or may be subject to inspections	22 (76%)	76 (87%)	27 (87%)
Workers have the right to take legal action against employers	14 (48%)	18 (21%)	7 (23%)
Potential Penalties for Employers who Pay Workers Less Than the Minimum Wage			
Employers may be fined	24 (83%)	74 (85%)	30 (97%)
Workers may receive compensation for lost wages	10 (34%)	39 (45%)	9 (29%)
Workplace business may be suspended	0 (0%)	5 (6%)	0 (0%)
Employers may be imprisoned	10 (34%)	25 (29%)	6 (19%)

Sources : World Policy Analysis Centre, Poverty Database and International Labour Organization, Global Wage Report 2008/09 (Geneva: International Labour Office, 2008).

Definitions: To determine *purchasing power parity (PPP)*, economists estimate the amount of money required to purchase the same bundle of goods and services across countries rather than using a simple exchange rate. *Low-income, middle-income,* and *high-income* refer to World Bank classifications of national income. Here, middle-income countries include those classified as lower-middle and upper-middle income.

Note : No minimum wage set by law or collective bargaining includes cases where there is no minimum wage legislation as well as where legislation provides a framework for establishing a minimum wage, but the country has not yet implemented one.

Table 6.2. Ensuring income protections for families during unemployment

	Low-Income	Middle-Income	High-Income
Unemployment Protections Guaranteed by Law			
No guaranteed unemployment protections	5 (16%)	12 (12%)	2 (4%)
Employers must compensate workers at the time of dismissal (severance pay)	25 (81%)	50 (49%)	7 (14%)
Government provides financial assistance during unemployment, self-employed excluded	1 (3%)	27 (26%)	25 (51%)
Government provides financial assistance during unemployment, self-employed coverage available	0 (0%)	13 (13%)	15 (31%)
Average Monthly Government-Provided Financial Assistance for an Unemployed Minimum Wage Worker, PPP-Adjusted			
No government-provided financial assistance	32 (100%)	64 (67%)	9 (22%)
$2 per day or less of financial assistance	0 (0%)	7 (7%)	0 (0%)
$2.01 - $4 per day of financial assistance	0 (0%)	5 (5%)	0 (0%)
$4.01 - $10 per day of financial assistance	0 (0%)	13 (14%)	6 (15%)
$10.01 - $20 per day of financial assistance	0 (0%)	5 (5%)	13 (32%)
$20.01 - $30 per day of financial assistance	0 (0%)	2 (2%)	8 (20%)
More than $30 per day of financial assistance	0 (0%)	0 (0%)	5 (12%)

Maximum Length of Government-Provided Financial Assistance During Unemployment

No government-provided financial assistance	32 (97%)	64 (67%)	9 (18%)
20 weeks or less of financial assistance available	0 (0%)	2 (2%)	1 (2%)
20.1 weeks - 26 weeks of financial assistance available	1 (3%)	6 (6%)	5 (10%)
26.1 weeks - 52 weeks of financial assistance available	0 (0%)	18 (19%)	16 (33%)
52.1 weeks - 78 weeks of financial assistance available	0 (0%)	1 (1%)	4 (8%)
78.1 weeks - 104 weeks of financial assistance available	0 (0%)	3 (3%)	5 (10%)
104.1 weeks - 156 weeks of financial assistance available	0 (0%)	2 (2%)	9 (18%)

Source : World Policy Analysis Centre, Poverty Database.

Notes : Severance pay may also be required when government unemployment benefits are available.
Self-employed excluded also includes cases where it is unknown whether self-employed coverage is available.
Self-employed coverage available includes both mandatory and voluntary coverage.

Table 6.3. Providing financial assistance to families with children

	Low-Income	Middle-Income	High-Income
Type of Government-Provided Family Benefits Available by Law			
No known family benefits	20 (63%)	48 (47%)	11 (23%)
Family benefits only in certain circumstances	1 (3%)	11 (11%)	6 (13%)
Means-tested family benefits available	0 (0%)	23 (23%)	8 (17%)
Family benefits available - not means tested	11 (34%)	20 (20%)	23 (48%)
Amount of Government-Provided Maternity and Birth Grants for First Child, PPP-Adjusted			
No birth or maternity grant available to first-time parents	24 (80%)	63 (65%)	23 (52%)
Less than $50 for first-time parents	5 (17%)	3 (3%)	0 (0%)
$50 - $149 for first-time parents	1 (3%)	7 (7%)	1 (2%)
$150 - $499 for first-time parents	0 (0%)	18 (19%)	7 (16%)
$500 - $999 for first-time parents	0 (0%)	4 (4%)	8 (18%)
$1,000 - $2,499 for first-time parents	0 (0%)	1 (1%)	3 (7%)
$2,500 or more for first-time parents	0 (0%)	1 (1%)	2 (5%)

Amount of Government-Provided Family Benefits Available to Low-Income Families with Two Preschool-Age Children (Age 4), PPP-Adjusted

No known family benefits available	21 (68%)	59 (63%)	17 (39%)
Less than $10 per month for eligible families	5 (16%)	3 (3%)	0 (0%)
$10 - $19.99 per month for eligible families	5 (16%)	5 (5%)	0 (0%)
$20 - $59.99 per month for eligible families	0 (0%)	12 (13%)	1 (2%)
$60 - $149.99 per month for eligible families	0 (0%)	9 (10%)	10 (23%)
$150 or more per month for eligible families	0 (0%)	5 (5%)	16 (36%)

Amount of Government-Provided Family Benefits Available to Low-Income Families with Two School-Age Children (Age 8), PPP-Adjusted

No known family benefits available	21 (68%)	60 (65%)	17 (39%)
Less than $10 per month for eligible families	5 (16%)	3 (3%)	0 (0%)
$10 - $19.99 per month for eligible families	5 (16%)	5 (5%)	0 (0%)
$20 - $59.99 per month for eligible families	0 (0%)	10 (11%)	1 (2%)
$60 - $149.99 per month for eligible families	0 (0%)	9 (10%)	10 (23%)
$150 or more per month for eligible families	0 (0%)	5 (5%)	16 (36%)

(continued)

Table 6.3 (*continued*)

Amount of Government- Provided Family Benefits Available to Low-Income Families with Two Teenage Children (Age 15), PPP-Adjusted			
No known family benefits available	27 (87%)	75 (81%)	27 (61%)
Less than $10 per month for eligible families	2 (6%)	0 (0%)	0 (0%)
$10 - $19.99 per month for eligible families	2 (6%)	2 (2%)	0 (0%)
$20 - $59.99 per month for eligible families	0 (0%)	5 (5%)	1 (2%)
$60 - $149.99 per month for eligible families	0 (0%)	7 (8%)	6 (14%)
$150 or more per month for eligible families	0 (0%)	4 (4%)	10 (23%)
Government-Provided Family Benefits Available for Child Care or School Costs			
No family benefits for child care or school costs	30 (100%)	87 (91%)	31 (69%)
Means-tested family benefits available	0 (0%)	3 (3%)	5 (11%)
Family benefits available - not means tested	0 (0%)	6 (6%)	7 (16%)
Family benefits available both with and without a means test	0 (0%)	0 (0%)	2 (4%)

Source : World Policy Analysis Centre, Poverty Database.

Definitions: Means-tested benefits are available only to families with incomes below a certain threshold.
Not means-tested benefits are available to families without considering their income.

Note : Only in certain circumstances includes cases where benefits are available only to specific subpopulations, such as single parents or orphans, or as benefits to fund specific aspects of life, such as housing allowances, birth grants, and school allowances.

Chapter 7

Equity and Discrimination

As a young girl in Jordan, where gender equity was not guaranteed, Aisha had limited opportunities.[1] *She never had the chance to learn to read or write and spent most of her youth caring for her chronically ill mother. This responsibility meant that she did not seek to marry until her mother died, by which time Aisha was old for marriage according to her community's norms. As a woman alone, she had little opportunity to earn an income. She married the first man who asked her; he beat her from the beginning of their marriage. Aisha miscarried early in her first pregnancy, and she was in the third trimester of her second pregnancy when her husband's abuse caused another miscarriage. Since she was not permitted to leave her home, no one was aware of the beatings. Rather than risk another miscarriage, Aisha decided to run away during her third pregnancy. She gave birth to a girl named Iman.*

Shortly after Iman was born, she was taken away by her father, who had tracked down Aisha's whereabouts. He took Iman across the border into Palestine and confined her to an institution, where she spent most of her childhood. Her mother continually struggled to get her back, but as a woman she had few legal rights with respect to her family; she finally succeeded 9 years later, only after Iman's father's death left Aisha with a legal right to custody.

Aisha wanted Iman to have equal opportunities and rights—an equal chance at education, equal opportunities to work, equal rights within the family, the chance to be independent—so that she could escape the limitations, losses, and abuses that had plagued Aisha's life.[2]

On the other side of the world, in Bolivia, inequities between indigenous and nonindigenous children have long started young. The results could be seen in the most basic indicator of education: literacy. In the mid-1990s, close to a quarter of men living in rural areas, who are almost exclusively indigenous, were illiterate, as were over half of rural women. In urban areas, where the nonindigenous population is concentrated, 96 percent of men and 86 percent of women were literate. Many indigenous children faced overt discrimination, but systemic inequity was an even greater barrier. Felix López described his experience at school: "Until I started school, I only spoke Aymara. I did not understand a word of Spanish. All the teachers spoke in Spanish, and the Aymaras in the class didn't understand anything. They would hit us with sticks because we couldn't pronounce Spanish words properly. . . . These traumas have stayed with us."[3] Until the mid-1990s, children in Bolivia were educated almost exclusively in Spanish, a second language for many indigenous people. As of 1994, the constitution guaranteed equal rights for indigenous people speaking different languages.[4]

The premise of this book is that equal chances for children matter. The importance of equal rights and opportunities for all children has achieved nearly universal international consensus—the UN Convention on the Rights of the Child, a powerful statement of these rights, has been ratified by 190 UN member states.[5]

Even beyond their inherent value, there are compelling reasons to care about equity and freedom from discrimination. The experience of unequal chances has a powerful impact on children's outcomes, from education and health in childhood to work and civic engagement in adulthood.

Discrimination can affect every aspect of a child's education, from school attendance to academic achievement. Experiencing discrimination has been shown to damage the grades, academic engagement, and motivation of African American, Asian American, and Latino students in the United States.[6] Widespread racism against the Roma in Europe continues to restrict their educational opportunities;[7] a study in Slovakia, for example, discovered that up to half of Roma children attending special primary schools had been wrongly assessed as in need of special education.[8] In Denmark, immigrant students experience lower expectations, less encouragement, and less pressure for academic achievement from their teachers than native Danish students; this explains a significant portion of the test-score gap between immigrant and nonimmigrant students.[9] Similarly, ethnic-minority adolescents in the Netherlands who perceive discrimination at school tend to disengage psychologically from their education.[10]

Discrimination in health-care delivery systems means that children are not always treated equally irrespective of their gender, ethnicity, or religion. For example, in the United States, white children with head injuries were 50 percent more likely than nonwhite children to receive head imaging even after socioeconomic, clinical, and hospital characteristics were taken into account.[11] In Egypt, health-care professionals were more likely to provide boys than girls with access to potentially lifesaving oral rehydration solutions to treat diarrhea,[12] one of the leading causes of severe child illness and death worldwide.[13] Discrimination from health-care providers is similarly a barrier to care for Roma children in Eastern Europe.[14]

A review of 134 studies documented that discrimination increases the frequency of illness and poor health, as well as limiting treatment.[15] Discrimination based on ethnicity, gender, sexual orientation, and other characteristics has been linked to poorer physical health outcomes from blood pressure to self-reported health.[16] Globally, self-reported health has been found to be highly predictive of the likelihood of serious illness or death.[17] Among youth, discrimination based on ethnicity has been linked to poorer physical health, as well as poorer mental and emotional health.[18] Discrimination against sexual and racial minorities has also been linked to an increase in detrimental health-related behaviors, such as smoking and alcohol use.[19] In one study, minorities who frequently experienced discrimination were more than twice as likely to smoke as their minority counterparts who experienced low levels of discrimination.[20]

Discrimination has also been clearly documented to affect mental health.[21] Experiences of racial discrimination at school and elsewhere are linked to depression among African American, Chinese American, and Latino adolescents in the United States.[22] The same phenomenon has been noted in South Africa, where perceived chronic discrimination is associated with psychological distress.[23] Similar results have been found for discrimination against lesbian, gay, and bisexual adolescents and adults.[24] In Spain, discrimination on various grounds, including national origin, religion, and gender, is associated with negative mental health outcomes. Men who felt discriminated against were more than 4 times as likely as men who did not to have mental health problems, even after controlling for age, social support, and marital status, and women who had experienced discrimination were 2.5 times as likely as women who had not to have poor mental health.[25]

Discrimination against children has lifelong effects. Poor health and low levels of educational attainment compromise children's options for the future. When girls are kept out of school, their chances of finding a job and achieving economic independence are severely curtailed; when ethnic-minority children are discriminated against at school by teachers or peers, their engagement and their school persistence markedly decrease, and this limits their work opportunities; and when children receive inadequate health care because of discrimination from parents or health-care providers, their poorer physical health can have long-term effects on their ability to work and their quality of life. As well, when parents' opportunities are limited by discrimination, children anticipate encountering the same treatment as adults, and this affects their aspirations for their work, family lives, and civic participation.

Much of this book has discussed what it would take to put equal chances into practice—making education affordable, facilitating access to health services, ensuring that parental working conditions allow for children's care, and preventing children from having to labor long hours or marry early. Government efforts in these areas exist within a national framework shaped by many factors—social, economic, historical, cultural, and political. Legally these efforts are shaped by whether equal-rights guarantees exist, commonly in foundational texts, such as constitutions. This chapter seeks to answer three questions. First, do constitutional guarantees of equal rights matter? Second, if they do, what rights would we want to see? Third, how common are these guarantees around the world?

Should We Care about Constitutions?

Most of this book looks at national policies and laws such as whether schools are free, whether it is illegal for children to work full-time at a young age, or whether employers have to provide maternity leave. The implications of laws and policies, if they are well enforced, are clear. Equally evident are the options for implementation, enforcement, and monitoring compliance—through budgets, programs, inspections, fines, and related mechanisms.

The rights expressed in constitutions tend to be broader, and the mechanisms for the implementation of constitutions are often one step removed. There are rarely regulators to determine how constitutions should be implemented or inspectors to determine whether guarantees of rights are respected. For constitutions to be effective, they must often be translated into laws and government policies. Constitutional promises of equal rights are often enforced by overturning laws or policies that do not comply. If they are another step removed from children's lives, how much do they matter?

While for other policy areas covered in this book, substantial research evidence exists from comparative studies across countries, longitudinal studies documenting the impact and effectiveness of change, and control trials of policy effects, we have far less of this type of information for constitutions. Countries can rarely serve as experimental controls for one another in examining constitutions. Constitutions change relatively infrequently, and when they do change, it is often because other events are occurring simultaneously in the political or social life of the country; this limits the utility of many longitudinal studies. What we do have is evidence of how constitutions can be and have been used, and it is the weight of this evidence that makes us believe that they are important to children's chances. Examples of how constitutions have been used to enhance children's opportunities and parents' rights follow.

First, constitutions can be used to challenge legislation limiting equal rights. In 2009, Afghanistan passed the Shi'i Personal Status Law, based on a particular interpretation of religious law that would be applicable to all people belonging to the Shi'a denomination of Islam. Under this legislation, women would be denied the rights to work and education without their husband's permission, with immense consequences for children, given the impact that a mother's education and access to resources have on a child's health and development. Custody of children would be granted exclusively to fathers or grandfathers, with no evaluation of the child's best interests. This law also seriously eroded other aspects of women's rights, such as by restricting them from leaving the house without a "legitimate purpose," requiring them to have sex with their husbands unless they were ill, and permitting men to withhold food from their wives if they refused to do so. This law was protested by members of Parliament, university faculty, civil society, and the international community. The opposition to this law drew heavily on women's right to equality, which was enshrined in Afghanistan's constitution, established just 5 years earlier. Domestic and international pressure, combined with the constitutional basis for equal rights in Afghanistan, resulted in the law being changed. Although the new version of the law was imperfect, it did not include many of the provisions most detrimental to women's equal rights and added some beneficial provisions, such as raising the age at which girls could be married from 9 to 16.[26]

Second, constitutional guarantees can be used to demand greater equity in the delivery of and access to basic services in many settings. In Canada, for example, the Charter of Rights and Freedoms, one of Canada's constitutional documents, prohibits discrimination based on mental or physical disability. The parents of Emily Eaton, a disabled student, argued for her rights under the charter, contending that she had a right to be educated in a regular classroom alongside other children. The court decided that children could not be segregated on the basis of disability unless doing so directly benefited their education.[27] Similarly, the right to education in Kenya's constitution and Children's Act were used by the Nyumbani Children's Home in Nairobi, Kenya, to advocate for HIV/AIDS-affected orphans, who were refused entry to local primary schools. The judge found that the constitution was unambiguous about children's right to education and that the government was responsible for ensuring that all children could go to school; as a result of the case, the schools were made to change their admission policies.[28]

Third, although constitutions do not eliminate interpersonal discrimination, they play an important role in setting norms. As the fundamental building blocks of a nation's government and laws, constitutions shape the rules that governments and societies must follow. Although constitutions often embody existing social norms, they can also be used to establish new ones. The United States Supreme Court's landmark *Brown v. Board of Education* decision in 1954 provides one example. In this case, the Court deemed racial segregation in public education to be unconstitutional at a time when racism was widespread. Before this decision, African American children in many southern states were required to attend different schools than white children. Their schools had fewer resources to pay teachers, fewer learning materials, and dilapidated facilities, among other marked disparities. *Brown v. Board of Education* established that the segregation of public education violated the Fourteenth Amendment of the U.S. Constitution, which guarantees equal protection under the law. This case set the stage for desegregation of education and other public services. Although implementation took time, it was a huge step forward for equal rights in the United States.[29] Since the 1950s, legal segregation has been eliminated throughout the country, de facto segregation has been reduced, and public racism has markedly declined.

There are more recent examples of constitutional rights forging ahead of social norms. In South Africa, a study examining surveys from 2003 to 2007 showed that 80 percent of citizens believed that sexual relations between same-sex adults were "wrong."[30] Nonetheless, gay and lesbian families in South Africa have been able to secure more rights because the constitution, which was written in 1996 and guarantees greater equality than social norms, prohibits discrimination on the grounds of sexual orientation. As a result, the Constitutional Court of South Africa ruled that defining common-law marriage as being between a man and a woman contravened the nation's constitutional guarantees of equality, and this terminology was subsequently amended to be gender neutral. Although the government appealed this decision, the court's ruling was reaffirmed in 2006. Same-sex partners in South Africa have also been guaranteed inheritance rights equal to those enjoyed by heterosexual partners.[31]

Barriers can break down after judicial rulings that establish grounds for nondiscrimination in education, labor, housing, family, and other spheres of life; as groups that have previously been isolated from one another begin to interact on a more equal footing, social stereotypes can diminish.[32] Although these examples are far from showing that constitutional guarantees will always have an impact, they do illustrate how constitutional rights can be an important tool for those working for equal opportunity, can contribute to greater equity ahead of social norms, and can be translated into changes in children's and families' daily lives.

Constitutional Rights around the World

The data presented in this chapter are the result of an intensive 5-year effort by our research team to build a comprehensive database of the rights and protections guaranteed in the world's constitutions. A team of researchers reviewed and analyzed constitutional texts and amendments through June 2011 from 191 countries to create the first detailed comparison of constitutions on equal rights; for more details on this database, see Appendix 1. Our database captures guarantees and denials of equal rights across a wide range of social groups. In this chapter we focus on three dimensions along which it is important to prohibit discrimination and guarantee equal rights: gender, race/ethnicity, and religion.

A Broad Basis of Equity

Gender equality plays an important role in the lives of children. When women's status and decision-making authority are higher, their children are better nourished. This has enormous implications: the International Food Policy Research Institute estimates that if women and men had equal status and influence in decision making, the number of malnourished children under the age of 3 would be reduced by 13.4 million in South Asia and 1.7 million in sub-Saharan Africa.[33] When women lack social equality, they may lack the ability to make important decisions concerning their children's health and welfare. For example, in a study in Gujarat, India, half the women interviewed stated that they required the approval of their husband or a parent-in-law before they could bring a sick child to the doctor.[34]

The approach countries take to addressing equity in constitutions varies. Some countries focus on the affirmative guarantee of equal rights for groups (for example, "Women and men enjoy equal rights") or of overall equality between groups ("The State guarantees equality between men and women"). Others make a guarantee of equality before the law ("Everyone is equal before the law regardless of race or ethnicity"). Most commonly, nations prohibit discrimination ("No person shall be discriminated against on the basis of his or her religion"). Instead of naming particular groups to be covered by a given protection, some nations make these guarantees generally, using language like "All persons shall be considered equal before the law." When countries endeavor to do one of these things but the language used is not categorical enough to be considered a guarantee, we give them credit for aspiring to the right or prohibition.[35]

With regard to gender, 73 countries explicitly guarantee equal rights on the basis of gender, 52 guarantee equality before the law for women and men, 18 guarantee overall equality between women and men, and 123 prohibit discrimination based on gender (Map 7.1). An additional 22 countries guarantee equal rights, overall equality, equality before the law, or prohibition of discrimination in general terms, without specifying gender. Although much of the world has taken at least one approach to guaranteeing or aspiring to equity, there are exceptions. The constitutions of 10 countries have no guaranteed or aspirational protection for gender equity in general or specifically.[36] Moreover, in 14 of the countries guaranteeing or aspiring to at least one approach to gender equity, the constitution also states that religious or customary law can prevail over the constitution.[37] Where this religious or customary law does not protect gender equity, this provision may seriously weaken any constitutional protections across gender.*

While all children with mothers, grandmothers, or other women as caregivers are impoverished by gender discrimination, children who are members of ethnic, religious, linguistic, or national minorities face additional risks. It is essential that both these children and their parents not be discriminated against because of their ethnicity, religion, country of origin, linguistic group, or other demographic characteristics. In the case of ethnicity, 125 countries prohibit discrimination based on ethnicity, 43 countries guarantee equal rights explicitly to persons of all ethnicities, 44 countries make this guarantee in regard

---

*World Policy Analysis Centre, Constitutions Database. Number of countries for which we have data: 191 (rights to equity).

Map 7.1. Do constitutions take at least one approach to gender equity?

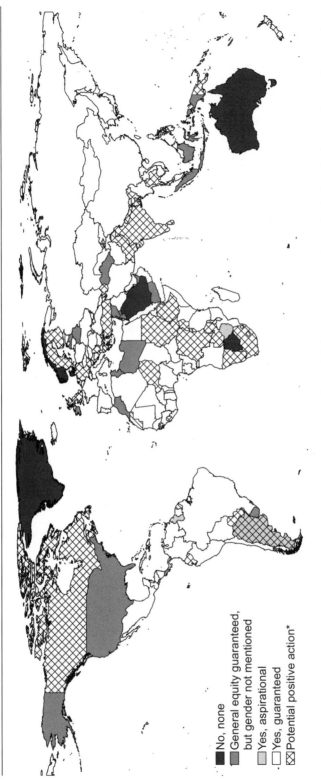

- ■ No, none
- ■ General equity guaranteed, but gender not mentioned
- ░ Yes, aspirational
- □ Yes, guaranteed
- ⊠ Potential positive action*

Approaches to equity include prohibitions of discrimination, guarantees of equal rights, guarantees of equality before the law, and overall guarantees of equality.
**Potential positive action* indicates that constitutions also include measures to promote equity for women.

Source: World Policy Analysis Centre, Constitutions Database

Map 7.2. Do constitutions take at least one approach to equity across ethnicity?

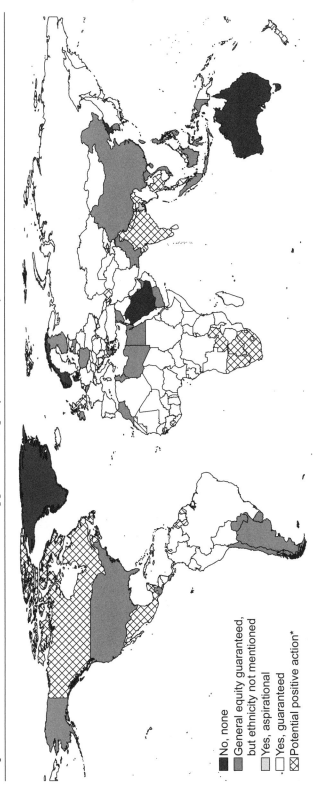

No, none

General equity guaranteed, but ethnicity not mentioned

Yes, aspirational

Yes, guaranteed

Potential positive action*

Approaches to equity include prohibitions of discrimination, guarantees of equal rights, guarantees of equality before the law, and overall guarantees of equality.

**Potential positive action* indicates that constitutions also include measures to promote equity on the basis of ethnicity.

Source: *World Policy Analysis Centre, Constitutions Database*

Map 7.3. Do constitutions take at least one approach to equity across religion?

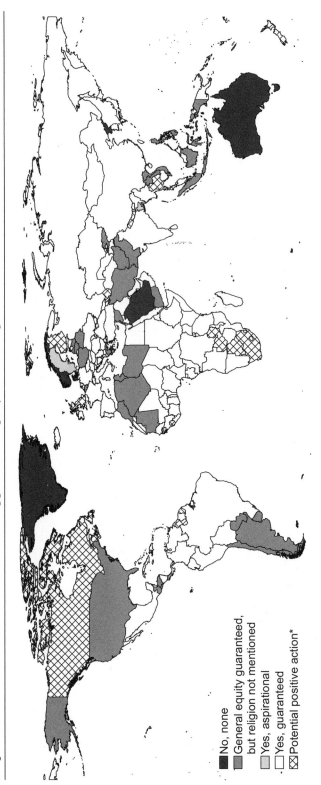

No, none

General equity guaranteed,
but religion not mentioned

Yes, aspirational

Yes, guaranteed

Potential positive action*

Approaches to equity include prohibitions of discrimination, guarantees of equal rights, guarantees of equality before the law, and overall guarantees of equality.
Potential positive action indicates that constitutions also include measures to promote equity on the basis of religion.

Source: *World Policy Analysis Centre, Constitutions Database*

to equality before the law, and 4 countries guarantee overall equality across ethnic groups (Map 7.2). The same number of countries make these guarantees in the case of religion, with the exception of the right to overall equality, which is explicitly granted in just 2 countries (Map 7.3). An additional 40 countries make one or more of these guarantees in general without specifying ethnicity or religion.[38] Seven countries do not protect equity across ethnicity or religion.*

Social and Economic Rights

Having looked at overall guarantees of equity and prohibitions of discrimination, we move on to these provisions in the specific areas of education for children and work for adults because of work's impact on family income.

As discussed earlier in this chapter, the impact of discrimination in education on the grounds of ethnicity, language, religion, and other factors is profound and long lasting. Gender equity in education has intergenerational effects: around the world, when girls receive more education, their children are more likely to have a chance to attend and complete school.[39] Girls' education also affects both their health and that of their children; children whose mothers have attended school are more likely to be immunized, to be better nourished, and to experience lower morbidity and mortality rates.[40] Discrimination in education against ethnic, religious, and other minorities likewise can have multigenerational effects. It affects children directly, and when parents' education was unnecessarily limited, it affects their children. As a result, there is perhaps no more important sphere than education in which to guarantee equal treatment for children.

Extremely few countries have explicitly prohibited discrimination in education in their constitutions. Just 12 countries prohibit discrimination in education specifically on the basis of gender, 16 countries specifically for religious groups, and 13 for ethnic groups. Four countries aspire to protect children from discrimination in education based on gender or ethnicity; 1 country prohibits discrimination in education based on ethnicity or religion, but may allow for exceptions.[41]

---

*World Policy Analysis Centre, Constitutions Database. Number of countries for which we have data: 191 (rights to equity).

Thirty-four countries have prohibited discrimination in education for all groups in general terms that could apply to ethnic groups, and 32 have general prohibitions that could apply across gender or religion. Even if this broader prohibition of discrimination in education is sufficient to protect girls and members of different ethnic or religious groups, there are no unequivocally guaranteed protections against discrimination in education for girls in the constitutions of 143 countries, for children across ethnic groups in 139 countries, and for children across religions in 142 countries.[*]

While education shapes children's daily lives and sets the stage for their future, an equally strong determinant of children's opportunities is their parents' access to resources. If a child's parents are unable to get decent jobs or receive less pay for their work because of labor-market discrimination, their children are far more likely to be raised in poverty and to lack basic necessities. The inequalities that parents face at work impoverish their children.

Few countries have chosen to include protection at work for ethnic or religious minorities in their constitution. Just 10 countries explicitly prohibit discrimination in work on the basis of ethnicity, and 8 on the basis of religion. Fewer than 20 countries have prohibited discrimination in work in general, without mentioning these specific social categories. In 163 countries, discrimination in work is not unequivocally prohibited either in general terms or specifically on the grounds of ethnicity in the constitution; the same is true in 165 countries on the basis of religion. More specific protection in the workplace can be offered by stipulations of equal pay for equal work, but this right is protected in just 21 countries across ethnicity, and 17 across religion. Many fewer countries have protected adults at work by explicitly prohibiting discrimination against these groups in hiring, promotions, or working conditions.[†]

Because of the priority they place on expenditures supporting their children's healthy development, women's access to resources has a particularly powerful impact on children. In many settings, women are

---

[*]World Policy Analysis Centre, Constitutions Database. Number of countries for which we have data: 191 (rights in education).

[†]World Policy Analysis Centre, Constitutions Database. Number of countries for which we have data: 191 (rights in work).

disadvantaged economically; their opportunities at work are compromised, and they are not paid as much as their male counterparts. Women's earnings amount to only 59 percent of men's earnings in East Asia and the Pacific, 58 percent of men's earnings in sub-Saharan Africa, 51 percent in Latin America and the Caribbean, 42 percent in South Asia, and 31 percent in the Middle East and North Africa.[42] When women have less access to resources, children suffer in families both with and without working fathers, and children benefit when women have greater influence over household resource allocation. For example, in Brazil, when women control a greater proportion of household income, expenditures on health and education increase, as does the nutrient content of the food consumed by their families.[43] In South Africa, expenditures on education increase as women's share of resources increases. Similarly, women's increased income and assets have been shown to benefit children from Ethiopia to Bangladesh to Indonesia.[44]

Moreover, disparities for women at work can affect the extent to which parents invest in their daughters. When social norms and widespread labor-market discrimination against women make it unlikely that women will get a job, parents anticipate few advantages from investing in their daughters' education. This is the case in Kenya, for example, where girls' school enrollment suffered because parents perceived limited returns from their daughters' education in the context of labor-market discrimination against women;[45] the right to equal economic opportunities became constitutionally guaranteed for women in Kenya only in the 2010 constitution.[46] In China, a study showed that when women's economic opportunities improve, the survival rates and educational attainment of girl children increase.[47]

Explicit prohibition of discrimination in work on the basis of gender is somewhat more common than on the basis of ethnicity or religion, but it appears in the constitutions of just 29 countries in guaranteed terms and 7 countries in aspirational terms. Ten additional countries prohibit discrimination in work in general, without specifying gender. Even if these general prohibitions are enough to protect women from workplace discrimination, women in 145 countries are not constitutionally protected from discrimination at work. Equal pay for equal work is more commonly addressed in the case of gender than for ethnicity or religion, but still, only a minority of countries (52) protect this key area in their constitution explicitly for gender in guaranteed or aspirational terms; an additional 10 discuss equal pay for equal work in general without specifying gender. Six countries guarantee or aspire to a prohibition of discrimination in hiring based on gender, 13 prohibit discrimination in promotions, and 20 prohibit discrimination in working conditions against women or men.*

Equity in Political Participation

Legislative and constitutional frameworks determine whether individuals have an equal right to participate in local and national governance regardless of their gender, ethnicity, religion, or other characteristics. Political participation is a crucial right because those who participate can shape the ways in which governments protect and promote the healthy development of all children.

The potential role of women in government provides an important example of this.[48] Currently, the overwhelming majority of the world's government leaders are men. Women are also underrepresented in parliaments: globally, they occupy less than 20 percent of parliamentary seats. The Arab states have the lowest level of female representation in parliaments at only 11 percent, and the Nordic countries have the highest level at 42 percent. The rest of the world falls somewhere in between: 23 percent of parliamentarians in the Americas are women; this figure is 21 percent in Europe (excluding the Nordic countries), 20 percent in sub-Saharan Africa, 18 percent in Asia, and 15 percent in the Pacific.[49] These disparities are important for women, but they are also significant for children. For example, in the United States, female legislators introduced legislation to promote child health three times as often as male legislators.[50] Similarly, in Argentina, Colombia, and Costa Rica, female legislators are more likely than males to sponsor bills related to children and families.[51] The situation is similar in national legislatures from Russia to Wales to New Zealand.[52] Equal representation in local government is just as important as it is in national government. In Norway, areas with more female local council members had greater child-care service coverage.[53] Since 1993, a third

---

*World Policy Analysis Centre, Constitutions Database. Number of countries for which we have data: 191 (rights in work).

of council-head positions in randomly selected villages in India have been reserved for women, and this has resulted in greater investments in drinking-water infrastructure, higher child immunization rates, and a 13 percent lower gap in school attendance between boys and girls.[54] Although many countries and an increasing number of male members of national and local governments support initiatives to improve the conditions children face, and although not all female members support child and family issues, on average, increasing women's political presence tends to increase the attention paid to these issues in government.

Adults' civic and political participation across ethnic groups, religions, and national origins also aids in ensuring that all children's needs are met. In India, for example, the reservation of state-level legislative seats for disadvantaged castes and tribes has been associated with increased targeted transfers benefiting these groups.[55] In the United States, African Americans in political office are more likely to support policies and initiatives targeting the interests of the African American population,[56] and the same applies for Latino legislators.[57] Individual impact on these issues increases with the power of the position held; although members of United States House committees or subcommittees influence committee activity on relevant bills, committee leaders have even more of an impact.[58]

Beyond these tangible benefits, experiences of equal civic participation can shape the vision that children have for their future. Role models have long been recognized as having an impact on the goals and achievement of children and youth, and their impact increases when children perceive them as more similar to themselves.[59] As one powerful example, in the United States, where African American children have historically been disadvantaged and as a result perceived their options as limited, Barack Obama's inauguration as the first black president had a rapid impact on raising children's aspirations and test scores.[60] In India, strong evidence shows that when adolescent girls see women in positions of political leadership, their career aspirations and educational attainment increase significantly.[61]

Most countries do not enshrine unequal treatment in political rights in their constitutions, but there are a few exceptions. For example, in the Maldives, individuals elected must be Sunni Muslim.

Some have sought to achieve greater equality through affirmative action. Sixteen countries have the option of reserving a portion of their legislative offices for women through quotas;* while quotas can lead to rapid growth in female legislative representation, the long-term advisability of quotas for any group can be debated. Are the preferences fair to those not receiving them? Is this action in fact advantageous to the marginalized group, or is it stigmatizing? Should the focus be on eliminating discriminatory treatment or on achieving certain quantifiable outcomes? In the section that follows, we discuss the advantages of addressing potential positive action in legislation instead of constitutions.

Building on a Constitutional Foundation

To have an adequate picture of the state of equal rights, it is critical to analyze laws as well as constitutions. While constitutions have some important advantages over regular legislation—their difficult amendment process makes the rights they enshrine more permanent—this same reality also means that it is difficult to add these rights where they are lacking. Constitutions developed more recently are more likely to have included many equal-rights and discrimination protections than constitutions written centuries ago. This raises the importance of looking also at equal-rights protections in regular legislation. It is clear that legislation fills a number of gaps. For example, the United States, recognizing inadequate constitutional protections, passed the Civil Rights Act of 1964 to guarantee equal opportunities at work across gender, ethnicity, and religion, among other characteristics.

There are currently no globally comparative data sources available on countries that guarantee equal rights across diverse groups in their legislation, as opposed to their constitutions. This gap must be filled in order to be able to fully analyze the most effective policies and to focus on change for the nations with the greatest inequities.

Looking at legislation is important for additional reasons. Where a history of discrimination exists, as it does on at least some dimensions in most countries, ensuring an equal chance for all will require more than equal rights in constitutions, as important as they are. Before any members of a marginalized group have held a high political office

---

*World Policy Analysis Centre, Constitutions Database. Number of countries for which we have data: 188 (rights in political participation).

or leadership positions in top companies, those positions may seem unattainable. When groups selecting the next leaders are made up of only one religion, ethnicity, or gender, they can easily bring a set of implicit biases to the selection process that privileges some groups over others. Moreover, a history of bias and discrimination can affect actual as well as perceived qualifications. Black South Africans had limited opportunities for advanced education in apartheid South Africa; as a result, immediately after the end of apartheid, there were disproportionately fewer black South Africans with advanced training in medicine, law, and other fields. When the upper echelons of business in the United States were largely closed to women, it meant at first that even committees seeking to consider women on an equal basis with men might find fewer female candidates with top executive experience. When recent immigrants in the United States, Britain, or France were relegated to the worst state schools because of the neighborhoods in which they lived, their training likewise suffered. Ensuring that all children have an equal chance will require transforming culture, eliminating biases that have little to do with quality from selection processes, and promoting policies that provide all groups with an equal foundation to compete.

From a legal standpoint, proactive laws to address past discrimination may be necessary. In a world in which all individuals are truly equal, such measures should not be permanently required. However, in contexts of profound bias or historical discrimination, it may not be possible to transition to full equity simply through constitutional or legal declarations prohibiting discrimination. When bias runs so deep that people cannot see beyond it, it may be necessary to take active steps to desegregate housing and ensure that children have an equal chance to grow up in safe and healthy neighborhoods. Similarly, when discrimination has prevented children from having an equal start in life, measures may be required to provide additional opportunities to disadvantaged groups in order to achieve equality in a timely fashion. Temporary preferential treatment that is intended to address past or deep discrimination is better embedded in policy or time-limited legislation than in constitutions; laws or policies can be passed on a time-limited basis either through passage and ready repeal or through a built-in sunset clause. Once all individuals have equal opportunities to develop and succeed, such measures should no longer be required.

Throughout this book we have noted the extent to which accomplishing each of the central goals for opportunity depends on achieving the others. Achieving equal rights for children is no exception. In many countries, discrimination has led to the long-term marginalization of a wide range of groups, including poorer access to education for children and youth, less access to jobs for adults as a result of educational limitations and discrimination, and living in concentrated poverty as a result of poorer work opportunities. Addressing educational, health, and income inequalities will increase the preparedness of all children and youth and facilitate the implementation of policies that decrease inequity. Likewise, addressing discrimination and equal rights will be essential to ensuring that all children have a chance at a healthy childhood and to develop to their full capacity.

Table 7.1. Overall constitutional protection of equity

	Equal Rights	Equality Before the Law	Equality	Prohibition of Discrimination
Approaches to Equity Based on Gender				
Constitution does not include any relevant protection	85 (45%)	42 (22%)	149 (78%)	46 (24%)
Constitution guarantees equal treatment to all citizens generally, but does not mention gender specifically	27 (14%)	97 (51%)	11 (6%)	16 (8%)
Constitution aspires to equal treatment based on gender	6 (3%)	0 (0%)	13 (7%)	5 (3%)
Constitution guarantees equal treatment based on gender, but allows for exceptions	0 (0%)	0 (0%)	0 (0%)	1 (1%)
Constitution guarantees equal treatment based on gender	73 (38%)	52 (27%)	18 (9%)	123 (64%)
Positive action may be taken to compensate for past discrimination or current inequalities on the basis of gender	6 (3%)	43 (23%)	1 (1%)	4 (2%)
Approaches to Equity Based on Ethnicity				
Constitution does not include any relevant protection	113 (59%)	43 (23%)	165 (86%)	47 (25%)
Constitution guarantees equal treatment to all citizens generally, but does not mention ethnicity specifically	34 (18%)	104 (54%)	13 (7%)	18 (9%)

(continued)

Table 7.1 (*continued*)

Constitution aspires to equal treatment based on ethnicity	1 (1%)	0 (0%)	9 (5%)	0 (0%)
Constitution guarantees equal treatment based on ethnicity, but allows for exceptions	0 (0%)	0 (0%)	0 (0%)	1 (1%)
Constitution guarantees equal treatment based on ethnicity	43 (23%)	44 (23%)	4 (2%)	125 (65%)
Positive action may be taken to compensate for past discrimination or current inequalities on the basis of ethnicity	0 (0%)	29 (15%)	1 (1%)	0 (0%)
Approaches to Equity Based on Religion				
Constitution does not include any relevant protection	114 (60%)	44 (23%)	171 (90%)	42 (22%)
Constitution guarantees equal treatment to all citizens generally, but does not mention religion specifically	33 (17%)	103 (54%)	14 (7%)	22 (12%)
Constitution aspires to equal treatment based on religion	1 (1%)	0 (0%)	4 (2%)	1 (1%)
Constitution guarantees equal treatment based on religion, but allows for exceptions	0 (0%)	0 (0%)	0 (0%)	1 (1%)
Constitution guarantees equal treatment based on religion	43 (23%)	44 (23%)	2 (1%)	125 (65%)

| Positive action may be taken to compensate for past discrimination or current inequalities on the basis of religion | 0 (0%) | 25 (13%) | 0 (0%) | 0 (0%) |

Source: World Policy Analysis Centre, Constitutions Database.

Definitions: Equal rights is a guarantee of being able to enjoy rights enshrined in the constitution. *Prohibition of discrimination* is a general protection against discrimination. *Equality before the law* is a guarantee of equal protection before the law. *Equality* is a guarantee of a general right to equality or equal opportunities. *Guaranteed with exceptions* includes cases where individuals can be treated disparately on the basis of gender, ethnicity, or religion for specified reasons, for example, where equality is guaranteed, except when the law "takes due account of physiological differences between persons of different sex or gender."

Note: Countries with an aspirational or guaranteed right could also have potential positive action.

Table 7.2. Constitutional guarantees of equality in education

Protection Against Discrimination in Education Based on Gender	Low-Income	Middle-Income	High-Income
Constitution does not include any relevant provisions specific to discrimination in education	25 (71%)	78 (74%)	40 (80%)
Constitution protects citizens against discrimination in education, but does not mention gender specifically	4 (11%)	22 (21%)	6 (12%)
Constitution aspires to protect citizens from discrimination in education on the basis of gender	3 (9%)	1 (1%)	0 (0%)
Constitution guarantees citizens protection from discrimination in education on the basis of gender, but allows for exceptions	0 (0%)	0 (0%)	0 (0%)
Constitution guarantees citizens protection from discrimination in education on the basis of gender	3 (9%)	5 (5%)	4 (8%)
Positive action may be taken to compensate for past discrimination or current inequalities on the basis of gender	5 (14%)	1 (1%)	1 (2%)

Protection Against Discrimination in Education Based on Ethnicity

Constitution does not include any relevant provisions specific to discrimination in education	27 (77%)	73 (69%)	39 (78%)
Constitution protects citizens against discrimination in education, but does not mention ethnicity specifically	4 (11%)	23 (22%)	7 (14%)
Constitution aspires to protect citizens from discrimination in education on the basis of ethnicity	1 (3%)	3 (3%)	0 (0%)
Constitution guarantees citizens protection from discrimination in education on the basis of ethnicity, but allows for exceptions	1 (3%)	0 (0%)	0 (0%)
Constitution guarantees citizens protection from discrimination in education on the basis of ethnicity	2 (6%)	7 (7%)	4 (8%)
Positive action may be taken to compensate for past discrimination or current inequalities on the basis of ethnicity	2 (6%)	4 (4%)	2 (4%)

(continued)

Table 7.2 (*continued*)

Protection Against Discrimination in Education Based on Religion			
Constitution does not include any relevant provisions specific to discrimination in education	27 (77%)	76 (72%)	39 (78%)
Constitution protects citizens against discrimination in education, but does not mention religion specifically	4 (11%)	21 (20%)	7 (14%)
Constitution aspires to protect citizens from discrimination in education on the basis of religion	0 (0%)	0 (0%)	0 (0%)
Constitution guarantees citizens protection from discrimination in education on the basis of religion, but allows for exceptions	1 (3%)	0 (0%)	0 (0%)
Constitution guarantees citizens protection from discrimination in education on the basis of religion	3 (9%)	9 (8%)	4 (8%)
Positive action may be taken to compensate for past discrimination or current inequalities on the basis of religion	1 (3%)	0 (0%)	2 (4%)

Source: World Policy Analysis Centre, Constitutions Database.

Definition: Low-income, middle-income, and high-income refer to World Bank classifications of national income. Here, middle-income countries include those classified as lower-middle and upper-middle income.

Note: Countries with an aspirational or guaranteed right could also have potential positive action.

Table 7.3. Constitutional guarantees of broad nondiscrimination at work

	Low-Income	Middle-Income	High-Income
Protection Against Discrimination in Work Based on Gender			
Constitution does not include any relevant provisions specific to discrimination in work	18 (51%)	89 (84%)	38 (76%)
Constitution protects citizens against discrimination in work, but does not mention gender specifically	4 (11%)	4 (4%)	2 (4%)
Constitution aspires to protect citizens from discrimination in work on the basis of gender	1 (3%)	3 (3%)	3 (6%)
Constitution guarantees citizens protection from discrimination in work on the basis of gender	12 (34%)	10 (9%)	7 (14%)
Positive action may be taken to compensate for past discrimination or current inequalities on the basis of gender	2 (6%)	3 (3%)	1 (2%)
Protection Against Discrimination in Work Based on Ethnicity			
Constitution does not include any relevant provisions specific to discrimination in work	22 (63%)	95 (90%)	46 (92%)
Constitution protects citizens against discrimination in work, but does not mention ethnicity specifically	8 (23%)	7 (7%)	2 (4%)
Constitution aspires to protect citizens from discrimination in work on the basis of ethnicity	1 (3%)	0 (0%)	0 (0%)

(continued)

Table 7.3 (continued)

Constitution guarantees citizens protection from discrimination in work on the basis of ethnicity	4 (11%)	4 (4%)	2 (4%)
Positive action may be taken to compensate for past discrimination or current inequalities on the basis of ethnicity	2 (6%)	0 (0%)	1 (2%)
Protection Against Discrimination in Work Based on Religion			
Constitution does not include any relevant provisions specific to discrimination in work	22 (63%)	97 (92%)	46 (92%)
Constitution protects citizens against discrimination in work, but does not mention religion specifically	10 (29%)	6 (6%)	2 (4%)
Constitution aspires to protect citizens from discrimination in work on the basis of religion	0 (0%)	0 (0%)	0 (0%)
Constitution guarantees citizens protection from discrimination in work on the basis of religion	3 (9%)	3 (3%)	2 (4%)
Positive action may be taken to compensate for past discrimination or current inequalities on the basis of religion	1 (3%)	0 (0%)	1 (2%)

Source : World Policy Analysis Centre, Constitutions Database.

Notes : Countries with an aspirational or guaranteed right could also have potential positive action. There are no countries that protect against discrimination in work with exceptions.

Table 7.4. Constitutional guarantees of nondiscrimination in hiring, promotion, and working conditions

	Hiring	Promotion	Working Conditions	Equal Pay for Equal Work
Specific Protections Against Discrimination in Work on the Basis of Gender				
Constitution does not include any relevant provision for protection of specific aspect of work	178 (93%)	176 (92%)	164 (86%)	129 (68%)
Constitution protects citizens against discrimination in an aspect of work, but does not mention gender specifically	7 (4%)	2 (1%)	7 (4%)	10 (5%)
Constitution aspires to protect citizens from discrimination in an aspect of work on the basis of gender	2 (1%)	4 (2%)	12 (6%)	10 (5%)
Constitution guarantees citizens protection from discrimination in an aspect of work on the basis of gender	4 (2%)	9 (5%)	8 (4%)	42 (22%)
Positive action may be taken to compensate for past discrimination or current inequalities on the basis of gender	3 (2%)	3 (2%)	13 (7%)	3 (2%)
Specific Protections Against Discrimination in Work on the Basis of Ethnicity				
Constitution does not include any relevant provision for protection of specific aspect of work	181 (95%)	186 (97%)	179 (94%)	154 (81%)
Constitution protects citizens against discrimination in an aspect of work, but does not mention ethnicity specifically	7 (4%)	3 (2%)	8 (4%)	16 (8%)
Constitution aspires to protect citizens from discrimination in an aspect of work on the basis of ethnicity	0 (0%)	0 (0%)	0 (0%)	0 (0%)

(continued)

Table 7.4 (*continued*)

Constitution guarantees citizens protection from discrimination in an aspect of work on the basis of ethnicity	3 (2%)	2 (1%)	4 (2%)	21 (11%)
Positive action may be taken to compensate for past discrimination or current inequalities on the basis of ethnicity	2 (1%)	2 (1%)	1 (1%)	0 (0%)
Specific Protections Against Discrimination in Work on the Basis of Religion				
Constitution does not include any relevant provision for protection of specific aspect of work	182 (95%)	186 (97%)	179 (94%)	155 (81%)
Constitution protects citizens against discrimination in an aspect of work, but does not mention religion specifically	7 (4%)	3 (2%)	9 (5%)	19 (10%)
Constitution aspires to protect citizens from discrimination in an aspect of work on the basis of religion	0 (0%)	0 (0%)	0 (0%)	0 (0%)
Constitution guarantees citizens protection from discrimination in an aspect of work on the basis of religion	2 (1%)	2 (1%)	3 (2%)	17 (9%)
Positive action may be taken to compensate for past discrimination or current inequalities on the basis of religion	2 (1%)	2 (1%)	1 (1%)	0 (0%)

Source: World Policy Analysis Centre, Constitutions Database.

Notes: Countries with an aspirational or guaranteed right could also have potential positive protections with exceptions. There are no countries that guarantee these specific protections with exceptions.

Chapter 8

Meeting Special Needs

Ngo Thi Hang, a 3-year-old girl with Down syndrome, required a great deal of care from her mother, with whom she lived in southern Viet Nam. Hang had a heart defect that needed regular medical attention; she went to see a doctor for routine care two to three times per month. Hang got sick often; she had been hospitalized five times already in her short life, each time for a week. Aside from her special care needs and hospitalizations, even dealing with common childhood illnesses was a financial challenge for her mother. She explained, "It costs 100,000 dong just for medicine, excluding the exam fee," nearly half of her average weekly income. When Hang had scarlet fever, her mother was forced to borrow money from a family member to cover costs.

Caring for Hang both increased her mother's need for money and diminished her ability to earn it. Her mother supported the family through her work as a seamstress, but she could not work as much while Hang was ill; meeting Hang's needs meant that sewing jobs went unfinished or delayed. No early intervention services or early childhood care was available that would meet Hang's needs. Her mother explained, "When she is fine, I can work 7 to 8 hours. When she is sick, I can only work 4 to 5 hours." When Hang was hospitalized, her mother could not work at all. She lost income not only from her reduced working hours, but also because some clients who paid her to sew clothing did not return.

Hang's mother was worried about sending her to school. She could not send her to a mainstream school because these schools were not equipped to meet even her most basic need, feeding her. The best education available would be at a local private school for children with special needs. "The tuition is 450,000 [dong] a month, too high for me to afford. But since I know that my child will have her full rights at that school, I will try my best to get her in. The government pays 200 to 300,000 a month; I will try to take care of the rest."[1]

The experience of Mason and Andrea Arnette in the United States could not have been more different in terms of services received. Mason and Andrea were twins who had been born 9 weeks prematurely, weighing just over a kilogram each. At 31 weeks gestation, their early birth took a toll. Mason's lungs were underdeveloped, leaving him with asthma severe enough that he was hospitalized repeatedly during his childhood. Both Mason and Andrea had learning disabilities and developmental problems, particularly in developing speech.

However, the services and care that Mason and Andrea received reduced the impact of their disabilities on their lives. The city made early intervention services available free of charge to families to provide developmental support. In the city's fully integrated public school system, children with and without disabilities shared schools and classrooms. At the same time, state law provided for additional services to support children with learning differences to succeed at school. Although the implementation of these policies and laws is imperfect and some families have difficulty accessing services, the experience of Mason and Andrea shows the important impact that they can have.

Mason and Andrea were carefully followed by professionals and assessed for special needs from the time of their premature birth. When they went home from the hospital, they were visited weekly to assess their development. From the age of 2, both received speech therapy to address their difficulties; by the time they were in the second grade, they no longer needed this assistance. An individualized education plan was developed for each of the children as soon as they entered school. Now 10 years old, they spent most of their time in a mainstream classroom at their local public school; twice a week, they were given extra attention from a tutor to ensure that their learning difficulties were not holding them back. Once or twice a year, their mother would go into the school to discuss her children's individualized education plans, goals for progress in the classroom, and the supports they would receive.[2] The United States had major holes in its safety net, especially in access to affordable health care, but the country had made a legislative commitment to providing equitable education for children with special needs.[3] The city and state where the Arnettes lived surpassed these national commitments, providing both greater educational supports and health-care services.

The experiences of Hang, Mason, and Andrea demonstrate the extent to which a child's environment and services received can shape their experience of disability. Children with disabilities face disadvantages in childhood in areas ranging from education to health that can limit their life chances. However, many of these barriers are as much a result of the social context in which disabled children and adults live as of the impairments themselves.

There are limitations inherent in certain impairments. However, the extent to which an impairment is truly disabling is fundamentally shaped by the context in which individuals find themselves. An inability to walk or climb stairs is less disabling when wheelchairs are available and all sidewalks and buildings are physically accessible. Being blind does not limit a child's ability to learn when all materials are available in audio or Braille formats. A child with Down syndrome can learn and interact with his or her peers in school when additional support is available. When depression is treated and understood and bias is reduced, it is not as limiting as it can be when health coverage is inadequate and discrimination is unchecked. As stated in the preamble of the UN Convention on the Rights of Persons with Disabilities, "Disability is an evolving concept and . . . disability results from the interaction between persons with impairments and attitudinal and environmental barriers that hinder their full and effective participation in society on an equal basis with others."[4] It is impossible to ensure that all children and youth have an equal chance at a full life without addressing the barriers faced by children with special needs. Numbering over 1 billion, people with disabilities make up one of the world's largest minority populations.[5]

Recognition of Equal Rights

Although the rights of persons across gender, ethnicity, and religion have enjoyed a high level of international consensus for decades, the rights of persons with disabilities have not always been as widely recognized. The Convention on the Rights of Persons with Disabilities (CRPD), a document that clearly outlines and endorses the rights of children and adults with disabilities, was adopted only in 2006, though it has quickly achieved a wide level of acceptance, with 153 nations as signatories and 109 ratifications by the end of 2011.[6] The CRPD both built on and provided support to national movements to ensure equal rights.

Because the realization of equal rights requires national guarantees, not just international ones, it is important to know whether children and adults with disabilities are guaranteed equal rights in national constitutions. Drawing on the comparative database that we created, for which we thoroughly reviewed original constitutional texts from 191 countries to analyze the rights and provisions they contain, we examined whether equal rights for children and adults with disabilities are guaranteed; for details on this database and the others used in this chapter, see Appendix 1. We would have liked additionally to compare country action through national laws, but these data are not yet systematically available.

The results of the data analysis show that few countries have confirmed their commitment to equal rights at a constitutional level (Map 8.1). Countries can approach the rights of persons with disabilities in various ways. They can guarantee that people with disabilities should enjoy rights on an equal basis with all others, they can guarantee overall equality for this group, they can prohibit discrimination on the basis of disability, and they can guarantee equality before the law irrespective of disability. In 35 countries, at least one of these approaches is taken.* In an additional 7 countries, at least one of these approaches is aspirational, meaning that it is mentioned in the constitution explic-

---

*World Policy Analysis Centre, Constitutions Database. Number of countries for which we have data: 191 (rights to equity). Map 8.1 is based on physical disability but is identical for people with mental health conditions or intellectual disabilities except in the case of Ireland, Thailand, and Zimbabwe, which explicitly mention only physical disability.

Map 8.1. Do constitutions take at least one approach to equity across disability?

No, none specific to disability
Yes, aspirational
Yes, guaranteed with exceptions*
Yes, guaranteed
Potential positive action**

Approaches to equity include prohibitions of discrimination, guarantees of equality before the law, and guarantees of overall equality.

**Guaranteed with exceptions* includes cases where equity is guaranteed for the disabled except if "their disability prevents them from exercising" their rights.

***Potential positive action* indicates that constitutions also include measures to promote equity for the disabled.

Source: *World Policy Analysis Centre, Constitutions Database*

itly in regard to disability, but that the language used is not strong enough to be considered a guarantee.[7]

While in our examination of constitutional equity across gender, ethnicity, and religion in the previous chapter the maps show both countries that explicitly guarantee equal rights and those that have a broad guarantee of equity that does not explicitly apply to the group in question, in the case of disability we focus on explicit protections because countries have not historically treated disability as grounds for equal rights when not explicitly guaranteed.

Some countries leave open the possibility of taking affirmative steps to ameliorate past discrimination and persistent disparities. In the maps and tables, we also indicate where a country has this "potential positive action." For example, Canada's Charter of Rights and Freedoms states that "every individual is equal before and under the law and has the right to the equal protection and equal benefit of the law without discrimination and, in particular, without discrimination based on . . . mental or physical disability. [This] does not preclude any law, program or activity that has as its object the amelioration of conditions of disadvantaged individuals or groups including those that are disadvantaged because of . . . mental or physical disability."

In 5 cases, countries guarantee equity for persons with disabilities but include caveats. For example, Ireland states that "all citizens shall, as human persons, be held equal before the law. This shall not be held to mean that the State shall not in its enactments have due regard to differences of capacity, physical and moral, and of social function." In Portugal, "Citizens with physical or mental disabilities shall fully enjoy the rights and shall be subject to the duties enshrined in this Constitution, save the exercise or fulfillment of those for which their condition renders them unfit." Mozambique, Angola, and Timor-Leste have similar language. These kinds of caveats are potentially problematic. When the state reserves the right to treat citizens differently because of differences in "capacity" or "fitness" to exercise their rights, the state's interpretation can determine whether discrimination is permitted.

However, the greatest gaps are in the 144 countries that make no explicit mention of disability in relation to equality before the law, overall equality, equal enjoyment of rights, or prohibition of discrimination. As in the case of rights to health and education, constitutions written more recently are more likely to include explicit guarantees of rights for people with disabilities than older constitutions. Over one-quarter of the constitutions adopted since 1990 have these guarantees, whereas less than 10 percent from the centuries before provide these protections.

Education is one of the most important aspects of life during childhood. Do national constitutions take steps to guarantee equity in education to children with disabilities? In general, the answer is no (Map 8.2). The constitutions of only 34 countries explicitly address the needs of children and youth with disabilities when they are discussing the right to education or the prohibition of discrimination in education. In some cases, the language used is quite strong. Thailand states that the education of persons with disabilities should be "on equal footing as others." Colombia makes clear that "the eradication of illiteracy and the education of individuals with physical or mental limitations or with exceptional capabilities are special obligations of the State." The Peruvian constitution contends that "no one should be prevented from receiving an adequate education on account of . . . mental or physical limitations." The Gambia states that "disabled persons shall be entitled to . . . protection against discrimination, in particular as regards access to health services, education and employment." In other countries, the goal is less strongly stated. Honduras simply states that "the State shall support and promote the education of disabled persons," and in Albania, "the State, within its constitutional powers and the means at its disposal, aims to supplement private initiative and responsibility with . . . specialized education and integration in society of disabled people." Three countries include caveats; those from Mozambique and Timor-Leste were discussed above. New Zealand explicitly prohibits discrimination on the basis of disability but also states that an educational establishment is permitted to refuse admission to a person "requiring special services or facilities that in the circumstances cannot reasonably be made available (being services or facilities that are required to enable the person to participate in the educational programme of that establishment or to enable the person to derive substantial benefits from that programme)." The vast majority of countries, 154, do not explicitly address equity in education for children and youth with disabilities in their constitutions.*

---

*World Policy Analysis Centre, Constitutions Database. Number of countries for which we have data: 191 (rights in education).

Map 8.2. Do constitutions guarantee disabled children's right to education?

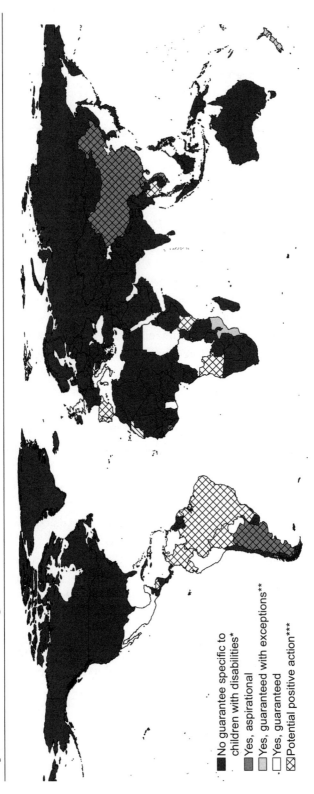

- No guarantee specific to children with disabilities*
- Yes, aspirational
- Yes, guaranteed with exceptions**
- Yes, guaranteed
- Potential positive action***

No guarantee specific to children with disabilities includes cases where the constitution does not mention educational rights or where the constitution guarantees education to all children, but does not specifically mention disability.
** *Guaranteed with exceptions* includes cases where education is guaranteed to disabled children, except if "their disability prevents them from exercising or fulfilling" their right to education.
*** *Potential positive action* indicates that constitutions also include measures to promote equity for the disabled.

Source: World Policy Analysis Centre, Constitutions Database

Beyond their needs during childhood, children with disabilities and their parents look to the experience of adults with disabilities to anticipate their future. The impact of role models on children and youth has long been recognized; when children see these role models as having similar attributes, their impact increases.[8] This has logical consequences for children with disabilities. As a blind child, it is much easier for you to stay motivated at school if you witness blind adults succeeding at work. If you are missing a limb and see that physically disabled adults in your society have leadership roles in the private sector, it is easier to dream of that possibility for yourself and more likely that others will invest in your chance of succeeding. If while you grapple with a bipolar disorder, you meet people with the same condition leading public organizations, it is much easier to imagine that possibility. As a parent with limited resources and a child with a chronic condition or disability, it is easier to justify an investment in the child's education when you have reasonable hope that the child will be able to find a job. This is not unique to children with disabilities; as has been discussed in Chapter 7 on equity and discrimination, the same effects occur for other groups. When women are succeeding in the workplace, girls' commitment to school and their parents' investments in their education both increase; when minority groups are able to participate in a nation's political and civic life, minority children's belief in what is possible for them changes.[9]

We examined all of the world's constitutions for guarantees of equal rights at work and in civic life. The constitutions of only 33 countries discuss the right to work or prohibit discrimination in work for people with disabilities; 13 of these do so in aspirational rather than guaranteed terms, and 4 have caveats. The minimum level of protection one would expect from all countries is reflected in Brazil's constitution, which includes a "prohibition of any discrimination with respect to wages and hiring criteria of disabled workers." The constitution does not state that people should be hired for a task they are unable to fulfill, but simply that they should not be discriminated against. These explicit constitutional protections exist in an extremely small number of countries.*

---

*World Policy Analysis Centre, Constitutions Database. Number of countries for which we have data: 191 (rights in work).

Even fewer countries explicitly ensure in their constitutions that the disabled will be able to vote and participate in the political process. The lack of proactive steps can leave substantial barriers to participation in place. Political participation of people with disabilities can be limited by everything from the inaccessibility of polling stations to discrimination from officials. For example, visual impairments that prevent a potential voter from seeing or reading the ballot or physical impairments that limit access to a voting booth can stand in the way of enfranchisement, affecting not only the rights of the individual but the likelihood that those elected may be pressed about the importance of equal rights. Four countries have special provisions to allow persons with physical disabilities to vote, although these provisions vary in strength. Kenya's constitution states that "legislation required . . . shall ensure that voting at every election . . . takes into account the special needs of (i) persons with disabilities; and (ii) other persons or groups with special needs." The constitutions of the Philippines and Uganda state that laws will be created to facilitate voting for persons with disabilities, and Malta permits the ballots of persons with visual or other impairments to be marked by voting officials if necessary.

Far from special provisions to ensure equal exercise of rights, in 3 countries, a voter can be disqualified on the basis of physical incapacity. Serbia requires "working ability" for voting, Uruguay suspends citizenship "by physical or mental ineptitude," and Namibia may suspend political rights on "grounds of infirmity."

Persons with mental health conditions or intellectual disabilities face much greater restrictions on their political rights than persons with physical disabilities. Forty-five countries reserve the right to deny the right to vote to the mentally incapacitated, using language such as "Parliament may enact a law imposing conditions restricting a citizen from exercising the right to vote by reason of any of the following grounds: . . . (b) being mentally infirm" (Tanzania) or "Rules may be laid down by law concerning the right to vote of persons otherwise entitled to vote who on Election Day are manifestly suffering from a seriously weakened mental state" (Norway). Some countries place distinct restrictions on persons who have been declared legally incompetent by a judge or medical professional, while others include blanket caveats not linked to legal or medical requirements. Although a certain level of capacity is inherent in the granting of the right to vote, potential denials of the right to vote for persons with disabilities with a mental health dimension, especially when the criteria are not clearly defined, leave open the possibility of denials of rights based solely on stigma, discrimination, and misconceptions about capacity. An understanding of the importance of this has led to decisions in Canada and in the European Union to make election laws more inclusive.[10]

Disparities on the Ground

As the previous section showed, equal rights for children and adults with disabilities have generally not been recognized constitutionally. In practice, how large are the disparities in children's opportunities and adults' experiences that shape expectations?

The educational chances of children with disabilities remain devastatingly limited in many settings. Around the world, children with disabilities are less likely to be enrolled in school than their nondisabled counterparts. A study of 13 low- and middle-income countries showed that enrollment rates for children with disabilities aged 6 to 11 ranged from 18 percent in Cambodia to 76 percent in South Africa and were between 30 and 60 percent in most countries. In Bolivia and Indonesia, children with disabilities were more than 50 percentage points less likely to be in school than nondisabled children; in Cambodia, Colombia, Jamaica, Mongolia, South Africa, and Zambia, this disparity was between 24 and 45 percentage points. The schooling deficit associated with disability is often even greater than that associated with more widely recognized sources of disadvantage, such as gender or poverty. In Bolivia, Indonesia, and Romania, for example, the disadvantage associated with disability was more than double that associated with wealth-based disadvantage, the next greatest source of disparity.[11] In India, the proportion of children with disabilities who are not in school is more than five times greater than the overall proportion of out-of-school children and four times greater even than that of the severely marginalized scheduled tribes.[12]

Even where the enrollment rates of disabled children are comparatively high, the disparities are still significant. For instance, in Bulgaria, 81 percent of children with disabilities aged 7 to 15 are enrolled in school, as are 71 percent in Jamaica and 76 percent in South Africa; however, enrollment rates among children without disabilities are 96 percent, 99 percent, and 96 percent, respectively.[13]

In some countries, the extent to which children face barriers to schooling differs according to their disability. In Burkina Faso, for example, 40 percent of children with an upper or lower limb impairment were enrolled in school, a rate not far below that of children without disabilities, but just 10 percent of 7- to 12-year-old children reported as deaf or "mute" were enrolled.[14] In Cape Verde, just 59 percent of children with mental health conditions or intellectual disabilities are enrolled in school, compared with an average enrollment rate of 73 percent for children with any disability and 88 percent for children without a disability.[15]

As one would expect after looking at enrollment data, global estimates of primary-school completion and secondary-school attendance are low for children with disabilities. From Estonia to the Philippines, less than one-third of these children move beyond primary school.[16] Studies in South Africa have found that disabled children complete an average of 3.5 years or less of schooling.[17] Even in countries like Costa Rica, with otherwise strong human development indicators, only 14 percent of children with disabilities receive a secondary education.[18] In nearby El Salvador, only 5 percent of children with disabilities complete secondary school. In Brazil, 1 in 10 disabled children completes the eighth grade.[19]

The disadvantages experienced by children with disabilities are compounded by the fact that their families tend to have more limited resources than the families of children without special needs. Their average income and earnings are often lower because of the restrictions that caring for a disabled child can place on employment.[20] As was the case for Hang's mother, parents frequently report that caring for a child with special needs is a barrier to work; they often end up quitting their jobs or cutting back on work hours in order to care for disabled children.[21] Living in poverty also places children at greater risk of disability because of the increased prevalence of malnutrition, greater exposure to risk factors for illness and injury, and environmental factors.[22] Poor children are more likely to be engaged in child labor, which exposes them to risks of accidents and injuries on the job. Moreover, poor children are at greater risk of having a curable or correctable impairment develop into a disability because of limited access to health care.[23]

The poverty often experienced by the families of children with disabilities can place further limitations on their access to education and health care. In the United States, among children with special healthcare needs, those from poor families were at least twice as likely to have an unmet need for routine or specialty health care as nonpoor children and were also more likely to have an unmet need for vision or hearing care, glasses, and hearing and communication aids. Cost was clearly a barrier to care. Uninsured children were 7.5 times more likely to lack access to needed routine care and more than 4 times more likely to lack access to needed specialty care than children who had access to health insurance; they were also more likely to lack the glasses, hearing aids, and mobility devices that they required, and less likely to access therapy services.[24]

The limited opportunities of children with disabilities during childhood shape their chances in adulthood as well. A study of 13 countries in Africa, Asia, Latin America, and Eastern Europe showed that having a disability is associated with living in poverty as an adult, and that much of this relationship is driven by educational disparities; each additional year of schooling completed is associated with a reduction in the probability of living in poverty of between 2 and 5 percentage points.[25] The connection between poverty and education makes sense because education is fundamentally tied to chances at work. When persons with disabilities receive limited education, their job possibilities are constrained.

Around the world, adults with disabilities face disadvantages in the labor market resulting from accessibility obstacles and discrimination, as well as educational disparities. In Latin America and the Caribbean, just 30 percent of persons with disabilities are in the workforce.[26] Similarly, in Asia, rates of unemployment among the disabled have been estimated as high as 80 percent in some countries.[27] In the member countries of the OECD, the average employment rate for adults with disabilities is 43 percent, ranging from a high of 61 percent in Iceland to a low of 18 percent in Poland.[28] According to South Africa's Department of Labour, just 1 percent of persons with disabilities in the country are formal sector employees, and they represent just 0.25 percent of public-sector employees.[29] In Eastern Europe, employment rates for disabled adults are between 20 and 60 percentage points lower than for nondisabled adults.[30] When disabled individuals are able to obtain a job, they are less likely to earn a decent wage. Ninety-eight percent of employed deaf adults in Sri Lanka earn less than $2 a day, and 81 percent earn less than $1 a day.[31] In Mexico, 37 percent of working adults with disabilities receive either no pay for their work or receive less than the minimum wage.[32] A study in Bangladesh found that the average incomes of adults with disabilities studied were 60 percent lower than the incomes of other adults.[33] In Moldova and Bulgaria, disabled employees earn at least 40 percent less than those without disabilities.[34] Poor adult outcomes lower family and community expectations for children and youth with disabilities.

What Policies Make a Difference?

It is clear that vastly more action must be taken for equal chances for children with disabilities to be made real. To improve their opportunities, children need to have access to affordable and high-quality education that meets their needs, their families require adequate resources to procure key services and equipment, and their parents need working conditions that enable them to provide essential care.

Ensuring Equal Opportunities in Education

There have been major debates over the years about how best to ensure that children with disabilities develop to their full potential, particularly at school. Some have argued that separate educational settings are better equipped to deal with the specialized learning needs of children with a wide range of disabilities. Logistically, it is easy to see advantages for a child with a hearing impairment in an educational setting where all teachers and students can communicate in sign language, for instance. At the same time, extensive evidence on the impact of inclusive education within mainstream schools versus separate education on the academic achievement of students with disabilities shows that the majority of students perform equally well or better in inclusive settings.[35]

Moreover, when the ultimate goal is for individuals with disabilities to be able to participate fully in the workplace, in civic life, and in all other spheres, segregating children eliminates the opportunity for children to learn from and about one another. As one would expect, when children with and without disabilities spend time together in the classroom, opportunities for social interaction between them increase, and the attitudes of children without disabilities toward children with special needs can improve, especially when this interaction is actively encouraged.[36] Education that separates children with disabilities and differences from their nondisabled peers sets the stage for the social exclusion that persons with disabilities commonly face throughout their lives.

Even if inclusive education did not have other benefits, separate education presents practical problems. Countries that seek to provide separate education often fail to supply enough classroom spaces. The disparity between the number of children and spaces can be enormous. For example, at a time when there were an estimated 260,000 children with disabilities who needed schooling in Cambodia and inclusive education was not provided, there were only eight special schools for children with physical disabilities, sensory disabilities, or multiple and severe disabilities. Together, they were able to educate just 500 children per year.[37] In Nicaragua, schools designed for children with special needs had space for only 1 in 40 of the children in need of special educational support.[38]

There may be a minority of cases in which inclusion is not in the best interest of the child because the child's condition and the school's accommodations prevent the child from developing to his or her full potential; however, the evidence supports that separate education should be the exception rather than the norm. Over the past few decades consensus has moved to support the inclusion of children with a wide range of physical, intellectual, and other differences in mainstream schools and classrooms. In 1994, this call was formalized internationally by the Salamanca Statement and Framework for Action on Special Needs Education, the product of a meeting organized by UNESCO that brought together 92 countries. This statement affirms that "regular schools with this inclusive orientation are the most effective means of combating discriminatory attitudes, creating welcoming communities, building an inclusive society and achieving education for all; moreover, they provide an effective education to the majority of children and improve the efficiency and ultimately the cost-effectiveness of the entire education system."[39] The CRPD echoes this endorsement of an inclusive approach. It requires that "persons with disabilities receive the support required, within the general education system, to facilitate their effective education," and that "effective individual support measures [be] required in environments that maximize academic and social development, consistent with the goal of full inclusion."[40]

We examined the extent to which countries around the world are including children with special needs in the public school system. To do this, our research team systematically analyzed the large amount of qualitative data contained in national reports to UNESCO to assess whether education for children with disabilities is publicly provided, and the extent to which these children are included with nondisabled children in classrooms or in schools. When countries report that children with special needs are integrated into the same classrooms as children without special needs, we consider this a high level of integration; when they attend the same schools but are not necessarily in the same classrooms, we consider this a medium level; and when education is publicly provided but in separate schools, we consider this a low level of integration. When education is publicly provided in the same system, schools, or classrooms, but children receive no additional supports to meet their needs, we do not give the country credit for having special education for children with disabilities.

The majority of the world's countries, 155, have some provision for special education in the public education system (Map 8.3). Of these, 73 countries have a high level of integration of children with and without special needs, meaning that children with and without disabilities are in the same classrooms, and there are additional supports for the children who need them. Sixty-two countries have a medium level of integration; in 20 countries, there are separate schools for disabled children within the public school system.*

While over three-quarters of high-income countries have a high level of integration, just 32 percent of middle-income countries and 21 percent of low-income countries are known to integrate students with special needs at the classroom level. At the other end of the scale, 5

---

*World Policy Analysis Centre, Education Database. Number of countries for which we have data: 163 (availability of inclusive special education).

Map 8.3. Is inclusive special education available for children with disabilities?

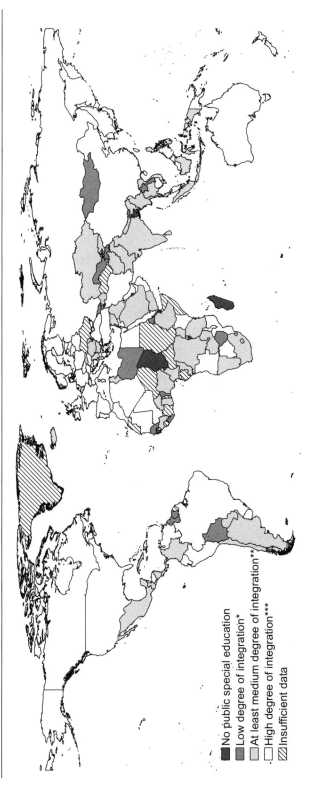

■ No public special education
■ Low degree of integration*
▨ At least medium degree of integration**
□ High degree of integration***
▨ Insufficient data

*Low degree of integration indicates that children are sent to separate schools within the public school system.
**At least medium degree of integration indicates that children may attend the same schools but not necessarily the same classrooms as other students.
***High degree of integration indicates that children with disabilities are able to be taught within the same classroom as other students.

Source: World Policy Analysis Centre, Education Database

low-income countries and 3 middle-income countries either have no special education or only nonpublic special education; all high-income countries have at least some public provision of education for children with special needs.

Although it is an important first step, simply examining which countries report that they are currently including children in their regular classrooms is clearly not sufficient to determine how much progress has been made in removing stereotypes, providing adequate training to teachers, and helping all children reach their maximum potential. Inclusive education is not just a matter of placing all children in the same classroom; it requires ensuring that each of these children is able to reach his or her full potential in education. Moreover, even if quality inclusive education is available for children with disabilities who attend school, if a substantial proportion of children with disabilities are not attending, a country is failing these children.

Inclusive schools and classrooms must be appropriately resourced to support all students successfully. Are children with disabilities being given the chance to learn and develop to their full potential? Quite simply, we do not know. Many children need to interact with the school curriculum in alternative ways to allow them to learn. Children with visual impairments need learning materials that they can touch or listen to; children who are deaf need access to interpreters or training in lipreading. We need to know the extent to which children have practical access to these learning materials. When safe and accessible transit options are not available, making the journey between school and home can be an insurmountable barrier. Once children are able to get to school, the buildings, classrooms, and facilities need to be made physically accessible to all children.

The extent and quality of teacher training on the most effective approaches to teaching children with a variety of special needs is critical, and no globally comparative data have yet been collected on this factor. Teachers need to be given training in how to integrate all children successfully into their classrooms. They need tools to adapt evaluation methods to the skills of different children so that goals are set high, but in a way that is achievable for each child.[41] Additional support staff to assist teachers with meeting all students' needs are often required.[42] In each of these areas, we need further globally comparative data.

Providing Adequate Resources and Care

Although one can debate the best way to make adequate resources available, whether by providing direct financial assistance or free or reduced-cost services, it is clear that many families face significant financial burdens in caring for their children with disabilities. Expenses related to health care, education, caregivers, and assistive devices are common. Around the world, the pattern is the same. Estimates vary, but the additional economic costs of caring for a child with a disability have been recognized in studies from Canada to China, from India to the United Kingdom, and from the United States to Sweden.[43] In Bangladesh, it has been estimated that a child with severe disabilities is three times as expensive to support as a child with average needs, and a disabled child's treatment and support equipment cost an average of 4 months' worth of income.[44] As discussed in an earlier section, the parents of children with disabilities often have lower earnings as well.

One of the ways to bridge the gap in resources faced by families is through direct financial assistance. Income support can mean that a disabled child's family has the financial capacity to pay for medical treatment, learning specialists, and other needed care. Income support reduces the chance that families will have to sacrifice the needs of their disabled child in favor of those of his or her siblings or vice versa, which can occur when resources are limited. Extensive detailed information on financial assistance was available through the Social Security Programs Throughout the World database and other sources, but these did not permit easy comparisons among countries. We analyzed this information to develop a quantitatively comparable database of poverty-reduction policy around the world. Here, we examine financial assistance designed solely for families with a disabled child through cash benefits, benefit supplements for families with disabled children available through general family benefit schemes, and resources available through programs targeting adults with disabilities that cover children as well.[45]

Even if all these types of benefit provision are included, just 58 countries provide a benefit or supplement specifically for families supporting children with disabilities (Map 8.4).* Over half of these countries

*World Policy Analysis Centre, Poverty Database. Number of countries for which we have data: 172 (availability of benefits for disabled children).

Map 8.4. Are benefits available to families with disabled children?

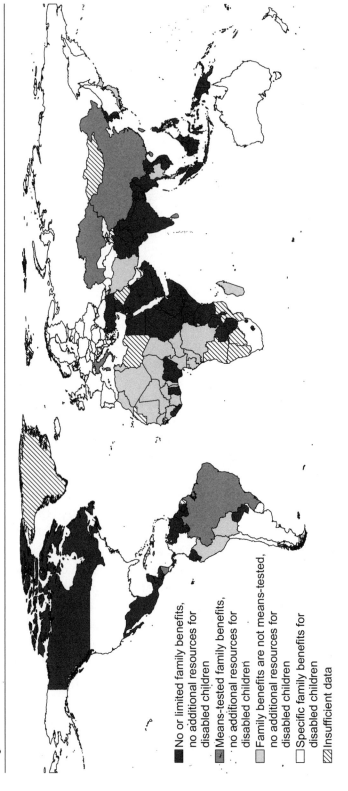

No or limited family benefits, no additional resources for disabled children

Means-tested family benefits, no additional resources for disabled children

Family benefits are not means-tested, no additional resources for disabled children

Specific family benefits for disabled children

Insufficient data

Source: World Policy Analysis Centre, Poverty Database

are high-income, in the company of 25 middle-income countries and 1 low-income country. If we include only benefits specifically targeted toward children with disabilities, 16 countries provide at least $500 per month, adjusted for purchasing power parity, for a low-income family with one severely disabled school-age child; 7 provide between $200 and $499.99 per month, 12 between $100 and $199.99, and 15 provide less than $100 per month. These figures are identical for younger children. Once a disabled child reaches adolescence, the number of countries providing financial assistance lowers to 47.*

Countries can also respond to the additional challenges faced by families supporting a child with a disability by providing assistance in a variety of other ways, including direct provision of free or subsidized care, assistive devices, and tax credits for disability-related expenditures. As of yet, there is no information source available on these programs in countries around the world.

Children with disabilities have better odds of equal chances when their parents are able to take the time they need to provide assistance, as well as when their families have the resources they need to support them. Although care provided by physicians, nurses, physical therapists, and other health-care providers is often essential, care provided on a daily basis at home is just as important. Children with cerebral palsy or paraplegia may go to a clinic for physical therapy, but the success of this therapy is often determined by the quality of its implementation at home. Physicians may determine which anticonvulsant is best for treating epilepsy, what should be done in case of an asthma attack, or how to treat diabetes, but ultimately the management of these chronic conditions relies on the ability of parents and children to follow monitoring and treatment protocols on a routine basis.[46] For parents to have the best understanding of what needs to be done, they need to be able to accompany their child to appointments and meet with their therapists. Moreover, parental availability to give emotional and other personal support at critical times can make an enormous difference to children's adaptation.[47]

If working parents are to be available to bring their child to receive health care or other needed services, they need to be able to take leave

---

*World Policy Analysis Centre, Poverty Database. Number of countries for which we have data: 164 (amount of benefits for disabled children).

from work without risking their jobs or incomes. A study of low-income households in the United States showed that parents were five times more likely to care for sick children themselves and to be available to bring them to health-care providers when necessary if they had access to paid leave that could be used for this purpose.[48] Although this is true for all children, the greater number of medical appointments required for children with special needs means that the availability of their parents or other caregivers is especially important. For example, in the United States, children with disabilities were hospitalized four times as often and for eight times as long as children without disabilities; they also saw a doctor twice as often and other health professionals five times as often as other children.[49]

Likewise, children with learning differences and disabilities affecting education do better with parental support. What children learn outside school while doing homework is often as important as what they learn in school.[50] At home, it is most often parents who shape the learning environment, so it should come as little surprise that parental involvement in learning at home makes a large difference in the developmental success of children with learning disabilities.[51] The ability of parents to respond well to their children's learning needs is strongly influenced by whether they are able to meet periodically with teachers to understand their children's needs and get guidance on the best way to proceed.[52] Parents whose children have learning disabilities or other conditions affecting school outcomes typically need to meet more often with teachers and learning specialists. When taking leave risks job loss, this can lead to untenable choices between meeting a child's educational needs and earning enough to support the family.

Our data, gathered from our systematic analysis of labor and other legislation around the world, show that in most of the world, labor laws do not guarantee parents the leave they need from work to meet their children's health and educational needs. As was discussed in greater detail in Chapter 5 on parenting, only 54 countries provide parents with paid leave specifically to meet their children's health needs, and 16 countries guarantee unpaid leave for this purpose. Even fewer countries, just 3 worldwide, provide either paid or unpaid leave specifically to meet children's educational needs. Some countries provide leave that can be taken for general family needs; 16 guarantee paid leave, and 3 guarantee unpaid leave. Others provide leave that can be taken at the

employee's discretion, but again this number is very small: 3 countries provide paid discretionary leave, and 7 provide unpaid leave. In 9
countries, paid leave can be taken in response to an emergency, and in
7 countries this leave is available unpaid, which could conceivably apply
to a child's health needs if acute but would probably not allow a parent
to address chronic health problems or long-term educational needs.*

Additional policies exist to support parental care at night for children
with disabilities. Information collected by the International Labour
Organization shows that at least 8 countries exempt parents from night
work if they are caring for a disabled child. Estonia, Italy, Kazakhstan,
Russia, and Slovenia have no upper age limit for this exemption; Moldova permits the exemption until the age of 16, and Lithuania until the
age of 18. Croatia's exemption is specific to a parent working part-time
to care for a disabled child up to the age of 7.[53]

Lingering Unknowns

The data we present in this chapter document the mixed results to date
in ensuring that all children with disabilities enjoy equal rights and opportunities. Ultimately, however, creating a society in which children
with disabilities truly have an equal chance is about much more than
the limited indicators we have discussed. If all these indicators showed
equity, it would be a huge improvement for the lives of children and
youth with disabilities, but much more is necessary in order to achieve
equality of opportunity. True equality of opportunity means that children and adults with disabilities are able to participate fully in society
every day and in all the ways in which other children and adults can. To
get a better picture of where nations stand on this much larger issue of
equity, much more needs to be known.

How many children have special needs, and what do they require in
order to meet their needs? This information is critical in order for
governments to ensure that all children are able to attend school with
sufficient supports and have access to the health care and assistive devices they might need, and to assess and address other barriers to full

---

*World Policy Analysis Centre, Adult Labour Database. Number of countries
for which we have data: 187 (health needs), 178 (educational needs), 182 (family
needs), 181 (discretionary), 181 (emergency).

participation for children and adults. Yet, even the number of children with disabilities is not known with much accuracy. For instance, surveys conducted in Colombia between 1993 and 1999 concluded that 2.1 percent, 12 percent, and 24 percent of the population had a disability.[54] In Ireland, the 2006 census reported a population disability rate of 9 percent, but the National Disability Survey conducted later that same year calculated a rate of 18.5 percent.[55] In Uzbekistan, although less than 4 percent of the population aged 7 and older is officially considered disabled, it is estimated that close to 12 percent has a serious difficulty or limitation in physical functioning.[56] Depending on the estimate, there could be between 6 million and 30 million children with disabilities in India.[57]

There is also much more we need to know in relation to legislation and provision of services. The CRPD calls on nations to pass legislation needed for the implementation of the provisions contained in this convention, including equity and nondiscrimination across all areas of life. Although all participating countries will have to submit reports on the steps they take to advance the goals of the convention, there is as of yet no systematic data on which countries have passed equal rights legislation. As well as facilitating citizens' ability to hold their governments accountable for their promises of equity, such information would serve as a resource for countries in the process of developing their own laws to learn from existing legislation. At the most basic level of service provision, do disabled children and adults have unfettered access to the built environment, from schools and health centers to workplaces and voting booths? This question cannot yet be answered comprehensively, but it appears that in many countries, the reality is far from this goal. In Thailand, for example, fewer than 1 percent of public buildings are accessible to mobility-impaired children or adults. As the International Disability Rights Monitor noted, Cambodia had no laws mandating the physical accessibility of public buildings or facilities.[58] Some countries have no legislation requiring accessibility: Belize, Honduras, and Suriname are just three examples.[59] Other countries, like Serbia and Ireland, apply their laws only to public buildings but not to private buildings, which make up the majority.[60] Some, like Peru, have legislation in place but exact no penalties for noncompliance.[61]

Do medical professionals have the training and experience to respond appropriately to the needs of persons with disabilities? Distance and physical inaccessibility can make accessing services next to impossible for many, as can communication barriers when the needs of patients with intellectual, developmental, or communication impairments are not addressed. Even where access to health services is generally very good, persons with disabilities often do not receive the care they need.[62] How often are assistive devices available? Systematic global data are lacking, but individual country statistics are deeply troubling. Only one in 4 people with disabilities in Viet Nam and Cambodia has access to needed assistive devices.[63] In Uzbekistan, only 4 percent of people with hearing impairments wear a hearing aid. In Tajikistan's capital city, Dushanbe, nearly 1 in 5 registered children with disabilities cannot afford to get the wheelchair they need. Glasses are taken for granted in much of the world, and the need for them is rarely considered disabling where they are widely available, but even these are not available to all those who need them, and in their absence basic functions like reading in school may not be possible. In Uzbekistan, for instance, more than half of people with vision difficulties are without glasses or contact lenses.[64]

These and other essential questions have not yet been answered or addressed on a global scale. By any estimate, disabled girls, boys, men, and women make up one of the world's largest minority communities, but they are among the last in most countries—and on the world stage—to have their rights recognized. Not only did the civil rights movement for people living with disabilities lag behind groups marginalized by demographics, but there was also a long-held tacit assumption that it made sense for the disabled to have fewer opportunities, less success, and worse outcomes; it was assumed that these were inherent in the differences. Now, it is increasingly recognized that the limitations faced by children and adults with disabilities are as often a result of the social context in which they find themselves as of intrinsic differences. In order to meet the needs of all their citizens and truly give all children an equal start, nations must do more to meet the needs of children with disabilities. No country can afford to miss out on the full contributions to society and the economy that can be made by millions of children and adults.

Table 8.1. Constitutional guarantees of rights for children and adults with disabilities

	Low-Income	Middle-Income	High-Income
Constitutional Protections of Equity for Persons with Disabilities			
Constitution does not guarantee any aspect of equal treatment specifically to persons with disabilities	23 (66%)	83 (78%)	38 (76%)
Constitution aspires to equal treatment for persons with disabilities in at least one way	1 (3%)	5 (5%)	1 (2%)
Constitution guarantees equal treatment for persons with disabilities in at least one way but allows for exceptions	1 (3%)	2 (2%)	2 (4%)
Constitution guarantees equal treatment for persons with disabilities in at least one way	10 (29%)	16 (15%)	9 (18%)
Positive action may be taken to promote equality for persons with disabilities	3 (9%)	10 (9%)	7 (14%)
Constitutional Protections of Education Rights for Children with Disabilities			
Constitution does not include any protection of education rights specific to children with disabilities	27 (77%)	85 (80%)	42 (84%)
Constitution aspires to protect education rights for children with disabilities	2 (6%)	4 (4%)	1 (2%)
Constitution guarantees education rights to children with disabilities but allows for exceptions	1 (3%)	1 (1%)	1 (2%)
Constitution guarantees education rights to children with disabilities	5 (14%)	16 (15%)	6 (12%)
Positive action may be taken to promote access to education and the full exercise of education rights for children with disabilities	3 (9%)	12 (11%)	3 (6%)

Constitutional Protections of Employment Rights for Adults with Disabilities

Constitution does not include any protection of employment rights specific to adults with disabilities	31 (89%)	82 (77%)	45 (90%)
Constitution aspires to protect employment rights for adults with disabilities	1 (3%)	11 (10%)	1 (2%)
Constitution guarantees employment rights to adults with disabilities but allows for exceptions	1 (3%)	2 (2%)	1 (2%)
Constitution guarantees employment rights to adults with disabilities	2 (6%)	11 (10%)	3 (6%)
Positive action may be taken to promote access to work and the full exercise of employment rights for adults with disabilities	2 (6%)	18 (17%)	4 (8%)

Source : World Policy Analysis Centre: Constitutions Database

Definitions: Protections of equity include prohibitions of discrimination, guarantees of equal rights, guarantees of equality before the law, and guarantees of overall equality.

Guaranteed with exceptions includes cases where equality is guaranteed for the disabled except if "their disability prevents them from exercising" their rights.

Low-income, middle-income, and *high-income* refer to World Bank classifications of national income. Here, middle-income countries include those classified as lower-middle and upper-middle income.

Note: Countries with an aspirational or guaranteed right could also have potential positive action.

Table 8.2. Financial and educational support for children with disabilities

	Low-Income	Middle-Income	High-Income
Availability of Inclusive Special Education for Children with Disabilities in Public Schools			
No special education for children with disabilities provided within the public school system	5 (18%)	3 (3%)	0 (0%)
Children with disabilities attend separate schools within the public system	5 (18%)	14 (16%)	1 (2%)
Children with disabilities may attend the same schools as their peers but are not necessarily taught within the same classrooms	12 (43%)	44 (49%)	6 (13%)
Children with disabilities are able to be taught within the same classrooms as their peers	6 (21%)	29 (32%)	38 (84%)
Government-Provided Family Benefits for Families of Children with Disabilities			
No known family benefits or benefits only in certain circumstances unrelated to disability	19 (61%)	50 (52%)	10 (22%)
Means-tested family benefits, but no additional support for families of children with disabilities	0 (0%)	6 (6%)	1 (2%)
Family benefits are not means-tested, but no additional support for families of children with disabilities	11 (35%)	15 (16%)	2 (4%)
Specific family benefits for children with disabilities	1 (3%)	25 (26%)	32 (71%)

Government-Provided Family Benefits for Low-Income Families with One Severely Disabled School-Age Child (Age 8), PPP-Adjusted

No specific family benefits for children with disabilities	30 (97%)	71 (76%)	13 (33%)
Less than $100 per month for eligible families	1 (3%)	11 (12%)	3 (8%)
$100 - $199.99 per month for eligible families	0 (0%)	6 (6%)	6 (15%)
$200 - $499.99 per month for eligible families	0 (0%)	3 (3%)	4 (10%)
$500 or more per month for eligible families	0 (0%)	2 (2%)	14 (35%)

Government-Provided Family Benefits for Low-Income Families with One Severely Disabled Teenage Child (Age 14), PPP-Adjusted

No specific family benefits for children with disabilities	30 (97%)	73 (78%)	15 (38%)
Less than $100 per month for eligible families	1 (3%)	12 (13%)	3 (8%)
$100 - $199.99 per month for eligible families	0 (0%)	5 (5%)	5 (13%)
$200 - $499.99 per month for eligible families	0 (0%)	2 (2%)	3 (8%)
$500 or more per month for eligible families	0 (0%)	2 (2%)	14 (35%)

Sources : World Policy Analysis Centre, Education Database and Poverty Database.

Definitions: Means-tested benefits are available only to families with incomes below a certain threshold.
Not-means-tested benefits are available to families without considering their income.
To determine *purchasing power parity (PPP),* economists estimate the amount of money required to purchase the same bundle of goods and services across countries rather than using a simple exchange rate.

Chapter 9

Changing Children's Chances

Isabella's life, take 1: Isabella lived in a small house with her parents and her two younger siblings. Her father cleaned city streets at night, and her mother worked in a textile factory; neither had completed more than a basic education. At the age of 14, Isabella was finally completing primary school. While she enjoyed learning and liked going to school to see her friends, her packed classroom was frequently too loud for her to concentrate, and she didn't like her teacher; she couldn't answer many of the questions that Isabella asked about math and geography. Like most teachers in her school, Isabella's had completed only a lower-secondary level of education herself, the minimum that primary school teachers were required to complete, and she was not well equipped with teaching strategies and background knowledge.

Isabella wouldn't be attending secondary school. The tuition fees required even in public schools were too much for her parents to afford, despite their two incomes. Since she had turned 11, Isabella had been working as well as going to school to add a little more income to her family's meager resources. With few laws against child labor and a minimum wage so low that many families couldn't make ends meet on parents' wages alone, almost everyone around her age that she knew worked somewhere in town. She worked most evenings, and one day on the weekend; she rarely had time to finish her homework, and she was often so tired at school that she dozed off. She had repeated the final year of primary three times. While it had taken her three extra years to finish primary school, many of her friends weren't in school at all.

Isabella's life, take 2: Isabella lived in a small house with her parents and her two younger siblings. Her father cleaned city streets at night, and her mother worked in a textile factory; neither had received more than a basic education. At the age of 11, Isabella was getting ready to enter secondary school. She enjoyed learning and liked going to school to see her friends; she was excited to start a new school with nearly all of them. Enrollment and attendance were high at the tuition-free local public school. Isabella dreamed of becoming a teacher herself, and she knew that meant that she would have to finish a college degree; it was required in order to teach.

Both of Isabella's parents earned the nationally guaranteed minimum wage. It was enough to keep the children fed, clothed, and in school. Isabella knew just one classmate who was already working, and he had to hide it very well because he was too young to work, and his employer could receive a huge fine if he was discovered. Her younger sister had been diagnosed with a learning disability that made it hard for her to learn to read. At first, her parents had been worried that they would not be able to afford the needed tutoring, but the principal had assured them that it was provided by the school for children who needed it. Her sister's teacher had been trained to adapt her teaching techniques to the needs of her students, and her sister received attention from a learning specialist once per week.

Millions of children's lives could be transformed if countries committed to giving all children an equal chance. This book began with the recognition that public policies as well as parents matter for children's chances, and sought to answer the question: where does the world stand when it comes to ensuring all children have an equal opportunity for healthy development? This final chapter presents some of the book's key findings, the results of a decade of investigation into laws and policies around the world, and highlights areas of success and failure. We go on to discuss proposed strategic steps that will enable the world to move forward on making equal chances for children a reality. Finally, we examine the specific and important roles that policymakers, individuals, organizations, and the private sector can play in this process of change.

Making Progress on Some of the Basics

Important progress has been made in many of the basic areas that are important for children and youth. This progress demonstrates the feasibility of significant change when there is political will for it.

In basic education, the world has come a long way. The majority of countries in the world, 166, have made primary education tuition-free, reducing the barriers to schooling faced by poor children, and primary schooling is compulsory in all but 15 countries.* These policy advances have yielded results—around the world, primary enrollment rates have increased substantially. In sub-Saharan Africa, for example, net primary enrollment rates jumped from 56 percent to 73 percent in just 8 years.[1] Additionally, nearly all countries have taken initial steps to address the educational needs of children with disabilities—all but 8 countries have public provision of some degree of special education.[†] Beyond education, countries have taken steps toward basic child protection in the area of labor. In 130 countries, the minimum age for hazardous work is set at 18.[‡]

Countries have taken steps to ensure that children are able to receive needed care from their parents and that fewer find themselves in extreme poverty. Although the minimum wage as an income-improving policy has been debated, studies from around the world have shown that minimum-wage increases can improve wages and reduce child poverty with no or minimal effects on employment rates.[2] Minimum wages can also contribute to wage increases in the informal economy.[3] In 167 countries, low-income working parents are protected by the establishment of a minimum wage through legislation or collective bargaining. Beyond an adequate earned income, families may need temporary income support to avoid falling into poverty during job transitions that involve periods of unemployment; we found that most countries, 163, recognize the need for income support during

---

* World Policy Analysis Centre, Education Database.
† World Policy Analysis Centre, Education Database.
‡ World Policy Analysis Centre, Child Labour Database.

this time through unemployment insurance or severance pay.* Income is also protected during periods of temporary leave to care for newborn children. Around the world, providing paid leave for new mothers is the norm; just 8 countries fail to do so.†

Falling Far Short of Equal Chances

While these and other global successes demonstrate the feasibility of improving conditions for children and families, the world is far from providing equal chances for healthy development for all children.

Secondary education is fundamental to employment opportunities and the ability to exit poverty, and has long-term implications for health. Yet far more work remains to make secondary education accessible: 120 countries make secondary education tuition-free until completion, but 38 countries have not eliminated this barrier.‡ The tuition charged makes accessing secondary and higher education unaffordable for children in the poorest families. Additionally, while most countries provide some special education for children with disabilities in the public system, less than half of countries, 73, include children with and without disabilities in the same classrooms, and in 28 countries they cannot even attend the same schools.§

If all children are to have a chance of success in school and beyond, more than the affordability of school is required; children need access to a quality education. Currently, even those children who can attend secondary school may be taught by teachers with little more education themselves. Despite evidence from around the world that higher educational levels among teachers benefit student learning,[4] in 48 countries, teachers at the lower secondary level are required to have completed no higher than a secondary level of education themselves. The same is true for upper secondary-school teachers in 30 countries.‖

Though most countries have set a minimum age for hazardous work at 18, these laws have far too many loopholes that allow employers to

---

*World Policy Analysis Centre, Poverty Database.
†World Policy Analysis Centre, Adult Labour Database.
‡World Policy Analysis Centre, Education Database.
§World Policy Analysis Centre, Education Database.
‖World Policy Analysis Centre, Education Database.

hire children younger than the minimum age. When exceptions to the stated minimum age are taken into account, children and youth under the age of 18 are not protected from performing hazardous work in 83 countries. Furthermore, children and youth should also be protected from long hours of labor at least until the end of secondary school, but in 103 countries, children can be working full-time under the age of 16, not old enough to allow for the completion of high school. Evidence from around the world shows that even work that is not full-time can hurt children's chances at school,[5] and many countries are not protecting children from working long hours on school days: in 118 countries, children can work more than 6 hours on school days at age 15 or younger.*

For girls, labor often comes in the form of domestic work, including paid work outside the home and unpaid work within their family's home or their husband's. Data from over 60 countries shows that as the number of hours that children work increases, whether they are doing market work, domestic work, or a combination, their school attendance decreases.[6] As well as making school dropout more likely,[7] early marriage leaves girls with less autonomy,[8] higher odds of abuse within their marriage,[9] and higher odds of illness, injury, and death during childbirth.[10] The minimum legal age for marriage remains too low to protect children in many countries and often also includes gender inequities. Girls can be married below the age of 18 in 99 countries. Among these, 42 countries do not protect girls from marriage at 15 or younger. Boys tend to be better protected than girls—only 64 countries allow boys to marry below the age of 18.†

While initial steps have been taken to ensure that parents can support their children, we have not yet come far enough. Although a minimum wage has been set in most of the world, in 40 countries this wage is so low that it would leave a family consisting of one working adult and one child living at or below the widely recognized poverty line of $2.00 per person per day, adjusted for purchasing power parity.‡ Children do not have the same opportunity to benefit from their father's early care as their mother's—only 81 countries provide paid

---

*World Policy Analysis Centre, Child Labour Database.
†World Policy Analysis Centre, Child Marriage Database.
‡World Policy Analysis Centre, Poverty Database.

leave for new fathers through paternity leave, parental leave, or a combination of both, and in nearly half these countries, fathers can take just 3 weeks or fewer of paid leave.* This discrepancy undermines gender equity at home and at work, as well as limiting children's time with their fathers from the beginning.

Parental availability is important beyond infancy, especially when children need support for their health or educational needs; evidence clearly shows that parental involvement makes a difference to children's outcomes.[11] Our data reveal that in much of the world, mothers and fathers risk income and job loss if they take time off from work to care for a sick child or address a child's educational needs, despite evidence that these work protections are affordable and do not impede countries from being economically competitive and having low unemployment rates.[12] Only 54 countries provide parents with paid leave specifically to meet their children's health needs, and 16 countries guarantee unpaid leave for this purpose. Even fewer countries, just 3 worldwide, provide either paid or unpaid leave specifically to meet children's educational needs.†

Beyond these legislative gaps, many of the lowest-income parents are working in the informal economy; these families are rarely guaranteed leave for children's needs, an income floor, or other protections. As just one example, though income protection during unemployment can be designed to include the self-employed (thus covering at least part of the informal economy), most countries have provided no safety net in case of job loss for these parents—the self-employed can opt to be included in government unemployment benefits in just 28 countries.‡

Is It All about the Money?

Is the failure to meet and raise standards simply a reflection of inadequate resources at the national level? There is little doubt that successful economies have more resources at their disposal to invest in children. Even when a higher-income country invests the same percentage

---

*World Policy Analysis Centre, Adult Labour Database.
†World Policy Analysis Centre, Adult Labour Database.
‡World Policy Analysis Centre, Poverty Database.

of gross domestic product (GDP) as a lower-income country, it will have more absolute dollars to invest in child health, education, and an income floor. Indeed, low-income countries are frequently among the countries with fewer services for children. Children in poor countries are less likely to have access to health professionals at birth and throughout childhood, more likely to be permitted to do hazardous or full-time work, and more likely to be taught by teachers with a low level of education and training, as just a few examples. On the other hand, economic resources are no guarantee of progressive policies—despite its powerful economy, the United States is one of only 8 countries in the world that does not guarantee paid maternal leave.

Could countries be funding more themselves? When it comes to investing in child health and education, although the final dollar amounts will differ, all nations should be expected to devote a reasonable proportion of their GDP, and many could be doing better. Over 80 percent of the countries that do not have enough health professionals to provide basic services spend less than 4 percent of their GDP on health. In the 29 countries where 50 percent or less of births are attended by skilled health personnel, 21 spend less than 3 percent of GDP on health. Close to one-third of the countries with at least 40 students per teacher in primary school spend less than 3 percent of their GDP on education. Of the 38 countries that begin charging tuition before the end of secondary school, 13 spend less than 4 percent of their GDP on education.[13]

Importantly, not all low- and middle-income countries are falling behind on children's chances—there are low- and middle-income countries that have been able to make important advances for children and families in many policy areas. For example, Chile has stronger child-labor laws than its neighbors, prohibiting full-time employment until age 18 with no major exceptions. Its child-labor rates are less than half those of economically similar Argentina.[14] Kenya makes education compulsory for 12 years, longer than all other countries in its region; spends more on education as a proportion of GDP than most of its neighbors; and has a higher minimum age for full-time employment than its neighbors. It is noteworthy that gross enrollment ratios in secondary education in Kenya are nearly double those in neighboring Uganda and Tanzania.[15] As well as paid maternal leave, Madagascar provides paid leave for children's health and for family needs, one year of breastfeeding breaks at work, and a wage premium for night work. Although many factors are likely to contribute, it is not surprising that Madagascar's infant and child mortality rates are among the lowest in sub-Saharan Africa, given the importance of breastfeeding and parental or quality adult care in infancy.[16] Despite its conflict-ridden history and ongoing problems, Sri Lanka is one of only two countries in South Asia that have free education from primary through university, and it makes schooling compulsory for 9 years. These policies are reflected in the outcomes of the country's children—primary enrollment and completion are close to 100 percent, over 90 percent of students progress to secondary school, and enrollment in higher education is rapidly increasing.[17]

Many protections, such as prohibiting discrimination or banning child marriage, have dramatic benefits with few financial costs. Moreover, many of the needed investments yield substantial economic gains for countries, as well as for the individuals affected. In the case of education, for example, studies from around the world have documented the economic returns to investment in terms of national economic growth.[18] A 50-country study found increasing the average amount of schooling completed by 1 year could raise GDP by 0.37 percent annually.[19] A study of 65 low-income, middle-income, and transition countries found that these nations forgo a staggering $92 billion in economic growth each year by failing to educate male and female children to the same level.[20] If OECD countries increased their average standardized test scores by 0.25 standard deviations in the next 20 years, they could expect a total increase of $115 trillion in aggregate GDP over the lifetime of those born in 2010.[21]

What Would It Take for All Children to Thrive?

If children in all countries, regardless of background, are going to have a chance to thrive and not just survive, a number of steps must be taken.

Set Our Sights Higher

Children's Chances has made the case that we need to set goals beyond the basics for children at home and around the world. These goals should and can transform the quality of life during childhood and how it affects adulthood. What components are essential to incorporate when we set those goals? The strengths and gaps in current global policies highlight the areas where action is needed.

First, the ability of parents to provide care during childhood is critical. We need to ensure that parental care is feasible not only when infants are born, but also when children are sick and when they are having trouble in school. Parents need to be able to earn an adequate income while caring for their children. Second, all children need access to the known and effective public health interventions that can prevent many of the leading causes of death, disease, and disability. In case of illness or disability, all children need access to affordable medical care to increase the odds that his or her quality of life will remain unaffected. Third, to be able to earn an income high enough to exit poverty, any individual is likely to need education at the secondary and postsecondary levels; all children should have realistic and affordable access to a high-quality secondary and postsecondary education. Inclusive education should be provided to children with special needs. Fourth, children need a chance at childhood without working such extensive hours that attending school or studying is impossible, and without being married and having to raise a family too young. Labor regulations should limit the hours that children can work until the end of secondary school, and laws should set an age of marriage high enough to protect young girls and boys. Finally, all children and adults need equal legal rights with discrimination prohibited. Children's opportunities and chance at healthy development should not be limited by their gender, disability status, ethnicity, religion, or other characteristics.

Recognize Critical Complementarities

To improve children's chances, we need to take a comprehensive approach. The responses that support children's healthy development depend on each other. Different actors in the global community have tended to focus on addressing individual aspects of the risks children face—in health, education, labor, and other areas—rather than improving their cumulative chances. But it is far more effective to address children's most important needs together than to target success in one area at a time. Success in one area has the potential to enhance success in other areas, and failure in one area increases the likelihood of failure in another.

The case of poverty, health, and education illustrates this well. When families are guaranteed a decent level of income, they are less likely to keep their children out of school to do paid labor or household chores and are better able to purchase the small supplies needed for school. Poor water and sanitation, leading to repeated bouts of diarrhea and malnutrition, impair children's chances at learning even before they start school. When children are in good health, they are more likely to succeed at school. At the same time, education profoundly affects health and poverty. When children receive more education during childhood, their health benefits throughout the life course. Around the world, higher educational attainment has been linked with better health and lower risks of mortality.[22] Education also deeply affects an individual's odds of living in poverty during adulthood and the chance that his or her children will be raised in poverty. Studies from high-, middle-, and low-income countries show that men and women who have completed more education are more likely to be employed than those with less, they are likely to earn more, and gender gaps in employment rates tend to decrease.[23]

These same interrelationships apply to other areas of child policy as well. Children's odds of suffering from pneumonia, for example, are strongly affected by their family income—their chances of becoming ill drastically increase when they are undernourished, when they live in overcrowded conditions, and when they are exposed to greater indoor air pollution,[24] as children living in poverty are more likely to be. Children living in poverty are also at higher risk of injury; this is true when they labor instead of going to school, live in poor-quality housing in urban slums, or are left alone or in poor care.[25]

Transform Knowledge into Action

Nations cannot be expected to act in the absence of knowledge of where they stand and where they should be heading. They need to understand where improvements are required, what works to address the key problems, and whether these actions are feasible. Individuals cannot press their governments to act without knowing what commitments have been made, whether the nation is living up to them, and what more needs to be done. Globally comparative sources of information on what makes a difference to children's life chances, where nations currently stand on the policies and outcomes that matter, and what changes need to be made are necessary.

As individuals, organizations, and policymakers work for change, they have been helped when clear information became available—as it did in efforts to reduce infant mortality—and hampered where there has been a dearth of information about where countries stand. While much more information would be useful, the World Policy Analysis Centre and this book have sought to break the ice on public policies and begin the process of making information widely and readily available on what all countries are doing—or failing to do—in giving children and youth an equal start.

Information on laws, policies, and implementation should be made readily available both to citizens within individual countries and to people around the world. It should be updated regularly and be easily comparable across countries. Although making this information publicly available benefits all children by showing nations a way forward and allowing citizens to hold governments accountable, this information is especially important for marginalized populations. When problems are invisible, marginalized children and families are the least likely to be able to afford to pay tuition, to have access to clean water, to study without having to labor, to have their basic needs met, or to have the political power to press for change in the absence of recognized problems. Democratizing access to information can make nations that are leaders or laggards visible, can change power dynamics, and can allow all people to hold their governments accountable for equal enjoyment of and access to rights and services.

Ensure Implementation

Once laws are enacted and policies are put in place, attention must focus on implementation. The legal cases discussed in this book tell two stories: first, that legal rights can transform our ability to give all children an equal chance; second, that these laws are not enough. If having child labor laws on paper were enough, groups in Nepal would not have had to sue the government for recruiting children and youth into the police force and army.[26] If guaranteeing equal rights for girls and women in the constitution were sufficient, national and international protesters would not have had to fight for equal rights for girls and women in Afghanistan in the face of new discriminatory legislation.[27] If prohibiting discrimination against persons with disabilities were enough, then the parents of a disabled girl in Canada would not have had to pursue a court case in order for their daughter to be included in the same classroom as her peers.[28]

Ensuring that rights are realized and services are delivered requires monitoring implementation and holding countries accountable for their commitments. If labor law prohibits children from working full-time under a given age, nations need to take steps to ensure that these children are not working, that their families are able to support themselves without this income, and that they are able to go to school. If schools are supposed to be tuition-free, we need to find out whether in practice students are not charged. Beyond tuition, additional expenses required for books, uniforms, or other school necessities can create significant financial obstacles for the poorest families. If discrimination is prohibited in public services, nations need to ensure that this prohibition is enforced and that members of all groups have equal access.

Ensuring that all children have equal chances will require paying attention to whether laws are being implemented equitably, as well as whether they are equitable in their design. Large disparities can be introduced in implementation. A common example is when the best public services are in neighborhoods serving the wealthiest children. Enforcement systems can also be differentially implemented across groups.

Global organizations could set up a system for reporting transparently what countries do on all the commitments that they have made; this system could build on national efforts. National statistical agencies and bilateral and multilateral organizations currently conduct hundreds of national surveys every year. If core indicators regarding children's basic needs, protection from child labor and child marriage, and the extent of access to quality education and health care were included, the world could track the degree and equity of implementation with powerful implications.

Contributing to Change

A mother from the American Midwest, a researcher in Pretoria, South Africa, a business executive in New Delhi, a student in Miami, Florida, and others have reached out to us after reading our past research findings on children and families to ask how they could make a difference. Each of us has something to contribute to changing children's chances around the world. So we hope you do not mind this book ending with examples of what we each can do.

Policymakers

If you are a policymaker, the steps are perhaps straightforward. Find out what your country is doing, and find out what barriers are still faced by parents and children. Are the laws and policies in place to ensure an equal chance? Are there critical holes in ensuring access to quality higher education, a chance at childhood free of the adult responsibilities of labor and family, the ability of parents and others to care for children in the community, and a life free of discrimination? If so, put the missing pieces in place. There are plenty of examples from countries in every region and at every income level that can be drawn on. If the laws and policies are in place but are not being implemented, focus there and hold governments to account for enforcement.

National government leaders have long employed rhetoric about the importance of the next generation, but their actions on the issue have been limited. Much can be done in rich and poor countries alike. As the data in Chapters 2 and 4 illustrate, there is substantial variation in the percentage of GDP being spent on children. Low-income countries have fewer dollars to spend, but those offering the poorest educational opportunities to children often invest particularly low percentages of GDP in children's education and health. They need to invest more, and the evidence shows doing so will pay dividends in national economic growth. In high-income countries, investments need to be made more equally across all children and youth. The high cost of rising inequalities in healthy development and educational outcomes is amply demonstrated in countries like the United States where national competitiveness in educational outcomes has fallen far behind and the economy is at risk of long-term stagnation.

Policymakers also have a role to play at a global level. When 189 countries came together in the year 2000 to agree on the Millennium Development Goals, basic standards were set that would matter to those worst off in countries around the world. Countries committed to advancing these goals and to reporting whether they had achieved measurable targets. The Millennium Development Goals were a huge step forward in terms of creating international consensus around key issues for children and adults worldwide.

As strong as this accomplishment was as a starting point, these goals are far too low to serve as an ending point. Take, for example, the goal of "eradicating extreme poverty and hunger." Although the shorthand is eradication, the actual goal is to cut the proportion of people living in poverty and hunger in half. Moreover, even though the goal was set in 2000, this halving was to occur from the benchmark level of 1990, not 2000, so that not as much actual progress was required. Even if the goal to halve poverty is met by 2015, 920 million people will still be living in extreme poverty on less than $1.25 per day.[29] The global goal for child mortality was a two-thirds reduction between 1990 and 2015. Even if this goal is met, there will still be more than 30 child deaths per 1,000 live births—a rate many times higher than what is achievable. In other areas relevant to children, while gender equity was made an explicit concern in education past the primary level, universal access to secondary and tertiary education was not.

As we approach the 2015 deadline for the Millennium Development Goals, attention is focused on the next round of targets. This is an opportunity for policymakers worldwide to set global goals high enough for children to truly thrive, and contribute to transforming children's chances.

Individuals and Organizations

Policymakers are not the only ones who can act. If you are a writer or reporter, have you written on children's issues lately? Far more print and Internet space is devoted to adults' needs than children's. Often the stories that are written tell of the individual traumas and resilience of a boy or girl, worth telling but leaving readers feeling that they have no role to play. You can help address that by writing about what can be done to change their circumstances. If you are a computer programmer, improving access to information relies greatly on your skills. It would make a world of difference to have such simple devices as a smartphone app that told consumers whether an item they are thinking of purchasing was made with child labor. Information combined with consumer action could dramatically change the economic incentives for using children as laborers. If you are a special-needs educator, the need for teachers to work around the world training other educators is enormous. We have highlighted some of the gaps in the number of trained teachers globally; the shortfall is even greater in the case of students with special needs. The list of what specialists can contribute goes on.

Everyone has a unique set of skills and background, but there are also common assets we all bring to making a difference in children's lives. As you cast your vote in an election, think about what candidates are committing to do to ensure that all children have an equal chance. Learn what your country is doing right, but also where it is lagging behind others. Anyone who wants more information on where his or her country could move forward can visit our website: http://www.chil drenschances.org. Let your representatives know that you care about these policies for children. All elected officials count e-mails, letters, and calls. Public officials respond to constituent concerns. The problem is that they rarely hear from constituents about the needs of children who are most marginalized. If every reader called his or her congressional representative or member of Parliament, it would make an enormous difference. If each reader not only called but over the course of a month talked five other people into calling or writing their representative, the ball would start rolling. If those who are already actively engaged made sure that every time they asked representatives to do more for children in their own community, they also asked representatives to do more for children in a poorer or more marginalized community, political leaders would begin to experience a sea change.

Although there is a great deal that every country can do for children within its own borders, the poorest countries will also need assistance if their children are to have an equal chance. At the time of this writing, overseas development assistance as a proportion of gross national income averages less than 0.3 percent in G7 countries.[30] If they were to increase this even to the 0.7 percent that they have promised at a series of international meetings, it would still represent a tiny fraction of their wealth but would be enough money to make a real difference in children's lives and the lives of many of those living in poverty. These resources can be used for education and public health measures that provide the foundation for equal chances. They do not replace, nor should they, countries' independent action, but they are an essential tool. The problem is that right now many citizens think that their country spends a great deal more on foreign assistance than it in fact does.[31] Let your representative know that you would like to see dollars spent on children worldwide.

For students who want to take action, there is little doubt that you have all the tools at your disposal. The power of recent student action like the antisweatshop movement and the movement to ensure that people around the world have access to essential medicines have powerfully demonstrated over and over again what student leadership, commitment, and innovation can do to move toward a more equitable global community.

Beyond individuals, if organizations and movements were to broaden their agendas to include the impact on equal chances for children, here too the results would be dramatic. Two examples are illustrative. MomsRising is a network in the United States, founded in 2006, that aims to educate the public and lobby for progress on issues affecting children and families and has rapidly come to play an important role in encouraging and passing child- and family-related policies and laws.[32] Given its origins, the overwhelming majority of its efforts are focused on American children. It would be transformative if 1 in 10 of its calls for action were about the world's children. The Occupy movement, which has spread across the world, has focused on inequalities experienced by adults, but those inequalities are often rooted in and reverberate in children's lives. If solutions proposed by movement members included a focus on what it would mean to give equal chances to children, here too the impact would be large.

Private-Sector Roles

Although this book has focused on what the public sector can do to ensure that all children have a fair start, in nearly every area there can also be an important role for the private sector. Whether or not laws guarantee adequate protections to working parents and children, companies should provide what is needed to support children's healthy development. The ability of families to meet many basic needs is heavily determined by income. It is critical that private companies pay a living wage to all their employees. This is as economically feasible as it is essential. In *Profit at the Bottom of the Ladder*, Harvard Business Press published the results of our 6-year global study documenting how firms in a wide range of economic sectors around the world have improved the working conditions, income, and assets of their lowest-level employees at the same time as becoming more successful financially.[33]

Parental working conditions beyond wages profoundly affect children's lives. Health provides one example. Child health depends on health-care services, but it also depends on the ability of parents to bring their children for preventive care, diagnosis, or treatment when they are ill or injured, and to follow up when they have chronic conditions. When parents' places of employment provide leave and flexibility, they are able to succeed at work while providing their children with the care they need. When workplaces create insurmountable barriers to meeting children's health needs and penalize those fathers and mothers who attempt to do so, their sons and daughters pay the price. The same is true for the ability of working parents to interact with their children's schools and address their educational needs.

Beyond its role as employer, the private sector produces goods that matter to children, and the accessibility of these goods is important. Businesses supplying materials for health-care services and education need to be profitable just like any other firm. Moreover, for these sectors to advance, firms need to be able to invest profits sufficiently in new product research and development. However, these objectives can be accomplished in a way that makes products affordable only in rich countries or in a way that makes them affordable to children across all income levels around the world. Pharmaceutical products provide an illustration of this. From hepatitis immunizations to HIV/AIDS treatment, when the same prices were set for affluent countries and poor countries, the results were few sales, little availability to people in poor countries, and similarly small financial returns from poor countries. When two-tier pricing schemes allowed pricing closer to marginal cost in poor countries and average cost in rich countries, the amount of economic return businesses received from low-income countries changed little (because there was little financial return beforehand), but the availability of essential medicines dramatically increased.[34]

In many of the areas discussed in this book, the combined efforts of the public and private sector will produce more than either alone. As just a few examples, when most companies want to pay a decent living wage, they are helped by a government floor that sets the minimum wage. This prevents the most exploitative companies from competing with lower prices based on unlivable wages and, as a result, makes it more feasible for other companies to pay wages they believe in. Similarly, in the case of child labor, companies who hire adults and pay reasonable wages should not have to compete with companies whose products cost far less because they are hiring children and paying them substandard wages while eliminating any chance they have at an education. When countries set up social insurance systems to pay for parental leave, both parents and companies benefit. When paid parental leave is guaranteed, employees are far more likely to return to the same employer after the birth or adoption of a new child than in the absence of this leave. Companies are able to retain skilled and knowledgeable workers, and children fare better. Likewise, public-sector policies that improve access to education and health benefit not only children and families but also companies that will profit from the resulting better-educated and healthier workforce. While private-sector leaders do not determine the laws, they are active both in national lawmaking and in global forums as individuals and with lobby groups that consider many of these issues. The positions that companies take in each of these areas will make a difference.

The world could be transformed as dramatically by national action devoted to giving all children an equal chance as it was by the industrial, communications, and transportation revolutions. If all children and youth were to receive health care, live free of child labor and child marriage, and get a good education beyond the primary level, the amount of human capital that we could turn to solving global problems would increase manyfold, and inequities both within and among countries would be reduced on a scale that has long been hoped for but rarely achieved. It is hard to imagine many things that would change individual and global realities more profoundly than if all children were given an equal chance.

Appendix 1

The World Policy
Analysis Centre

The World Policy Analysis Centre is an initiative that I lead at the Institute for Health and Social Policy at McGill University. This initiative aims to significantly improve the level and quality of comparative data on public policies available to people in countries around the world, to global and national policymakers, to civil society and private-sector leaders, and to researchers. The World Policy Analysis Centre to date includes, among other components, education, discrimination, equity, health, disability, family, parental labor, child labor, child marriage, and income policies as well as social, economic, civil, and political rights. Each of the databases spans a wide range of topics important to children and adults, from which we selected the elements we felt were most critical for children to present in this book. This appendix details the overall approach to database construction, as well as describing in greater detail the processes followed for the particular topics and variables used in this book. Further information is available at http://www.childrenschances.org.

Building the World Policy Analysis Centre

When we were determining what types of laws, rights, and policies should be included in the data center, we gave priority to policies that are supported in two ways: with research evidence on their importance to human development, health, or well-being in a variety of geographic, social, and economic circumstances; and with widespread global consensus on their value. If a policy mattered only under a very particular set of circumstances, it was unlikely to make our list.

Data Sources

In selecting data sources to analyze, we had several priorities. Did the source provide primary data on the question we were looking for? For example, if we were looking for information about labor protections, we would always rather read the labor laws themselves (a primary source) than a secondary summary or description of them. Primary sources allowed us to better understand the law or policy and helped us avoid errors that might have been introduced in the secondary sources. Working with primary sources also had the advantage of enabling us to provide links to actual legislation and constitutions for those interested in passing new laws or creating reform in their countries. Documents were reviewed in their original language or in a translation into one of the UN's official languages.

When legislation was not available, either because it had not been collected or because we were examining areas that are often not legislated, such as education policy, we gave priority to country reports on their policies submitted to international organizations. We recognize the limitations of country reports, primarily that countries may claim to be doing more than they in fact are in order to cast a more favorable light on their approach, but this limitation is partially mitigated by countries' awareness that nongovernmental organizations and experts will have the opportunity to make recorded comments on the accuracy of many reports to the UN that are linked to international agreements. We turned to official country reports for two reasons. First, as we reviewed the reports, it became clear that many countries do acknowledge gaps in their laws, policies, and programs. For example, many countries that charge tuition for education acknowledge this in their reports to the International Bureau of Education. Second, we saw them as a source for initial mapping that national governments, having filed the reports themselves, would find valid.

Although we used primary data and global sources whenever possible, we also used secondary sources when information was unclear or lacking on particular countries, or when a substantial number of countries were missing even from the most comprehensive sources. In choosing these secondary sources, we gave priority to those that were comparable across multiple countries, such as regional sources. When we were using information sources that covered a limited number of countries, we aimed to ensure that the information they contained could be made consistent with our other sources.

Coding Frameworks

Conceptually, frameworks had to be developed that allowed the comparison of laws and policies across all the world's countries, even when there was a great deal of variation in the approach taken by individual nations. Questions that originally seemed simple to answer across all countries rarely were. For instance, countries do not simply prohibit or allow child labor below a certain age; many permit work below the minimum age in certain industries or under specific conditions. Once children are allowed to work, there is a range of legislation addressing when they can work, for how long, and under what conditions. As another example, we originally thought that the minimum wage could be captured by a few currency figures. However, we found enormous variation in everything from how the minimum wage was set to how it was determined whether and when it was increased to who was exempted. The minimum wage was straightforward compared with analyzing a question like equal rights in constitutions. What domains should constitutions cover in providing equal rights? Does it matter if they have a general equal-protection clause but do not spell out specific groups? Which named groups should be captured, and how can this be done consistently? As well, citizens are rarely simply denied or granted certain rights; these rights are subject to provisions regarding whether they can be denied under certain circumstances, whether the nation guarantees the right or just aspires to it, whether positive action can be taken for certain populations, and whether citizens are permitted to defend the right in court, among others.

In developing analytic approaches for each policy area, we began with the essential features, based in intrinsic characteristics of the policy, research evidence on important features, and global agreement where it existed. For example, in the case of child labor, international agreements and the evidence base distinguish light work from general employment and hazardous work. In the case of equal rights in constitutions, international agreements have forged consensus on the importance of equal rights across a wide range of features, including gender, ethnicity, and disability, among others; they also underscore the importance of equal rights in social and economic as well as civil and political areas.

After determining a set of key features, research-team members read laws and policies from 20 to 30 countries to develop closed-ended categories according to which these features could be coded while capturing the full variety of approaches taken by countries. They then tested this coding system on an additional 10 to 20 nations before implementing it for all countries.

Our priority was to ensure that the richness and variety of approaches that different countries took were well captured. At times, research teams would have already analyzed 60 to 80 countries before coming across single countries whose approach to a particular problem was different enough in important ways that it could not be adequately captured within the coding scheme. In these cases, the coding scheme was revised to add the elements necessary to capture new features of legislation and policymaking that had presented themselves. All previously coded nations were reviewed to determine whether the revised coding system would alter how they were analyzed. In other words, the new coding system, better adapted to the full variety of approaches nations around the world take, was applied in the end to all countries.

The data sources available contained systematic information on legislation and policies but not on implementation. To ensure consistent approaches across countries, reports that contained comprehensive information on policies but only limited incidental information on implementation were coded only for policies. Obtaining systematic sources of information on implementation should be a pressing priority for global organizations.

Coding Process

Coding is the process by which an individual researcher takes a piece of information on legislation, policy, or constitutions and translates it into a set of features that can be mapped, quantitatively analyzed, and readily understood and shared. For example, a researcher would review many pieces of labor legislation and use them to answer such questions as the following: At what age can children or youth engage in hazardous work? How many hours are they permitted to work per day or per week? To capture this information as reliably as possible, coding was carried out as often as possible by team members fluent in the relevant language of the original documents or in the language into which it had been translated by a UN source.

Although the coding was designed to be as straightforward as possible to increase reliability, some questions required judgment calls. To make our approach transparent and consistent, the rules for making these judgments were captured systematically in a codebook used by all involved in the particular database.

Policies, laws, constitutions, reports, and secondary sources were coded independently twice, and the results of each coding were compared to minimize human error. Where there was disagreement due to human error and the answer was straightforward, the coding was corrected. Where researchers arrived at different conclusions based on judgment, the two researchers discussed the best answer on the basis of coding guidelines and coded their consensus answer. Where they did not agree, a team meeting was called to determine the best way to proceed.

Accuracy, Analysis, and Updating

Nations that were outliers on particular policies were verified using external sources whenever possible. We recognize that even with all the efforts to provide information that is as accurate as possible, errors in version 1.0 are nearly inevitable. The UN and other sources we used may not always have the most up-to-date legislation where primary data were used. Any error or omission in national reports that we used will also be reflected in our data. Finally, even with the double coding, the research team can make errors. We look forward to receiving feedback from readers if they believe that any individual countries have been placed in the wrong category. We will update country reports in our databases when we receive new primary sources of legislation or policy, indicating that changes should be made.

National and Subnational Levels

Until now, the information in the World Policy Analysis Centre has focused largely on the national level. However, in federal systems, states or provinces may legislate a variety of areas relevant to children. In some cases, omitting subnational legislation is not a significant omission—in China, for example, laws can be passed by provinces as well as the national government, but most legislation is in fact passed nationally. In other countries, like the United States, labor legislation may be equally passed by the federal government and by states, but historically, once most states have had guarantees, these have typically become federal. However, in other federal contexts, like Canada, federal and provincial jurisdictions are quite distinct. Many social policies are under the jurisdiction only of provinces. In this case, not having subnational information is a greater omission.

Currently, our data on parental working conditions and some child labor laws incorporate subnational data for the United States, Canada, India, China, and Australia. In cases where all states or provinces provide a guarantee, we credit the country with a national guarantee. Where some states lack protections, the country is recorded as guaranteeing all its citizens only the amount of the lowest state guarantee. In the future, we hope that a team will be able to search for and analyze state and provincial policies and laws in all federal systems for each relevant policy area.

Education Database

Several sources of global data were analyzed to create the Education Database. Reports produced by UNESCO's International Bureau of Education for its fifth (2003), sixth (2006/2007), and seventh editions (2010/2011, as much as available as of February 2012) were all systematically analyzed by our research team to translate this wealth of qualitative data into a quantitatively comparable dataset.[1] These reports profile the education systems of 161 countries, largely on the basis of national reports submitted to the UN. We chose to use these reports as the principal source for several reasons. These reports were the most comprehensive source of data on educational systems and policies available covering a majority of countries. Moreover, these reports were prepared using similar structures and consistently reported the same kinds of information across countries. Also used were reports on the development of education submitted by national governments for the 48th International Conference on Education (2008),[2] which are available for 116 countries and focus particularly on special education, allowing the inclusion of much more information on this topic than would have been available from the International Bureau of Education reports alone.

When information on policies affecting access to and quality of education was incomplete in these sources, they were supplemented by analyzing information available through the following sources:

- Planipolis contains education policies and assessment reports from UNESCO member states and allowed some missing information to be filled in.[3]

- The Millennium Development Goals Reports (2003–2009) and the Education for All Mid-Decade Assessment Reports were used to confirm or fill in information when it was lacking, most often regarding whether education at various levels was free and/or compulsory.[4]

- Eurydice—Network on Education Systems and Policies in Europe was used to fill in missing information for European countries. It consists of encyclopedia-like entries on the educational systems of 33 countries.[5]

- The World Bank's report *Financing Higher Education in Africa* provided information on tuition fees in higher education in African countries.[6]

- *The State of the Right to Education Worldwide—Free or Fee: 2006 Global Report*, a report by Katrina Tomasevski, the UN Special Rapporteur on the Right to Education, was the source of some information when no additional sources were available regarding tuition fees.[7]

Education "plans" were not included when they focused only on goals for the future rather than on the present situation. In federal states where education policies vary according to state or province, our data show what the majority of states or provinces do.

Information on Variables

DEFINING PRIMARY AND SECONDARY EDUCATION

Countries define primary and secondary education in different ways. In order to increase the comparability of policies across countries, it was necessary to look at the number of years of education in each country and to define primary and secondary in a similar way across nations. UNESCO also adjusts for comparability in reporting its outcomes for countries. In the Education Database, when countries explicitly define lower and upper secondary and do not split primary, these divisions are used. When countries split lower and upper primary and do not split secondary education, we consider lower primary as primary education and upper primary as equivalent to lower secondary education. If primary education is not explicitly split but lasts more than 8 years and consists of "stages" or "levels," again we consider the lower stage as primary and the upper stage as lower secondary. In the few cases in which countries have split both primary and secondary education into upper and lower levels, lower and upper primary are considered primary education (as long as combined they last 8 or fewer years), and the country's definitions of lower and upper secondary are used. For countries that do not split primary or secondary into levels, we apply the general secondary data to both levels of secondary. In the maps and tables presented in this book, "beginning secondary education" refers to the policy in place during the first year of what our database considers lower secondary education. "Finishing secondary education" refers to the policy in place in the final year of upper secondary education.

TUITION FEES

Information on tuition fees examines whether tuition is charged for education in the public school system. When there is a private school system parallel to the public one that charges tuition, as long as the public system is tuition-free, the country is considered to be tuition-free because children do have access to tuition-free education. These data include only tuition fees required to attend school, not any additional fees that may be required, such as for textbooks or uniforms, because of a lack of reliable and comparable information on this subject on a large number of countries.

COMPULSORY EDUCATION

Compulsory education can be delineated by an age range, a number of years, or a level of education. These have been analyzed to create comparable information on the age until which education is compulsory by using available information on the duration of particular educational levels and the standard age to begin school.

TEACHER EDUCATION AND TRAINING

Data on teacher education and training capture the minimum level of education that national policy requires teachers to have completed in order to instruct students at different levels, as well as whether they are required to have completed some specialized teacher training (the nature and duration of which can vary across countries). If no information was available on whether teacher training is required, but the level of education required is known, the country appears in the maps and tables at the corresponding level of education without teacher training. When a country requires three years of postsecondary education, we consider this equivalent to a bachelor's degree for the purpose of comparability across countries.

INCLUSIVE SPECIAL EDUCATION

The variable "inclusive special education" captures whether the public school system makes special education available to children with disabilities. Countries are considered to have a high level of integration when children with and without disabilities are integrated within the same classrooms; a medium level when they attend the same schools but different classrooms, or when policy reports do not clearly indicate whether they are able to attend the same classrooms; and a low level of integration when special education is publicly provided but occurs in separate schools. When education is publicly provided at any level of integration, but children with disabilities receive no additional supports to meet their needs, the country is not given credit for special education.

Child Labour Database

In order to build the Child Labour Database, original labor legislation from each country was analyzed. First, a country's labor code was carefully reviewed to identify all provisions related to child labor. This legislation was located primarily through the International Labour Organization (ILO)'s NATLEX database.[8] Not all laws pertinent to child labor are contained within the labor code. To ensure that all relevant legal provisions were included in the database, team members also searched NATLEX in five languages for a comprehensive list of terms related to children and youth, young ages in years, types of work prohibited for children and youth, hazardous and illegal forms of labor, and child development in order to identify any other pieces of legislation that may be applicable. All laws identified through this process were also reviewed and coded where relevant.

NATLEX is managed by the ILO's International Labour Standards Department. It is designed to remain current, although delays may occur in updating it, especially if the country's legislation is not in one of the ILO's three official languages.

When labor legislation was not available through NATLEX, researchers attempted to locate this legislation through the following global sources:

- Countries' websites
- Foreign Law Guide[9]
- World Legal Information Institute[10]
- Global Legal Information Network[11]
- Lexadin[12]
- GlobaLex[13]

The following additional sources were also consulted for specific countries when necessary:

- Pacific Islands Legal Information Institute[14]
- Commonwealth Legal Information Institute[15]

In some cases, hard copies of legislation were examined at the ILO's headquarters in Geneva, as well as at McGill and Harvard universities' law libraries.

The data reflect a systematic review of available legislation as of March 2012 (data were not collected on the newest UN nation, South Sudan, which became a member in July 2011).

This database gives credit to countries for protections guaranteed to all citizens. In the case of countries where child labor legislation exists at a subnational level, this legislation was reviewed when available from the sources used. If all subnational governments had legislation regarding a particular work regulation, the country was given credit for having this protection in place. When not all parts of the country were covered by the same legislation or types of protections, the least protective standards were coded as the minimum guarantee for the country.

Information on Variables

MINIMUM AGE FOR HAZARDOUS WORK

Information on the minimum age for hazardous work shows the minimum age at which a child is permitted to do hazardous work. In order to determine the age at which children are permitted to do hazardous work, researchers first had to determine what kind of work should be considered hazardous, with the recognition that the professions considered hazardous can vary by country. If a country explicitly defined hazardous work in its legislation, its own definition was used. For countries that do not define hazardous work, we use the International Labour Organization's categorization of hazardous work:

(a) work which exposes children to physical, psychological or sexual abuse; (b) work underground, under water, at dangerous heights or in confined spaces; (c) work with dangerous machinery, equipment and tools, or which involves the manual handling or transport of heavy loads; (d) work in an unhealthy environment which may, for example, expose children to hazardous substances, agents, or processes, or to temperatures, noise levels, or vibrations damaging to their health; (e) work under particularly difficult conditions such as work for long hours or during the night or work where the child is unreasonably confined to the premises of the employer.[16]

In some cases, there is no minimum age for hazardous work, but there is a minimum age for general employment; in these cases, the minimum age for general employment is applied to the minimum age for hazardous work on the assumption that if children are not permitted to work, they will not be permitted to do hazardous work, and conversely, if hazardous work is not regulated separately, then children will be able to do hazardous work once they reach the minimum working age. When data were not available either on the minimum age for hazardous work or the minimum age for general employment, the country appears as having insufficient data.

Some countries include exceptions to the minimum age for hazardous work that would allow children to do this work at a younger age under specified conditions. The types of exceptions that countries can have are exceptions for specific types of work, often agricultural; for educational, vocational, personal development, apprenticeship, or volunteer work; when minister or government approval is granted; when working with family members; when a medical certificate is provided; when there is unlikely to be any harm to health, safety, or morals; or under force majeure (extraordinary circumstances, such as war). In this book, when it is stated that exceptions are taken into account, this includes all these exceptions except no harm to health, safety, and morals (because in this case the work would no longer be hazardous) and force majeure.

MINIMUM AGE FOR FULL-TIME WORK

Information on the minimum age for full-time work shows the minimum age at which a child is permitted to do full-time work, subject only to parental permission. We use 35 or more hours of work per week as a measure of full-time employment.

For this variable, the number of hours of work permitted per week while school is in session is the preferred measurement. If a weekly limit is not available, we calculate the number of hours permitted using the number of hours of work permitted on a school day, the number of hours of work permitted on a nonschool day, and the number of days of rest guaranteed per week through the following equation: $5 \times$ (daily hours of work on a school day) $+ (2 - \text{days of rest}) \times$ (daily hours of work on a nonschool day). When the number of hours of work permitted on a school day is not specified, we calculate this variable by using the number of hours of work permitted on any day and the number of days of rest guaranteed per week: $(7 - \text{guaranteed days of rest}) \times$ (daily hours of work).

When a country guarantees up to 36 hours of rest, it is given credit for 1 day of rest per week. When a country guarantees between 37 and 48 hours, it is given credit for 2 days of weekly rest. When labor legislation does not specify a child-specific rest period, the rest period guaranteed to working adults is applied.

Some countries differentiate the number of hours of work permitted for a child at a given age based on whether or not the child is enrolled in school, with a larger number of hours permitted if a child is not enrolled. In these cases, after children reach the age at which education is no longer compulsory, we apply the number of hours permitted if a child is not enrolled in school.

Some countries prohibit work during school hours and during the night but set no maximum on work hours. In these countries, it is assumed that full-time work is permitted because if a child is not permitted to work during school hours (a 6-hour school day is assumed) and for 12 hours during the night but there are no other restrictions, the child still has 6 hours available to work on school days and 12 hours per day on weekends.

When a younger working age is permitted with only the requirement that a parent grant permission, this younger age is used. Additionally, the hashing on Map 3.3 showing the minimum age for full-time work indicates that there are exceptions that we consider major loopholes allowing children to work at an age younger than the official minimum age. These exceptions fall into the categories of work with family members; specific types of work, such as agricultural, temporary, or seasonal; when the work is termed essential to the child or family; or upon minister or government approval or request.

HOURS OF WORK PERMITTED ON SCHOOL DAYS

A nation's stated maximum number of hours permitted on a school day is used whenever available to measure this variable directly. When countries do not specify hours allowed on a school day, we use the maximum number of hours permitted per day (not specific to a school day) because it is assumed that these regulations will also apply to school days. When countries state that work is prohibited during school hours but do not specify particular hour limitations, a 6-hour school day is assumed and is combined with data on hours of rest guaranteed at night; the resulting number of hours is used to represent the hours of work permitted on school days.

When a child is permitted to work at a younger age subject only to parental permission, this younger age appears in the maps and tables. However, legislation may allow for other exceptions to be made to this minimum age, and this variable does not capture this information because there was insufficient information available to code at what age children could work specified hours when exceptions are considered. This is an important area for future research, particularly in cases where the exceptions are common.

HOURS OF REST AT NIGHT

The variable "hours of rest at night" captures the number of uninterrupted hours off work at night that children are guaranteed at particular ages. The legislation often states that night work is prohibited (without specifying hours), that work is prohibited between certain hours, and/or that a certain number of hours off from work (for example, 11) must be given to children and youth.

If a country specifies only that work by children and youth is limited to a given number of hours per day, it is not coded as prohibiting night work because the working hours could occur at night if there are no restrictions on night work.

Exceptions to night-work protections are important, as they are in other areas of child labor legislation. Unfortunately, due to the nature of labor regulations on night work, we were not able to systematically analyze at what age children and youth might have to work nights once exceptions are taken into account.

TYPE OF WORK PERMITTED AT A GIVEN AGE

The variable "type of work permitted at a given age" evaluates the type of work (none, light work, general employment, hazardous work) permitted at a given age when exceptions are taken into account.

When light work is defined by national legislation, the country's definition is used. Light work is defined by the ILO as work that is not likely to be harmful to children's health or development and is not likely to be detrimental to their schooling or vocational training; as a result, when a country does not explicitly define light work, we consider work "light" when legislation specifies that it cannot harm the child's health or development or impede his or her schooling, or when the legislation explicitly distinguishes work that can be done at a younger age than general employment. General employment refers to work that is not specified as hazardous or light.

In measuring the age at which different types of work are allowed, we take into account common exceptions. In particular, if an exception means that many children may not be protected by the legislation or that protections can be voided without this necessarily being clearly in the best interest of the child or youth, the age at which protection stops for "excepted" children and youth is used. Because of the greater dangers of hazardous work, we do not credit countries with providing adequate protection at a given age if there are any exceptions other than force majeure or when the work cannot harm the child. For general employment and light work, we do not credit countries with adequately protecting children at a given age if they allow child labor when it is conducted with family members; in specific sectors, such as agriculture; when the work is temporary or seasonal; or upon minister or government approval or request.

A handful of countries also make an exception for work that is termed essential for the child or his or her family. Because there is no way to ensure that this exception would truly be made in the best interests of the child, this kind of exception is also considered a loophole that lowers the minimum age.

Child Marriage Database

The Child Marriage Database was created by first analyzing the most recent reports submitted by countries to the monitoring committees of the Convention on the Rights of the Child (CRC) and the Convention on the Elimination of All Forms of Discrimination against Women (CEDAW), including question-and-answer periods, as well as the reports detailing the committees' concluding observations.[17] These conventions are those most relevant to child marriage regulations because of their concern with children and with women. This review was completed in March 2012 and included all reports for sessions held between 2005 and early 2012.

For countries where data were not available or were incomplete, information was drawn from legislative sources listed through the country's government or legislative website, as well as through legal reference sites such as the Lexadin World Law Guide[18] and the Foreign Law Guide.[19]

In the very few cases where CEDAW reports, CRC reports, and original legislation were not available, and in some cases to clarify or complete an area, information was drawn from the Emory Law Legal Profiles,[20] the *Guide pratique international de l'état civil*,[21] and the Legislation of INTERPOL Member States on Sexual Offences against Children compendium, which collects information on sexual activity with children and the laws framing its legality or illegality.[22]

Information on Variables

LEGAL AGE OF MARRIAGE

The minimum age of marriage captured in our database is the youngest age at which a girl or boy can be married with no restrictions or subject only to the permission of his or her parents.

PROTECTION OF CHILDHOOD

The variable "protection of childhood" draws on data from the Child Labour Database, the Child Marriage Database, and the Education Database. It shows the ages when labor is prohibited, marriage is prohibited, and education is compulsory.

Here, labor refers to general employment and takes into account exceptions allowing younger children to work. The age of marriage used is the age at which a child can marry subject only to parental permission; if the age of marriage differs between girls and boys, the younger age is used. Also included is the age until which education is compulsory.

Adult Labour Database

The Adult Labour Database was created through a systematic review of labor legislation and information on social security systems available as of March 2012. The labor legislation was located primarily through the ILO's NATLEX database.[23]

When full-text labor legislation was not available through NATLEX, researchers located this legislation through country websites, as well as other sources, such as the World Bank's Doing Business Law Library,[24] Lexadin,[25] and the World Legal Information Institute.[26] In some cases, hard copies of legislation were examined at the ILO's headquarters in Geneva, as well as at McGill and Harvard universities' law libraries.

The Social Security Programs Throughout the World database, based on data from the International Social Security Association and other supplemental sources, was used to complement legislative information about paid-leave policies. Specifics, such as wage-replacement rates, are not included in some labor codes but rather are mandated by social security policies. Social Security Programs Throughout the World also included information on some countries for which we were unable to locate a labor code. Reports were reviewed for every country included in our database.[27]

Additional information to fill in gaps was drawn from the following sources:

- Some additional regional secondary sources, such as the Council of Europe Family Policy Database[28] and the *International Review of Leave Policies and Related Research*,[29] were used to clarify information or fill in missing details.

- The International Labour Organization's Maternity Protection Database and Working Time Database were used to supplement information on maternity and working time policies when primary sources were unavailable.[30]

- In a small number of cases, information on maternal leave and breastfeeding breaks was clarified or corroborated with information compiled by the World Alliance for Breastfeeding Action[31] and the United Nations' 2005 *The World's Women* data and report.[32]

Where subnational legislation was reviewed, a country was given credit for a policy only if it was present in all provinces or states.

Information on Variables

MATERNAL AND PATERNAL LEAVE

The data on leave for new mothers and new fathers presented in this book include paid leave specifically designated for the parent in question, as well as the total amount of paid leave that is available to either parent. Duration is reported in weeks. When legislation stipulates duration in months, a multiplier of 4.3 was used to calculate the number of weeks. When legislation stipulates duration in working days, this was divided by the standard length of the working week if this information was available; when this information was not available, a 5.5-day working week was assumed (this number was chosen to accommodate differences in the standard length of the work week, which tends to be 5, 5.5, or 6, depending on the country). We report the leave available under normal conditions and not the maximum duration when leave periods can be extended in extraordinary circumstances, such as childbirth complications.

The maximum wage-replacement rate during leave presented in this book shows the highest level of wage replacement available during leave when wage-replacement rates vary over the course of the leave.

AVAILABILITY OF BREASTFEEDING BREAKS AT WORK

The information on availability of breastfeeding breaks at work shows whether women are guaranteed the right to breaks for breastfeeding upon their return to work after childbirth. The amount allowed can be specified in a variety of ways, including a number of hours of leave each day to breastfeed, the opportunity to shorten the workday by a given amount of time to breastfeed, or allowance to take a particular number of breaks of a specified duration. Breastfeeding breaks are commonly guaranteed for a set length of time that is indicated either by a number of months after returning to work or by a child's age.

LEAVE FOR CHILDREN'S NEEDS

Leave specifically designated for children's health needs is sometimes written in language that permits a parent to use this leave for any of a child's health needs, but sometimes is available only in the case of serious illness or hospitalization. When leave to meet a child's health or educational needs is made available only to women, it was not included. Our variable captures leave available to both men and women because of the implications for gender equity.

Some countries offer a broader category of leave for family or discretionary leave either in place of or in addition to leave specifically targeting children's health and education. Family leave is a kind of leave provided by countries that can be taken for a variety of family or household needs; these needs are specified to a greater or lesser extent depending on the country. For example, Botswana states that "workers are allowed 20 days of additional paid leave per year for events directly affecting the worker's household which cannot be deducted from the worker's paid annual leave." Singapore states that an employee "shall be entitled to childcare leave of 2 days" if he or she has a child under the age of 7 and that "an employer shall pay an employee who is entitled to childcare leave his gross rate of pay for every day of such leave that is taken by the employee."

Discretionary leave is offered in more general terms. For instance, Thailand states that "an employee is entitled to take leave for essential errands in accordance with work rules and regulations," and Hungary states that "employees shall be exempted from the requirement of availability and from work duty . . . for any duration of absence due to personal or family reasons, or as justified by unavoidable external reasons." Emergency leave is offered for urgent needs. For example, the Maldives states that "Special annual leave of 10 days [can be] granted to an employee for extraordinary circumstances."

WAGE PREMIUMS FOR EVENING AND NIGHT WORK

Information on whether a wage premium is guaranteed for work carried out during evening or night hours, as well as on the level of this premium, is captured. In some cases, the employer may have the right to provide time off instead of a wage premium.

Constitutions Database

The Constitutions Database is a comprehensive analysis of the rights and protections contained in constitutions around the world. This database contains data on 191 countries, all of the United Nations' member countries as of June 2011 with the exception of Fiji and South Sudan. (Fiji's constitution was suspended as of June 2011, and the new state of South Sudan did not yet have one.)

This database relies exclusively on primary constitutional texts in force as of June 2011, in a constitution's original language whenever possible or translated into English, French, or Spanish when this was not possible. Additional legislation was included in the database only when the constitution explicitly referenced it. Although the vast majority of countries have codified written constitutions, a few countries (e.g., the United Kingdom, Canada, New Zealand, Israel, and Libya) either have no written codified constitution or have a series of constitutional laws rather than a single text. In both cases, those documents or laws that are considered to be constitutional either by the country itself or by the legal community were identified.[33]

Based on 37 international conventions, a framework of rights and protections was established to permit constitutional characteristics to be compared. The database collects information across 14 social categories: age, citizenship, sex/gender, race/ethnicity, religion, language, national origin, sexual orientation, parentage, social position, intellectual disability or mental health condition, physical disability, social disability, and prisoner status.

Information on Variables

GUARANTEED VERSUS ASPIRATIONAL

A right is considered aspirational instead of guaranteed if the language used is not authoritative enough to be considered a guarantee, for example, when a right is dependent on the state's ability to provide it, when a right appears only in the constitution's preamble, or when it is explicitly stated to be nonenforceable. If the right appears only in the preamble but the preamble is stated to be an integral part of the constitution, the right is considered guaranteed.

RIGHTS IN EDUCATION

One of the most fundamental social and economic rights that constitutions can address is education. Constitutions can protect education rights in various ways, from prohibiting discrimination in education or guaranteeing a right to education in broad terms to guaranteeing that education will be free and compulsory for a given length of time. Some constitutions also protect the right to education for particular groups, such as children with disabilities or persons from different language groups.

In this book, we have examined general rights to education and rights to specified levels of education; constitutional stipulations of free and/or compulsory education; the right to education for children with disabilities; prohibitions of discrimination in education across gender, ethnicity, religion, and disability; and provisions for education for different linguistic groups. Although the full database captures distinctions in education rights guaranteed only to children versus rights that also apply to adults, because this book focuses on children, any education right that includes all children has been reported as a universal guarantee.

We consider a right to education as guaranteed or aspirational for a particular level (primary, secondary, and tertiary) if the constitution explicitly protects that level of education, as well as if it protects the right to free and/or compulsory education at that level (for example, a guarantee of free primary education is considered a guarantee of primary education). If the constitution protects the right to education "at all levels," we consider this to be a specific guarantee for primary, secondary, and tertiary education.

When the constitution does not attach the rights to education, free education, or compulsory education to a specific level or "all levels" of education, it is assumed that they necessarily apply at the primary level as the most basic level of education. For example, the right to compulsory education is interpreted as a guarantee of primary education. These rights are considered specific guarantees at the secondary level only when they are specified to extend for at least 11 years or until age 16.

Provisions that grant rights to education without specifying that the right is protected at a specific level, at "all levels," or for a given length of time are not applied to secondary and higher education because several constitutions make it clear that states often equate the "right to education" with primary education. One example is the Brazilian constitution: "Article 206. Education shall be provided on the basis of the following principles: . . . IV—free public education in official schools; . . . Article 208. The duty of the State towards education shall be fulfilled by ensuring the following: I—mandatory and free elementary education, including the assurance of its free offer to all those who did not have access to it at the proper age; II—progressive universalization of free high-school education."

The prohibition of discrimination in education is considered to be guaranteed to particular social groups (in this book, across gender, ethnicity, religion, and disability) only when a prohibition of discrimination in education is explicitly guaranteed to these groups.

The right to separate education for different linguistic groups is captured separately in the database in its various formulations. Some countries guarantee the right to education in one of the country's official languages, or in one of a given selection of languages. Some countries grant the right to education to all in the language of their choosing. Others guarantee education for particular national or linguistic minorities in their own language. Some countries in Latin America also make guarantees of education for indigenous groups in an indigenous language. It is important to note that not all of these guarantees imply state provision of education in the chosen language.

The right to education is considered to be protected for children with disabilities when the following are explicitly granted to children with disabilities or are granted in general *and* the constitution states that persons with disabilities enjoy rights on an equal basis: the right to education, the right to education at all levels, the right to compulsory education, the right to free education, and the prohibition of discrimination in education. Some countries discuss persons with physical disabilities, some discuss persons with mental health conditions or intellectual disabilities, and some discuss persons with disabilities in general. Results presented in this book show rights for all disabled children, either because the guarantee is provided to those with both physical and mental health conditions or because the constitution broadly guarantees the right to all children with disabilities.

RIGHTS TO HEALTH

Constitutions can deal with health-related rights in a variety of ways. Some countries broadly guarantee the right to health by using terms such as "health," "health security," and "overall well-being." Some countries guarantee the right to medical services, including terms such as "curative services," "health-care services," or "disease treatment," or discussion of the state's responsibility to restore/rehabilitate health. Some countries also protect the right to public health, including the "defense of public health," "access to preventive services," "illness prevention," and so on. Each of these can be guaranteed in broad terms, such as the statement of a right to public health, and/or can be phrased more specifically, such as access to immunizations and health education. The broad right was considered guaranteed when it was made explicit, or when these types of specifics appeared within a broader applicable context; for example, if access to immunizations was mentioned within the context of the protection of public health or disease prevention, the right to public health was considered granted, but if it appeared alone, the overall right to public health was not considered guaranteed.

RIGHTS AT WORK

There are many ways in which constitutions can address equal rights at work. In this book, we present information on the general prohibition of discrimination in work based on gender, ethnicity, and religion; protections of specific aspects of work life across these groups; and protection of disabled adults' rights at work.

Constitutions can prohibit discrimination in work in general or in specific aspects of work, such as hiring, working conditions, or promotions. In each of these cases, constitutions sometimes prohibit discrimination against all persons in general terms and sometimes list particular groups to whom this protection applies. This book's tables show separately countries that prohibit discrimination in general in work, hiring, promotions, and working conditions, and countries that make explicit mention of gender, ethnicity, and religion in relation to these protections.

Equal pay for equal work tends to be treated differently in constitutions—it normally appears as a positive guarantee of the right to equal pay for equal work rather than a prohibition of discrimination in remuneration. In some cases, the guarantee of equal pay for equal work is made explicitly across gender, ethnicity, and religion. In others, the guarantee is made in general, but elsewhere in the constitution it is specified that these groups must enjoy their rights equally with others.

Disabled adults' rights at work can be protected in a variety of ways. The right to work can be guaranteed in general, there can be a prohibition of discrimination in work generally, and there can be prohibitions of discrimination in specific aspects of work, such as hiring, promotions, and working conditions. These work protections are considered to apply specifically to persons with disabilities when they are guaranteed explicitly to persons with disabilities, or when these protections are granted in general *and* the constitution states that persons with disabilities enjoy relevant categories of rights on an equal basis.

APPROACHES TO EQUITY

Constitutions can take different approaches to equity. Most commonly, nations prohibit discrimination using language such as "No person shall be discriminated against on the basis of his or her religion." Some make positive guarantees of equal rights, for example, "Women and men enjoy equal rights." They can also guarantee overall equality between groups, such as "The State guarantees equality between men and women." In other cases, constitutions guarantee equality before the law, for example, "Everyone is equal before the law regardless of his or her race or ethnicity." This book maps all these approaches to equity based on gender, ethnicity, religion, and disability.

Although provisions that prohibit discrimination or guarantee equality are relatively straightforward, general equal-rights guarantees are more complex because they may specify certain rights or groups of rights that particular groups should enjoy equally. In the database, we make a distinction between countries that guarantee that everyone enjoys equal rights and those that specify that everyone is equal in the enjoyment of specific categories of rights, such as economic and social rights or political rights. In this book, a country is given credit for having a broad guarantee of equal rights when the constitution guarantees equality in the exercise of all rights, fundamental or basic rights, human rights, both political and social rights, both public and private rights, or both individual and social rights.

POTENTIAL POSITIVE ACTION

Positive action is a measure or measures that may be taken to compensate for past or current inequalities. Positive action can be framed in guaranteed terms, for example, Bolivia's stipulation that "the State shall adopt measures of affirmative action to promote the effective integration of disabled persons into the productive, economic, political, social, and cultural sphere, without any discrimination whatsoever," or in terms that leave open the possibility for positive action, such as Bangladesh's provision that "the State shall not discriminate against any citizen on grounds only of religion, race, caste, sex, or place of birth. . . . Nothing in this article shall prevent the State from making special provision in favour of women." Guaranteed and possible positive action are grouped together as potential positive action for the purposes of this book's maps and tables.

CITIZENS VERSUS RESIDENTS

In this book, we were not able to present all the aspects of rights guarantees that we would have liked to and that we have begun to capture in the database. One of these was the distinction between rights guaranteed to all citizens and those guaranteed to all residents. In an age of increasing migration, it is critical that rights be guaranteed to all children regardless of their citizenship. Because of the nature of the data, constitutional maps best capture citizens' rights.

Poverty Database

The data on family, unemployment, and disability benefits are drawn primarily from a review of relevant legislation and details of social security systems. Legislative texts were accessed via the ILO's NATLEX database and official government gazettes.[34] Social Security Programs Throughout the World reports were analyzed because of their systematic updating.[35] The International Social Security Association conducts an Annual Survey on Development and Trends that is used to inform Social Security Programs Throughout the World, along with other supplemental sources. For European countries not included in Social Security Programs Throughout the World or for which data are incomplete, information was drawn from the European Union's Mutual Information System on Social Protection,[36] and some data for European countries not belonging to the European Union were drawn from the Mutual Information System on Social Protection of the Council of Europe.[37] Only laws and policies existing at a national level are included.

Data pertaining to minimum-wage policies were drawn primarily from legislative texts accessed via the ILO's NATLEX database and official government gazettes, as well as the ILO's TRAVAIL Database of Conditions of Work and Employment Laws.[38] When these sources did not yield recent data on minimum-wage rates, information was drawn from the U.S. Department of State's Human Rights Reports.[39] All data used in building the minimum-wage database were based on observations relevant to the years 2010 and 2011.

Information on Variables

MINIMUM WAGE

Countries address the minimum wage in a wide variety of ways. The minimum wage can be set by a state authority or wage board or by collective bargaining. When it is set by collective bargaining, nonunionized workers may or may not be covered, and the state may or may not have the right to set a separate minimum for unprotected workers. When the minimum wage is set legislatively, some minimum wages vary by occupation, by sector, or by region of the country; some countries set different minimum wages for particular categories of workers, such as youth, piece-rate workers, or new hires. Who is covered by the minimum wage also differs—in many cases, certain types of employees have separate regulations (such as public-sector workers or civil servants), and in others particular categories of workers are excluded from minimum-wage protections, such as casual workers or employees of small businesses. Countries also define different minimum-wage adjustment and enforcement mechanisms.

In this book, we present whether countries have a minimum wage, its level, and its enforcement mechanisms. When the level of the minimum wage varies by occupation, sector, region, or other feature and several levels exist, researchers coded the lowest established minimum wage. In exceptional cases where it was clear that although some workers would receive a lower minimum wage, a higher minimum level would apply to the vast majority, this higher wage was coded. For example, in the United States, the federal minimum-wage level does not apply to tipped employees, who are guaranteed a lower minimum level with the assumption that combined with the tips they receive, this will be at least equal to the general minimum-wage level.

The level of minimum wages established through collective bargaining is generally not shown because it differs per sector, with the exception of three countries. Belgium and Croatia have a collectively bargained national minimum-wage level below which collectively bargained sectoral minimum-wage levels cannot be set; in Greece, we were able to determine the amount of the lowest collectively bargained minimum wage, and that level has been coded.

UNEMPLOYMENT BENEFITS

Countries provide income protection during unemployment through at least three broad mechanisms: government unemployment benefits, guarantees of severance pay, or a combination of both. The duration and amount of unemployment benefits can vary according to employment status and history, family status, age, and other factors. Eligibility to receive these benefits can be contingent on a minimum period of employment, the specific type of employment (e.g., full-time, casual), age, and other factors. In some cases, certain categories of workers, such as agricultural workers, artisans, or the self-employed, are excluded from unemployment benefits. When unemployment benefits include the self-employed, this can be on a voluntary or a mandatory basis.

When the duration or amount of benefits provided varies, the absolute minimum and maximum lengths and levels under ordinary circumstances are reported. When analyzing the duration of unemployment benefits, all durations were converted into weeks for the purposes of comparability. When legislation refers to calendar days explicitly or implicitly, the conversion of 7 days per week is used; when legislation refers to working days, we use a conversion of 5 working days per week. When legislation establishes the length of benefits in months, we consider 1 month equivalent to 4.3 weeks.

In this book, we present information on whether unemployment benefits are provided by the government, whether employers are required to provide severance pay in the absence of benefits, and the maximum duration of unemployment benefits. We also present the amount of benefits that an unemployed person previously earning the minimum wage would receive, drawing on the benefit calculation formula, national floor of unemployment benefits, and minimum-wage levels included in this database.

FAMILY BENEFITS

In regard to family or disability benefits, the database captures only benefits provided on a statutory basis—that is, established by law. Because the Social Security Programs Throughout the World database offers very limited detail on nonstatutory programs (and by definition there are no legislative documents that detail them), these were not included in the database. Additionally, only cash benefits are captured because of a lack of consistent and reliable information on other types of benefits, such as tax benefits.

In designing policies, countries take different approaches to family assistance. In some countries, benefits are subject to a means test; in others, they differ according to family composition, including the age of the child and the number of children. In order to provide a concrete and comparable image of the financial support offered to families across countries, we calculated benefit levels for sample families with a specified number of children of a specified age. When benefits differed according to income level, the lowest income bracket was used because we were particularly concerned with what financial support would be available to families with the greatest need. For families with preschool-age children, the calculation was made assuming a family with two 4-year-old children. For families with school-age children, the calculation was made assuming a family with two 8-year-old children. For families with teenaged children, the calculation was made assuming a family with two 15-year-old children.

In some cases, nations also provide benefit supplements for particular events or periods in a child's life. In this book, we examine whether countries provide a birth or maternity grant; when the amount of this grant differs on the basis of birth order, we present information on grants available for the first child. We also examine grants available for child care or school.

Some countries provide benefit supplements for families supporting a child with a disability; these are also examined in this book. We analyzed information on these benefits, whether they are provided to families through disability benefit systems or through family benefit systems. Some countries adjust the amount of these benefits on the basis of the age of the child, the family's income, the amount of benefits received through other schemes, and/or the nature of the child's disability. For the purposes of comparability, we examine the benefits provided to families in the lowest income bracket with one child with the most severe level of disability at a given age.

Data Analysis and Disaggregation

The data presented in the tables are often disaggregated into low-, middle-, and high-income countries. For these categories, we use the

World Bank's November 2011 classification of income groups, the most recent available. For the regional classifications used in the text, we use the World Bank's classifications.

The purchasing power parity conversions used in this book's data are from the United Nations Statistics Division's Millennium Development Goals Database, updated as of 29 August 2011, available at http://data.un.org/Data.aspx?q=PPP+datamart[MDG]&d=MDG&f =seriesRowID%3a699 (accessed 21 March 2012).

Appendix 2

Interview Data

Project on Global Working Families

At Harvard University, I founded and led the Project on Global Working Families. For this project, we analyzed extensive survey data on 55,000 families, collected policy data on labor policies worldwide, and conducted qualitative interviews in 14 countries. Over 2,000 in-depth, open-ended interviews were conducted with parents, child-care providers, teachers, health-care providers, and employers in the United States, Canada, Russia, Norway, Ireland, Botswana, South Africa, Honduras, Mexico, Peru, India, China, Viet Nam, and Australia. The open-ended structure of the in-depth interviews, geared toward understanding the challenges faced by working parents and their children around the world, allowed the respondents to tell their stories and raise what they saw as the most important issues. All interviewees during this project were guaranteed confidentiality, and their names have been changed. I have drawn on some of these interviews from Botswana, Mexico, the United States, and Viet Nam in the anecdotes that open many of this book's chapters.

In some countries, interviews targeted special populations, experiences (such as families in economic transitions or after a disaster), or employers (across size or sector). Most of the interviews presented in this book are drawn from representative samples of families using public services.

In Botswana, working parents were recruited for interviews at government health clinics in three cities (Gaborone, Lobatse, and Molepolole). Interviews were conducted, and the overall response rate was 96 percent. Demographic information collected from nonrespondents showed no significant differences between respondents and nonrespondents in marital status, educational attainment, or work in the formal versus the informal economy.

In Mexico, interviewees were recruited at health clinics in two cities, Mexico City and San Cristóbal de las Casas; clinics were carefully chosen to ensure variation in the respondents' occupation, socioeconomic status, family structure, and ethnicity. The response rate was 87 percent, and there were no significant differences between respondents and nonrespondents in ethnicity, number of children, marital status, and whether they did formal or informal work.

In the United States, the Urban Working Families Study interviewed a random sample of families using a city's services, as well as supplemental samples of low-income families living in subsidized housing and of unilingual Spanish speakers. The response rate was 82 percent, and no significant differences were found with respect to education, ethnicity, employment status, and family structure.

In Viet Nam, samples of working parents in different economic and living situations were recruited at three sites in Ho Chi Minh City and its surrounding urban and periurban areas. The response rates were 77 percent for mothers and 89 percent for fathers. There were no significant differences between respondents and nonrespondents regarding marital status, educational attainment, or work in the formal or the informal economy.

Population Health: Moving from Evidence to Effective Policy

At the Institute for Health and Social Policy at McGill University, I led a 6-year initiative, Population Health: Moving from Evidence to Effective Policy, funded by the Max Bell Foundation. One of its principal components was a series of case studies of effective policy programs around the world.

For each of 5 themes, a list of between 200 and 500 potential case-study sites was carefully narrowed down to a final list of 10 case studies to be conducted (6 in the program's pilot cohort). The initiative's first cohort focused on companies and countries that provide good working conditions for low-skilled workers while succeeding economically. The second cohort focused on policies and programs addressing educational inequalities. The third cohort focused on increasing equity in civic participation, the fourth on environmental sustainability, and the final cohort on equity for persons with disabilities. During 6 years, fellows examined policies and programs in a total of 26 countries around the world: Argentina, Bangladesh, Barbados, Bolivia, Brazil, Cameroon, Canada, Colombia, Denmark, Ecuador, Ghana, Iceland, India, Jordan, Malawi, Mali, Nepal, Nicaragua, Norway, Paraguay, Peru, Sweden, Tanzania, the United Kingdom, the United States, and Zambia.

In this book, we draw on only a minute portion of this initiative—a few of the over 2,000 interviews conducted around the world. Interviewees were guaranteed confidentiality when they were service recipients or ordinary citizens, and their names have been changed, but real names have been used when an individual's position in an organization made anonymity impossible.

Notes

1. Within Our Reach

1. World Bank, World Development Indicators, "Mortality Rate, Under-5 (per 1,000)" and "Mortality Rate, Infant (per 1,000 Live Births)," available at http://databank.worldbank.org (accessed 10 February 2012).

2. UNESCO Institute for Statistics, "Regional Youth (15–24) Literacy Rate (%). Total," available at http://stats.uis.unesco.org/unesco/TableViewer/tableView .aspx?ReportId=201 (accessed 15 March 2011).

3. S. O. Rutstein, "Factors Associated with Trends in Infant and Child Mortality in Developing Countries during the 1990s," *Bulletin of the World Health Organization* 78, no. 10 (2000): 1256–1270.

4. Deaths from pneumonia fell from 44 to fewer than 1 per 1,000; deaths from diarrhea were reduced from 29 per 1,000 to fewer than 1 in 10,000. Neonatal mortality, or mortality in the first 28 days of life, dramatically declined.

5. J. Jiménez and M. I. Romero, "Reducing Infant Mortality in Chile: Success in Two Phases," *Health Affairs* 26, no. 2 (2007): 458–465.

6. United Nations Statistics Division, Millennium Development Goals Indicators, "2.1 Net Enrolment Ratio in Primary Education," available at http://mdgs .un.org/unsd/mdg/Data.aspx, last updated 14 July 2009 (accessed 26 January 2010); United Nations Statistics Division, Millennium Development Goals Indicators, "2.2 Proportion of Pupils Starting Grade 1 Who Reach Last Grade of Primary," available at http://mdgs.un.org/unsd/mdg/Data.aspx, last updated 14 July 2009 (accessed 26 January 2010).

7. International Labour Organization, *The End of Child Labour: Within Reach* (Geneva: International Labour Office, 2006), 13–14; A. Dewees and S. J. Klees, "Social Movements and the Transformation of National Policy: Street and Working Children in Brazil," *Comparative Education Review* 39, no. 1 (1995): 76–100; World Bank, *Brazil: Eradicating Child Labor*, Report no. 21858-BR (Washington,

D.C.: World Bank, 2001); Y.-T. Yap, G. Sedlacek, and P. F. Orazem, "Limiting Child Labor through Behavior-Based Income Transfers: An Experimental Evaluation of the PETI Program in Rural Brazil" (working paper, February 2001), available at http://siteresources.worldbank.org/INTISPMA/Resources/38370411 53333441931/11375_orazem-peti-brazil.pdf (accessed 24 February 2010).

8. R. Paes de Barros and R. Mendonca, "Trabalho infantil no Brasil: Rumo à erradicacão," *Mercado de Trabalho* 41 (2009), available at https://ipea.gov.br/agencia /images/stories/PDFs/mercadodetrabalho/03_NT_TrabalhoInfantil.pdf (accessed 3 February 2012).

9. Global movements to support free education helped reverse the negative effects of fees that were imposed under structural adjustment policies.

10. Instituto Mexicano del Seguro Social, http://www.imss.gob.mx (accessed 2 March 2009).

11. J. Heymann and A. Earle, *Raising the Global Floor: Dismantling the Myth That We Can't Afford Good Working Conditions for Everyone* (Stanford, Calif.: Stanford University Press, 2010). For details about the Project on Global Working Families, see J. Heymann, *Forgotten Families: Ending the Growing Crisis Confronting Children and Working Parents in the Global Economy* (New York: Oxford University Press, 2006), and the Institute for Health and Social Policy, McGill University, http://www.mcgill.ca/ihsp (accessed 28 July 2010).

12. "NGO Helps End Child Soldier Hire in Nepal," *Hindustan Times*, 16 December 2005; "Case Filed against Nepal's Child Soldier Recruitment Policy," *Hindustan Times*, 24 June 2005; "Supreme Court Bars Under-Age Recruitment in Nepal," *Xinhua News Agency*, 16 December 2005.

2. Beyond Basic Education

1. This interview took place in November 1999. This amount was converted using the World Bank's data in "PPP Conversion Factor, Private Consumption (LCU per International $)"; this factor was 6 for Mexico in 1999. World Bank, *World Development Indicators*, available at http://data.worldbank.org/indicator (accessed 31 March 2011).

2. Interview, Project on Global Working Families (Mexico, 23 November 1999). The name of this interviewee has been changed to protect confidentiality.

3. UNESCO, *Education for All Global Monitoring Report 2010: Reaching the Marginalized* (Paris: UNESCO, 2010), 57–59.

4. UNESCO defines gross enrollment as follows: "Total enrolment in a specific level of education, regardless of age, expressed as a percentage of the population in the official age group corresponding to this level of education" (ibid., 447). We use "Arab states" here because this is the terminology used by UNESCO, from whom these data come; in our analyses, we use "Middle East and North Africa" because our database follows World Bank regional guidelines.

5. UNESCO, "Policy Paper 04," Education for All Global Monitoring Report Policy Paper (Paris: UNESCO, 2012).

6. M. Bruneforth, "Social Background and a Typology of Out-of-School Children in 27 Countries" (background paper for *EFA Global Monitoring Report 2010*), cited in UNESCO, *Education for All Global Monitoring Report 2010*, 59.

7. UNESCO, "Policy Paper 04."

8. UNESCO, *Education for All Global Monitoring Report 2011: The Hidden Crisis* (Paris: UNESCO, 2011), 47.

9. UNESCO, *Education for All Global Monitoring Report 2010*, 155.

10. Campaign 2000, *2010 Report Card on Child and Family Poverty in Canada: 1989–2010* (Toronto: Campaign 2000, 2010).

11. UNESCO, *Education for All Global Monitoring Report 2010*.

12. Ibid.

13. Ibid.

14. E. Field and A. Ambrus, "Early Marriage, Age of Menarche, and Female Schooling Attainment in Bangladesh," *Journal of Political Economy* 166, no. 5 (2008): 881–930.

15. UNESCO, *Education for All Global Monitoring Report 2010*.

16. Economic and Social Commission for Western Asia, *Where Do Arab Women Stand in the Development Process? A Gender-Based Statistics Analysis* (New York: United Nations, 2004).

17. For example, data from 2005 show that 17 percent of women graduated with education-related degrees, compared with 7 percent of men, while 21 percent of men and 5 percent of women graduated with an engineering degree. S. Vincent-Lancrin, "The Reversal of Gender Inequalities in Higher Education: An On-going Trend," in *Higher Education to 2030*, vol. 1, *Demography* (Paris: OECD, 2008): 274.

18. Status of treaty ratifications: United Nations Treaty Collection, "3. International Covenant on Economic, Social and Cultural Rights," available at http://treaties.un.org/Pages/ViewDetails.aspx?src=TREATY&mtdsg_no=IV-3&chapter=4&lang=en (accessed 24 January 2012); United Nations Treaty Collection, "Convention on the Rights of the Child," available at http://treaties.un.org/Pages/ViewDetails.aspx?src=TREATY&mtdsg_no=IV-11&chapter=4&lang=en (accessed 24 January 2012).

19. A right is considered aspirational if it is written in language that is not authoritative (e.g., the State "should," "endeavors to," "promotes"), if it is explicitly dependent on the state's ability to provide it, or if it is explicitly nonenforceable. It is also considered aspirational if it appears only in the preamble of the constitution when the preamble is not described as an integral part of the constitution in question.

20. The 5 countries guaranteeing education in a given selection of languages are Iraq, Paraguay, Romania, South Africa, and Sri Lanka.

21. The 9 countries guaranteeing the right to education in the language of one's own choosing are Azerbaijan, Belarus, Ecuador, Kazakhstan, Iraq, Moldova, Namibia, the Russian Federation, and Uganda.

22. The 7 countries guaranteeing indigenous peoples the right to education in an indigenous language are Argentina, Bolivia, Brazil, Ecuador, Guatemala, Nicaragua, and Venezuela.

23. The 19 countries guaranteeing education for national or linguistic minorities in their own language are Albania, Austria, Bulgaria, Canada, Colombia, Czech Republic, Estonia, Hungary, India, Macedonia, Mongolia, Montenegro, Nepal, Nicaragua, Romania, Serbia, Slovakia, Slovenia, and Ukraine.

24. Interview, Population Health: Moving from Evidence to Effective Policy (Malawi, 7 July 2008).

25. United Nations Statistics Division, Millennium Development Goals Indicators, "2.1 Net Enrolment Ratio in Primary Education," available at http://mdgs .un.org/unsd/mdg/Data.aspx, last updated 14 July 2009 (accessed 26 January 2010).

26. United Nations Statistics Division, Millennium Development Goals Indicators, "2.2 Proportion of Pupils Starting Grade 1 Who Reach Last Grade of Primary," available at http://mdgs.un.org/unsd/mdg/Data.aspx, last updated 14 July 2009 (accessed 26 January 2010).

27. World Bank, *Cambodia: Halving Poverty by 2015? Poverty Assessment 2006* (Washington, D.C.: World Bank, 2006); World Bank, *Uganda: Poverty and Vulnerability Assessment* (Washington, D.C.: World Bank, 2006); World Bank, *Malawi: Poverty and Vulnerability Assessment; Investing in Our Future, Synthesis Report; Main Findings and Recommendations* (Washington, D.C.: World Bank, 2007); Y. Tsujita, "Implications of Migration and Schooling for Urban Educational Disparity: A Study of Delhi Slum Children," in S. Hirashima, H. Oda, and Y. Tsujita, eds., *Inclusiveness in India: A Strategy for Growth and Equality* (Basingstoke, U.K.: Palgrave Macmillan, 2011), 136–173.

28. World Bank, *Education in Sierra Leone: Present Challenges, Future Opportunities* (Washington, D.C.: World Bank, 2007), cited in UNESCO, *Education for All Global Monitoring Report 2010*, 166.

29. C. Cameron, *Education Decisions in Slums of Dhaka, Bangladesh* (Glasgow, U.K.: British Association of International and Comparative Education, 2008), cited in UNESCO, *Education for All Global Monitoring Report 2010*, 165.

30. UNESCO Institute for Statistics, "Gross Enrolment Ratio. Primary. Total" and "Net Enrolment Rate. Primary. Total," 2005–2010, available at http:// stats.uis.unesco.org/ (accessed 3 July 2012).

31. World Bank and Burundi Government, *Republic of Burundi: Public Expenditure Management and Financial Accountability Review (PEMFAR); Improving Allocative Efficiency and Governance of Public Expenditure and Investing in Public Capital to Accelerate Growth and Reduce Poverty* (Washington, D.C.: World Bank Report No. 42160-BI, 2008), cited in UNESCO, *Education for All Global Monitoring Report 2010*, 166.

32. K. Deininger, "Does Cost of Schooling Affect Enrollment by the Poor? Universal Primary Education in Uganda," *Economics of Education Review* 22, no. 3 (2003): 291–305.

33. Structural adjustment programs were conditions associated with receiving loans or assistance from the World Bank and the International Monetary Fund. X. Bonal, "Plus ça change . . . : The World Bank Global Education Policy and the Post-Washington Consensus," *International Studies in Sociology of Education* 12, no. 1 (2002): 3–22.

34. H. D. Nielsen, *Moving toward Free Primary Education: Policy Issues and Implementation Challenges* (New York: UNICEF, 2009).

35. K. Inoue and M. Oketch, "Implementing Free Primary Education Policy in Malawi and Ghana: Equity and Efficiency Analysis," *Peabody Journal of Education* 83, no. 1 (2008): 41–70.

36. P. Oreopoulos, *Canadian Compulsory School Laws and Their Impact on Educational Attainment and Future Earnings* (Ottawa: Statistics Canada, 2005); P. Oreopoulos, "The Compelling Effects of Compulsory Schooling: Evidence from Canada," *Canadian Journal of Economics* 39, no. 1 (2006): 22–52.

37. P. Oreopoulos, "Estimating Average and Local Average Treatment Effects of Education When Compulsory Schooling Laws Really Matter," *American Economic Review* 96, no. 1 (2006): 152–175.

38. G. Brunello, M. Fort, and G. Weber, "Changes in Compulsory Schooling, Education, and the Distribution of Wages in Europe," *Economic Journal* 119, no. 536 (2009): 516–539.

39. M. Dayioglu, "Patterns of Change in Child Labour and Schooling in Turkey: The Impact of Compulsory Schooling," *Oxford Development Studies* 33, no. 2 (June 2005): 195–210.

40. Men born in the first quarter of the year in the cohorts examined were approximately 10 percent more likely to have dropped out of high school than men born in the fourth quarter. J. D. Angrist and A. B. Krueger, "Does Compulsory School Attendance Affect Schooling and Earnings?," *Quarterly Journal of Economics* 106, no. 4 (1991): 979–1014.

41. T. Zhang and Z. Minxia, "Universalizing Nine-Year Compulsory Education for Poverty Reduction in Rural China," *Review of Education* 52 (2006): 261–285.

42. K. Tomasevski, *The State of Education Worldwide—Free or Fee: 2006 Global Report* (Copenhagen: UN Special Rapporteur on the Right to Education, 2006), 237.

43. Interview, Population Health: Moving from Evidence to Effective Policy.

44. A. Riddell, "The Introduction of Free Primary Education in Sub-Saharan Africa" (background paper for UNESCO, *Education for All Global Monitoring Report 2003/4: Gender and Education for All* [Paris: UNESCO, 2003]).

45. Interview, Population Health: Moving from Evidence to Effective Policy (Tanzania, 14/15 July 2008).

46. UNESCO-BREDA, *Dakar+7*: EFA Top Priority for Integrated Sector-Wide Policies (Dakar: UNESCO Regional Office for Education in Africa, 2007).

47. UNESCO-OREALC, *Los aprendizajes de los estudiantes de América Latina y el Caribe: Primer reporte de los resultados del Segundo Estudio Regional Comparativo y Explicativo* [*Student Achievement in Latin America and the Caribbean: Results of the Second Regional Comparative and Explanatory Study*] (Santiago: UNESCO Regional Bureau for Education in Latin America and the Caribbean, Latin American Laboratory for Assessment of the Quality of Education, 2008), cited in UNESCO, *Education for All Global Monitoring Report 2010*, 106.

48. J. Das, P. Pandey, and T. Zajonc, *Learning Levels and Gaps in Pakistan*, Policy Research Working Paper 4067 (Washington, D.C.: World Bank, 2006), cited in UNESCO, *Education for All Global Monitoring Report 2010*, 107.

49. I. Mullis, M. Martin, and P. Foy, *TIMSS 2007 International Mathematics Report: Findings from IEA's Trends in International Mathematics and Science Study at the Fourth and Eighth Grades* (Chestnut Hill, Mass.: Boston College, Lynch School of Education, TIMSS and PIRLS International Study Center, 2008), cited in UNESCO, *Education for All Global Monitoring Report 2010*, 105.

50. UNESCO, *Education for All Global Monitoring Report 2005: The Quality Imperative* (Paris: UNESCO, 2004); K. Cuc Nguyen, M. Wu, and S. Gillis, "Factors Influencing Achievement Levels in SACMEQ II—Botswana: An Application of Structural Equation Monitoring" (paper presented at the International Invitational Education Policy Conference, Paris, France, Fall 2005); M. Urquiola,

"Identifying Class Size Effects in Developing Countries: Evidence from Rural Bolivia," *Review of Economics and Statistics* 88, no. 1 (2006): 171–177.

51. This study found that if class sizes were decreased by 10 students, scores on the tests examined in this study would go up by 5 points. J. D. Willms and M. A. Somer, "Family, Classroom, and School Effects on Children's Educational Outcomes in Latin America," *School Effectiveness and School Improvement* 12, no. 4 (2001): 409–445.

52. J.-W. Lee and R. J. Barro, "Schooling Quality in a Cross-Section of Countries," *Economica* 68, no. 272 (2001): 465–488.

53. G. Peevely, L. Hedges, and B. A. Nye, "The Relationship of Class Size Effects and Teacher Salary," *Journal of Education Finance* 31, no. 1 (2005): 101–109; A. B. Krueger, "Economic Considerations and Class Size," *Economic Journal* 113, no. 485 (2003): F34–F63; C. Januszka and L. Dixon-Krauss, "Class Size: A Battle between Accountability and Quality Instruction," *Childhood Education* 84, no. 3 (2008): 167–170.

54. E. A. Hanushek, "The Failure of Input-Based Schooling Policies," *Economic Journal* 113, no. 485 (2003): F64–F98.

55. J. D. Finn and C. M. Achilles, "Tennessee's Class Size Study: Findings, Implications, Misconceptions," *Educational Evaluation and Policy Analysis* 21, no. 2 (1999): 97–109; UNESCO, *Education for All Global Monitoring Report 2005*.

56. Finn and Achilles, "Tennessee's Class Size Study."

57. J. D. Finn, "Small Classes in American Schools: Research, Practice, and Politics," *Phi Delta Kappan* 83, no. 7 (2002): 551–560; Januszka and Dixon-Krauss, "Class Size"; L. Ilon and A. H. Normore, "Relative Cost-Effectiveness of School Resources in Improving Achievement," *Journal of Education Finance* 31, no. 3 (2006): 238–254; P. Blatchford, P. Bassett, H. Goldstein, and C. Martin, "Are Class Size Differences Related to Pupils' Educational Progress and Classroom Processes? Findings from the Institute of Education Class Size Study of Children Aged 5–7 Years," *British Educational Research Journal* 29, no. 5 (2003): 709–730.

58. UNESCO Institute for Statistics, "Pupil-teacher Ratio. Primary," 1999–2011 (most recent year available), available at http://stats.uis.unesco.org (accessed 20 June 2012). Number of countries for which data are available: 180.

59. In cases where the country does not divide secondary into lower and upper secondary, the value given for secondary education as a whole is used for both lower and upper secondary. UNESCO Institute for Statistics, "Pupil-teacher Ratio. Lower Secondary, Secondary, Upper Secondary," 1999–2011 (most recent year available), available at http://stats.uis.unesco.org (accessed 20 June 2012). Number of countries for which data are available: 175 (lower secondary pupil-to-teacher ratio), 176 (upper secondary pupil-to-teacher ratio).

60. Organisation for Economic Co-operation and Development, "Chapter 4: Teachers' Pay and Conditions," in *Education at a Glance Analysis* (Paris: OECD Publishing, 1996), 55–65; B. Hansson and E. Charbonnier, *Education at a Glance 2010* (Paris: OECD Publishing, 2010); M. C. O'Sullivan, "Teaching Large Classes: The International Evidence and a Discussion of Some Good Practice in Ugandan Primary Schools," *International Journal of Educational Development* 26, no. 1 (2006): 24–27; UNESCO, *Teachers in a Changing World* (Geneva: UNESCO, 1998); M. Zymelman and J. DeStefano, *Primary School Teachers' Salaries in Sub-Saharan Africa* (Washington, D.C.: World Bank. 1989).

61. Willms and Somer, "Family, Classroom, and School Effects on Children's Educational Outcomes in Latin America."

62. K. Michaelowa, "Primary Education Quality in Francophone Sub-Saharan Africa: Determinants of Learning Achievement and Efficiency Considerations," *World Development* 29, no. 10 (2001): 1699–1716.

63. D. D. Goldhaber and D. J. Brewer, "Evaluating the Effect of Teacher Degree Level on Educational Performance," in W. J. J. Fowler, ed., *Developments in School Finance, 1996: Fiscal Proceedings from the Annual NCES State Data Conference, July 1996* (Washington, D.C.: U.S. Government Printing Office, 1997), 197–210; B. Rowan, F.-S. Chiang, and R. J. Miller, "Using Research on Employees' Performance to Study the Effects of Teachers on Student Achievement," *Sociology of Education* 70, no. 4 (1997): 256–284.

64. C. T. Clotfelter, H. F. Ladd, and J. L. Vigdor, "Teacher Credentials and Student Achievement: Longitudinal Analysis with Student Fixed Effects," *Economics of Education Review* 26, no. 6 (2007): 673–682; Goldhaber and Brewer, "Evaluating the Effect of Teacher Degree Level on Educational Performance."

65. S. R. Khandker, *Education Achievements and School Efficiency in Rural Bangladesh*, World Bank Discussion Paper no. 319 (Philadelphia: World Bank, 1996).

66. UNESCO, *Education for All Global Monitoring Report 2005*.

67. T. Konold, B. Jablonski, A. Nottingham, L. Kessler, S. Byrd, S. Imig, R. Berry, and R. McNergney, "Adding Value to Public Schools: Investigating Teacher Education, Teaching, and Pupil Learning," *Journal of Teacher Education* 59, no. 4 (2008): 300–312.

68. These agreements include, among others, the Universal Declaration of Human Rights (1948), the Convention against Discrimination in Education (1960), the International Covenant on Civil and Political Rights (1966), the International Covenant on Economic, Social and Cultural Rights (1966), the International Convention on the Elimination of All Forms of Racial Discrimination (1965), the Convention on the Elimination of All Forms of Discrimination against Women (1979), the Convention on the Rights of the Child (1989), and the Convention on the Rights of Persons with Disabilities (2006).

69. UNESCO, "The EFA Movement," available at http://www.unesco.org/en/efa/the-efa-movement/ (accessed 1 February 2010).

70. UNESCO, *Education for All Global Monitoring Report 2010*.

71. Ibid.

72. Ibid., 370–371.

73. UNESCO has found that the effect of instructional time is even more significant in low-income countries than it is in industrialized nations. Studies of 40 years of results from the International Association for the Evaluation of Educational Achievement covering 50 countries show that student performance in math, science, and foreign language improves as time spent on the subjects in school increases. UNESCO, *Education for All Global Monitoring Report 2005*. This positive relationship between instructional time and student outcomes, including test scores and repetition rates, has been confirmed around the world. Lee and Barro, "Schooling Quality in a Cross-Section of Countries"; J. H. Marshall, "School Quality and Learning Gains in Rural Guatemala," *Economics of Education Review* 28, no. 2 (2009): 207–216; J. S. Pischke, "The Impact of Length of the

School Year on Student Performance and Earnings: Evidence from the German Short School Years," *Economic Journal* 117, no. 523 (2007): 1216–1242.

74. A. J. Dowd, "A Day in School: Are Students Getting an Opportunity to Learn?" (paper presented at the Comparative and International Education Society Conference, Charleston, S.C., 24 March 2009); J. DeStefano and N. Elaheebocus, *School Effectiveness in Woliso, Ethiopia: Measuring Opportunity to Learn and Early Grade Reading Fluency* (Washington, D.C.: USAID/Save the Children USA, 2009); both cited in UNESCO, *Education for All Global Monitoring Report 2010*, 114; UNESCO, *Education for All Global Monitoring Report 2005*.

75. UNESCO, *Education for All Global Monitoring Report 2005*; F. Jalal, M. Samani, M. C. Chang, R. Stevenson, A. B. Ragatz, and S. D. Negara, *Teacher Certification in Indonesia: A Strategy for Teacher Quality Improvement* (Indonesia: Development Education Program, World Bank, 2009).

76. N. Chaudhury, J. Hammer, M. Kremer, K. Muralidharan, and F. H. Rogers, "Missing in Action: Teacher and Health Worker Absence in Developing Countries," *Journal of Economic Perspectives* 20, no. 1 (2006): 91–116.

77. UNESCO, *Education for All Global Monitoring Report 2005*; Jalal et al., *Teacher Certification in Indonesia*.

78. UNESCO, *Education for All Global Monitoring Report 2005*.

79. L. Pritchett, "Toward a New Consensus for Addressing the Global Challenge of the Lack of Education," in B. Lomborg, ed., *How to Spend $50 Billion to Make the World a Better Place* (Cambridge: Cambridge University Press, 2006), 57–70; A. Barrett, S. Ali, J. Clegg, E. Hinostroza, J. Lowe, J. Nikel, M. Novelli, G. Oduro, M. Pillay, L. Tikly, and G. Yu, "Initiatives to Improve the Quality of Teaching and Learning" (background paper for UNESCO, *Education for All Global Monitoring Report 2008: Education for All by 2015* [Paris: UNESCO, 2007]).

80. In francophone Africa, the availability of textbooks has been shown to have a strong positive effect on student outcomes; all else being equal, in classes where each student had both a French and a mathematics textbook, students scored between 6.6 and 8 percentage points higher on assessments than students in classes without textbooks. Michaelowa, "Primary Education Quality in Francophone Sub-Saharan Africa." In Latin America, the availability of school materials such as maps and calculators, as well as the size of the school library, has a positive impact on test scores. Willms and Somers, "Family, Classroom, and School Effects on Children's Educational Outcomes in Latin America." In Namibia, Tanzania, the Philippines, and China, when more textbooks were available, test scores rose in a range of school subjects. T. Godana and J. M. Ashipala, *The Impact of Educational Quality on Rates of Return to Education in Namibia*, NEPRU Working Paper no. 106 (Windhoek: Namibian Economic Policy Research Unit, 2006); A. V. Y. Mbelle, *The Impact of Reforms on the Quality of Primary Education in Tanzania*, Research Report 08.1 (Dar es Salaam: Research on Poverty Alleviation, 2008); Y. H. Du and Y. M. Hu, "Student Academic Performance and the Allocation of School Resources: Results from a Survey of Junior Secondary Schools," *Chinese Education and Society* 41, no. 5 (2008): 8–20; UNESCO, *Education for All Global Monitoring Report 2005*; E. A. Jamison, D. T. Jamison, and E. A. Hanushek, "The Effects of Education Quality on Income Growth and Mortality Decline," *Economics of Education Review* 26, no. 6 (2007): 771–788. Other materials, such as blackboards in the classroom, can also have an

impact. A. U. Ahmed and M. Arends-Kuenning, "Do Crowded Classrooms Crowd Out Learning? Evidence from the Food for Education Program in Bangladesh," *World Development* 34, no. 4 (2006): 665–684.

81. F. E. Aboud, "Evaluation of an Early Childhood Preschool Program in Rural Bangladesh," *Early Childhood Research Quarterly* 21, no. 1 (2006): 46–60; P. Sammons, K. Elliot, K. Sylva, E. Melhuish, I. Siraj-Blatchford, and B. Taggart, "The Impact of Pre-school on Young Children's Cognitive Attainments at Entry to Reception," *British Educational Research Journal* 30, no. 5 (2004): 691–712; K. A. Magnuson, C. Ruhm, and J. Waldfogel, "Does Prekindergarten Improve School Preparation and Performance?," *Economics of Education Review* 26, no. 1 (2007): 33–51; S. Berlinski, S. Galiani, and P. Gertler, "The Effect of Pre-primary Education on Primary School Performance," *Journal of Public Economics* 93, nos. 1–2 (2009): 219–234; J. Waldfogel and F. Zhai, "Effects of Public Preschool Expenditures on the Test Scores of Fourth Graders: Evidence from TIMSS," *Educational Research and Evaluation* 14, no. 1 (2008): 9–28; World Bank, *Brazil Early Childhood Development: A Focus on the Impact of Preschools*, Report No. 22841-BR (Washington, D.C.: World Bank, 2001); W. S. Barnett and L. N. Masse, "Comparative Benefit-Cost Analysis of the Abecedarian Program and Its Policy Implications," *Economics of Education Review* 26, no. 1 (2007): 113–125; K. M. Gorey, "Early Childhood Education: A Meta-analytic Affirmation of the Short- and Long-Term Benefits of Educational Opportunity," *School Psychology Quarterly* 16, no. 1 (2001): 9–30; J. Currie, "Early Childhood Education Programs," *Journal of Economic Perspectives* 15, no. 2 (2001): 213–238; A. Reynolds, J. A. Temple, D. L. Robertson, and E. A. Mann, "Age 21 Cost-Benefit Analysis of the Title I Chicago Child-Parent Centers," *Educational Evaluation and Policy Analysis* 24, no. 4 (2002): 267–303; D. Deming, "Early Childhood Intervention and Life-Cycle Skill Development: Evidence from Head Start," *American Economic Journal: Applied Economics* 1, no. 3 (2009): 111–134; F. A. Campbell, B. H. Wasik, E. Pungello, M. Burchinal, O. Barbarin, K. Kainz, J. J. Sparling, and C. T. Ramey, "Young Adult Outcomes of the Abecedarian and CARE Early Childhood Educational Interventions," *Early Childhood Research Quarterly* 23, no. 4 (2008): 452–466.

82. World Bank, *Brazil Early Childhood Development*; Barnett and Masse, "Comparative Benefit-Cost Analysis of the Abecedarian Program and Its Policy Implications."

83. Gorey, "Early Childhood Education."

84. Currie, "Early Childhood Education Programs"; Reynolds et al., "Age 21 Cost-Benefit Analysis of the Title I Chicago Child-Parent Centers."

85. Berlinski et al., "Effect of Pre-primary Education on School Performance."

86. This study controlled for socioeconomic status, including income and parental levels of education. Deming, "Early Childhood Intervention and Life-Cycle Skill Development."

87. Control groups were used to assess program effects. Campbell et al., "Young Adult Outcomes of the Abecedarian and CARE Early Childhood Educational Interventions."

88. UNESCO, *Education for All Global Monitoring Report 2007: Strong Foundations; Early Childhood Care and Education* (Paris: UNESCO, 2006).

89. One country, Afghanistan, has over 40 students per teacher but information was not available on its educational expenditures.

90. UNESCO Institute for Statistics, "Public Expenditure on Education as % of GDP," 1999–2011 (most recent year available), available at http://stats.uis.unesco.org (accessed 20 June 2012). Number of countries for which data are available: 172.

91. Employment rates for men and women with a tertiary education are an average of 9 percentage points higher than employment rates for those with only an upper secondary education. In some countries, including Greece, Poland, and Turkey, this difference is more than 12 percentage points. OECD, *Education at a Glance 2008: OECD indicators* (Paris: OECD, 2008).

92. In Malaysia, for example, men's employment rates increase from 88 percent among those with no education to 95 percent or above among those with an upper secondary or tertiary education. UNESCO Institute for Statistics and OECD, *Education Trends in Perspective—Analysis of the World Education Indicators* (Paris: UIS/OECD, 2005).

93. UNESCO Institute for Statistics and OECD, *Financing Education: Investments and Returns* (Paris: UIS/OECD, 2002).

94. OECD, *Education at a Glance 2008.*

95. UNESCO Institute for Statistics and OECD, *Financing Education.*

96. O. Ashenfelter and A. B. Krueger, "Estimates of the Economic Return to Schooling from a New Sample of Twins," *American Economic Review* 84, no. 5 (1994): 1157–1173; O. Ashenfelter and C. Rouse, "Income, Schooling, and Ability: Evidence from a New Sample of Identical Twins," *Quarterly Journal of Economics* 113, no. 1 (1998): 253–284.

97. UNESCO Institute for Statistics and OECD, *Financing Education.*

98. E. A. Hanushek and L. Wößmann, *Education Quality and Economic Growth* (Washington, D.C.: World Bank, 2007).

99. In the Philippines, for example, an additional year of education is estimated to increase income by 5 to 7 percent. Jamison, Jamison, and Hanushek, "Effects of Education Quality on Income Growth and Mortality Decline." This effect can be even greater in other countries, such as Chile, where it has been estimated to be between 7 and 19 percent even when other determinants of income are taken into account. UNESCO Institute for Statistics and OECD, *Financing Education.*

100. UNESCO Institute for Statistics and OECD, *Education Trends in Perspective.*

101. UNESCO, *EFA Global Monitoring Report 2009: Overcoming Inequality; Why Governance Matters* (Oxford: UNESCO, 2008).

102. Plan International, *Paying the Price: The Economic Cost of Failing to Educate Girls* (Surrey, U.K.: Plan International, 2008).

103. OECD, *The High Cost of Low Educational Performance* (Paris: OECD Publishing, 2010).

3. A Chance at Childhood

1. This interview took place in August 2001. This amount was converted using the World Bank's data in "PPP Conversion Factor, Private Consumption (LCU per International $)"; this factor was 5,221 for Viet Nam in 2001. World Bank, *World Development Indicators*, available at http://data.worldbank.org/indicator (accessed 21 March 2011).

2. Interview, Project on Global Working Families (Viet Nam, 9 August 2001). The name of this interviewee has been changed to protect confidentiality.

3. S. Bessell, "The Politics of Child Labour in Indonesia: Global Trends and Domestic Policy," *Pacific Affairs* 72 (1999): 353–371; S. Hertel, *Unexpected Power: Conflict and Change among Transnational Activists* (Ithaca, N.Y.: Cornell University Press, 2006); G. Myrstad, "What Can Trade Unions Do to Combat Child Labour?," *Childhood* 6 (1999): 75–88; D. Smolin, "Strategic Choices in the International Campaign against Child Labor," *Human Rights Quarterly* 22 (2000): 942–987; D. Smolin, "Conflict and Ideology in the International Campaign against Child Labour," *Hofstra Labor and Employment Law Journal* 16 (1999): 383–426; World Bank, "World Bank Global Child Labor Program Update, 2003," available at http://web.worldbank.org/WBSITE/EXTERNAL/TOP ICS/EXTSOCIALPROTECTION/EXTCL/0,,contentMDK:20254161~menu PK:754419~pagePK:148956~piPK:216618~theSitePK:390553,00.html? (accessed 2 July 2007).

4. R. Paes de Barros and R. Mendonca, "Trabalho infantil no Brasil: Rumo à erradicacão," *Mercado de Trabalho* 41 (2009), available at https://ipea.gov.br/agencia /images/stories/PDFs/mercadodetrabalho/03_NT_TrabalhoInfantil.pdf (accessed 3 February 2012).

5. International Labour Organization, *Accelerating Action against Child Labour*, Report of the Director-General, International Labour Conference, 99th Session (Geneva: ILO, 2010).

6. This ILO Statistical Information and Monitoring Programme on Child Labour (SIMPOC) study covered 16 countries: Azerbaijan, Burkina Faso, Cambodia, Colombia, Ecuador, El Salvador, Guatemala, Kyrgyzstan, Malawi, Mali, Mongolia, the Philippines, Senegal, Sri Lanka, Turkey, and Ukraine. F. Blanco Allais, *Assessing the Gender Gap: Evidence from SIMPOC Surveys* (Geneva: Statistical Information and Monitoring Programme on Child Labour [SIMPOC], International Programme on the Elimination of Child Labour, ILO, 2009).

7. International Labour Organization, *Accelerating Action against Child Labour*.

8. Blanco Allais, *Assessing the Gender Gap*.

9. For additional information on the ILO's global call to action on child labor, see International Labour Organization, *The End of Child Labour: Within Reach*, Report of the Director-General, International Labour Conference, 95th Session (Geneva: ILO, 2006). For additional examples of actors calling for further passage and implementation of child-labor-related legislation, see E. A. Archampong, "The Impact of Child Labor Laws in Ghana: A Critical Assessment" (master of law thesis, Queen's University, September 2001); K. Bakirci, "Child Labour and Legislation in Turkey," *International Journal of Children's Rights* 10 (2002): 55–72; K. Basu and P. H. Van, "The Economics of Child Labor," *American Economic Review* 88, no. 3 (1998): 412–427; K. Basu, "Child Labor: Cause, Consequence, and Cure, with Remarks on International Labor Standards," *Journal of Economic Literature* 37 (1999): 1083–1119; K. Basu and Z. Tzannatos, "The Global Child Labor Problem: What Do We Know and What Can We Do?," *World Bank Economic Review* 17, no. 2 (2003): 147–173; K. Basu, "Child Labor and the Law: Notes on Possible Pathologies," *Economics Letters* 87, no. 2 (2005): 169–174; Bessell, "Politics of Child Labour in Indonesia"; G. Betcherman, J. Fares, A. Luinstra,

and R. Prouty, "Child Labor, Education, and Children's Rights," in P. Alston and M. Robinson, eds., *Human Rights and Development: Towards Mutual Reinforcement* (New York: Oxford University Press, 2005): 173–200; J. Blagbrough, "Child Domestic Labour: A Modern Form of Slavery," *Children and Society* 22 (2008): 179–190; M. Bonnet, "Child Labour in Africa," *International Labour Review* 132, no. 3 (1993): 371–389; M. Caesar-Leo, "Child Labour: The Most Visible Type of Child Abuse and Neglect in India," *Child Abuse Review* 8 (1999): 75–86; M. Doepke and F. Zilibotti, *Voting with Your Children: A Positive Analysis of Child Labor Laws*, UCLA Department of Economics Working Paper no. 828 (Los Angeles: UCLA, February 2003); M. Doepke and F. Zilibotti. "The Macroeconomics of Child Labor Regulation," *American Economic Review* 95, no. 5 (2005): 1492–1524; C. Grootaert and R. Kanbur, "Child Labor: A Review," Policy Research Working Paper 1454 (Washington, D.C.: World Bank, Office of the Vice President, Development Economics, May 1995); C. Grootaert and R. Kanbur. "Child Labour: An Economic Perspective," *International Labour Review* 134, no. 2 (1995): 187–203; E. J. Kongnyuy, A. Y. Kongnyuy, and E. D. Richter, "Child Labour in Cameroon," *Internet Journal of World Health and Societal Politics* 5, no. 1 (2008), available at http://www.ispub.com/journal/the-internet-journal-of-world-health-and-societal -politics/volume-5-number-1/child-labour-in-cameroon.html (accessed 22 June 2012); M. Murshed, "Unraveling Child Labor and Labor Legislation," *Journal of International Affairs* 55, no. 1 (2001): 169–189; C. M. A. Nicholson, "The Impact of Child Labor Legislation on Child-Headed Households in South Africa," *Thomas Jefferson Law Review* 30 (2008): 407–427; M. E. Nielsen, "The Politics of Corporate Responsibility and Child Labour in the Bangladeshi Garment Industry," *International Affairs* 81, no. 3 (2005): 559–580; J. Otis, E. Mayers Pasztor, and E. J. McFadden, "Child Labor: A Forgotten Focus for Child Welfare," *Child Welfare* 80, no. 5 (2001): 611–622.

10. T. Fasih, *Analyzing the Impact of Legislation on Child Labor in Pakistan*, World Bank Policy Research Working Paper no. 4399 (Washington, D.C.: World Bank, November 2007).

11. Blanco Allais, *Assessing the Gender Gap.*

12. Reliable data on the other worst forms of child labor are unavailable. International Labour Organization, *Accelerating Action against Child Labour.*

13. A. Swift, "Let Us Work!," *New Internationalist* 292 (1997): 21–23; M. F. C. Bourdillon, "Child Labour and Education: A Case Study from South-eastern Zimbabwe," *Journal of Social Development in Africa* 15, no. 2 (2000): 5–32; H. A. Patrinos and G. Psacharopoulos, "Educational Performance and Child Labor in Paraguay," *International Journal of Educational Development* 15, no. 1 (1995): 47–60; D. Chernichovsky, "Socioeconomic and Demographic Aspects of School Enrolment and Attendance in Rural Botswana," *Economic Development and Cultural Change* 33 (1985): 319–332.

14. For example, in Bolivia and Venezuela, a working child's educational attainment is reduced by about 2 years compared with that of nonworking children. G. Psacharopoulos, "Child Labor versus Educational Attainment—Some Evidence from Latin America," *Journal of Population Economics* 10, no. 4 (1997): 377–386. Similarly, in Brazil, child labor before age 12 is estimated to reduce the number of years of education completed by approximately 2 years. N. Ilahi, P. Orazem, and G. Sedlacek, "The Implications of Child Labor for Adult Wages,

Income, and Poverty" (2001), available at http://www.grade.org.pe/Eventos/nip
_conference/private/sedlacek-%20child_labor%20retros.pdf (accessed 18 February 2010). For other examples of studies showing the educational disadvantage
experienced by child laborers, see S. Doocy, B. Crawford, C. Boudreaux, and
E. Wall, "The Risks and Impacts of Portering on the Well-Being of Children in
Nepal," *Journal of Tropical Pediatrics* 53, no. 3 (2007): 165–170; R. Ray, "The Determinants of Child Labour and Child Schooling in Ghana," *Journal of African
Economies* 11, no. 4 (2002): 561–590, cited in E. V. Edmonds, "Defining Child Labour: A Review of the Definitions of Child Labour in Policy Research" (working
paper for the Statistical Information and Monitoring Programme on Child
Labour, International Programme on the Elimination of Child Labour, ILO,
Geneva, November 2008), 34.

15. K. Beegle, R. Dehejia, and R. Gatti, *Why Should We Care about Child Labor? The Education, Labor Market, and Health Consequences of Child Labor,* World
Bank Policy Working Paper no. 3479 (Washington, D.C.: World Bank, 2005).

16. G. Bonnet, "Marginalization in Latin America and the Caribbean"
(background paper for and cited in UNESCO, *Education for All Global Monitoring
Report 2010: Reaching the Marginalized* [Oxford: Oxford University Press,
2010]), 111; M. A. Sánchez, P. F. Orazem, and V. Gunnarsson, "The Impact of
Child Labor Intensity on Mathematics and Language Skills in Latin America,"
in P. F. Orazem, G. Sedlacek, and Z. Tzannatos, eds., *Child Labor and Education
in Latin America: An Economic Perspective* (New York: Palgrave Macmillan,
2009), 117–130, cited in UNESCO, *Education for All Global Monitoring Report
2010,* 168.

17. V. Gunnarsson, P. F. Orazem, and M. A. Sánchez, "Child Labor and
School Achievement in Latin America," *World Bank Economic Review* 20, no. 1
(2006): 31–54.

18. D. Post and S. Pong, "Employment during Middle School: The Effects on
Academic Achievement in the U.S. and Abroad," *Educational Evaluation and Policy
Analysis* 22, no. 3 (2000): 273–298.

19. C. Heady, "The Effect of Child Labor on Learning Achievement," *World
Development* 31, no. 2 (2003): 385–398.

20. M. Fetuga, O. F. Njokanma, and T. A. Ogunlesi, "Do Working Children
Have Worse Academic Performance?," *Indian Journal of Pediatrics* 74, no. 10
(2007): 933–936; C. Dustmann, J. Micklewright, N. Rajah, and S. Smith, "Earning and Learning: Educational Policy and the Growth of Part-Time Work
by Full-Time Pupils," *Fiscal Studies* 17, no. 1 (1996): 79–103; H. Akabayashi and
G. Psacharopoulos, "The Trade-off between Child Labour and Human Capital
Formation: A Tanzanian Case Study," *Journal of Development Economics* 35 (1999):
120–140.

21. Edmonds, "Defining Child Labour."

22. Blanco Allais, *Assessing the Gender Gap.*

23. Ray, "Determinants of Child Labour and Child Schooling in Ghana,"
cited in Edmonds, "Defining Child Labour," 34.

24. Akabayashi and Psacharopoulos, "Trade-off between Child Labour and
Human Capital Formation."

25. B. Fuller, L. Dellagnelo, A. Strath, E. S. Barretto Bastos, M. Holanda
Maia, K. Socorro Lopes de Matos, A. L. Portela, and S. Lerche Vieira, "How

to Raise Children's Early Literacy? The Influence of Family, Teacher, and Classroom in Northeast Brazil," *Comparative Education Review* 43, no. 1 (1999): 1–35.

26. J. H. Lillydahl, "Academic Achievement and Part-Time Employment of High School Students," *Journal of Economic Education* 21, no. 3 (1990): 307–316.

27. R. D'Amico, "Does Working during High School Impair Academic Progress?," *Sociology of Education* 57, no. 3 (1984): 152–164.

28. Edmonds, "Defining Child Labour."

29. R. Assad, D. Levison, and N. Zibani, *The Effect of Child Work on Schooling: Evidence from Egypt*, Economic Research Forum Working Paper no. 0111 (Cairo: Economic Research Forum, revised 2005). Additional work by these authors shows that for girls, "a 10 percent increase in the probability of work reduces the probability of being in school by 6 percentage points." R. Assad, D. Levison, and N. Zibani, "The Effect of Domestic Work on Girls' Schooling: Evidence from Egypt," *Feminist Economics* 16, no. 1 (2010): 79–128.

30. H. Phoumin, "Human Capital and Hours Worked of Children in Cambodia: Empirical Evidence for Policy Implications," *Asian Economic Journal* 22, no. 1 (2008): 25–46.

31. O. O'Donnell, F. C. Rosati, and E. van Doorslaer, "Health Effects of Child Work: Evidence from Rural Vietnam," *Journal of Population Economics* 18, no. 3 (2005): 437–467; F. C. Rosati and R. Straub, "Does Work during Childhood Affect the Health of Guatemalan Adults?," *Review of Economics of the Household* 5, no. 1 (2007): 83–95; S. A. E. Cortez, M. A. Barbieri, M. Pereira Saraiva, H. Bettiol, A. A. Moura da Silva, and V. Cunha Cardoso, "Does Child Labour Affect Final Height?," *Occupational Medicine* 57 (2007): 118–125; I. S. Martins, F. M. Fisher, and D. C. Oliveira, "Crescimento e trabalho de estudantes de ensino fundamental e medio em São Paulo, Brasil," *Revista de Saúde Publica* 36, no. 1 (2002): 19–25, cited in Cortez et al., "Does Child Labour Affect Final Height?", 122; A. Cigno and F. Rosati, *Why Do Indian Children Work, and Is It Bad for Them?*, IZA Discussion Paper No. 115 (Bonn: Institute for the Study of Labor, 2000).

32. C. L. Castro, S. Gormly, and A. R. Ritualo, "The SIMPOC Philippine Survey of Children 2001: A Data Source for Analyzing Occupational Injuries to Children," *Public Health Reports* 120, no. 6 (2005): 631–640; Doocy et al., "Risks and Impacts of Portering on the Well-Being of Children in Nepal"; I. A. Nuwayhid, J. Usta, M. Makarem, A. Khudr, and A. El-Zein, "Health of Children Working in Small Industrial Shops," *Occupational and Environmental Medicine* 62, no. 2 (2005): 86–94; R. R. Tiwari, A. Saha, J. R. Parikh, and H. N. Saiyed, "Injuries and Injury Care among Child Labourers in Gem Polishing Industries in Jaipur, India," *Journal of Occupational Health* 46, no. 3 (2004): 216–219; A. D. Woolf, "Health Hazards for Children at Work," *Journal of Toxicology—Clinical Toxicology* 40, no. 4 (2002): 477–482.

33. D. L. Mull and S. R. Kirkhorn, "Child Labor in Ghana Cocoa Production: Focus upon Agricultural Tasks, Ergonomic Exposures, and Associated Injuries and Illnesses," *Public Health Reports* 120, no. 6 (2005): 649–655; B. Saddik, A. Williamson, I. Nuwayhid, and D. Black, "The Effects of Solvent Exposure on Memory and Motor Dexterity in Working Children," *Public Health Reports* 120, no. 6 (2005): 657–663.

34. R. Harari and M. Cullen, "Childhood Lead Intoxication Associated with Manufacture of Roof Tiles and Ceramics in the Ecuadorian Andes," *Archives of Environmental Health* 50, no. 5 (1995): 393; L. S. R. Ide and D. L. Parker, "Hazardous Child Labor: Lead and Neurocognitive Development," *Public Health Reports* 120, no. 6 (2005): 607–610; Nuwayhid et al., "Health of Children Working in Small Industrial Shops."

35. Blagbrough, "Child Domestic Labour"; UNICEF, "Child Domestic Work," *Innocenti Digest* 5 (1999): 1–20; International Labour Organization, *Hazardous Child Domestic Work: A Briefing Sheet* (Geneva: ILO, 2007); R. Silva-de-Alwis, *Legislative Reform on Child Domestic Labour: A Gender Analysis*, Legislative Reform Initiative Paper Series (New York: UNICEF Division of Policy and Planning, 2008); A. Matsuno and J. Blagbrough, *Child Domestic Labour in Southeast and East Asia: Emerging Good Practices to Combat It* (Bangkok: International Programme on the Elimination of Child Labour, 2006).

36. Nuwayhid et al., "Health of Children Working in Small Industrial Shops"; O'Donnell, Rosati, and van Doorslaer, "Health Effects of Child Work"; F. C. Wolff and Maliki, "Evidence on the Impact of Child Labor on Child Health in Indonesia, 1993–2000," *Economics and Human Biology* 6, no. 1 (2007): 143–169.

37. Rosati and Straub, "Does Work during Childhood Affect the Health of Guatemalan Adults?"

38. A. L. Kassouf, M. McKee, and E. Mossialos, "Early Entrance to the Job Market and Its Effect on Adult Health," *Health Policy and Planning* 16, no. 1 (2001): 21–28.

39. At the time of database construction, the United Nations had 192 member nations (South Sudan had not yet become a member). The Child Labor Database includes 192 countries, but 3 had no labor legislation available. Thus we examined the legislation of 189 countries.

40. International Labour Organization, "C182 Worst Forms of Child Labour Convention, 1999," available at http://www.ilo.org/ilolex/cgi-lex/convde.pl?C182 (accessed 19 February 2010).

41. International Labour Organization, "Recommendation 190: Recommendation Concerning the Prohibition and Immediate Action for the Elimination of the Worst Forms of Child Labour," available at http://www.ilo.org/public/english /standards/relm/ilc/ilc87/com-chir.htm (accessed 12 March 2012).

42. Types of exceptions in legislation include sectoral work, especially agricultural; educational/vocational/apprenticeship positions; volunteer and personal development opportunities; work with minister or government approval or request; work with family members; work with a medical certificate; work as a result of detention or judicial order; jobs for which there is no harm to health, safety, and morals; and force majeure.

43. Office of the United Nations High Commissioner for Human Rights, "Convention on the Rights of the Child," available at http://www2.ohchr.org /english/law/crc.htm#art32 (accessed 19 July 2010).

44. The 6 countries with no minimum age for full-time employment are Australia, India, Micronesia, New Zealand, Pakistan, and Tonga.

45. The 5 countries with a minimum age for full-time work of less than 14 are Bhutan, Dominica, Guinea, the Solomon Islands, and Sudan.

46. International Labour Organization, "C138 Minimum Age Convention, 1973," available at http://www.ilo.org/ilolex/cgi-lex/convde.pl?C138 (accessed 19 February 2010).

47. International Labour Organization, *Accelerating Action against Child Labour.*

48. When a country stipulates hour restrictions for working children of a given age but specifies a lower hour limit when the child is enrolled in school, this lower limit is applied until the age at which schooling is no longer compulsory. After this age, the higher number of hours is applied.

49. "Article 7, 1. National laws or regulations may permit the employment or work . . . on light work which is—(a) not likely to be harmful to their health or development; and (b) not such as to prejudice their attendance at school, their participation in vocational orientation or training programmes approved by the competent authority or their capacity to benefit from the instruction received." International Labour Organization, "C138 Minimum Age Convention, 1973," available at http://www.ilo.org/ilolex/cgi-lex/convde.pl?C138 (accessed 22 February 2012).

50. J. Owens, "Classification and Epidemiology of Childhood Sleep Disorders," *Primary Care: Clinics in Office Practice* 35, no. 3 (2008): 533–546; P. C. Zee and F. W. Turek, "Sleep and Health: Everywhere and in Both Directions," *Archives of Internal Medicine* 166, no. 16 (2006): 1686–1688; L. M. O'Brien, "The Neurocognitive Effects of Sleep Disruption in Children and Adolescents," *Child and Adolescent Psychiatric Clinics of North America* 18, no. 4 (2009): 813–823; A. R. Wolfson and M. A. Carskadon, "Understanding Adolescents' Sleep Patterns and School Performance: A Critical Appraisal," *Sleep Medicine Reviews* 7, no. 6 (2003): 491–506; J. Lim and D. F. Dinges, "Sleep Deprivation and Vigilant Attention," *Annals of the New York Academy of Sciences* 1129 (2008): 305–322; M. W. Chee and L. Y. Chuah, "Functional Neuroimaging Insights into How Sleep and Sleep Deprivation Affect Memory and Cognition," *Current Opinion in Neurology* 21, no. 4 (2008): 417–423; G. Fallone, C. Acebo, J. T. Arnedt, R. Seifer, and M. A. Carskadon, "Effects of Acute Sleep Restriction on Behavior, Sustained Attention, and Response Inhibition in Children," *Perceptual and Motor Skills* 93, no. 1 (2001): 213–229; G. Fallone, C. Acebo, R. Seifer, and M. A. Carskadon, "Experimental Restriction of Sleep Opportunity in Children: Effects on Teacher Ratings," *Sleep* 28, no. 12 (2005): 1561–1567; K. Fredriksen, J. Rhodes, R. Reddy, and N. Way, "Sleepless in Chicago: Tracking the Effects of Adolescent Sleep Loss during the Middle School Years," *Child Development* 75, no. 1 (2004): 84–95.

51. International Labour Organization, "R146 Minimum Age Recommendation, 1973," available at http://www.ilo.org/ilolex/cgi-lex/convde.pl?R146 (accessed 25 February 2011).

52. As with the maps detailed in earlier sections, we include hazardous work permitted routinely or with any exception other than force majeure, and other types of work permitted either routinely or with requirements that are not sufficiently protective. For example, if a country's official age of general employment is 16, but 14-year-olds are allowed to work in agriculture, then the country would appear in the category "not protected from general employment" at age 14 because these youth could work in agriculture. When exceptions are granted down to a specified age, we use that age as the minimum age for work. When no age is

given, we assume a child of any age can perform the indicated type of work, unless another law provides protection. For example, when exceptions to the minimum age for hazardous work have no minimum age attached to them, we assume the child can work under this exception as long as he or she is old enough to legally be generally employed.

53. S. Mathur, M. Greene, and A. Malhotra, *Too Young to Wed: The Lives, Rights, and Health of Young Married Girls* (Washington, D.C.: International Center for Research on Women, 2003).

54. UNICEF, "Achieving the MDGs with Equity," *Progress for Children* 9 (September 2010).

55. Mathur, Greene, and Malhotra, *Too Young to Wed.*

56. UNICEF, *Early Marriage: A Harmful Traditional Practice* (New York: UNICEF, 2005); B. Mensch, "The Transition to Marriage," in C. B. Lloyd, ed., *Growing Up Global: The Changing Transitions to Adulthood in Developing Countries*, Committee on Population, Board on Children, Youth, and Families, Division of Behavioral and Social Sciences and Education, National Research Council, and Institute of Medicine (Washington, D.C.: National Academies Press, 2005), 416–505.

57. R. Jensen and R. Thornton, "Early Female Marriage in the Developing World," *Gender and Development* 11, no. 2 (2003): 9–19.

58. S. Jain and K. Kurz, "New Insights on Preventing Child Marriage: A Global Analysis of Factors and Programs" (report prepared by the International Center for Research on Women for the United States Agency for International Development, April 2007); Mensch, "Transition to Marriage."

59. UNICEF, *Early Marriage: A Harmful Traditional Practice.*

60. Jensen and Thornton, "Early Female Marriage in the Developing World"; Mensch, "Transition to Marriage"; Jain and Kurz, "New Insights on Preventing Child Marriage."

61. C. B. Lloyd and B. S. Mensch, "Marriage and Childbirth as Factors in Dropping out of School: An Analysis of DHS Data from Sub-Saharan Africa," *Population Studies* 62, no. 1 (2008): 1–13; T. Tuwor and M.-A. Sossou, "Gender Discrimination and Education in West Africa: Strategies for Maintaining Girls in School," *International Journal of Inclusive Education* 12, no. 4 (2008): 363–379.

62. E. Field and A. Ambrus, "Early Marriage, Age of Menarche, and Female Schooling Attainment in Bangladesh," *Journal of Political Economy* 166, no. 5 (2008): 881–930.

63. UNICEF, *Early Marriage; A Harmful Traditional Practice;* Mensch, "Transition to Marriage"; Jain and Kurz, "New Insights on Preventing Child Marriage"; Jensen and Thornton, "Early Female Marriage in the Developing World."

64. M. J. Hindin and A. O. Fatusi, "Adolescent Sexual and Reproductive Health in Developing Countries: An Overview of Trends and Interventions," *International Perspectives on Sexual and Reproductive Health* 35, no. 2 (2009): 58–62; UNICEF, "Early Marriage: Child Spouses," *Innocenti Digest* 7 (March 2001); UNICEF, *Early Marriage: A Harmful Traditional Practice;* R. Savitridina, "Determinants and Consequences of Early Marriage in Java, Indonesia," *Asia-Pacific Population Journal* 12, no. 2 (1997): 25–48; A. Raj, N. Saggurti, D. Balaiah, and J. G. Silverman, "Prevalence of Child Marriage and Its Effect on Fertility and Fertility-Control Outcomes of Young Women in India: A Cross-Sectional,

Observational Study," *Lancet* 373, no. 9678 (2009): 1883–1889; Jain and Kurz, "New Insights on Preventing Child Marriage"; Mathur, Greene, and Malhotra, *Too Young to Wed.*

65. Jain and Kurz, "New Insights on Preventing Child Marriage"; Mathur, Greene, and Malhotra, *Too Young to Wed;* Hindin and Fatusi, "Adolescent Sexual and Reproductive Health in Developing Countries"; S. Clark, "Early Marriage and HIV Risks in Sub-Saharan Africa," *Studies in Family Planning* 35, no. 3 (2004): 149–160; S. Clark, J. Bruce, and A. Dude, "Protecting Young Women from HIV/AIDS: The Case against Child and Adolescent Marriage," *International Family Planning Perspectives* 32, no. 2 (2006): 79–88; UNICEF, *Early Marriage: A Harmful Traditional Practice.*

66. Mathur, Greene, and Malhotra, *Too Young to Wed.*

67. Field and Ambrus, "Early Marriage, Age of Menarche, and Female Schooling Attainment in Bangladesh."

68. UNICEF, *Early Marriage: A Harmful Traditional Practice;* S. Singh and R. Samara, "Early Marriage among Women in Developing Countries," *International Family Planning Perspectives* 22, no. 4 (1996): 148–157; M. Ertem, G. Saka, A. Ceylan, and V. Deger, "The Factors Associated with Adolescent Marriages and Outcomes of Adolescent Pregnancies in Mardin Turkey," *Journal of Comparative Family Studies* 39, no. 2 (2008): 229–239; Raj et al., "Prevalence of Child Marriage and Its Effect on Fertility and Fertility-Control Outcomes of Young Women in India"; Jain and Kurz, "New Insights on Preventing Child Marriage"; Mathur, Greene, and Malhotra, *Too Young to Wed.*

69. Mathur, Greene, and Malhotra, *Too Young to Wed.*

70. K. A. Annan, *We the Children* (New York: UNICEF, 2001).

71. N. M. Nour, "Health Consequences of Child Marriage in Africa," *Emerging Infectious Diseases* 12, no. 11 (2006): 1644–1649; N. M. Nour, "Child Marriage: A Silent Health and Human Rights Issue," *Reviews in Obstetrics and Gynecology* 197, no. 1 (2009): 51–56; L. Wall, "Dead Mothers and Injured Wives: The Social Context of Maternal Morbidity and Mortality among the Hausa of Northern Nigeria," *Studies in Family Planning* 29, no. 4 (1998): 341–370; L. S. Zabin and K. Kiragu, "The Health Consequences of Adolescent Sexual and Fertility Behavior in Sub-Saharan Africa," *Studies in Family Planning* 29, no. 2 (1998): 210–233.

72. UNICEF, "Early Marriage: Child Spouses"; Save the Children, *Children Having Children: State of the World's Mothers 2004* (Westport, Conn.: Save the Children, 2004).

73. L. Meyer, C. J. Ascher-Walsh, R. Norman, A. Idrissa, H. Herbert, O. Kimso, and J. Wilkinson, "Commonalities among Women Who Experienced Vesicovaginal Fistulae as a Result of Obstetric Trauma in Niger: Results from a Survey Given at the National Hospital Fistula Center, Niamey, Niger," *American Journal of Obstetrics and Gynecology* 197, no. 1 (2007): 90.e1–90.e4; G. S. Melah, A. A. Massa, U. R. Yahaya, M. Bukar, D. D. Kizaya, and A. U. El-Nafaty, "Risk Factors for Obstetric Fistulae in North-eastern Nigeria," *Journal of Obstetrics and Gynaecology* 27, no. 8 (2007): 819–823; A. Holme, M. Breen, and C. MacArthur, "Obstetric Fistulae: A Study of Women Managed at the Monze Mission Hospital, Zambia," *Bjog: An International Journal of Obstetrics and Gynaecology* 114, no. 8 (2007): 1010–1017; Nour, "Health Consequences of Child Marriage in Africa";

Hindin and Fatusi, "Adolescent Sexual and Reproductive Health in Developing Countries"; D. O. Onolemhemhem and C. C. Ekwempu, "An Investigation of Sociomedical Risk Factors Associated with Vaginal Fistula in Northern Nigeria," *Women and Health* 28, no. 3 (1999): 103–116; Jain and Kurz, "New Insights on Preventing Child Marriage."

74. E. P. Ghararo and K. N. Agholor, "Aspects of Psychosocial Problems of Patients with Vesico-vaginal Fistula," *Journal of Obstetrics and Gynaecology* 29, no. 7 (2009): 644–647; Melah et al., "Risk Factors for Obstetric Fistulae in Northeastern Nigeria."

75. Mathur, Greene, and Malhotra, *Too Young to Wed*.

76. Jain and Kurz, "New Insights on Preventing Child Marriage."

77. Mathur, Greene, and Malhotra, *Too Young to Wed*; Nour, "Health Consequences of Child Marriage in Africa"; V. Sharma, J. Katz, L. C. Mullany, S. K. Khatry, S. C. Leclerq, S. R. Shrestha, G. L. Darmstadt, and J. M. Tielsch, "Young Maternal Age and the Risk of Neonatal Mortality in Rural Nepal," *Archives of Pediatric and Adolescent Medicine* 162, no. 9 (2008): 828–835; Ertem et al., "Factors Associated with Adolescent Marriages and Outcomes of Adolescent Pregnancies in Mardin Turkey"; Raj et al., "Prevalence of Child Marriage and Its Effect on Fertility and Fertility-Control Outcomes of Young Women in India"; UNICEF, "Early Marriage: Child Spouses"; A. O. Igwebe and G. O. Udigwe, "Teenage Pregnancy: Still an Obstetric Risk," *Journal of Obstetrics and Gynaecology* 21, no. 5 (2001): 478–481; B. Banerjee, G. Pandey, D. Dutt, B. Sengupta, M. Mondal, and S. Deb, "Teenage Pregnancy: A Socially Inflicted Health Hazard," *Indian Journal of Community Medicine* 34, no. 3 (2009): 227–231; Jain and Kurz, "New Insights on Preventing Child Marriage"; S. Shawky and W. Milaat, "Cumulative Impact of Early Maternal Marital Age during the Childbearing Period," *Paediatric and Perinatal Epidemiology* 15, no. 1 (2001): 27–33.

78. M. Muleta and G. Williams, "Postcoital Injuries Treated at the Addis Ababa Fistula Hospital," *Lancet* 354, no. 9195 (1999): 2051–2052; K. G. Santhya, N. Haberland, F. Ram, R. K. Sinha, and S. K. Mohanty, "Consent and Coercion: Examining Unwanted Sex among Married Young Women in India," *International Family Planning Perspectives* 33, no. 3 (2007): 124–132; D. F. Flake, "Individual, Family, and Community Risk Markers for Domestic Violence in Peru," *Violence against Women* 11, no. 3 (2005): 353–373; N. Gottschalk, "Uganda: Early Marriage as a Form of Sexual Violence," *Forced Migration Review* 27 (2007): 51–53; Hindin and Fatusi, "Adolescent Sexual and Reproductive Health in Developing Countries"; P. Ebigbo, "Child Abuse in Africa: Nigeria as Focus," *International Journal of Early Childhood* 35, no. 1 (2003): 95–113; P. Ouis, "Honourable Traditions? Honour Violence, Early Marriage and Sexual Abuse of Teenage Girls in Lebanon, the Occupied Palestinian Territories and Yemen," *International Journal of Children's Rights* 17, no. 3 (2009): 445–474; UNICEF, *Early Marriage; A Harmful Traditional Practice*; Jain and Kurz, "New Insights on Preventing Child Marriage"; Mathur, Greene, and Malhotra, *Too Young to Wed*.

79. Proportion of women who had been emotionally abused, married at the age of 15 or younger: 43 percent; under 18: 41 percent; 16–20: 39 percent; 21–25: 34 percent; 26–30: 29 percent; 30 or older: 28 percent. Proportion of women who had been physically abused, married at the age of 15 or younger: 20 percent; under 18: 18 percent; 16–20: 16 percent; 21–25: 12 percent; 26–30: 8 percent; 30 or older:

7 percent. Proportion of women who had been sexually abused, married at the age of 15 or younger: 17 percent; under 18: 14 percent; 16–20: 13 percent; 21–25: 11 percent; 26–30: 7 percent; 30 or older: 5 percent. Jensen and Thornton, "Early Female Marriage in the Developing World."

80. Twelve percent of women married under age 18 had been beaten in the past year, compared with 5 percent of women married between the ages of 21 and 25 and 4 percent of women married at age 26 or older. Ibid.

81. Before building this database, we considered using data from the United Nations Statistics Division's Gender Info 2007, which presents data on the minimum legal age for marriage. We did not use these data for two reasons. First, the different conditions under which children can marry at different ages (parental permission, pregnancy, and so on) were not captured consistently. Second, we came across a number of inconsistencies in the data that raised questions about their reliability. For example, although Gender Info stated that girls in Spain can marry at the age of 12 with parental consent, a report by the Committee on the Convention on the Rights of the Child (CRC/C/15/Add. 185 of 13 June 2002) states that a "judge may authorize marriages as low as 14 years of age in exceptional circumstances."

82. Of the 6 countries that allow boys to marry at the age of 13 or younger, 3 are in sub-Saharan Africa, 2 are in the Middle East and North Africa, and 1 is in the Americas. Of the 15 countries that permit boys to marry at 14 or 15, 10 are in the Americas, 3 are in East Asia and the Pacific, 1 is in the Middle East and North Africa, and 1 is in sub-Saharan Africa. Of the 43 countries that allow boys to marry at age 16 or 17, 17 are in the Americas, 11 are in Europe and Central Asia, 8 are in sub-Saharan Africa, 4 are in East Asia and the Pacific, and 3 are in the Middle East and North Africa.

83. World Bank, "The Twin Challenges of Eliminating Child Labour and Achieving EFA: Evidence and Policy Options from Mali and Zambia" (working paper, April 2009); International Labour Organization, *End of Child Labour*; International Labour Organization, "Effective Abolition of Child Labour," available at http://www.ilo.org/declaration/principles/abolitionofchildlabour/lang–en /index.htm (accessed 28 February 2012).

84. The importance of crafting effective laws to address early marriage has been highlighted by a UNICEF Legislative Reform Initiative paper on child marriage and the law that includes detailed recommendations on laws and implementation, some of which are discussed in this section. R. de Silva-de-Alwis, "Child Marriage and the Law" (Legislative Reform Initiative Paper Series, UNICEF Division of Policy and Planning, January 2008).

85. Ibid.; UNICEF, "Early Marriage: Child Spouses."

86. UNICEF, "Achieving the MDGs with Equity."

87. Silva-de-Alwis, "Child Marriage and the Law"; Mensch, "Transition to Marriage."

88. Government of Liberia, *Combined Second, Third, and Fourth Country Report to the United Nations Committee on the Rights of the Child* (July 2009), available at http://www2.ohchr.org/english/bodies/crc/docs/CRC.C.LBR.2-4.pdf (accessed 31 March 2011).

89. International Labour Organization, *End of Child Labour*; A. Dewees and S. J. Klees, "Social Movements and the Transformation of National Policy: Street

and Working Children in Brazil," *Comparative Education Review* 39, no. 1 (1995): 76–100.

90. This conditional cash transfer program provided stipends to mothers of children aged 7 to 14 on the condition that the child or children would go to school, attend after-school activities, and not work. World Bank, *Brazil: Eradicating Child Labor*, Report no. 21858-BR (Washington, D.C.: World Bank, 2001).

91. Y.-T. Yap, G. Sedlacek, and P. F. Orazem, "Limiting Child Labor through Behavior-Based Income Transfers: An Experimental Evaluation of the PETI Program in Rural Brazil" (working paper, February 2001), available at http://site resources.worldbank.org/INTISPMA/Resources/383704-1153333441931/11375 _orazem-peti-brazil.pdf (accessed 24 February 2010).

92. International Labour Organization, *Eliminating Child Labour: The Promise of Conditional Cash Transfers* (Geneva: ILO, 2006); H. Tabatabai, *Conditional Cash Transfers and Child Labour: Experiences and Opportunities* (Geneva: International Programme on the Elimination of Child Labour, ILO, 2010); M. Arends-Kuenning and S. Amin, "School Incentive Programs and Children's Activities: The Case of Bangladesh," *Comparative Education Review* 48, no. 3 (2004): 295–317.

93. Yap, Sedlacek, and Orazem, "Limiting Child Labor through Behavior-Based Income Transfers."

94. A. de Janvry, F. Finan, E. Sadoulet, and R. Vakis, "Can Conditional Cash Transfer Programs Serve as Safety Nets in Keeping Children at School and from Working When Exposed to Shocks?," *Journal of Development Economics* 79 (2006): 349–373.

95. International Programme on the Elimination of Child Labour, *Investing in Every Child: An Economic Study of the Costs and Benefits of Eliminating Child Labour* (Geneva: ILO, 2003).

96. UNICEF, "Early Marriage: Child Spouses"; UNICEF, *Early Marriage: A Harmful Traditional Practice*; International Planned Parenthood Federation and the Forum on Marriage and the Rights of Women and Girls, *Ending Child Marriage: A Guide for Global Policy Action* (London: International Planned Parenthood Federation and the Forum on Marriage and the Rights of Women and Girls, 2006); F. D. Chowdhury, "The Socio-cultural Context of Child Marriage in a Bangladeshi Village," *International Journal of Social Welfare* 13, no. 3 (2004): 244–253; Mathur, Greene, and Malhotra, *Too Young to Wed*; N. Otoo-Oyortey and S. Pobi, "Early Marriage and Poverty: Exploring Links and Key Policy Issues," *Gender and Development* 11, no. 2 (2003): 42–51; Jensen and Thornton, "Early Female Marriage in the Developing World."

97. UNICEF, *Early Marriage: A Harmful Traditional Practice*.

98. For information on the impact of social norms, see Mathur, Greene, and Malhotra, *Too Young to Wed*. An additional element that may need to be addressed is that families may need to be convinced of the value of sending both boys and girls to school. UNICEF, "Early Marriage: Child Spouses." They may also need to learn about the legal age of marriage, the risks of early marriage for children, and the other options available to their children besides marriage. P. Subramanian, "Determinants of the Age at Marriage of Rural Women in India," *Family and Consumer Sciences Research Journal* 37, no. 2 (2008): 160–166; Mathur, Greene,

and Malhotra, *Too Young to Wed*. A cultural focus on a girl's virginity and the dependence of a family's honor on this "purity" also tend to encourage early marriage; marrying a daughter off at a young age decreases the amount of time during which a family must concern itself with keeping her "untouched." Mathur, Greene, and Malhotra, *Too Young to Wed*; UNICEF, "Early Marriage: Child Spouses." Husbands and in-laws may also have a preference for younger girls. Field and Ambrus, "Early Marriage, Age of Menarche, and Female Schooling Attainment in Bangladesh"; Jensen and Thornton, "Early Female Marriage in the Developing World." When dowry payments increase with a girl's age, families have an additional incentive to marry their daughters off quickly in order to minimize their financial burden. Field and Ambrus, "Early Marriage, Age of Menarche, and Female Schooling Attainment in Bangladesh."

99. A. S. Erulkar and E. Muthengi, "Evaluation of Berhane Hewan: A Program to Delay Child Marriage in Rural Ethiopia," *International Perspectives on Sexual and Reproductive Health* 35, no. 1 (2009): 6–14.

100. UNICEF, *Early Marriage: A Harmful Traditional Practice*; L. Davids, "Female Subordination Starts at Home: Consequences of Young Marriage and Proposed Solutions," *Regent Journal of International Law* 5 (2007): 299–324; Jain and Kurz, "New Insights on Preventing Child Marriage;" D. P. Lindstrom and C. B. Paz, "Alternative Theories of the Relationship of Schooling and Work to Family Formation: Evidence from Mexico," *Social Biology* 48, nos. 3–4 (2001): 278–297; Mathur, Greene, and Malhotra, *Too Young to Wed*.

101. S. O. Gyimah, "Cohort Differences in Women's Educational Attainment and the Transition to First Marriage in Ghana," *Population Research and Policy Review* 28, no. 4 (2009): 455–471; Lindstrom and Paz, "Alternative Theories of the Relationship of Schooling and Work to Family Formation"; Mathur, Greene, and Malhotra, *Too Young to Wed*.

102. Mensch, "Transition to Marriage."

103. L. M. Bates, J. Maselko, and S. R. Schuler, "Women's Education and the Timing of Marriage and Childbearing in the Next Generation: Evidence from Rural Bangladesh," *Studies in Family Planning* 38, no. 2 (2007): 101–112.

104. UNICEF, *Early Marriage: A Harmful Traditional Practice*.

105. J. Raynor and K. Wesson, "The Girls' Stipend Program in Bangladesh," *Journal of Education for International Development* 2, no. 2 (2006): 1–12.

106. Jensen and Thornton, "Early Female Marriage in the Developing World"; Jain and Kurz, "New Insights on Preventing Child Marriage"; Mensch, "Transition to Marriage."

107. Mathur, Greene, and Malhotra, *Too Young to Wed*.

4. Beyond Survival to Health

1. Interview, Project on Global Working Families (Mexico, 4 April 2000). The name of this interviewee has been changed to protect confidentiality.

2. World Health Organization, *Packages of Interventions for Family Planning, Safe Abortion Care, Maternal, Newborn and Child Health* (Geneva: World Health Organization, 2010); World Health Organization and UNICEF, *Countdown to 2015 Decade Report (2000–2010) with Country Profiles: Taking Stock of Maternal, Newborn and Child Survival* (Washington, D.C.: WHO and UNICEF, 2010).

3. World Health Organization and UNICEF, *Countdown to 2015 Decade Report (2000–2010) with Country Profiles.*

4. World Health Organization, "Newborn Death and Illness" (September 2011), available at http://www.who.int/pmnch/media/press_materials/fs/fs_newborndealth_illness/en/index.html (accessed 22 May 2012).

5. World Health Organization and UNICEF, *Countdown to 2015 Decade Report (2000–2010) with Country Profiles.*

6. C. Hertzman and C. Power, "A Life Course Approach to Health and Human Development," in J. Heymann, C. Hertzman, M. L. Barer, and R. G. Evans, eds., *Healthier Societies: From Analysis to Action* (New York: Oxford University Press, 2006); C. B. Forrest and A. W. Riley, "Childhood Origins of Adult Health: A Basis for Life-Course Health Policy," *Health Affairs* 23, no. 5 (2004): 155–164.

7. World Health Organization, "Young People: Health Risks and Solutions," Fact Sheet no. 345 (August 2011), available at http://www.who.int/mediacentre/factsheets/fs345/en/index.html (accessed 27 February 2012).

8. UNICEF, "Achieving the MDGs with Equity," *Progress for Children* 9 (September 2010).

9. World Health Organization and UNICEF, *World Report on Child Injury Prevention* (Geneva: World Health Organization, 2008).

10. J. H. DiLiberti, "The Relationship between Social Stratification and All-Cause Mortality among Children in the United States: 1968–1992," *Pediatrics* 105, no. 1 (2000): e2–e7.

11. T. Blakely, J. Atkinson, C. Kiro, A. Blaiklock, and A. D'Souza, "Child Mortality, Socioeconomic Position, and One-Parent Families: Independent Associations and Variation by Age and Cause of Death," *International Journal of Epidemiology* 32, no. 3 (2003): 410–418.

12. UNICEF, "Achieving the MDGs with Equity."

13. UNICEF and World Health Organization, *Diarrhoea: Why Children are Still Dying and What Can Be Done* (New York: UNICEF/WHO, 2009).

14. UNICEF, "Achieving the MDGs with Equity."

15. S. Egerter, K. Marchi, C. Cubbin, and P. Braveman, *Disparities in Maternal and Infant Health: Are We Making Progress? Lessons from California* (Menlo Park, Calif.: Henry J. Kaiser Family Foundation, Fall 2004).

16. In all but two Indian states, immunization coverage rates were higher for boys than for girls. In the northern region, which had the greatest difference in immunization coverage rates between boys and girls aged 12 to 47 months, girls had 0.58 times the odds of receiving the BCG tuberculosis vaccination compared with boys, 0.58 times the odds of receiving the diphtheria, pertussis, and tetanus vaccination, 0.59 times the odds of receiving the polio vaccination, and 0.63 times the odds of receiving the measles vaccination. P. Arokiasamy, "Regional Patterns of Sex Bias and Excess Female Child Mortality in India," *Population* 59, no. 6 (2004): 833–864.

17. S. Li, C. Zhu, and M. W. Feldman, "Gender Differences in Child Survival in Contemporary Rural China: A County Study," *Journal of Biosocial Science* 36 (2004): 83–109; J. Li, "Gender Inequality, Family Planning, and Maternal and Child Care in a Rural Chinese County," *Social Science and Medicine* 59 (2004): 695–708.

18. G. Hazarika, "Gender Differences in Children's Nutrition and Access to Health Care in Pakistan," *Journal of Development Studies* 37, no. 1 (2000): 73–92.

19. UNICEF Thematic Group on Violence against Disabled Children, *Summary Report: Violence against Disabled Children* (New York: UNICEF, 2005).

20. G. Jones, R. W. Steketee, R. E. Black, Z. A. Bhutta, S. S. Morris, and the Bellagio Child Survival Study, "How Many Child Deaths Can We Prevent This Year?," *Lancet* 362, no. 9377 (2003): 65–71.

21. UNICEF, "Achieving the MDGs with Equity."

22. UNICEF, *State of the World's Children—Special Edition: Celebrating 20 Years of the Convention on the Rights of the Child* (New York: UNICEF, 2009).

23. World Health Organization, *WHO Vaccine-Preventable Diseases: Monitoring System, 2009 Global Summary* (Geneva: World Health Organization, 2009).

24. Herd immunity occurs when a large-enough proportion of the population has been immunized against a disease that even nonimmunized individuals are largely protected because of the greatly reduced odds that a nonimmunized individual will come into contact with the contagious disease. World Health Organization, "Workshop on Herd Effects on Vaccine Effectiveness," available at http://www.who.int/vaccine_research/about/gvrf/Session6_Clemens_report WHE.pdf (accessed 18 February 2011).

25. World Health Organization, Global Health Observatory Data Repository, 2009–2010, available at http://apps.who.int/ghodata/ (accessed 7 May 2012). Number of countries for which data are available: 191.

26. UNICEF and World Health Organization, *Diarrhoea*. "One DALY [disability-adjusted life year] can be thought of as one lost year of 'healthy' life. The sum of these DALYs across the population, or the burden of disease, can be thought of as a measurement of the gap between current health status and an ideal health situation where the entire population lives to an advanced age, free of disease and disability." World Health Organization, "Metrics: Disability-Adjusted Life Year (DALY)," available at http://who.int/healthinfo/global_burden_disease /metrics_daly/en/ (accessed 10 July 2012).

27. UNICEF and World Health Organization, *Diarrhoea*.

28. J. Bartram and S. Cairncross, "Hygiene, Sanitation, and Water: Forgotten Foundations of Health," *PLoS Medicine* 7, no. 11 (2010): e1000367 (9 pages).

29. World Health Organization, Global Health Observatory Data Repository, 2010, available at http://apps.who.int/ghodata/ (accessed 7 May 2012). Number of countries for which data are available: 167.

30. Ibid. Number of countries for which data are available: 167.

31. World Health Organization and UNICEF, *World Report on Child Injury Prevention*.

32. Ibid.

33. World Health Organization, Global Health Observatory Data Repository, 2007, available at http://apps.who.int/ghodata/ (accessed 7 May 2012). Number of countries for which data are available: 171 (road safety strategy), 172 (child restraints law), 174 (motorcycle helmet law).

34. World Health Organization, *WHO Report on the Global Tobacco Epidemic, 2009: Implementing Smoke-Free Environments* (Geneva: WHO, 2009).

35. World Health Organization, Global Health Observatory Data Repository, 2010. Number of countries for which data are available: 191.

36. World Health Organization, *WHO Report on the Global Tobacco Epidemic, 2009.*

37. The WHO Framework Convention on Tobacco Control, adopted in 2003, is the first treaty negotiated by WHO member states and contains legally binding provisions for its 172 parties, as well as a framework for action. This convention promotes six policies for tobacco control: monitoring tobacco use and prevention policies; protecting the population from exposure to tobacco smoke; providing help to those who want to quit; warning consumers about the dangers of tobacco; mandating bans on tobacco advertising, promotion, and sponsorship; and increasing the price of tobacco products by raising taxes on them. World Health Organization, "WHO Framework Convention on Tobacco Control," available at http://www.who.int/fctc/en/ (accessed 7 March 2011).

38. World Health Organization, *Break the Tobacco Marketing Net: Tobacco-Free Youth* (Geneva: World Health Organization, 2008).

39. Ibid.; World Health Organization, *WHO Report on the Global Tobacco Epidemic, 2009.*

40. World Health Organization, Global Health Observatory Data Repository, 2010. Number of countries for which data are available: 189.

41. World Health Organization, *WHO Report on the Global Tobacco Epidemic, 2009.*

42. World Health Organization, Global Health Observatory Data Repository, 2010. Number of countries for which data are available: 191.

43. World Health Organization, *Global Strategy to Reduce the Harmful Use of Alcohol* (Geneva: World Health Organization, 2010).

44. World Health Organization, *Global Status Report: Alcohol Policy* (Geneva: World Health Organization, 2004).

45. The following countries have no minimum legal age for alcohol purchase: Armenia, Azerbaijan, Belgium, Benin, Burundi, Cambodia, the Central African Republic, China, Equatorial Guinea, Eritrea, Guinea-Bissau, India, Italy, Jamaica, Japan, Laos, Liberia, Mali, Nicaragua, São Tomé and Principe, Sierra Leone, Timor-Leste, Togo, and Ukraine. World Health Organization, Global Health Observatory Data Repository, 2008, available at http://apps.who.int/ghodata/ (accessed 7 May 2012). Number of countries for which data are available: 151.

46. We reviewed information available from the World Health Organization, the Joint United Nations Programme on HIV/AIDS (UNAIDS), the United Nations Population Division (UNPD), and several international NGOs. We found global data to be limited but available on a few important outcome measures. For example, there were data on adolescent fertility rates. While information on this outcome is essential, so too is a better understanding of what countries are doing to try to address youth needs. We were able to find only one relevant policy indicator from the UNPD that has a yes/no answer to whether a country has "policies to reduce adolescent fertility," but lacks the specificity needed to understand their content and efficacy. The limited outcomes data available also include crucial information on HIV prevalence rates among youth. These important data illuminate the risks currently faced by girls. Unfortunately, the data on what is being done about this is limited in nature and geographic scope.

47. World Health Organization and UNICEF, *Countdown to 2015 Decade Report (2000–2010) with Country Profiles.*

48   World Health Organization, *World Health Statistics 2011* (Geneva: WHO, 2011). Number of countries for which data are available: 183.

49. UNICEF and World Health Organization, *Pneumonia: The Forgotten Killer of Children* (New York and Geneva: UNICEF/WHO, 2006).

50. World Health Organization and UNICEF, *Countdown to 2015 Decade Report (2000–2010) with Country Profiles.*

51. P. E. Petersen, D. Bourgeois, H. Ogawa, S. Estupinian-Day, and C. Ndiaye, "The Global Burden of Oral Diseases and Risks to Oral Health," *Bulletin of the World Health Organization* 83, no. 9 (2005): 661–669; P. E. Petersen, *World Oral Health Report 2003* (Geneva: World Health Organization, 2003); R. C. Williams, A. H. Barnett, N. Claffey, M. Davis, R. Gadsby, M. Kellett, G. Y. Lip, and S. Thackray, "The Potential Impact of Periodontal Disease on General Health: A Consensus View," *Current Medical Research and Opinion* 24, no. 6 (2008): 1635–1643; A. Sheiham, "Oral Health, General Health and Quality of Life," *Bulletin of the World Health Organization* 83, no. 9 (2005): 644–645.

52. World Health Organization, *World Health Statistics 2011.* Number of countries for which data are available: 180.

53. World Health Organization, UNICEF, UN Population Fund, and World Bank, *Trends in Maternal Mortality: 1990 to 2010* (Geneva: World Health Organization, 2012).

54. World Health Organization, "Infant Mortality," Global Health Observatory Data Repository, available at http://www.who.int/gho/urban_health/out comes/infant_mortality_text/en/index.html (accessed 22 May 2012).

55. World Health Organization, *World Health Report 2005: Making Every Mother and Child Count* (Geneva: WHO, 2005).

56. World Health Organization et al., *Trends in Maternal Mortality.*

57. World Health Organization, *Making a Difference in Countries: Strategic Approach to Improving Maternal and Newborn Survival and Health* (Geneva: WHO, 2006).

58. World Health Organization, *Packages of Interventions.*

59. M. Kamrul Islam and U.-G. Gerdtham, *The Costs of Maternal-Newborn Illness and Mortality* (Geneva: World Health Organization, 2006).

60. World Health Organization, *World Health Statistics 2011.* Number of countries for which data are available: 176.

61. Organisation for Economic Co-operation and Development, OECD Health Data 2011, available at http://stats.oecd.org (accessed 23 June 2012). Number of countries for which data are available: 34.

62. World Health Organization, "Maternal Mortality Ratio (per 100 000 Live Births)—Interagency Estimates, 2008," Global Health Observatory Data Repository, available at http://apps.who.int/ghodata/ (accessed 26 February 2012).

63. World Health Organization, "Infant Mortality Rate (Probability of Dying between Birth and Age 1 per 1000 Live Births), 2010," Global Health Observatory Data Repository, available at http://apps.who.int/ghodata/ (accessed 26 February 2012).

64. World Bank, "GDP per Capita, PPP (current international $)," available at http://databank.worldbank.org (accessed 8 May 2012); Human Rights Watch,

Well Oiled: Oil and Human Rights in Equatorial Guinea (New York: Human Rights Watch, 2009).

65. World Health Organization, *World Health Statistics 2011*.

66. H. Matsuura, "Does Constitutional Right to Health Matter? Cross-Country Evidence," portion of unpublished doctoral dissertation, Harvard School of Public Health, Boston, Mass. Using our own data, we have also confirmed an association between health rights and indicators of health care service delivery.

67. A right is considered aspirational if it is written in language that is not authoritative (e.g., the State "should," "endeavors to," "promotes"), if it is explicitly dependent on the state's ability to provide it, or if it is explicitly nonenforceable. It is also considered aspirational when it appears only in the preamble of the constitution when the preamble is not described as an integral part of the constitution in question.

68. World Health Organization, Global Health Observatory Data Repository, 2009–2010. Number of countries for which data are available: 189. Somalia has a DTP3 immunization rate of less than 85 percent and fewer than half of births are attended by skilled personnel, but data on health expenditures were not available.

69. UN Millennium Project, "The 0.7% Target: An In-Depth Look," available at http://www.unmillenniumproject.org/press/07.htm (accessed 16 February 2011).

70. Reported assistance as a percentage of GDP (which is less than gross national product because it does not include international productivity) is 0.53 percent in the United Kingdom, 0.36 percent in Germany, 0.3 percent in Australia and Canada, and 0.2 percent in the United States. Overseas development assistance figures from OECDStat, "Net Disbursements, ODA, Current Prices (USD Millions)," 2009, available at http://stats.oecd.org (accessed 16 February 2011); GDP figures from World Bank, "GDP (Current US$)," available at http://databank.worldbank.org/ddp/home.do (accessed 16 February 2011).

71. Australian AID, *Australian Multilateral Assessment March 2012: Global Fund to Fight AIDS, Tuberculosis and Malaria (the Global Fund)* (Australia: Commonwealth of Australia, 2012).

72. Stockholm International Water Institute with World Health Organization and Norwegian Agency for Development Cooperation, *Making Water a Part of Economic Development* (2005), available at http://www.siwi.org/documents/Resources/Reports/CSD_Making_water_part_of_economic_development_2005.pdf (accessed 16 February 2011).

73. P. R. Hunter, A. M. MacDonald, and R. C. Carter, "Water Supply and Health," *PLoS Medicine* 7, no, 11 (2010): e1000361 (9 pages).

74. J. Sachs, *Macroeconomics and Health: Investing in Health for Economic Development*, Report of the Commission on Macroeconomics and Health (Geneva: World Health Organization, 2001).

75. J. Ehreth, "The Global Value of Vaccination," *Vaccine* 21, no. 7–8 (2003): 596–600.

76. Centers for Disease Control and Prevention, "Crude and Age-Adjusted Percentage of Civilian, Noninstitutionalized Population with Diagnosed Diabetes, United States, 1980–2010," available at http://www.cdc.gov/diabetes/statistics/prev/national/figage.htm (accessed 26 February 2012).

77. Diabetes Quebec and the Canadian Diabetes Association, *Diabetes: Canada at the Tipping Point* (2011), available at http://www.diabetes.ca/documents/get-involved/WEB_Eng.CDA_Report_.pdf (accessed 26 February 2012).

5. Parents and Children

1. Interview, Project on Global Working Families (United States, 20 June 1997). The name of this interviewee has been changed to protect confidentiality.

2. D. Hernandez, "Children's Changing Access to Resources: A Historical Perspective," in K. Hansen and A. Garey, eds., *Families in the U.S.: Kinship and Domestic Politics* (Philadelphia: Temple University Press, 1998), 201–215.

3. Population Division of the Department of Economic and Social Affairs of the United Nations Secretariat, *World Population Prospects: The 2006 Revision* and *World Urbanization Prospects; The 2007 Revision*, available at http://esa.un.org/unup/p2k0data.asp (accessed 29 July 2010).

4. Among interviewed parents with at least one child under 5 years of age, just 45 percent in Mexico, 32 percent in Botswana, and 44 percent in Viet Nam were able to rely on extended family members for help and did not need to provide assistance to extended family members themselves. J. Heymann, *Forgotten Families: Ending the Growing Crisis Confronting Children and Working Parents in the Global Economy* (New York: Oxford University Press, 2006).

5. For 1960 figures, see World Bank, *World Development Indicators 2002* (Washington, D.C.: World Bank, 2002), CD-ROM; for 2009 figures, see World Bank, World Development Indicators, "Labor Force, Female (% of Total Labor Force)," available at http://data.worldbank.org/ (accessed 23 January 2012).

6. D. Thomas, "The Distribution of Income and Expenditure within the Household," *Annales d'Économie et de Statistique* 29 (1993): 109–135; A. R. Quisumbing and L. C. Smith, "Intrahousehold Allocation, Gender Relations, and Food Security in Developing Countries," in S. E. Frandsen, P. Pinstrup-Andersen, and F. Cheng, eds., *Case Studies in Food Policy for Developing Countries*, vol. 1, *Policies for Health, Nutrition, Food Consumption, and Poverty* (Ithaca, N.Y.: Cornell University Press, 2009), 195–207.

7. These estimates are based on detailed household survey information from a sample of widely divergent countries. Heymann, *Forgotten Families*, 7, 12.

8. World Health Organization, *Packages of Interventions for Family Planning, Safe Abortion Care, Maternal, Newborn and Child Health* (Geneva: World Health Organization, 2010); World Health Organization and UNICEF, *Countdown to 2015 Decade Report (2000–2010) with Country Profiles: Taking Stock of Maternal, Newborn and Child Survival* (Washington, D.C.: WHO and UNICEF, 2010).

9. J. P. Shonkoff and D. A. Phillips, eds., *From Neurons to Neighborhoods: The Science of Early Childhood Development* (Washington, D.C.: National Academy Press, 2000).

10. E. Anisfeld and E. Lipper, "Early Contact, Social Support, and Mother-Infant Bonding," *Pediatrics* 72, no. 1 (1983): 79–83; M. E. Lamb, "Early Contact and Maternal-Infant Bonding: One Decade Later," *Pediatrics* 70, no. 5 (1982): 763–768; P. G. Mertin, "Maternal-Infant Attachment: A Developmental Perspec-

tive," *Australian and New Zealand Journal of Obstetrics and Gynaecology* 26, no. 4 (1986): 280–283; A. M. Taubenheim, "Paternal-Infant Bonding in the First-Time Father," *JOGN Nursing* 10, no. 4 (1981): 261–264.

11. This study controlled for gross domestic product (GDP) per capita, total and government health expenditures, female literacy, and basic health care and public health provision. J. Heymann, A. Raub, and A. Earle, "Creating and Using New Data Sources to Analyze the Relationship between Social Policy and Global Health: The Case of Maternal Leave," *Public Health Reports* 126, no. 3 (2011): 127–134.

12. In OECD countries, a 10-week extension of paid parental leave is associated with a reduction in infant mortality rates of 2.6 percent, post-neonatal mortality rates of 4.1 percent, and child mortality rates of 3 percent. S. Tanaka, "Parental Leave and Child Health across OECD Countries," *Economic Journal* 115 (2005): F7–F28.

13. In the countries studied, a 10-week increase in paid leave is associated with a reduction in infant mortality of between 2.5 and 3.4 percent. C. J. Ruhm, "Parental Leave and Child Health," *Journal of Health Economics* 19, no. 6 (2000): 931–960.

14. N. Leon-Cava, C. Lutter, J. Ross, and M. Luann, *Quantifying the Benefits of Breastfeeding: A Summary of the Evidence* (Washington, D.C.: Pan American Health Organization, 2002); S. Ip, M. Chung, G. Raman, P. Chew, N. Magula, D. DeVine, T. Trikalinos, and J. Lau, "Breastfeeding and Maternal and Infant Health Outcomes in Developed Countries" (prepared for Agency for Healthcare Research and Quality, AHRQ Publication 07-E007, Rockville, Md., April 2007); C. Dennis, "Breastfeeding Initiation and Duration: A 1990–2000 Literature Review," *Journal of Obstetric, Gynecologic and Neonatal Nursing* 31, no. 1 (2002): 12–32; A. S. Cunningham, D. B. Jelliffe, and E. F. P. Jelliffe, "Breast-feeding and Health in the 1980s: A Global Epidemiologic Review," *Journal of Pediatrics* 118, no. 5 (1991): 659–666; J. M. Jason, P. Nieburg, and J. S. Marks, "Mortality and Infectious Disease Associated with Infant-Feeding Practices in Developing Countries," *Pediatrics* 74 (1984): 702–727; K. G. Dewey, M. Jane Heinig, and L. A. Nommsen-Rivers, "Differences in Morbidity between Breastfed and Formula-Fed Infants. Part 1," *Journal of Pediatrics* 126 no. 5 (1995): 696–702.

15. G. Aniansson, B. Alm, B. Andersson, A. Hakansson, P. Larsson, O. Nylen, H. Peterson, P. Rigner, M. Svanborg, and H. Sabharwal, "A Prospective Cohort Study on Breast-feeding and Otitis Media in Swedish Infants," *Pediatric Infectious Disease Journal* 13, no. 3 (1994): 183–188; C. Arnold, S. Makintube, and G. Istre, "Daycare Attendance and Other Risk Factors for Invasive Haemophilus Influenzae Type B Disease," *American Journal of Epidemiology* 138, no. 5 (1993): 333–340; A. Bener, S. Denic, and S. Galadari, "Longer Breastfeeding and Protection against Childhood Leukaemia and Lymphomas," *European Journal of Cancer* 37, no. 2 (2001): 234–238; M. Cerqueriro, P. Murtagh, A. Halac, M. Avila, and M. Weissenbacher, "Epidemiologic Risk Factors for Children with Acute Lower Respiratory Tract Infection in Buenos Aires, Argentina: A Matched Case-Control Study," *Reviews of Infectious Diseases* 12, suppl. 8 (1990): S1021–S1028; T. L. Creek, A. Kim, L. Lu, A. Bowen, J. Masunge, W. Arvelo, M. Smit, O. Mach, K. Legwaila, L. Zaks, T. Finkbeiner, L. Povinelli, M. Maruping, G. Ngwaru, G. Tebele, C. Bopp, N. Puhr, S. P. Johnston, A. J. Dasilva, C. Bern, R. S. Beard, and M. K.

Davis, "Hospitalization and Mortality among Primarily Nonbreastfed Children during a Large Outbreak of Diarrhea and Malnutrition in Botswana, 2006," *Journal of Acquired Immune Deficiency Syndrome* 53, no. 1 (2010): 14–19; B. Duncan, J. Ey, C. Holberg, A. Wright, F. Martinez, and L. Taussig, "Exclusive Breast-feeding for at Least 4 Months Protects against Otitis Media," *Pediatrics* 91, no. 5 (1993): 867–872; R. G. Feachem and M. A. Koblinsky, "Interventions for the Control of Diarrhoeal Diseases among Young Children: Promotion of Breast-feeding," *Bulletin of the World Health Organization* 62, no. 2 (1984): 271–291; P. Howie, J. Forsyth, S. Ogston, A. Clark, and C. Florey, "Protective Effect of Breast Feeding against Infection," *British Medical Journal* 300, no. 6716 (1990): 11–16; E. Klement, R. V. Cohern, J. Boxman, A. Joseph, and S. Reif, "Breastfeed-ing and Risk of Inflammatory Bowel Disease: A Systematic Review with Meta-analysis," *American Journal of Clinical Nutrition* 80, no. 5 (2004): 1342–1352; P. Lepage, C. Munyakazi, and P. Hennart, "Breastfeeding and Hospital Mortal-ity in Children in Rwanda," *Lancet* 318, no. 8242 (1981): 409–411; R. M. Martin, D. Gunnell, C. G. Owen, and G. D. Smith, "Breastfeeding and Childhood Can-cer: A Systematic Review with Meta-analysis," *International Journal of Cancer* 117, no. 6 (2005): 1020–1031; A. J. Naylor and A. Morrow, eds., *Developmental Readiness of Normal Full Term Infants to Progress from Exclusive Breastfeeding to the Introduc-tion of Complementary Foods: Reviews of the Relevant Literature Concerning Infant Immunologic, Gastrointestinal, Oral Motor and Maternal Reproductive and Lacta-tional Development* (Washington, D.C.: Wellstart International and the LINK-AGES Project/Academy for Educational Development, 2001); V. Sadauskaite-Kuehne, J. Ludvigsson, Z. Padaiga, E. Jasinskiene, and U. Samuelsson, "Longer Breastfeeding Is an Independent Protective Factor against Development of Type 1 Diabetes Mellitus in Childhood," *Diabetes/Metabolism Research and Reviews* 20, no. 2 (2004): 150–157; X. O. Shu, M. S. Linet, M. Steinbuch, W. Q. Wen, J. D. Buckley, J. P. Neglia, J. D. Potter, G. H. Reaman, and L. L. Robison, "Breastfeed-ing and Risk of Childhood Acute Leukemia," *Journal of the National Cancer Insti-tute* 91, no. 20 (1999): 1765–1772; X. O. Shu, J. Clemens, W. Zheng, D. M. Ying, B. T. Ji, and F. Jin, "Infant Breastfeeding and the Risk of Childhood Lymphoma and Leukaemia," *International Journal of Epidemiology* 24, no. 1 (1995): 27–32; C. J. Watkins, S. R. Leeder, and R. T. Corkhill, "The Relationship between Breast and Bottle Feeding and Respiratory Illness in the First Year of Life," *Journal of Epidemiology and Community Health* 33, no. 3 (1979): 180–182; A. Wright, C. Hol-berg, F. Martinez, W. Morgan, and L. Taussig, "Breast Feeding and Lower Re-spiratory Tract Illness in the First Year of Life," *British Medical Journal* 299, no. 6705 (1989): 946–949; J. W. Anderson, B. M. Johnstone, and D. T. Remley, "Breast-feeding and Cognitive Development: A Meta-analysis," *American Journal of Clinical Nutrition* 70, no. 4 (1999): 525–535; E. L. Mortensen, K. F. Michaelsen, S. A. Sanders, and J. M. Reinisch, "The Association between Duration of Breast-feeding and Adult Intelligence," *Journal of the American Medical Association* 287, no. 18 (2002): 2365–2371; M. S. Kramer, F. Aboud, E. Mironova, I. Vanilovich, R. W. Platt, L. Matush, S. Igumnov, E. Fombonne, N. Bogdanovich, T. Ducruet, J. P. Collet, B. Chalmers, E. Hodnett, S. Davidovsky, O. Skugarevsky, O. Trofi-movich, L. Kozlova, and S. Shapiro, "Breastfeeding and Child Cognitive Devel-opment: New Evidence from a Large Randomized Trial," *Archives of General Psychiatry* 65, no. 5 (2008): 578–584; M. Gdalevich, D. Mimouni, M. David, and

M. Mimouni, "Breast-feeding and the onset of atopic dermatitis in childhood: A systematic review and meta-analysis of prospective studies," *Journal of the American Academy of Dermatology* 45, no. 4 (2001): 487–647.

16. Leon-Cava et al., *Quantifying the Benefits of Breastfeeding.*

17. For more information on the connection between breastfeeding and pneumonia, see UNICEF and World Health Organization, *Pneumonia: The Forgotten Killer of Children* (New York: UNICEF and WHO, 2006). Mothers can also benefit from breastfeeding, with documented results that include accelerated postpartum weight loss and reduced premenopausal breast cancer risk, as well as potential reduced risk for other diseases, from ovarian cancer to osteoporosis. See Ip et al., "Breastfeeding and Maternal and Infant Health Outcomes in Developed Countries"; E. B. Schwarz, R. M. Ray, A. M. Stuebe, M. A. Allison, R. B. Ness, M. S. Freiberg, and J. A. Cauley, "Duration of Lactation and Risk Factors for Maternal Cardiovascular Disease," *Obstetrics and Gynecology* 113 (2009): 974–982; S. J. Reeder, L. L. Martin, and D. Koniak-Griffin, *Maternity Nursing: Family, Newborn, and Women's Health Care,* 18th ed. (Philadelphia: Lippincott, 1997); P. T. Ellison, "Breastfeeding, Fertility, and Maternal Condition," in P. Stuart-Macadam and K. A. Dettwyler, eds., *Breastfeeding: Biocultural Perspectives* (New York: Aldine de Gruyter, 1995); G. Palmer and S. Kemp, "Breastfeeding Promotion and the Role of the Professional Midwife," in S. F. Murray, ed., *Baby Friendly Mother Friendly* (London: Mosby, 1996), 1–23; Leon-Cava et al., *Quantifying the Benefits of Breastfeeding;* S. M. Enger, R. K. Ross, A. Paganini-Hill, and L. Bernstein, "Breastfeeding Experience and Breast Cancer Risk among Postmenopausal Women," *Cancer Epidemiology, Biomarkers and Prevention* 7 (1998): 365–369; and K. B. Michels, W. C. Willett, B. A. Rosner, J. E. Manson, D. J. Hunter, G. A. Colditz, S. E. Hankinson, and F. E. Speizer, "Prospective Assessment of Breastfeeding and Breast Cancer Incidence among 89,887 Women," *Lancet* 347, no. 8999 (1996): 431–436.

18. R. Khanam, H. S. Nghiem, and L. B. Connelly, "Does Maternity Leave Affect Child Health? Evidence from Parental Leave in Australia Survey" (31st Australian Conference of Health Economists [AHES 2009], Darwin City, Australia, 1–2 Oct 2009).

19. M. O'Brien, "Fathers, Parental Leave Policies, and Infant Quality of Life: International Perspectives and Policy Impact," *Annals of the American Academy of Political and Social Science* 624 (2009): 190–213.

20. For example, these fathers were 75 percent more likely to change the baby's diaper more than once per day than fathers who had not taken leave. L. Nepomnyaschy and J. Waldfogel, "Paternity Leave and Fathers' Involvement with Their Young Children," *Community, Work and Family* 10, no. 4 (2007): 427–453.

21. S. Tanaka and J. Waldfogel, "Effects of Parental Leave and Work Hours on Fathers' Involvement with Their Babies," *Community, Work and Family* 10, no. 4 (2007): 409–426.

22. M. Page and M. S. Wilhelm, "Postpartum Daily Stress, Relationship Quality, and Depressive Symptoms," *Contemporary Family Therapy: An International Journal* 29, no. 4 (2007): 237–251.

23. J. Waldfogel, "Family and Medical Leave: Evidence from the 2000 Surveys," *Monthly Labor Review* 124, no. 9 (September 2001): 17–23.

24. Tanaka, "Parental Leave and Child Health across OECD Countries."

25. Ruhm, "Parental Leave and Child Health."

26. Khanam, Nghiem, and Connelly, "Does Maternity Leave Affect Child Health?"

27. H. Mandel, "Winners and Losers: The Consequences of Welfare State Policies for Gender Wage Inequality," *European Sociological Review* 28, no. 2 (2012): 241–262; B. R. Bergmann, "Long Leaves, Child Well-Being, and Gender Equality," *Politics and Society* 36 (2008): 350–359; M. Estévez-Abe, "Gender Bias in Skills and Social Policies: The Varieties of Capitalism Perspective on Sex Segregation," *Social Politics: International Studies in Gender, State and Society* 12, no. 2 (2005): 180–215.

28. F. E. Aboud, "Evaluation of an Early Childhood Preschool Program in Rural Bangladesh," *Early Childhood Research Quarterly* 21, no. 1 (2006): 46–60; P. Sammons, K. Elliot, K. Sylva, E. Melhuish, I. Siraj-Blatchford, and B. Taggart, "The Impact of Pre-school on Young Children's Cognitive Attainments at Entry to Reception," *British Educational Research Journal* 30, no. 5 (2004): 691–712; K. A. Magnuson, C. Ruhm, and J. Waldfogel, "Does Prekindergarten Improve School Preparation and Performance?," *Economics of Education Review* 26, no. 1 (2007): 33–51; S. Berlinski, S. Galiani, and P. Gertler, "The Effect of Pre-primary Education on School Performance," *Journal of Public Economics* 93, nos. 1–2 (2009): 219–234; J. Waldfogel and F. Zhai, "Effects of Public Preschool Expenditures on the Test Scores of Fourth Graders: Evidence from TIMSS," *Educational Research and Evaluation* 14, no. 1 (2008): 9–28; World Bank, *Brazil Early Childhood Development: A Focus on the Impact of Preschools*, Report no. 22841-BR (Washington, D.C.: World Bank, 2001); W. S. Barnett and L. N. Masse, "Comparative Benefit-Cost Analysis of the Abecedarian Program and Its Policy Implications," *Economics of Education Review* 26, no. 1 (2007): 113–125; K. M. Gorey, "Early Childhood Education: A Meta-analytic Affirmation of the Short- and Long-Term Benefits of Educational Opportunity," *School Psychology Quarterly* 16, no. 1 (2001): 9–30; J. Currie, "Early Childhood Education Programs," *Journal of Economic Perspectives* 15, no. 2 (2001): 213–238; A. Reynolds, J. A. Temple, D. L. Robertson, and E. A. Mann, "Age 21 Cost-Benefit Analysis of the Title I Chicago Child-*Parent Centers*," *Educational* Evaluation and Policy Analysis 24, no. 4 (2002): 267–303; D. Deming, "Early Childhood Intervention and Life-Cycle Skill Development: Evidence from Head Start," *American Economic Journal: Applied Economics* 1, no. 3 (2009): 111–134; F. A. Campbell, B. H. Wasik, E. Pungello, M. Burchinal, O. Barbarin, K. Kainz, J. J. Sparling, and C. T. Ramey, "Young Adult Outcomes of the Abecedarian and CARE Early Childhood Educational Interventions," *Early Childhood Research Quarterly* 23, no. 4 (2008): 452–466.

29. For example, in Germany, women are guaranteed 14 weeks of paid maternity leave, men are not guaranteed any paid paternity leave, and mothers and fathers are collectively entitled to 52 weeks of paid leave. We examine the maximum amount of leave available to the parent under consideration; in Germany, new mothers can take up to 66 weeks of paid leave, and new fathers up to 52 weeks. However, if a father were to take 52 weeks of leave, only 14 would be available to the mother. The information presented in these maps cannot be combined to show the total amount of leave that a couple could take.

30. Australia provides a flat-rate payment during maternity leave. Botswana, Kiribati, the Solomon Islands, and Tuvalu replace 25 percent of women's wages during maternity leave.

31. International Labour Organization, "C3 Maternity Protection Convention, 1919," available at http://www.ilo.org/ilolex/cgi-lex/convde.pl?C003 (accessed 28 July 2010); International Labour Organization, "C183 Maternity Protection Convention, 2000," available at http://www.ilo.org/ilolex/cgi-lex/convde.pl?C183 (accessed 28 July 2010); International Labour Organization, "R191 Maternity Protection Recommendation, 2000," available at http://www.ilo.org/ilolex/cgi-lex/convde.pl?R191 (accessed 28 July 2010).

32. B. Brandth and E. Kvande, "Flexible Work and Flexible Fathers," *Work, Employment and Society* 15, no. 2 (2001): 251–267; R. Eriksson, "Parental Leave in Sweden: The Effects of the Second Daddy Month" (Swedish Institute for Social Research Working Paper Series, no. 9, 2005).

33. Organisation for Economic Co-operation and Development, *Babies and Bosses: Reconciling Work and Family Life*, vol. 4 (Paris: Organisation for Economic Co-operation and Development, 2005).

34. A. C. Gielen, R. R. Faden, P. O'Campo, C. H. Brown, and D. M. Paige, "Maternal Employment during the Early Postpartum Period: Effects on Initiation and Continuation of Breast-feeding," *Pediatrics* 87, no. 3 (1991): 298–305; G. Ong, M. Yap, F. L. Li, and T. B. Choo, "Impact of Working Status on Breastfeeding in Singapore," *European Journal of Public Health* 15, no. 4 (2005): 424–430; Y. C. Chen, Y.-C. Wu, and W.-C. Chie, "Effects of Work-Related Factors on the Breastfeeding Behavior of Working Mothers in a Taiwanese Semiconductor Manufacturer: A Cross-Sectional Survey," *BMC Public Health* 6, no. 160 (2006): 22 pages, available at http://www.biomedcentral.com/content/pdf/1471-2458-6 -160.pdf (accessed 10 August 2012); S. S. Hawkins, L. J. Griffiths, C. Dezateux, and C. Law, "Millennium Cohort Study Child Health Group: The Impact of Maternal Employment on Breast-feeding Duration in the UK Millennium Cohort Study," *Public Health Nutrition* 10, no. 9 (2007): 891–896; C. J. Gatrell, "Secrets and Lies: Breastfeeding and Professional Paid Work," *Social Science and Medicine* 65, no. 2 (2007): 393–404; Dennis, "Breastfeeding Initiation and Duration"; L. Berger, J. Hill, and J. Waldfogel, "Maternity Leave, Early Maternal Employment and Child Health and Development in the US," *Economic Journal* 115, no. 501 (2005): F29–F47; S. Guendelman, J. L. Kosa, M. Pearl, S. Graham, J. Goodman, and M. Kharrazi, "Juggling Work and Breastfeeding: Effects of Maternity Leave and Occupational Characteristics," *Pediatrics* 123, no. 1 (2010): e38–e46; J. Baxter, "Breastfeeding, Employment and Leave: An Analysis of Mothers Growing Up in Australia," *Family Matters*, no. 80 (2008): 17–26; A. R. Cooklin, S. M. Donath, and L. H. Amir, "Maternal Employment and Breastfeeding: Results from the Longitudinal Study of Australian Children," *Acta Paediatrica* 97, no. 5 (2008): 620–623; L. D. Lindberg, "Women's Decisions about Breastfeeding and Maternal Employment," *Journal of Marriage and Family* 58 (1996): 239–251; V. Escriba, C. Colomer, R. Mas, and R. Grifol, "Working Conditions and the Decision to Breast-feed in Spain," *Health Promotion International* 9 (1994): 251–258.

35. UNESCO, *Education for All Global Monitoring Report 2007: Strong Foundations: Early Childhood Care and Education* (Paris: UNESCO, 2006).

36. A. George and J. Hancock, "Reducing Pediatric Burn Pain with Parent Participation," *Journal of Burn Care and Rehabilitation* 14 (1993): 104–107; P. A. LaRosa Nash and J. M. Murphy, "An Approach to Pediatric Perioperative Care: Parent-Present Induction," *Nursing Clinics of North America* 32 (1997): 183–199; S. J. Palmer, "Care of Sick Children by Parents: A Meaningful Role," *Journal of Advanced Nursing* 18 (1993): 185–191; I. Kristensson-Hallström, G. Elander, and G. Malmfors, "Increased Parental Participation on a Paediatric Surgical Day-Care Unit," *Journal of Clinical Nursing* 6 (1997): 297–302; T. McGraw, "Preparing Children for the Operating Room: Psychological Issues," *Canadian Journal of Anaethesia* 41, no. 11 (1994): 1094–1103; J. Cleary, O. P. Gray, D. J. Hall, P. H. Rowlandson, C. P. Sainsbury, and M. M. Davies, "Parental Involvement in the Lives of Children in Hospitals," *Archives of Disease in Childhood* 61, no. 8 (1986): 779–787; M. W. Gauderer, J. L. Lorig, and D. W. Eastwood, "Is There a Place for Parents in the Operating Room?," *Journal of Pediatric Surgery* 24, no. 7 (1989): 705–706; R. S. Hannallah and J. K. Rosales, "Experience with Parents' Presence during Anesthesia Induction in Children," *Canadian Anesthetists Society Journal* 30, no. 3, pt. 1 (1983): 286–289; M. R. H. Taylor and P. O'Connor, "Resident Parents and Shorter Hospital Stay," *Archives of Disease in Childhood* 64, no. 2 (1989): 274–276; M. A. Schuster, P. J. Chung, and K. D. Vestal. "Children with Health Issues." *Future of Children* 21, no. 2 (2011): 91–116; P. Mahaffy, "The Effects of Hospitalization on Children Admitted for Tonsillectomy and Adenoidectomy," *Nursing Review* 14 (1965): 12–19; J. Robertson, *Young Children in Hospital* (London: Tavistock, 1970).

37. C. L. Hanson, M. J. DeGuire, A. M. Schinkel, S. W. Henggeler, and G. A. Burghen, "Comparing Social Learning and Family Systems Correlates of Adaptation in Youths with IDDM," *Journal of Pediatric Psychology* 17, no. 5 (1992): 555–572; K. W. Hamlett, D. S. Pellegrini, and K. S. Katz, "Childhood Chronic Illness as a Family Stressor," *Journal of Pediatric Psychology* 17, no. 1 (1992): 33–47; A. M. LaGreca, W. F. Auslander, P. Greco, D. Spetter, E. B. Fisher, and J. V. Santiago, "I Get By with a Little Help from My Family and Friends: Adolescents' Support for Diabetes Care," *Journal of Pediatric Psychology* 20, no. 4 (1995): 449–476; B. J. Anderson, J. P. Miller, W. F. Auslander, and J. V. Santiago, "Family Characteristics of Diabetic Adolescents: Relationship to Metabolic Control," *Diabetes Care* 4, no. 6 (1981): 586–594; S. T. Hauser, A. M. Jacobson, P. Lavori, J. I. Wolfsdorf, R. D. Herskowitz, J. E. Milley, R. Bliss, D. Wertlieb, and J. Stein, "Adherence among Children and Adolescents with Insulin-Dependent Diabetes Mellitus over a Four-Year Longitudinal Follow-up: II. Immediate and Long-Term Linkages with the Family Milieu," *Journal of Pediatric Psychology* 15, no. 4 (1990): 527–542; C. Wolman, M. D. Resnick, L. J. Harris, and R. W. Blum, "Emotional Well-Being among Adolescents with and without Chronic Conditions," *Adolescent Medicine* 15, no. 3 (1994): 199–204.

38. T. A. Waugh and D. L. Kjos, "Parental Involvement and the Effectiveness of an Adolescent Day Treatment Program," *Journal of Youth and Adolescence* 21 (1992): 487–497; M. M. Richards, M. J. Bowers, T. Lazicki, D. Krall, and A. K. Jacobs, "Caregiver Involvement in the Intensive Mental Health Program: Influence on Changes in Child Functioning," *Journal of Child and Family Studies* 17 (2008): 241–252.

39. Centers for Disease Control and Prevention (CDC), National Immunization Program, *Estimated Vaccination Coverage with Individual Vaccines and Selected*

Vaccination Series among Children Nineteen to Thirty-Five Months-of-Age by State (Atlanta, Ga.: CDC, 2001); World Health Organization, *WHO Vaccine Preventable Diseases: Monitoring System* (Geneva: WHO, Department of Vaccines and Biologicals, 2000).

40. No leave is available in Haiti and Indonesia. The unpaid leave in the United States covers serious illnesses, such as those requiring hospitalization, but not preventive care. For more information on the impact of parents' work schedules on children's immunization, see J. Coreil, A. Augustin, N. A. Halsey, and E. Holt, "Social and Psychological Costs of Preventive Child Health Services in Haiti," *Social Science and Medicine* 38, no. 2 (1994): 231–238; K. Streatfield and M. Singarimbun, "Social Factors Affecting the Use of Immunization in Indonesia," *Social Science and Medicine* 27, no. 11 (1988): 1237–1245; L. K. McCormick, L. K. Bartholomew, M. J. Lewis, M. W. Brown, and I. C. Hanson, "Parental Perceptions of Barriers to Childhood Immunization: Results of Focus Groups Conducted in an Urban Population," *Health Education Research* 12, no. 3 (1997): 355–362; C. Lannon, V. Brack, J. Stuart, M. Caplow, A. McNeill, W. C. Bordley, and P. Margolis, "What Mothers Say about Why Poor Children Fall Behind on Immunizations—A Summary of Focus Groups in North Carolina," *Archives of Pediatrics and Adolescent Medicine* 149, no. 10 (1995): 1070–1075; V. P. Niederhauser and M. Markowitz, "Barriers to Immunizations: Multiethnic Parents of Under- and Unimmunized Children Speak," *Journal of the American Academy of Nurse Practitioners* 19, no. 1 (2007): 15–23; A. M. Paschal, J. V. Maryman, and J. Oler-Manske, "How Can Immunization Coverage in Urban Counties Be Improved? A Pilot Study of a Kansas County," *American Journal of Infection Control* 37, no. 5 (2009): 423–425.

41. A. Riddell, *Factors Influencing Educational Quality and Effectiveness in Developing Countries: A Review of Research* (Eschborn: German Development Cooperation [GTZ], 2008); A. Reynolds, "Comparing Measures of Parental Involvement and Their Effects on Academic Achievement," *Early Childhood Research Quarterly* 7, no. 3 (1992): 441–462; S. Christenson, T. Rounds, and D. Gorney, "Family Factors and Student Achievement: An Avenue to Increase Students' Success," *School Psychology Quarterly* 7 (1992): 178–206; D. Miller and M. Kelley, "Interventions for Improving Homework Performance: A Critical Review," *School Psychology Quarterly* 6 (1991): 174–185; M. M. Englund, B. Egeland, and W. A. Collins, "Exceptions to High School Dropout Predictions in a Low-Income Sample: Do Adults Make a Difference?," *Journal of Social Issues* 64, no. 1 (2008): 77–94; J. Fantuzzo, G. Davis, and M. Ginsburg, "Effects of Parental Involvement in Isolation or in Combination with Peer Tutoring on Student Self-Concept and Mathematics Achievement," *Journal of Educational Psychology* 87, no. 2 (1995): 272–281.

42. C. Desforges and A. Abouchaar, "The Impact of Parental Involvement, Parental Support, and Family Education on Pupil Achievement and Adjustment: A Literature Review" (DFES Research Report 433, Department for Education and Skills, Nottingham, UK, 2003), available at http://publications.dcsf.gov.uk /eOrderingDownload/RR433.pdf (accessed February 24, 2009); A. Reynolds, "A Structural Model of First-Grade Outcomes for an Urban, Low Socioeconomic Status, Minority Population," *Journal of Educational Psychology* 81, no. 4 (1989): 594–603; A. Reynolds, "Early Schooling of Children at Risk," *American Educational Research Journal* 28, no. 2 (1991): 392–422.

43. J. Griffith, "Relation of Parental Involvement, Empowerment, and School Traits to Student Academic Performance," *Journal of Educational Research* 90, no. 1 (1996): 33–41.

44. National Center for Education Statistics, *Fathers' Involvement in Their Children's Schools*, NCES 98-091 (Washington, D.C.: U.S. Department of Education, 1997).

45. H. Aturupane, P. Glewwe, and S. Wisniewski, "The Impact of School Quality, Socio-economic Factors and Child Health on Students' Academic Performance: Evidence from Sri Lankan Primary Schools," *Education Economics* (2011): 1–37.

46. G. van der Werf, B. Creemers, and H. Guldemond, "Improving Parental Involvement in Primary Education in Indonesia: Implementation, Effects, and Costs," *School Effectiveness and School Improvement* 12, no. 4 (2001): 447–466.

47. K. Callahan, J. Rademacher, and B. Hildreth, "The Effect of Parent Participation in Strategies to Improve the Homework Performance of Students Who Are at Risk," *Remedial and Special Education* 19, no. 3 (1998): 131–141; T. Keith, P. Keith, G. Troutman, P. Bickley, P. Trivette, and K. Singh, "Does Parental Involvement Affect Eighth-Grade Student Achievement? Structural Analysis of National Data," *School Psychology Review* 22 (1993): 474–476; P. Fehrmann, T. Keith, and T. Reimers, "Home Influences on School Learning: Direct and Indirect Effects of Parental Involvement on High School Grades," *Journal of Educational Research* 80, no. 6 (1987): 330–337; L. Feinstein and J. Symons, "Attainment in Secondary School," *Oxford Economic Papers* 51, no. 2 (1999): 300–321.

48. Education Support Program, *Monitoring School Dropouts: Albania, Kazakhstan, Latvia, Mongolia, Slovakia, and Tajikistan* (Budapest: Open Society Institute, 2007).

49. National Center for Education Statistics, *Fathers' Involvement in Their Children's Schools*.

50. Heymann, *Forgotten Families*.

51. A. Earle and S. J. Heymann, "What Causes Job Loss among Former Welfare Recipients? The Role of Family Health Problems," *Journal of the American Medical Women's Association* 57 (2002): 5–10.

52. S. J. Heymann, A. Earle, and B. Egleston, "Parental Availability for the Care of Sick Children," *Pediatrics* 98, no. 2, pt. 1 (1996): 226–230.

53. S. J. Heymann, S. Toomey, and F. Furstenberg, "Working Parents: What Factors Are Involved in Their Ability to Take Time Off from Work When Their Children Are Sick?," *Archives of Pediatric and Adolescent Medicine* 153 (August 1999): 870–874; J. Heymann, *The Widening Gap: Why America's Working Families Are in Jeopardy and What Can Be Done about It* (New York: Basic Books, 2000).

54. Providing 1.5 to 2 weeks of paid leave per year is equivalent to a 2–3 percent increase in wage and salary costs and less than that in total compensation costs.

55. Bureau of Labor Statistics, *Workers on Flexible and Shift Schedules in 2004*, USDL 05-1198 (Washington, D.C.: Bureau of Labor Statistics, July 2005).

56. F. Ramb, "Employment Gender Gap in the EU Is Narrowing," *Eurostat: Statistics in Focus*, vol. 99, European Commission (2008), available at http://epp.eurostat.ec.europa.eu/cache/ITY_OFFPUB/KS-SF-08-099/EN/KS-SF-08-099-EN.PDF (accessed 5 April 2011).

57. J. Heymann, "What Happens during and after School: Conditions Faced by Working Parents Living in Poverty and Their School-Age Children," *Journal of Children and Poverty* 6, no. 1 (2000): 5–20.

58. J. Hsueh and H. Yoshikawa, "Working Nonstandard Schedules and Variable Shifts in Low-Income Families: Associations with Parental Psychological Well-Being, Family Functioning, and Child Well-Being," *Developmental Psychology* 43, no. 3 (2007): 620–632; S. Daniel, J. Grzywacz, E. Leerkes, J. Tucker, and W. Han, "Nonstandard Maternal Work Schedules during Infancy: Implications for Children's Early Behavior Problems," *Infant Behavior and Development* 32, no. 2 (2009): 195–207; E. Rosenbaum and C. Morett, "The Effect of Parents' Joint Work Schedules on Infants' Behavior over the First Two Years of Life: Evidence from the ECLSB," *Maternal and Child Health Journal* 13, no. 6 (2009): 732–744; W. Han, "Maternal Work Schedules and Child Outcomes: Evidence from the National Survey of American Families," *Children and Youth Services Review* 28, no. 9 (2006): 1039–1059; L. Strazdins, R. Korda, L. L. Lim, D. H. Broom, and R. M. D'Souza, "Around-the-Clock: Parent Work Schedules and Children's Well-Being in a 24-H Economy," *Social Science and Medicine* 59, no. 7 (2004): 1517–1527; A. Dockery, J. Li, and G. Kendall, "Parents' Work Patterns and Adolescent Mental Health," *Social Science and Medicine* 68, no. 4 (2009): 689–698.

59. S. J. Heymann and A. Earle, "The Impact of Parental Working Conditions on School-Age Children: The Case of Evening Work," *Community, Work and Family* 4, no. 3 (2001): 305–325; Heymann, *Widening Gap.*

60. This study controlled for income and other family characteristics. Heymann, *Widening Gap.*

61. The quality of the home environment is assessed using the Home Observation Measure of the Environment (HOME) score. A measure of the extent and nature of parents' engagement, the physical environment, and enrichment opportunities present in the home, the HOME score is very predictive of children's cognitive and social development, as well as academic outcomes. The quality of a child's home environment decreases by 11 percent when his or her mother works evenings or nights, and by 8 percent when his or her father does so. Heymann and Earle, "Impact of Parental Working Conditions on School-Age Children."

62. International Labour Organization, TRAVAIL Legal Database of Conditions of Work and Employment, available at http://www.ilo.org/dyn/travail/trav main.home (accessed 25 May 2012).

63. J. Heymann and A. Earle, *Raising the Global Floor: Dismantling the Myth That We Can't Afford Good Working Conditions for Everyone* (Stanford, Calif.: Stanford University Press, 2010).

64. The 34 OECD countries consist of 24 European countries, Australia, Canada, Chile, Israel, Japan, the Republic of Korea, Mexico, New Zealand, Turkey, and the United States. Organisation for Economic Co-operation and Development, "Members and Partners," available at http://www.oecd.org/pages/0,3417 ,en_36734052_36761800_1_1_1_1_1,00.html (accessed 10 July 2012).

65. OECD nations agreed on the following definition of unemployed persons: "Working-age individuals who are not working and are available for and actively seeking work. The unemployment rate is then equal to the number of unemployed persons as a percentage of civilian employees, the self-employed, unpaid

family workers and the unemployed." Further information on the selection and development of this definition of unemployment can be found through Eurostat, European Commission, http://europa.eu.int/comm/eurostat/ (accessed 27 February 2009).

66. Twelve countries fell into this category: Australia, Austria, Denmark, Iceland, Japan, the Republic of Korea, Luxembourg, Mexico, the Netherlands, New Zealand, Norway, and the United Kingdom.

67. An organization developed and led by business leaders, the WEF also brings government officials, civil society, and academic researchers to meet with top business executives. From 1987 to 2005, the WEF's index was named the Growth Competitiveness Index; its name was changed to the Global Competitiveness Index in 2006/2007. World Economic Forum, "Our Organization," http://www.weforum.org/en/about/Our%20Organization/index.htm (accessed 26 February 2009).

68. These nations were Australia, Austria, Belgium, Canada, Denmark, Finland, France, Germany, Japan, the Netherlands, Norway, Singapore, Sweden, Switzerland, the United Kingdom, and the United States.

69. Although there are some administrative costs associated with leave, these are very small for short periods of leave. In addition, the loss of employee productivity while employees are not at work is partially offset by the fact that when employees are worrying about their sick children, they are not working at full productivity when they are at work; moreover, being able to care for their children reduces the number of days affected.

6. Meeting Basic Needs

1. This interview took place in October 2000. This amount was converted using the World Bank's data in "PPP Conversion Factor, Private Consumption (LCU per international $)"; this factor was 3 for Botswana in 2000. World Bank, World Development Indicators, available at http://data.worldbank.org/indicator (accessed 21 March 2011).

2. Interview, Project on Global Working Families (Botswana, 5 October 2000). The name of this interviewee has been changed to protect confidentiality.

3. S. Chen and M. Ravaillon, "The Developing World Is Poorer Than We Thought, but No Less Successful in the Fight against Poverty," *Quarterly Journal of Economics* 125, no. 4 (2010): 1577–1625.

4. UNICEF, "Achieving the MDGs with Equity," *Progress for Children* 9 (September 2010).

5. This figure ranges from under 5 percent in Denmark and Sweden to over 20 percent in the United States, Poland, Mexico, and Turkey. Organisation for Economic Co-operation and Development (OECD), *Growing Unequal? Income Distribution and Poverty in OECD Countries* (Paris: OECD Publications, 2008), 137–138.

6. In addition, the proportion of households reporting an inability to heat their homes adequately ranges from 1 percent in Austria, Japan, and Sweden to 56 percent in Portugal. The proportion of households reporting an inability to afford a healthy diet ranges from 1 percent in Denmark and Ireland to 53 percent in Turkey. The proportion of households reporting restricted access to health care

ranges from 1 percent in Denmark to 33 percent in Turkey. OECD, *Growing Unequal?*, 182.

7. In the Middle East and North Africa, rates of under-5 mortality are 2.6 times higher for children in the poorest quintile of households than for children in the richest quintile; in South Asia, these rates are 2.7 times higher; and in East Asia and the Pacific, they are 2.8 times higher. UNICEF, "Achieving the MDGs with Equity."

8. The infant mortality rate for the most affluent quintile is 4 per 1,000 live births, compared with 8.1 in the least affluent quintile. A child's risk of accidental death is 16 per 100,000 in the most affluent quintile, compared with 83 in the least affluent. World Health Organization, *Closing the Health Inequalities Gap: An International Perspective* (Copenhagen: WHO, 2005).

9. In 72 low- and middle-income countries, 45 percent of children living in rural areas and 29 percent in urban areas have stunted growth. These figures exclude China. UNICEF, "Achieving the MDGs with Equity." A study of 42 countries in Latin America, Africa, and Asia shows that in some nations, such as Bangladesh, Guatemala, India, and Pakistan, more than half of children under 5 have stunted growth. More than 30 percent are stunted in an additional 19 countries. T. B. Heaton, R. Forste, J. P. Hoffmann, and D. Flake, "Cross-National Variation in Family Influences on Child Health," *Social Science and Medicine* 60, no. 1 (2005): 97–108.

10. This global figure comes from UNICEF, "Achieving the MDGs with Equity." Additionally, studies have shown that in South Africa and Uganda, growing up in one of the poorest families increases the odds of stunting or being underweight three- to eightfold. E. Zere and D. McIntyre, "Inequities in Under-Five Child Malnutrition in South Africa," *International Journal for Equity in Health* 11, no. 2 (2003): 7–16; I. M. Engebretsen, T. Tylleskar, H. Wamani, C. Karamagi, and J. K. Tumwine, "Determinants of Infant Growth in Eastern Uganda: A Community-Based Cross-Sectional Study," *BMC Public Health* 8 (2008): 418–429. In Bangladesh, the risk of stunting for children in the poorest quintile, who had no access to piped water and electricity and almost no access to adequate sanitation facilities, was double that of children in the wealthiest. M. Giashuddin, M. Kabir, and M. Hasan, "Economic Disparity and Child Nutrition in Bangladesh," *Indian Journal of Pediatrics* 72, no. 6 (2005): 481–487.

11. R. E. Black, L. H. Allen, Z. A. Bhutta, L. E. Caulfield, M. de Onis, M. Ezzati, C. Mathers, and J. Rivera, "Maternal and Child Undernutrition: Global and Regional Exposures and Health Consequences," *Lancet* 371, no. 9626 (2008): 5–22.

12. The proportion of underweight children under age 5 is 48 percent in South Asia, 27 percent in sub-Saharan Africa, 14 percent in the Middle East and North Africa and in East Asia and the Pacific, and 6 percent in Latin America and the Caribbean. UNICEF, "Achieving the MDGs with Equity."

13. G. Fanjiang and R. E. Kleinman, "Nutrition and Performance in Children," *Current Opinion in Clinical Nutrition and Metabolic Care* 10 (2007): 342–347.

14. K. Alaimo, C. M. Olson, E. A. J. Frongillo, and R. Briefel, "Food Insufficiency, Family Income, and Health in US Preschool and School-Aged Children," *American Journal of Public Health* 91, no. 5 (2001): 781–786.

15. J. Cook, "Arkansas, Texas and Arizona Lead the Nation in Child Food Insecurity," Children's HealthWatch, July 1, 2010, available at http://www.child renshealthwatch.org/page.php?id=228 (accessed 10 August 2010).

16. The micronutrient malnutrition that can result from insufficient or poor-quality food has serious consequences. Zinc deficiency, for example, leads to an increased risk of diarrhea, pneumonia, and malaria. A child deficient in vitamin A has a higher risk of blindness or serious illness than a child without this deficiency. Iron deficiency can lead to anemia, as well as poorer cognitive performance; iodine deficiency can similarly affect cognitive performance, along with other effects on health and development. Black et al., "Maternal and Child Undernutrition;" UNICEF, *State of the World's Children 2005: Childhood under Threat* (New York: UNICEF, 2004); A. Tomkins, "Malnutrition, Morbidity, and Mortality in Children and Their Mothers," *Proceedings of the Nutrition Society* 59 (2000): 135–146.

17. OECD, *Growing Unequal?*

18. Fanjiang and Kleinman, "Nutrition and Performance in Children"; E. E. Oyhenart, L. E. Castro, L. M. Forte, M. L. Sicre, F. A. Quintero, M. A. Luis, M. F. Torres, M. E. Luna, M. F. Cesani, and A. B. Orden, "Socioenvironmental Conditions and Nutritional Status in Urban and Rural Schoolchildren," *American Journal of Human Biology* 20, no. 4 (2008): 399–405; E. C. Chambers, C. S. Duarte, and F. M. Yang, "Household Instability, Area Poverty, and Obesity in Urban Mothers and Their Children," *Journal of Health Care for the Poor and Underserved* 20, no. 1 (2009): 122–133; T. Lobstein, L. Baur, and R. Uauy, "Obesity in Children and Young People: A Crisis in Public Health," *Obesity Reviews* 5, suppl. 1 (2004): 4–85.

19. Lobstein, Baur, and Uauy, "Obesity in Children and Young People."

20. The proportion of children who lack access to adequate water supplies ranges from 53 percent in sub-Saharan Africa to 7 percent in Latin America and the Caribbean; for adequate sanitation, this range is from 61 percent in South Asia to 10 percent in East Asia and the Pacific. D. Gordon, S. Nandy, C. Pantazis, S. Pemberton, and P. Townsend, *Child Poverty in the Developing World* (Bristol, U.K.: Policy Press, 2003); UNICEF, *State of the World's Children 2005*.

21. UNICEF, "Achieving the MDGs with Equity."

22. UNICEF and World Health Organization, *Diarrhoea: Why Children Are Still Dying and What Can Be Done* (New York/Geneva: UNICEF/WHO, 2009); M. Emch, "Diarrheal Disease Risk in Matlab, Bangladesh," *Social Science and Medicine* 49, no. 4 (1999): 519–530.

23. J. T. Lee, J. Y. Son, H. Kim, and S. Y. Kim, "Effect of Air Pollution on Asthma-Related Hospital Admissions for Children by Socioeconomic Status Associated with Area of Residence," *Archives of Environmental and Occupational Health* 61, no. 3 (2006): 123–130; M. H. Benício, M. U. Ferreira, M. R. A. Cardoso, S. C. Konno, and C. A. Monteiro, "Wheezing Conditions in Early Childhood: Prevalence and Risk Factors in the city of São Paulo, Brazil," *Bulletin of the World Health Organization* 82, no. 7 (2004): 516–522; L. Séguin, B. Nikiéma, L. Gauvin, M.-V. Zunzunegui, and Q. Xu, "Duration of Poverty and Child Health in the Quebec Longitudinal Study of Child Development: Longitudinal Analysis of a Birth Cohort," *Pediatrics* 119, no. 5 (2007): e1063–e1070; G. W. Evans, "The Environment of Childhood Poverty," *American Psychologist* 59, no. 2 (2004): 77–92.

24. World Health Organization and UNICEF, *World Report on Child Injury Prevention* (Geneva: World Health Organization, 2008); M. Brownell, D. Friesen, and T. Mayer, "Childhood Injury Rates in Manitoba—Socioeconomic Influences," *Canadian Journal of Public Health—Revue Canadienne de Sante Publique* 93 (2002): S50–S56; A. J. D'Souza, T. A. Blakely, and A. Woodward, "The Effect of Eradicating Poverty on Childhood Unintentional Injury Mortality in New Zealand: A Cohort Study with Counterfactual Modelling," *Journal of Epidemiology and Community Health* 62, no. 10 (2008): 899–904.

25. J. D. McLeod and M. J. Shanahan, "Trajectories of Poverty and Children's Mental Health," *Journal of Health and Social Behavior* 37, no. 3 (1996): 207–220; E. L. Lipman, D. R. Offord, and M. H. Boyle, "What If We Could Eliminate Child Poverty? The Theoretical Effect on Child Psychosocial Morbidity," *Social Psychiatry and Psychiatric Epidemiology* 31, no. 5 (1996): 303–307; B. Jablonska, L. Lindberg, F. Lindblad, and A. Hjern, "Ethnicity, Socio-economic Status and Self-Harm in Swedish Youth: A National Cohort Study," *Psychological Medicine* 39, no. 1 (2009): 87–94.

26. B. J. Goosby, "Poverty Duration, Maternal Psychological Resources, and Adolescent Socioemotional Outcomes," *Journal of Family Issues* 28, no. 8 (2007): 1113–1134.

27. A study using longitudinal data from the United States that followed low-income children for 5 years showed that children who lived in poverty for only part of this time exhibited fewer antisocial behavioral problems than children who were poor for most or all of the 5-year period examined. McLeod and Shanahan, "Trajectories of Poverty and Children's Mental Health." Another U.S. study confirms these findings and shows that longer durations of poverty increase levels of maternal depression, with detrimental effects on adolescent psychological health. Goosby, "Poverty Duration, Maternal Psychological Resources, and Adolescent Socioemotional Outcomes."

28. UNICEF, "Achieving the MDGs with Equity."

29. Ibid.

30. OECD, *Growing Unequal?*, 182.

31. A. Case, A. Fertig, and C. Paxson, "The Lasting Impact of Childhood Health and Circumstance," *Journal of Health Economics* 24, no. 2 (2005): 365–389.

32. Body mass index is calculated by dividing an individual's weight by the square of his or her height. It is used as a proxy for body fat. A high body mass index indicates that an individual is overweight or obese. R. Poulton, A. Caspi, B. J. Milne, W. M. Thomson, A. Taylor, M. R. Sears, and T. E. Moffitt, "Association between Children's Experience of Socioeconomic Disadvantage and Adult Health: A Life-Course Study," *Lancet* 360, no. 9346 (2002): 1640–1645.

33. In Norway, men and women who were disadvantaged as children are more likely to die of cardiac disease as adults. O. Naess, B. H. Strand, and G. D. Smith, "Childhood and Adulthood Socioeconomic Position across 20 Causes of Death: A Prospective Cohort Study of 800 000 Norwegian Men and Women," *Journal of Epidemiology and Community Health* 61, no. 11 (2007): 1004–1009. In Sweden, a similar relationship among childhood social class and adult illness holds for stroke and heart disease. D. A. Lawlor, J. A. C. Sterne, P. Tynelius, G. Davey Smith, and F. Rasmussen, "Association of Childhood Socioeconomic Position with Cause-Specific Mortality in a Prospective Record Linkage Study of 1,839,384 Individuals,"

American Journal of Epidemiology 164, no. 9 (2006): 907–915. Eighteen of 22 studies looking at European populations found that those adults who had experienced deprivation or poor socioeconomic circumstances as children were more likely to die prematurely as adults. B. Galobardes, J. W. Lynch, and G. D. Smith, "Is the Association between Childhood Socioeconomic Circumstances and Cause-Specific Mortality Established? Update of a Systematic Review," *Journal of Epidemiology and Community Health* 62, no. 5 (2008): 387–390. The risks apply not only to families living in long-term poverty but also to families exposed to economic shocks. The Health and Retirement Study in the United States, a study that included examining functional limitations in retirement, found that those adults who had been exposed to economic shocks during childhood were more likely to have some degree of physical or mental health limitations as older adults. S. Haas, "Trajectories of Functional Health: The 'Long Arm' of Childhood Health and Socioeconomic Factors," *Social Science and Medicine* 66, no. 4 (2008): 849–861.

34. F. Blanco Allais and P. Quinn, "Marginalisation and Child Labour" (background paper for UNESCO, *Education for All Global Monitoring Report 2010: Reaching the Marginalized* [Oxford: Oxford University Press, 2010]); Understanding Children's Work, "The Twin Challenges of Eliminating Child Labour and Achieving EFA: Evidence and Policy Options from Mali and Zambia" (background paper for UNESCO, *Education for All Global Monitoring Report 2010*).

35. J. Heymann, *Forgotten Families: Ending the Growing Crisis Confronting Children and Working Parents in the Global Economy* (New York: Oxford University Press, 2006).

36. UNESCO Institute for Statistics, *Children Out of School: Measuring Exclusion from Primary Education* (Montreal: UNESCO Institute for Statistics, 2005).

37. In many countries including Cambodia, Ghana, Guatemala, Nigeria, and Yemen, coming from the poorest quintile of households more than doubles a youth's risk of completing fewer than 4 years of education. UNESCO, *Education for All Global Monitoring Report 2010*, 140.

38. Ibid.

39. World Bank, *Cambodia: Halving Poverty by 2015? Poverty Assessment 2006* (Washington, D.C.: World Bank, 2006); World Bank, *Uganda: Poverty and Vulnerability Assessment* (Washington, D.C.: World Bank, 2006); World Bank, *Malawi: Poverty and Vulnerability Assessment; Investing in Our Future, Synthesis Report; Main Findings and Recommendations* (Washington, D.C.: World Bank, 2007); Y. Tsujita, "Deprivation of Education: A Study of Slum Children in Delhi, India" (background paper for *EFA Global Monitoring Report 2010*); all cited in UNESCO, *Education for All Global Monitoring Report 2010*, 166.

40. Séguin et al., "Duration of Poverty and Child Health in the Quebec Longitudinal Study of Child Development."

41. Chen and Ravaillon, "The Developing World Is Poorer Than We Thought, but No Less Successful in the Fight against Poverty"; M. Ravallion and S. Chen, "China's (Uneven) Progress against Poverty," *Journal of Development Economics* 82 (2007): 1–42.

42. G. J. Duncan, L. Gennetian, and P. Morris, "Effects of Welfare and Antipoverty Programs on Participants' Children," *Focus* 25, no. 2 (2007–2008): 3–12.

43. N. Kristensen and W. Cunningham, *Do Minimum Wages in Latin America and the Caribbean Matter? Evidence from 19 Countries*, World Bank Policy Research

Working Paper no. 3870 (2006); D. F. Angel-Urdinola, "Can a Minimum Wage Increase Have an Adverse Impact on Inequality? Evidence from Two Latin American Economies," *Journal of Economic Inequality* 6, no. 1 (2008): 57–71; D. Neumark and S. Adams, "Do Living Wage Ordinances Reduce Urban Poverty?," *Journal of Human Resources* 38, no. 3 (2003): 490–521; R. V. Burkhauser and J. J. Sabia, "The Effectiveness of Minimum-Wage Increases in Reducing Poverty: Past, Present, and Future," *Contemporary Economic Policy* 25, no. 2 (2007): 262–281; A. Leigh, "Does Raising the Minimum Wage Help the Poor?," *Economic Record* 83, no. 263 (2007): 432–445; K. Bird and C. Manning, "Minimum Wages and Poverty in a Developing Country: Simulations from Indonesia's Household Survey," *World Development* 36, no. 5 (2008): 916–933.

44. Neumark and Adams, "Do Living Wage Ordinances Reduce Urban Poverty?"; D. Morgan and K. Kickham, "Children in Poverty: Do State Policies Matter?," *Social Science Quarterly* 82, no. 3 (2001): 478–493; R. Mincy, "Raising the Minimum Wage: Effects on Family Poverty," *Monthly Labor Review* 113, no. 7 (1990): 18–25; R. H. DeFina, "The Impact of State Minimum Wages on Child Poverty in Female-Headed Families," *Journal of Poverty* 12, no. 2 (2008): 155–174.

45. G. Cooke and K. Lawton, *Working out of Poverty: A Study of the Low-Paid and the "Working Poor"* (London: Institute for Public Policy Research, 2008); D. Piachaud and H. Sutherland, "How Effective Is the British Government's Attempt to Reduce Child Poverty?" (CASE Paper 38, Centre for Analysis of Social Exclusion, March 2000).

46. Organisation for Economic Co-operation and Development, *OECD Employment Outlook 1998: Towards an Employment-Centred Social Policy* (Paris: OECD Publishing, 1998); J. Rutkowski, "The Minimum Wage: Curse or Cure?" (World Bank, 2003), available at http://siteresources.worldbank.org/INTECONEVAL/Resources/MinimumWageNoteJul03v2.pdf (accessed 20 June 2012); S. Devereux, "Can Minimum Wages Contribute to Poverty Reduction in Poor Countries?," *Journal of International Development* 17 (2005): 899–912; C. Saget, "Poverty Reduction and Decent Work in Developing Countries: Do Minimum Wages Help?," *International Labour Review* 140, no. 3 (2001): 237–269.

47. J. Rodgers and J. Rubery, "The Minimum Wage as a Tool to Combat Discrimination and Promote Equality," *International Labour Review* 142, no. 4 (2003): 543–556.

48. T. H. Gindling and K. Terrell, "The Effect of Minimum Wages on Actual Wages in Formal and Informal Sectors in Costa Rica," *World Development* 33, no. 11 (2005): 1905–1921.

49. This study determined impact by checking whether there was a spike in wages in the informal economy associated with the minimum wage. This was clearly demonstrated in 14 of the 19 countries examined. In the other 5 countries, because there was no spike, the authors were unable to determine whether there was no effect or whether it raised or lowered wages. Kristensen and Cunningham, *Do Minimum Wages in Latin America and the Caribbean Matter?*

50. Saget, "Poverty Reduction and Decent Work in Developing Countries."

51. When minimum wages are set through collective bargaining, typically groups representing entire sectors or professions negotiate with organizations of employers to establish a minimum wage that applies to most or all workers. Even if employers in a particular sector do not hold membership in the organization for

that sector, they must honor the sectoral or professional minimum wages set by collective agreement.

52. International Labour Organization, *Global Wage Report 2008/09* (Geneva: International Labour Office, 2008). Number of countries for which data are available: 100.

53. For details on these studies, see UNESCO, "Distance Learning for Adults: Radio ECCA Project for Socioeconomic Development," Effective Literacy Practice (2009), available at http://www.unesco.org/uil/litbase/?menu=4& programme=7 (accessed 14 September 2010); UNESCO, "Harnessing the Power and Potential of Adult Learning and Education for a Viable Future" (prepared for CONFINTEA VI: Sixth International Conference on Adult Education, Belém, Brazil, December 2009), available at http://www.unesco.org/fileadmin/MULTI MEDIA/INSTITUTES/UIL/confintea/pdf/working_documents/confinteavi_ framework_en.pdf (accessed 11 July 2012); UNESCO, "Community-Based Adult Learning and Development Programme," Effective Literacy Practice (2009), available at http://www.unesco.org/uil/litbase/?menu=8&programme=31 (accessed 14 September 2010); UNESCO, "National Literacy Program in Namibia," Effective Literacy Practice (2009), available at http://www.unesco.org/uil/litbase/?menu=8 &programme=15 (accessed 14 September 2010); R. Hayman, "The Contribution of Post-basic Education and Training (PBET) to Poverty Reduction in Rwanda: Balancing Short-Term Goals and Long-Term Visions in the Face of Capacity Constraints" (Post-Basic Education and Training Working Paper no. 3, Centre of African Studies, 2005); APPEAL Resource and Training Consortium, *Income-Generating Programmes for Poverty Alleviation through Non-formal Education* (Bangkok: UNESCO, 2003); M. Wallenborn, "Skills Development for Poverty Reduction (SDPR): The Case of Tajikistan," *International Journal of Educational Development* 29, no. 6 (2009): 550–557; International Labour Organization, *Working out of Poverty*, Report of the Director General, International Labour Conference, 91st Session (Geneva: ILO, 2003); and J. Blanden, F. Buscha, P. Sturgis, and P. Urwin, "The Effect of Lifelong Learning on Intra-generational Social Mobility: Evidence from Longitudinal Data in the United Kingdom" (report commissioned by the Department for Innovation, Universities and Skills, March 2008). Additionally, adult education programs can have less tangible effects, such as increasing the independence of participating women and allowing them the chance for greater mobility and economic participation. J. Cameron and S. Cameron, "The Economic Benefits of Increased Literacy" (background paper for UNESCO, *Education for All Global Monitoring Report 2006* [Paris: UNESCO, 2005]); T. Westell, "Measuring Non-academic Outcomes in Adult Literacy Programs—A Literature Review" (2005), available at http://www.nald.ca/fulltext/measuring /measuring.pdf (accessed 14 September 2010).

54. A. Robinson-Pant, "The Social Benefits of Literacy" (background paper for UNESCO, *Education for All Global Monitoring Report 2006*); UNESCO, "Family Basic Education (FABE)," Effective Literacy Practice (2009), available at http://www.unesco.org/uil/litbase/?menu=9&targetgroup=8&programme=9 (accessed 14 September 2010).

55. Bureau of Labor Statistics, "Number of Jobs Held, Labor Market Activity, and Earnings Growth among the Youngest Baby Boomers: Results from a Longitudinal Survey" (Economic News Release, USDL-10-1243, 10 September 2010).

56. C. Macaulay, "Job Mobility and Job Tenure in the UK," *Labour Market Trends* (November 2003): 541–550.

57. Eight percent of adults without a high-school diploma were unemployed, compared with 5 percent of high-school graduates and 2.5 percent of university graduates. Bureau of Labor Statistics, "Number of Jobs Held, Labor Market Activity, and Earnings Growth."

58. International Labour Organization, "Unemployment by Level of Education Attainment," in *Key Indicators of the Labour Market*, available at http://kilm .ilo.org/KILMnet/ (accessed 28 February 2012); Organization for Economic Cooperation and Development, *Education at a Glance 2011—Highlights* (Paris: OECD Publishing, 2011).

59. National Employment Law Project, "A Year of Unbalanced Growth: Industries, Wages, and the First 12 Months of Job Growth after the Great Recession" (data brief, February 2011), available at http://www.nelp.org/page /-/Justice/2011/UnbalancedGrowthFeb2011.pdf?nocdn=1 (accessed 28 February 2012).

60. Severance pay is compensation that must be provided by an employer to an employee upon termination from his or her job.

61. For the 4 countries where we were unable to determine whether unemployment benefits apply to the self-employed—Angola, Bahrain, Mongolia, and Seychelles—a conservative assumption was made that they did not provide this coverage. They were mapped together with those countries which provide government-funded benefits but do not cover the self-employed.

62. International Labour Organization, *Women and Men in the Informal Economy: A Statistical Picture* (Geneva: ILO, 2002).

63. These amounts are calculated by inputting the minimum wage (captured elsewhere in our databases) into the benefit-calculation formula. If the calculated benefit amount for minimum-wage workers is less than the designated national floor of unemployment benefits, the national floor is used. If we were unable to calculate the amount of benefits a worker earning the minimum wage would receive, the national floor of unemployment benefits was substituted.

64. A. Barrientos and J. DeJong, "Reducing Child Poverty with Cash Transfers: A Sure Thing?," *Development Policy Review* 24, no. 5 (2006): 537–552; E. Duflo, "Child Health and Household Resources in South Africa: Evidence from the Old Age Pension Program," *American Economic Review* 90, no. 2 (2000): 393–398; M. Forster and I. Toth, "Child Poverty and Family Transfers in the Czech Republic, Hungary and Poland," *Journal of European Social Policy* 11, no. 4 (2001): 324–341; M. Matsaganis, C. O'Donoghue, H. Levy, M. Coromaldi, M. Mercader-Prats, C. Farinha Rodrigues, S. Toso, and P. Tsakloglou, "Child Poverty and Family Transfers in Southern Europe" (Institute for the Study of Labor Discussion Paper no. 1509, March 2005); W.-H. Chen and M. Corak, "Child Poverty and Changes in Child Poverty," *Demography* 45, no. 3 (2008): 537–553; D. Engster and H. O. Stensota, "Do Family Policy Regimes Matter for Children's Well-Being?," *Social Politics* 18, no. 1 (2011): 82–124.

65. C. Paxson and N. Schady, *Does Money Matter? The Effects of Cash Transfers on Child Health and Development in Rural Ecuador*, World Bank Policy Research Working Paper no. 4226 (May 2007). The World Policy Analysis Centre's Poverty Database captures only benefits provided by law, that is, on a statutory basis;

the Bono de Desarrollo Humano is not statutory and thus is not included in this database.

66. E. V. Edmonds and N. Schady, "Poverty Alleviation and Child Labor" (National Bureau of Economic Research Working Paper no. 15345, September 2009); N. Schady and M. C. Araujo, *Cash Transfers, Conditions, School Enrollment, and Child Work: Evidence from a Randomized Experiment in Ecuador*, World Bank Policy Research Working Paper no. 3930 (June 2006).

67. L. C. H. Fernald, P. J. Gertler, and L. M. Neufeld, "Role of Cash in Conditional Cash Transfer Programmes for Child Health, Growth, and Development: An Analysis of Mexico's Oportunidades," *Lancet* 371, no. 9615 (2008): 828–837. Oportunidades is a conditional cash transfer program, not a government cash benefit policy, and thus does not appear in this chapter's maps.

68. Minister of Community Development and Social Services and German Technical Cooperation, "Final Evaluation Report: Kalomo Social Cash Transfer Scheme" (Social Safety Net Project, September 2007). This program does not appear in this chapter's maps because it was in place for only one district in Zambia rather than being available on a national level.

69. R. Himaz, "Welfare Grants and Their Impact on Child Health: The Case of Sri Lanka," *World Development* 36, no. 10 (2008): 1843–1857.

70. For this calculation, when benefits differed according to income level, the lowest income bracket was used. For families with preschool-age children, a family with two 4-year-old children was assumed in making the calculation; for families with school-age children, a family with two 8-year-old children was assumed; and for families with teenage children, a family with two 15-year-old children was assumed.

71. K. Milligan and M. Stabile, "Do Child Tax Benefits Affect the Wellbeing of Children? Evidence from Canadian Child Benefit Expansions," *American Economic Journal—Economic Policy* 3 (2011): 175–205.

72. G. Dahl and L. Lochner, "The Impact of Family Income on Child Achievement: Evidence from the Earned Income Tax Credit" (National Bureau of Economic Research Working Paper no. 14599, December 2008).

7. Equity and Discrimination

1. Jordan does not guarantee overall equity for women. The constitution guarantees equal rights, overall equality, and equality before the law and prohibits discrimination in general, but it does not explicitly mention gender in these guarantees, nor does it explicitly guarantee equity for women in work or education. For example, the constitution states in Article 6(i) that "Jordanians shall be equal before the law. There shall be no discrimination between them as regards to their rights and duties on grounds of race, language, or religion."

2. Interview, Population Health: Moving from Evidence to Effective Policy (Jordan, 12 July 2009). The name of this interviewee has been changed to protect confidentiality.

3. Interview, Population Health: Moving from Evidence to Effective Policy (Bolivia, 9 July 2008); B. Lambert, "Improving Indigenous Children's Educational Access and Outcomes through Intercultural Bilingual Education," in J. Heymann and A. Cassola, eds., *Lessons in Educational Equality: Successful Ap-*

proaches to Intractable Problems around the World (New York: Oxford University Press, 2011), 222–245.

4. The 1994 constitution guaranteed "equal enjoyment of rights, liberties, and guarantees recognized by this Constitution, without distinction based on race, sex, language . . ." It also guaranteed the special rights of indigenous groups. Bolivia's most recent constitution, passed in 2008, similarly guarantees equal rights for indigenous groups.

5. United Nations Treaty Collection, "Convention on the Rights of the Child: Status of Ratifications," available at http://treaties.un.org/Pages/View Details.aspx?src=TREATY&mtdsg_no=IV-11&chapter=4&lang=en (accessed 1 February 2012).

6. E. C. Alfaro, A. J. Umaña-Taylor, M. A. Gonzales-Backen, M. Y. Bámaca, and K. H. Zeiders, "Latino Adolescents' Academic Success: The Role of Discrimination, Academic Motivation, and Gender," *Journal of Adolescence* 32 (2009): 941–962; C. Smalls, R. White, T. Chavous, and R. Sellers, "Racial Ideological Beliefs and Racial Discrimination Experiences as Predictors of Academic Engagement among African American Adolescents," *Journal of Black Psychology* 33, no. 3 (2007): 299–330; A. D. Benner and S. Y. Kim, "Experiences of Discrimination among Chinese-American Adolescents and the Consequences for Socioemotional and Academic Development," *Developmental Psychology* 45, no. 6 (2009): 1682–1694; C. A. Wong, J. S. Eccles, and A. Sameroff, "The Influence of Ethnic Discrimination and Ethnic Identification on African American Adolescents' School and Socioemotional Adjustment," *Journal of Personality* 71, no. 6 (2003): 1197–1232; D. S. DeGarmo and C. R. Martinez Jr., "A Culturally Informed Model of Academic Well-Being for Latino Youth: The Importance of Discriminatory Experiences and Social Support," *Family Relations* 55, no. 3 (2006): 267–278; J. S. Eccles, C. A. Wong, and S. C. Peck, "Ethnicity as a Social Context for the Development of African-American Adolescents," *Journal of Social Psychology* 44 (2006): 407–426.

7. R. Russinov, "Equal Opportunity in Education: Eliminating Discrimination against Roma," *UN Chronicle* 44, no. 3 (2007): 34–35; T. Smith, "Recognising Difference: The Romani 'Gypsy' Child Socialisation and Education Process," *British Journal of Sociology of Education* 18, no. 2 (1997): 243–256; D. Cudworth, "There Is a Little Bit More than Just Delivering the Stuff: Policy, Pedagogy, and the Education of Gypsy/Traveller Children," *Critical Social Policy* 28, no. 3 (2008): 361–377.

8. UNESCO, *Education for All Global Monitoring Report 2010: Reaching the Marginalized* (Oxford: Oxford University Press, 2010).

9. B. S. Rangvid, "Sources of Immigrants' Underachievement: Results from PISA-Copenhagen," *Education Economics* 15, no. 3 (2007): 293–326.

10. M. Verkuyten and P. Brug, "Educational Performance and Psychological Disengagement among Ethnic-Minority and Dutch Adolescents," *Journal of Genetic Psychology* 164, no. 2 (2003): 189–200.

11. R. Mannix, F. T. Bourgeois, S. A. Schutzman, A. Bernstein, and L. K. Lee, "Neuroimaging for Pediatric Head Trauma: Do Patient and Hospital Characteristics Influence Who Gets Imaged?," *Academic Emergency Medicine* 17, no. 7 (2010): 694–700.

12. K. M. Yount, "Provider Bias in the Treatment of Diarrhea among Boys and Girls Attending Public Facilities in Minia, Egypt," *Social Science and Medicine*

56 (2003): 753–768. This study found that 12 percent of girls versus 45 percent of boys were given oral rehydration solution (ORS) by health providers, health providers recommended that ORS be administered at home for 8 percent of girls versus 43 percent of boys, and girls had 0.6 times lower adjusted odds than boys of being administered ORS.

13. UNICEF and World Health Organization, *Diarrhoea: Why Children Are Still Dying and What Can Be Done* (New York/Geneva: UNICEF/WHO, 2009).

14. B. Rechel, C. M. Blackburn, N. J. Spencer, and B. Rechel, "Access to Health Care for Roma Children in Central and Eastern Europe: Findings from a Qualitative Study in Bulgaria," *International Journal for Equity in Health* 8, no. 1 (2009): 24–33.

15. E. A. Pascoe and L. S. Richman, "Perceived Discrimination and Health: A Meta-analytic Review," *Psychological Bulletin* 135, no. 4 (2009): 531–554.

16. D. M. Huebner and M. C. Davis, "Perceived Antigay Discrimination and Physical Health Outcomes," *Health Psychology* 26, no. 5 (2007): 627–634; Y. Paradies, "A Systematic Review of Empirical Research on Self-Reported Racism and Health," *International Journal of Epidemiology* 35 (2006): 888–901; K. Sanders-Phillips, B. Settles-Reaves, D. Walker, and J. Brownlow, "Social Inequality and Racial Discrimination: Risk Factors for Health Disparities in Children of Color," *Pediatrics* 124 (2009): S176–S186; C. Borrell, C. Muntaner, D. Gil-González, L. Artazcoz, M. Rodríguez-Sanz, I. Rohlfs, K. Pérez, M. García-Calvente, R. Villegas, and C. Álvarez-Dardet, "Perceived Discrimination and Health by Gender, Social Class, and Country of Birth in a Southern European Country," *Preventive Medicine* 50 (2010): 86–92.

17. S. Miilunpalo, I. Vuori, P. Oja, M. Pasanen, and H. Urponen, "Self-Rated Health Status as a Health Measure: The Predictive Value of Self-Reported Health Status on the Use of Physician Services and on Mortality in the Working-Age Population," *Journal of Clinical Epidemiology* 50, no. 5 (1997): 517–528; M. R. Benjamins, R. A. Hummer, I. W. Eberstein, and C. B. Nam, "Self-Reported Health and Adult Mortality Risk: An Analysis of Cause-Specific Mortality," *Social Science and Medicine* 59, no. 6 (2004): 1297–1306.

18. K. Pantzer, L. Rajmil, C. Tebé, F. Codina, V. Serra-Sutton, M. Ferrer, U. Ravens-Sieberer, M. C. Simeoni, and J. Alonso, "Health Related Quality of Life in Immigrants and Native School Aged Adolescents in Spain," *Journal of Epidemiology and Community Health* 60 (2006): 694–698.

19. Huebner and Davis, "Perceived Antigay Discrimination and Physical Health Outcomes"; Paradies, "A Systematic Review of Empirical Research on Self-Reported Racism and Health"; Pascoe and Richman, "Perceived Discrimination and Health"; D. H. Chae, D. T. Takeuchi, E. M. Barbeau, G. G. Bennett, J. Lindsay, and N. Krieger, "Unfair Treatment, Racial/Ethnic Discrimination, Ethnic Identification, and Smoking among Asian Americans in the National Latino and Asian American Study," *American Journal of Public Health* 98, no. 3 (2008): 485–492.

20. H. Landrine, E. A. Klonoff, I. Corral, S. Fernandez, and S. Roesch, "Conceptualizing and Measuring Ethnic Discrimination in Health Research," *Journal of Behavioral Medicine* 29, no. 1 (2006): 79–94.

21. Borrell et al., "Perceived Discrimination and Health by Gender, Social Class, and Country of Birth in a Southern European Country"; A. Llácer, J. del

Amo, A. García-Fulgueiras, V. Ibañez-Rojo, R. García-Pino, I. Jarrín, D. Díaz, A. Fernández-Liria, V. García-Ortuzar, L. Mazarrasa, M. A. Rodríguez-Arenas, and M. V. Zunzunegui, "Discrimination and Mental Health in Ecuadorian Immigrants in Spain," *Journal of Epidemiology and Community Health* 63 (2009): 766–772; Sanders-Phillips et al., "Social Inequality and Racial Discrimination."

22. T. R. Coker, M. N. Elliott, D. E. Kanouse, J. A. Grunbaum, D. C. Schwebel, M. J. Gilliland, S. R. Tortolero, M. F. Peskin, and M. A. Schuster, "Perceived Racial Discrimination among Fifth-Grade Students and Its Association with Mental Health," *American Journal of Public Health* 99, no. 5 (2009): 878–884; Wong, Eccles, and Sameroff, "Influence of Ethnic Discrimination and Ethnic Identification"; V. M. Nyborg and J. F. Curry, "The Impact of Perceived Racism: Psychological Symptoms among African American Boys," *Journal of Clinical Child and Adolescent Psychology* 32, no. 2 (2003): 258–266; G. H. Brody, Y. Chen, V. M. Murry, X. Ge, R. L. Simons, F. X. Gibbons, M. Gerrard, and C. E. Cutrona, "Perceived Discrimination and the Adjustment of African American Youths: A Five-Year Longitudinal Analysis with Contextual Moderation Effects," *Child Development* 77, no. 5 (2006): 1170–1189; R. L. Simons, V. Murry, V. McLoyd, K. Lin, C. Cutrona, and R. D. Conger, "Discrimination, Crime, Ethnic Identity, and Parenting as Correlates of Depressive Symptoms among African American Children: A Multilevel Analysis," *Development and Psychopathology* 14 (2002): 371–393; Benner and Kim, "Experiences of Discrimination among Chinese-American Adolescents"; M. L. Greene, N. Way, and K. Pahl, "Trajectories of Perceived Adult and Peer Discrimination among Black, Latino, and Asian American Adolescents: Patterns and Psychological Correlates," *Developmental Psychology* 42, no. 2 (2006): 218–238.

23. D. R. Williams, H. M. Gonzalez, S. Williams, S. A. Mohammed, H. Moomal, and D. J. Stein, "Perceived Discrimination, Race, and Health in South Africa," *Social Science and Medicine* 67 (2008): 441–452.

24. T. R. Coker, S. B. Austin, and M. A. Schuster, "The Health and Health Care of Lesbian, Gay, and Bisexual Adolescents," *Annual Review of Public Health* 31 (2010): 457–477; V. M. Mays and S. D. Cochran, "Mental Health Correlates of Perceived Discrimination among Lesbian, Gay, and Bisexual Adults in the United States," *American Journal of Public Health* 91, no. 11 (2001): 1869–1876.

25. Borrell et al., "Perceived Discrimination and Health by Gender, Social Class, and Country of Birth in a Southern European Country"; Llácer et al., "Discrimination and Mental Health in Ecuadorian Immigrants in Spain."

26. "Shi'i Family Law Needs to Abide by Constitution, Universal Values—Afghan Daily," *BBC Monitoring South Asia*, 10 April 2009; J. Boone, "'Worse than the Taliban'—New Law Rolls Back Rights for Afghan Women," *Guardian*, 31 March 2009; "Afghan Ministers, Rights Activists Oppose Women Rights Violations under New Law," *BBC Monitoring South Asia*, 9 April 2009; "Afghan Civil, Rights Organizations Call for Review of Law on Women," *BBC Monitoring South Asia*, 7 April 2009; T. Coghlan, "The Bravest Women in Kabul: Protesters March against Sex Slavery Law," *Times*, 16 April 2009; A. Gopal, "Afghanistan's Controversial Law Emboldens Women's Rights Activists," *Christian Science Monitor*, 16 April 2009; A. Hodge, "Karzai Risks Wrath of West over Shia Law," *Australian*, 19 August 2009; J. Page, "Karzai Approves 'Marital Rape' Law; West Split over

Response to 'No Sex, No Food' Legislation," *Times*, 17 August 2009; R. Reid, "Speak Out for Women's Rights," *Canberra Times*, 20 August 2009.

27. L. Vanhala, "Twenty-five Years of Disability Equality? Interpreting Disability Rights in the Supreme Court of Canada," *Common Law World Review* 39 (2010): 27–47.

28. "Kenyan Govt. Sued over Discriminatory School Access for HIV Infected Children," *Xinhua News Agency*, 7 January 2004; "Children Sue State over School Admission," *All Africa*, 8 January 2004; "Nairobi Primary Schools Have to Admit HIV Orphans," *Dow Jones International News*, 9 January 2004; "Education: Agreement to Admit HIV-Positive Children into Nairobi's Public Schools Approved," *AIDS Weekly*, 9 February 2004; M. Lacey, "Court Allows Kenyan Pupils with HIV into Schools," *New York Times*, 10 January 2004; T. Maliti, "Kenya to Let HIV-Positive Kids in School," *Associated Press Newswires*, 10 January 2004.

29. Brown Foundation for Educational Equity, Excellence, and Research, "Brown vs. Board of Education: About the Case," available at http://brownvboard .org/summary/ (accessed 5 August 2010); J. T. Patterson, *Brown v. Board of Education: A Civil Rights Milestone and Its Troubled Legacy* (New York: Oxford University Press, 2001).

30. B. Roberts and V. Reddy, "Pride and Prejudice: Public Attitudes towards Homosexuality," *HSRC Review* 6, no. 4 (2008), available at http://www.hsrc.ac.za /HSRC_Review_Article-121.phtml (accessed 10 August 2010).

31. "S. Africa Says to Appeal Gay Marriage Court Ruling," *Reuters News*, 22 December 2004; "The Vitality of Difference," *Mail and Guardian Online*, 13 December 2005; "Govt to Respect Concourt Gay Marriage Ruling," *South African Press Association*, 1 December 2005; "Final Seal of Approval for South Africa Gay Marriage Law," *Agence France Presse*, 30 November 2006; C. Benjamin, "South Africa: Citizens 'Still Think Homosexuality Is Wrong,'" *All Africa*, 9 December 2008; T. Trengove Jones, "'My Mother Believed I'd Go to Hell,'" *Sunday Times*, 31 January 2010; "South Africa Court Rules for Gay Rights," *Associated Press*, 24 November 2006; C. Timberg, "S. Africa OKs Gay Marriage," *Kitsap Sun*, 2 December 2005.

32. T. F. Pettigrew and L. R. Tropp, "A Meta-analytic Test of Intergroup Contact Theory," *Journal of Personality and Social Psychology* 90, no. 5 (2006): 751–783.

33. L. C. Smith, U. Ramakrishnan, A. Ndiaye, L. Haddad, and R. Martorell, "The Importance of Women's Status for Child Nutrition in Developing Countries" (Research Report 131, International Food Policy Research Institute, Washington, D.C., 2003).

34. L. Visaria, "Female Autonomy and Fertility Behaviour: An Exploration of Gujarat Data," in *Proceedings of the International Population Conference, Montreal*, vol. 4 (Liege, Belgium: International Union for the Scientific Study of Population, 1993), 263–275, cited in ORC Macro, *A Focus on Gender: Collected Papers on Gender Using DHS Data* (Calverton, Md.: USAID, 2005).

35. A right is considered aspirational if it is written in language that is not authoritative (e.g., the State "should," "endeavors to," "promotes"), if it is explicitly dependent on the state's ability to provide it, or if it is explicitly nonenforceable. It is also considered aspirational when it appears only in the preamble of the consti-

tution when the preamble is not described as an integral part of the constitution in question.

36. One country has a provision that could be interpreted to explicitly permit differential treatment, but this depends on its application. Zimbabwe's constitution states that "nothing contained in or done under the authority of any law that discriminates between persons on the grounds of their sex or gender shall be held to be in contravention . . . to the extent that the law in question . . . (b) takes due account of physiological differences between persons of different sex or gender."

37. The countries that state that religious or customary law may prevail over the constitution are Ethiopia, the Gambia, Iran, Kenya, Lesotho, Malaysia, the Maldives, the Marshall Islands, Samoa, Sierra Leone, Swaziland, Tuvalu, Zambia, and Zimbabwe.

38. Additionally, one country, Bangladesh, guarantees at least one approach to equity across ethnicity and religion but has a potential exception. The constitution of Bangladesh has a provision allowing laws to abridge certain rights, including the right to nondiscrimination, in order to give effect to the fundamental principles that the constitution aspires to. Since one of these fundamental principles is social and economic equality between women and men, this provision is not interpreted as a potential abridgment of the right to gender equality. However, since racial and religious equality are not among the principles in the name of which the contravening law could be passed, these guarantees are still considered to have certain possible exceptions attached to them.

39. In low- and middle-income countries, children are twice as likely to be out of school if their mothers have never been educated as they are if their mothers have received some education. UNICEF, "A Report Card on Gender Parity and Primary Education," *Progress for Children* 2 (April 2005). Research in Brazil demonstrated that as a mother's years of schooling increase, the probability that her daughters will labor as children decreases, and the probability of school attendance for both sons and daughters increases. P. M. Emerson and A. Portela Souza, "Bargaining over Sons and Daughters: Child Labor, School Attendance, and Intrahousehold Gender Bias in Brazil" (Working Paper no. 02-W13, Department of Economics, Vanderbilt University, May 2002).

40. World Bank, "Education and Development," Education Advisory Service, World Bank, Washington, D.C., available at http://siteresources.worldbank.org /EDUCATION/Resources/278200-1099079877269/547664-1099080118171/Ed ucationBrochure.pdf (accessed 22 March 2010).

41. Bangladesh prohibits discrimination in education across ethnicity and religion, but has a potential exception. The constitution of Bangladesh has a provision allowing laws to abridge certain rights, including the right to nondiscrimination, in order to give effect to the fundamental principles that the constitution aspires to. Since one of these fundamental principles is social and economic equality between women and men, this provision is not interpreted as a potential abridgment of the right to gender equality. However, since racial and religious equality are not among the principles in the name of which the contravening law could be passed, these guarantees are still considered to have certain possible exceptions attached to them.

42. Based on data from "Ratio of Estimated Female to Male Earned Income," in United Nations Development Programme, *Human Development Report 2009*

(New York: UNDP, 2009), 186–189. Globally, there is also a significant gender gap in asset ownership. According to Peru's living-standard measurement survey, only 13 percent of agricultural land parcels were owned by women, whereas 74 percent were owned by men and an additional 13 percent were owned jointly by a man and a woman. The same survey in Paraguay showed that 27 percent of farms were owned by women, while men owned 70 percent. In Nicaragua, 16 percent of landowners were women, while 81 percent were men. C. D. Deere and M. Leon, "The Gender Asset Gap: Land in Latin America," *World Development* 31, no. 6 (2003): 925–947. Only 5 percent of registered landholdings in Kenya were owned by women. In northern Nigeria, men's wealth at the time of marriage was more than 7 times greater than women's, and the wealth gap between genders widened over time. C. D. Deere and C. R. Doss, "The Gender Asset Gap: What Do We Know and Why Does It Matter?," *Feminist Economics* 12, no 1 (2006): 1050. The value of men's assets at marriage was more than 11 times greater than women's assets in Bangladesh, almost 6 times greater in Ethiopia, and 2.5 times greater in South Africa. A. R. Quisumbing and J. A. Maluccio, "Intrahousehold Allocation and Gender Relations: New Empirical Evidence" (Policy Research Report on Gender and Development, Working Paper Series no. 2, World Bank, October 1999).

43. D. Thomas, "The Distribution of Income and Expenditure within the Household," *Annales d'Économie et de Statistique* 29 (1993): 109–135.

44. In Bangladesh, when women have more assets at the time of marriage, household expenditures on children's clothing and education increase. In Indonesia, women's landownership has a positive impact on the portion of household resources spent on health care and education. Similarly, in Ethiopia, when women bring more land and livestock into the marriage, a greater share of the household's budget is spent on food, and girls complete more schooling. Quisumbing and Maluccio, "Intrahousehold Allocation and Gender Relations."

45. C. Buchmann, "Family Structure, Parental Perceptions, and Child Labor in Kenya: What Factors Determine Who Is Enrolled in School?," *Social Forces* 78, no. 4 (2000): 1349–1378.

46. As of 2010, Kenya's new constitution states that "women and men have the right to equal treatment, including the right to equal opportunities in political, economic, cultural and social spheres."

47. N. Qian, "Missing Women and the Price of Tea in China: The Effect of Sex-Specific Earnings on Sex Imbalance," *Quarterly Journal of Economics* 123, no. 3 (2008): 1251–1285.

48. The impact of female political participation is so significant for children that UNICEF targeted this area for improvement in its *State of the World's Children* report. UNICEF, *The State of the World's Children 2007: Women and Children; The Double Dividend of Gender Equality* (New York: UNICEF, 2006).

49. Inter-Parliamentary Union, "Women in Politics: 2012," updated February 2012, available at http://www.ipu.org/pdf/publications/wmnmap12_en.pdf (accessed 8 May 2012).

50. M. M. Davis and A. M. Upston, "State Legislator Gender and Other Characteristics Associated with Sponsorship of Child Health Bills," *Ambulatory Pediatrics* 4, no. 4 (2004): 295–302.

51. Although both male and female legislators in these countries displayed a high level of support for children and family issues, when they were asked to pri-

oritize policy areas, female legislators were more likely than males to rank these issues as a "high" or "very high" priority. L. A. Schwindt-Bayer, "Female Legislators and the Promotion of Women, Children, and Family Policies in Latin America" (background paper for UNICEF, *State of the World's Children 2007*). Female legislators in Argentina were nearly 10 percent more likely than men to make child and family issues a policy priority, measured as a proportion of related bills introduced in the Chamber of Deputies. M. P. Jones, "Legislator Gender and Legislator Policy Priorities in the Argentine Chamber of Deputies and the United States House of Representatives," *Policy Studies Journal* 25, no. 4 (1997): 613–629.

52. Compared with their male counterparts, female legislators in the Russian Duma were more supportive of policies addressing child care, parental leave and benefits, and domestic violence, regardless of their party ideology. I. Shevchenko, "Who Cares about Women's Problems? Female Legislators in the 1995 and 1999 Russian State Dumas," *Europe-Asia Studies* 54, no. 8 (2002): 1201–1222. In the National Assembly of Wales, female representatives were far more likely than males to participate in discussion and debate regarding child-care concerns. S. Childs, J. Lovenduski, and R. Campbell, *Women at the Top 2005: Changing Numbers, Changing Politics?* (London: Hansard Society, 2005). Similarly, analyses of 25 years of parliamentary debate in New Zealand revealed that female members of the House of Representatives were significantly more likely to initiate discussion on both child care and parental leave. S. Grey, "Does Size Matter? Critical Mass and New Zealand's Women MPs," *Parliamentary Affairs* 5 (2002): 19–29.

53. K. A. Bratton and L. P. Ray, "Descriptive Representation, Policy Outcomes, and Municipal Day-Care Coverage in Norway," *American Journal of Political Science* 46, no. 2 (2002): 428–437.

54. L. Beaman, E. Duflo, R. Pande, and P. Topalova, "Women Politicians, Gender Bias, and Policy-Making in Rural India" (background paper for UNICEF, *State of the World's Children 2007*).

55. R. Pande, "Can Mandated Political Representation Increase Policy Influence for Disadvantaged Minorities? Theory and Evidence from India," *American Economic Review* 93, no. 4 (2003): 1132–1151.

56. M. Bradbury and J. Kellough, "Representative Bureaucracy: Exploring the Potential for Active Representation in Local Government," *Journal of Public Administration Research and Theory* 18, no. 4 (2008): 697–714; K. Whitby and G. Krause, "Race, Issue Heterogeneity and Public Policy: The Republican Revolution in the 104th US Congress and the Representation of African-American Policy Interests," *British Journal of Political Science* 31, no. 3 (2001): 555–572; M. Minta, "Legislative Oversight and the Substantive Representation of Black and Latino Interests in Congress," *Legislative Studies Quarterly* 34, no. 2 (2009): 193–218.

57. K. Bratton, "The Behavior and Success of Latino Legislators: Evidence from the States," *Social Science Quarterly* 87, no. 5 (2006): 1136–1157.

58. K. Gamble, "Black Political Representation: An Examination of Legislative Activity within US House Committees," *Legislative Studies Quarterly* 32, no. 3 (2007): 421–447.

59. M. K. Pleiss and J. F. Feldhussen, "Mentors, Role Models, and Heroes in the Lives of Gifted Children," *Educational Psychologist* 30, no. 3 (1995): 159–169;

S. Zirkel, "Is There a Place for Me? Role Models and Academic Identity among White Students and Students of Color," *Teachers College Record* 104, no. 2 (2002): 357–376; P. Lockwood and Z. Kunda, "Superstars and Me: Predicting the Impact of Role Models on the Self," *Journal of Personality and Social Psychology* 73, no. 1 (1997): 91–103; D. M. Anderson, L. A. Bedini, and L. Moreland, "Getting All Girls into the Game: Physically Active Recreation for Girls with Disabilities," *Journal of Park and Recreation Administration* 23, no. 4 (2005): 78–103.

60. D. M. Marx, S. J. Ko, and R. A. Friedman, "The 'Obama Effect': How a Salient Role Model Reduces Race-Based Performance Differences," *Journal of Experimental Social Psychology* 45, no. 4 (2009): 953–956.

61. L. Beaman, E. Duflo, R. Pande, and P. Topalova, "Female Leadership Raises Aspirations and Educational Attainment for Girls: A Policy Experiment in India," *Science*, January 2012, 1–8.

8. Meeting Special Needs

1. Interview, Project on Global Working Families (Viet Nam, 11 September 2001). The name of this interviewee has been changed to protect confidentiality.

2. Interview, Project on Global Working Families (United States, 27 June 1997). The name of this interviewee has been changed to protect confidentiality.

3. This guarantee was made through the Individuals with Disabilities Education Act. For more information, see U.S. Department of Education, "Building the Legacy: IDEA 2004," available at http://idea.ed.gov/ (accessed 28 February 2012).

4. Office of the United Nations High Commissioner for Human Rights, "Convention on the Rights of Persons with Disabilities," available at http://www2.ohchr.org/english/law/disabilities-convention.htm (accessed 15 April 2011).

5. World Health Organization and World Bank, *World Report on Disability* (Geneva: World Health Organization, 2011).

6. United Nations Treaty Collection, "Convention on the Rights of Persons with Disabilities," available at http://treaties.un.org/Pages/ViewDetails.aspx?src=TREATY&mtdsg_no=IV-15&chapter=4&lang=en (accessed 27 January 2012).

7. A right is considered aspirational if it is written in language that is not authoritative (e.g., the State "should," "endeavors to," "promotes"), if it is explicitly dependent on the state's ability to provide it, or if it is explicitly nonenforceable. It is also considered aspirational when it appears only in the preamble of the constitution when the preamble is not described as an integral part of the constitution in question.

8. M. K. Pleiss and J. F. Feldhussen, "Mentors, Role Models, and Heroes in the Lives of Gifted Children," *Educational Psychologist* 30, no. 3 (1995): 159–169; S. Zirkel, "Is There a Place for Me? Role Models and Academic Identity among White Students and Students of Color," *Teachers College Record* 104, no. 2 (2002): 357–376; P. Lockwood and Z. Kunda, "Superstars and Me: Predicting the Impact of Role Models on the Self," *Journal of Personality and Social Psychology* 73, no. 1 (1997): 91–103; D. M. Anderson, L. A. Bedini, and L. Moreland, "Getting All Girls into the Game: Physically Active Recreation for Girls with Disabilities," *Journal of Park and Recreation Administration* 23, no. 4 (2005): 78–103.

9. See, for example, C. Buchmann, "Family Structure, Parental Perceptions, and Child Labor in Kenya: What Factors Determine Who Is Enrolled in School?," *Social Forces* 78, no. 4 (2000): 1349–1378; L. Beaman, E. Duflo, R. Pande, and P. Topalova, "Female Leadership Raises Aspirations and Educational Attainment for Girls: A Policy Experiment in India," *Science*, January 2012, 1–8; D. M. Marx, S. J. Ko, and R. A. Friedman, "The 'Obama Effect': How a Salient Role Model Reduces Race-Based Performance Differences," *Journal of Experimental Social Psychology* 45, no. 4 (2009): 953–956.

10. In 1993, Canada eliminated from its Elections Act the provision that excluded people with "mental disease" from voting. D. Davidson and M. Lapp, "The Evolution of Federal Voting Rights for Canadians with Disabilities," *Electoral Insight* 6, no. 1 (April 2004): 15–21. In 2010, a European Court of Human Rights ruling in a case brought by an individual with manic depression declared that the Hungarian constitution's blanket denial of the right to vote for people under guardianship violated the European Convention on Human Rights. European Court of Human Rights, *Case of Alajos Kiss v. Hungary*, application no. 38832/06, judgment, Strasbourg (20 May 2010), available at http://www.unhcr .org/refworld/pdfid/4bf665f58.pdf (accessed 28 February 2012).

11. D. Filmer, "Disability, Poverty, and Schooling in Developing Countries: Results from 14 Household Surveys," *World Bank Economic Review* 22, no. 1 (2008): 141–163. This study covered 13 countries; the title references 14 surveys because 2 from Cambodia were used.

12. World Bank, "People with Disabilities in India: From Commitments to Outcomes" (World Bank Human Development Unit, South Asia Region, July 2009).

13. C. Mete, ed., *Economic Implications of Chronic Illness and Disability in Eastern Europe and the Former Soviet Union* (Washington, D.C.: World Bank, 2008); Filmer, "Disability, Poverty, and Schooling in Developing Countries."

14. J.-F. Kobiané and M. Bougma, *Rapport d'analyse du thème IV: Instruction, alphabétisation et scolarisation* (Ouagadougou, Burkina Faso: Institut National de la Statistique et de la Démographie, 2009).

15. D. Echevin, "Employment and Education Discrimination against Disabled People in Cape Verde," *Applied Economics* 45, no. 7 (2013): 857–875.

16. UNICEF, *Innocenti Insight: Children and Disability in Transition in CEE/ CIS and Baltic States* (Florence, Italy: UNICEF, 2005); International Disability Rights Monitor, *Regional Report of Asia* (Chicago: Center for International Rehabilitation, 2005).

17. M. Loeb, A. H. Eide, J. Jelsma, M. ka Toni, and S. Maart, "Poverty and Disability in Eastern and Western Cape Provinces, South Africa," *Disability and Society* 23, no. 4 (2008): 311–321.

18. P. Dudzik, A. Elwan, and R. L. Metts, *Disability Policies, Statistics, and Strategies in Latin America and the Caribbean: A Review* (Washington, D.C.: Inter-American Development Bank, 2002).

19. International Disability Rights Monitor, *Regional Report of the Americas* (Chicago: Center for International Rehabilitation, 2004).

20. A. Elwan, "Poverty and Disability: A Survey of the Literature" (Social Protection Discussion Paper no. 9932, December 1999); M. K. Meyers, A. Lukemeyer, and T. Smeeding, "The Cost of Caring: Childhood Disability and

Poor Families," *Social Service Review* 72, no. 2 (1998): 209–233; K. A. Kuhlthau and J. M. Perrin, "Child Health Status and Parental Employment," *Archives of Pediatrics and Adolescent Medicine* 155, no. 12 (2001): 1346–1350; J. Shearn and S. Todd, "Maternal Employment and Family Responsibilities: The Perspectives of Mothers of Children with Intellectual Disabilities," *Journal of Applied Research in Intellectual Disabilities* 13, no. 3 (2000): 109–131.

21. For information on caring for children with special needs as a barrier to work, see Meyers, Lukemeyer, and Smeeding, "Cost of Caring"; Shearn and Todd, "Maternal Employment and Family Responsibilities"; D. Anderson, S. Dumont, P. Jacobs, and L. Azzaria, "The Personal Costs of Caring for a Child with a Disability: A Review of the Literature," *Public Health Reports* 122 (2007): 3–16; and A. Lukemeyer, M. K. Meyers, and T. Smeeding, "Expensive Children in Poor Families: Out-of-Pocket Expenditures for the Care of Disabled and Chronically Ill Children in Welfare Families," *Journal of Marriage and Family* 62, no. 2 (2000): 399–415. These barriers can lead to reduced income; in Romania, for example, households with a disabled child had 65 percent of the income of households without disabled children. UNICEF, *Innocenti Insight: Children and Disability in Transition in CEE/CIS and Baltic States.*

22. For a review of the evidence, see T. Emmett and E. Alant, "Women and Disability: Exploring the Interface of Multiple Disadvantage," *Development Southern Africa* 23, no. 4 (2006): 445–460.

23. Dudzik, Elwan, and Metts, *Disability Policies, Statistics, and Strategies in Latin America and the Caribbean.*

24. M. L. Mayer, A. C. Skinner, and R. T. Slifkin, "Unmet Need for Routine and Specialty Care: Data from the National Survey of Children with Special Health Care Needs," *Pediatrics* 113, no. 2 (2004): e109–e115; S. C. Dusing, A. C. Skinner, and M. L. Mayer, "Unmet Need for Therapy Services, Assistive Devices, and Related Services: Data from the National Survey of Children with Special Health Care Needs," *Ambulatory Pediatrics* 4, no. 5 (2004): 448–454.

25. Filmer, "Disability, Poverty, and Schooling in Developing Countries."

26. International Disability Rights Monitor, *Regional Report of the Americas.*

27. International Disability Rights Monitor, *Regional Report of Asia.*

28. Organisation for Economic Co-operation and Development, "Sickness, Disability, and Work" (background paper for High-Level Forum, Stockholm, May 2009), available at http://www.oecd.org/dataoecd/42/15/42699911.pdf (accessed 21 February 2012).

29. A. K. Dube, "The Role and Effectiveness of Disability Legislation in South Africa," Disability Knowledge and Research Series (March 2005).

30. Mete, *Economic Implications of Chronic Illness and Disability in Eastern Europe and the Former Soviet Union.*

31. P. Parnes, D. Cameron, N. Christie, L. Cockburn, G. Hashemi, and K. Yoshida, "Disability in Low-Income Countries: Issues and Implications," *Disability and Rehabilitation* 31, no. 14 (2009): 1170–1180.

32. International Disability Rights Monitor, *Regional Report of the Americas.*

33. D. Foley and J. Chowdhury, "Poverty, Social Exclusion and the Politics of Disability: Care as a Social Good and the Expenditure of Social Capital in Chuadanga, Bangladesh," *Social Policy and Administration* 41, no. 4 (2007): 372–385.

34. Mete, *Economic Implications of Chronic Illness and Disability in Eastern Europe and the Former Soviet Union.*

35. For additional details on inclusive educational outcomes for children with disabilities, see N. M. Ruijs and T. T. D. Peetsma, "Effects of Inclusion on Students with and without Special Educational Needs Reviewed," *Educational Research Review* 4 (2009): 67–79; N. Ruijs, T. Peetsma, and I. van der Veen, "The Presence of Several Students with Special Educational Needs in Inclusive Education and the Functioning of Students with Special Educational Needs," *Educational Review* 62, no. 1 (2010): 1–37; C. Fore III, S. Hagan-Burke, M. D. Burke, R. T. Boon, and S.Smith, "Academic Achievement and Class Placement in High School: Do Students with Learning Disabilities Achieve More in One Class Placement than Another?," *Education and Treatment of Children* 31, no. 1 (2008): 55–72; M. S. Klompas, "Inclusive Education of Primary School Aged Children with Down Syndrome in Gauteng Province, South Africa" (diss., University of Witwatersrand, 2008); D. Leach and M. L. Duffy, "Supporting Students with Autism Spectrum Disorders in Inclusive Settings," *Intervention in School and Clinic* 45, no. 31 (2009): 31–37; and P. Foreman, M. Arthur-Kelly, S. Pascoe, and B. Smyth-King, "Evaluating the Educational Experiences of Students with Profound and Multiple Disabilities in Inclusive and Segregated Classroom Settings: An Australian Perspective," *Research and Practice for Persons with Severe Disabilities* 29, no. 3 (2004): 183–193. Evidence is also clear that inclusion does not negatively affect the achievement of students without disabilities. T. E. Scruggs, M. A. Mastropieri, and K. A. McDuffie, "Co-teaching in Inclusive Classrooms: A Metasynthesis of Qualitative Research," *Exceptional Children* 73, no. 4 (2007): 392–416; N. M. Ruijs, I. van der Veen, and T. T. D. Peetsma, "Inclusive Education and Students without Special Educational Needs," *Educational Research* 52, no. 4 (2010): 351–390; A. Kalambouka, P. Farrell, A. Dyson, and I. Kaplan, "The Impact of Placing Pupils with Special Educational Needs in Mainstream Schools on the Achievement of Their Peers," *Educational Research* 49, no. 4 (2007): 365–382.

36. H. Nakken and S. J. Pijl, "Getting Along with Classmates in Regular Schools: A Review of the Effects of Integration on the Development of Social Relationships," *International Journal of Inclusive Education* 6, no. 1 (2002): 47–61; P. C. Favazza, L. Phillipsen, and P. Kumar, "Measuring and Promoting Acceptance of Young Children with Disabilties," *Exceptional Children* 66, no. 4 (2000): 491–508.

37. Y. Takamine, "Disability Issues in East Asia: Review and Ways Forward" (World Bank Working Paper no. 29299, May 2004).

38. G. L. Porter, *Disability and Education—Toward an Inclusive Approach* (New York: Inter-American Development Bank, 2001).

39. World Conference on Special Needs Education: Access and Quality, "The Salamanca Statement and Framework for Action on Special Needs Education" (Salamanca, Spain, 7–10 June 1994), available at http://www.unesco.org/education /pdf/SALAMA_E.PDF (accessed 22 July 2012).

40. Office of the United Nations High Commissioner for Human Rights, "Convention on the Rights of Persons with Disabilities."

41. As well as being important for integrating children and adapting evaluation methods, relevant training also improves teachers' attitudes toward inclusion, which are crucial for its success. For more information, see R. E. Janney, M. E. Snell, M. K. Beers, and M. Raynes, "Integrating Students with Moderate

and Severe Disabilities into General Education Classes," *Exceptional Children* 61, no. 5 (1995): 425–439; C. S. Ching, C. Forlin, and A. M. Lan, "The Influence of an Inclusive Education Course on Attitude Change of Pre-service Secondary Teachers in Hong Kong," *Asia-Pacific Journal of Teacher Education* 35, no. 2 (2007): 161–179; A. K. Van Reusen, A. R. Shoho, and K. S. Barker, "High School Teacher Attitudes towards Inclusion," *High School Journal* 84, no. 2 (2000): 7–20; H. Sari, "The Influence of an In-Service Teacher Training (INSET) Programme on Attitudes towards Inclusion by Regular Classroom Teachers Who Teach Deaf Students in Primary Schools in Turkey," *Deafness and Education International* 9, no. 3 (2007): 131–146; R. Rose, L. Kaikkonen, and K. Koiv, "Estonian Vocational Teachers' Attitudes towards Inclusive Education for Students with Special Educational Needs," *International Journal of Special Education* 22, no. 3 (2007): 97–108; S. Lohrmann and E. M. Boggs, "Elementary Education Teachers' Beliefs about Essential Supports Needed to Successfully Include Students with Developmental Disabilities Who Engage in Challenging Behaviors," *Research and Practice for Persons with Severe Disabilities* 31, no. 2 (2006): 157–173; and J. Campbell, L. Gilmore, and M. Cuskelly, "Changing Student Teachers' Attitudes towards Disability and Inclusion," *Journal of Developmental and Intellectual Disability* 28, no. 4 (2003): 369–379.

42. Porter, *Disability and Education;* S. Sze, "A Literature Review: Pre-service Teachers' Attitudes towards Students with Disabilities," *Education* 130, no. 1 (2009): 53–56; J. Suter and M. Giangreco, "Numbers That Count: Exploring Special Education and Paraprofessional Service Delivery in Inclusion-Oriented Schools," *Journal of Special Education* 43, no. 2 (2009): 81–93; N. K. French, "Working Together: Resource Teachers and Paraeducators," *Remedial and Special Education* 19, no. 6 (1998): 357–368.

43. Anderson et al., "Personal Costs of Caring for a Child with a Disability"; N. Xiong, L. Yang, Y. Yu, J. Hou, J. Li, H. Liu, Y. Zhang, and Z. Jiao, "Investigation of Raising Burden of Children with Autism, Physical Disability and Mental Disability in China," *Research in Developmental Disabilities* 32 (2011): 306–311.

44. A. Marriott and K. Gooding, "Social Assistance and Disability in Developing Countries" (DFID and Sightsavers International, July 2007).

45. These data show only funds provided specifically for families supporting a disabled child. It should be noted that families may also receive other benefits through a general family benefits scheme or other sources. For preschool, a 4-year-old child is assumed. For school age, an 8-year-old child is assumed. For adolescence, a 15-year-old child is assumed.

46. A. M. LaGreca, W. F. Auslander, P. Greco, D. Spetter, E. B. Fisher Jr., and J. V. Santiago, "I Get By with a Little Help from My Family and Friends: Adolescents' Support for Diabetes Care," *Journal of Pediatric Psychology* 20, no. 4 (1995): 449–476; S. T. Hauser, A. M. Jacobson, P. Lavori, J. I. Wolfsdorf, R. D. Herskowitz, J. E. Milley, R. Bliss, D. Wertlieb, and J. Stein, "Adherence among Children and Adolescents with Insulin-Dependent Diabetes Mellitus over a Four-Year Longitudinal Follow-Up: II. Immediate and Long-Term Linkages with the Family Milieu," *Journal of Pediatric Psychology* 15, no. 4 (1990): 527–542; C. Hovinga, M. Asato, R. Manjunath, J. W. Wheless, S. J. Phelps, R. D. Sheth, J. E. Pina-Garza, W. M. Zingaro, and L. S. Haskins, "Association of Non-adherence to

Antiepileptic Drugs and Seizures, Quality of Life, and Productivity: Survey of Patients with Epilepsy and Physicians," *Epilepsy and Behavior* 13, no. 2 (2008): 316–322; S. H. Simpson, "A Meta-analysis of the Association between Adherence to Drug Therapy and Mortality," *British Medical Journal* 333, no. 7557 (2006): 15–21.

47. C. Wolman, M. D. Resnick, L. J. Harris, and R. W. Blum, "Emotional Well-Being among Adolescents with and without Chronic Conditions," *Journal of Adolescent Health* 15, no. 3 (1994): 199–204; K. W. Hamlett, D. S. Pellegrini, and K. S. Katz, "Childhood Chronic Illness as a Family Stressor," *Journal of Pediatric Psychology* 17, no. 1 (1992): 33–47.

48. S. J. Heymann, S. Toomey, and F. Furstenberg, "Working Parents: What Factors Are Involved in Their Ability to Take Time Off from Work When Their Children Are Sick?," *Archives of Pediatric and Adolescent Medicine* 153 (1999): 870–874.

49. P. W. Newacheck, M. Inkelas, and S. E. Kim, "Health Services Use and Health Care Expenditures for Children with Disabilities," *Pediatrics* 114 (2004): 79–85.

50. F. Davis, "Understanding Underachievers," *American Education* 20, no. 10 (1984): 12–14; M. Gajria and S. J. Salend, "Homework Practices of Students with and without Learning Disabilities: A Comparison," *Journal of Learning Disabilities* 28, no. 5 (1995): 291–296; S. J. Salend and J. Schliff, "An Examination of the Homework Practices of Teachers of Students with Learning Disabilities," *Journal of Learning Disabilities* 22, no. 10 (1989): 621–623.

51. H. Cooper and B. Nye, "Homework for Students with Learning Disabilities—The Implications of Research for Policy and Practice," *Journal of Learning Disabilities* 27, no. 8 (1994): 470–479; C. R. Vinograd-Bausell, R. B. Bausell, W. Proctor, and B. Chandler, "Impact of Unsupervised Parent Tutors on Word Recognition Skills," *Journal of Special Education* 20, no. 1 (1986): 83–90; J. D. Austin, "Homework Research in Mathematics," *School Science and Mathematics* 79 (1979): 115–121; S. J. Salend and M. Gajria, "Increasing the Homework Completion Rates of Students with Mild Disabilities," *Remedial and Special Education* 16, no. 5 (1995): 271–278; E. J. Cancio, R. P. West, and K. R. Young, "Improving Mathematics Homework Completion and Accuracy of Students with EBD through Self-Management and Parent Participation," *Journal of Emotional and Behavioral Disorders* 12, no. 1 (2004): 9–22.

52. J. Hewison, "The Long Term Effectiveness of Parental Involvement in Reading: A Follow-up to the Haringey Reading Project," *British Journal of Educational Psychology* 58, no. 1 (1988): 184–190; J. Tizard, J. Hewison, and W. N. Schofield, "Collaboration between Teachers and Parents in Assisting Children's Reading," *British Journal of Educational Psychology* 52 (1982): 1–15.

53. International Labour Organization, TRAVAIL Database of Conditions of Work and Employment Laws, available at http://www.ilo.org/dyn/travail/trav main.home (accessed 25 May 2012).

54. Dudzik, Elwan, and Metts, *Disability Policies, Statistics, and Strategies in Latin America and the Caribbean.*

55. World Health Organization and World Bank, *World Report on Disability.*

56. Mete, *Economic Implications of Chronic Illness and Disability in Eastern Europe and the Former Soviet Union.*

57. N. Singal, "Inclusive Education in India: International Concept, National Interpretation," *International Journal of Disability, Development, and Education* 53, no. 3 (2006): 351–369.

58. International Disability Rights Monitor, *Regional Report of Asia.*

59. International Disability Rights Monitor, *Regional Report of the Americas.*

60. International Disability Rights Monitor, *Regional Report of Europe* (Chicago: Center for International Rehabilitation, 2007).

61. International Disability Rights Monitor, *Regional Report of the Americas.*

62. J. Robertson, H. Roberts, and E. Emerson, *Health Checks for People with Learning Disabilities: A Systematic Review of Evidence,* Improving Health and Lives: Learning Disabilities Observatory (2010), available at http://www.improving healthandlives.org.uk/uploads/doc/vid_7646_IHAL2010–04HealthChecksSystemticReview.pdf (accessed 30 January 2011); E. Emerson and S. Baines, *Health Inequalites and People with Learning Disabilities in the UK: 2010,* Improving Health and Lives: Learning Disabilities Observatory (2010), available at http://www.improving healthandlives.org.uk/uploads/doc/vid_7479_IHaL2010–3HealthInequality2010 .pdf (accessed 30 January 2011).

63. International Disability Rights Monitor, *Regional Report of Asia.*

64. Mete, *Economic Implications of Chronic Illness and Disability in Eastern Europe and the Former Soviet Union.*

9. Changing Children's Chances

1. UNESCO, *Education for All Global Monitoring Report 2010: Reaching the Marginalized* (Paris: UNESCO, 2010), 347.

2. D. Neumark and S. Adams, "Do Living Wage Ordinances Reduce Urban Poverty?," *Journal of Human Resources* 38, no. 3 (2003): 490–521; D. Morgan and K. Kickham, "Children in Poverty: Do State Policies Matter?," *Social Science Quarterly* 82, no. 3 (2001): 478–493; R. Mincy, "Raising the Minimum Wage: Effects on Family Poverty," *Monthly Labor Review* 113, no. 7 (1990): 18–25; R. H. DeFina, "The Impact of State Minimum Wages on Child Poverty in Female-Headed Families," *Journal of Poverty* 12, no. 2 (2008): 155–174; G. Cooke and K. Lawton, *Working out of Poverty: A Study of the Low-Paid and the "Working Poor"* (London: Institute for Public Policy Research, 2008); D. Piachaud and H. Sutherland, "How Effective Is the British Government's Attempt to Reduce Child Poverty?" (CASE Paper 38, Centre for Analysis of Social Exclusion, March 2000); Organisation for Economic Co-operation and Development, *OECD Employment Outlook 1998: Towards an Employment-Centred Social Policy* (Paris: OECD Publishing, 1998); J. Rutkowski, "The Minimum Wage: Curse or Cure?" (World Bank, 2003), available at http://siteresources.worldbank.org/INTECONEVAL/Re sources/MinimumWageNoteJul03v2.pdf (accessed 20 June 2012); S. Devereux, "Can Minimum Wages Contribute to Poverty Reduction in Poor Countries?," *Journal of International Development* 17 (2005): 899–912; C. Saget, "Poverty Reduction and Decent Work in Developing Countries: Do Minimum Wages Help?," *International Labour Review* 140, no. 3 (2001): 237–269; J. Rodgers and J. Rubery, "The Minimum Wage as a Tool to Combat Discrimination and Promote Equality," *International Labour Review* 142, no. 4 (2003): 543–556; T. H. Gindling and K. Terrell, "The Effect of Minimum Wages on Actual Wages in

Formal and Informal Sectors in Costa Rica," *World Development* 33, no. 11 (2005): 1905–1921; N. Kristensen and W. Cunningham, *Do Minimum Wages in Latin America and the Caribbean Matter? Evidence from 19 Countries*, World Bank Policy Research Working Paper no. 3870 (2006).

3. Rodgers and Rubery, "Minimum Wage as a Tool to Combat Discrimination and Promote Equality"; Gindling and Terrell, "Effect of Minimum Wages on Actual Wages in Formal and Informal Sectors in Costa Rica"; Kristensen and Cunningham, *Do Minimum Wages in Latin America and the Caribbean Matter?*; Saget, "Poverty Reduction and Decent Work in Developing Countries."

4. J. D. Willms and M. A. Somer, "Family, Classroom, and School Effects on Children's Educational Outcomes in Latin America," *School Effectiveness and School Improvement* 12, no. 4 (2001): 409–445; K. Michaelowa, "Primary Education Quality in Francophone Sub-Saharan Africa: Determinants of Learning Achievement and Efficiency Considerations," *World Development* 29, no. 10 (2001): 1699–1716; D. D. Goldhaber and D. J. Brewer, "Evaluating the Effect of Teacher Degree Level on Educational Performance," in W. J. J. Fowler, ed., *Developments in School Finance, 1996: Fiscal Proceedings from the Annual NCES State Data Conference, July 1996* (Washington, D.C.: U.S. Government Printing Office, 1997), 197–210; B. Rowan, F.-S. Chiang, and R. J. Miller, "Using Research on Employees' Performance to Study the Effects of Teachers on Student Achievement," *Sociology of Education* 70, no. 4 (1997): 256–284.

5. G. Psacharopoulos, "Child Labor versus Educational Attainment—Some Evidence from Latin America," *Journal of Population Economics* 10, no. 4 (1997): 377–386; N. Ilahi, P. Orazem, and G. Sedlacek, "The Implications of Child Labor for Adult Wages, Income, and Poverty" (2001), available at http://www.grade .org.pe/Eventos/nip_conference/private/sedlacek-%20child_labor%20retros.pdf (accessed 18 February 2010); S. Doocy, B. Crawford, C. Boudreaux, and E. Wall, "The Risks and Impacts of Portering on the Well-Being of Children in Nepal," *Journal of Tropical Pediatrics* 53, no. 3 (2007): 165–170; R. Ray, "The Determinants of Child Labour and Child Schooling in Ghana," *Journal of African Economies* 11, no. 4 (2002): 561–590, cited in E. V. Edmonds, "Defining Child Labour: A Review of the Definitions of Child Labour in Policy Research" (working paper for the Statistical Information and Monitoring Programme on Child Labour, International Programme on the Elimination of Child Labour, ILO, Geneva, November 2008), 34; G. Bonnet, "Marginalization in Latin America and the Caribbean" (background paper for and cited in UNESCO, *Education for All Global Monitoring Report 2010*), 111; M. A. Sánchez, P. F. Orazem, and V. Gunnarsson, "The Impact of Child Labor Intensity on Mathematics and Language Skills in Latin America," in P. F. Orazem, G. Sedlacek, and Z. Tzannatos, eds., *Child Labor and Education in Latin America: An Economic Perspective* (New York: Palgrave Macmillan, 2009), 117–130, cited in UNESCO, *Education for All Global Monitoring Report 2010*, 168; V. Gunnarsson, P. F. Orazem, and M. A. Sánchez, "Child Labor and School Achievement in Latin America," *World Bank Economic Review* 20, no. 1 (2006): 31–54; D. Post and S. Pong, "Employment during Middle School: The Effects on Academic Achievement in the U.S. and Abroad," *Educational Evaluation and Policy Analysis* 22, no. 3 (2000): 273–298; C. Heady, "The Effect of Child Labor on Learning Achievement," *World Development* 31, no. 2 (2003): 385–398; M. Fetuga, O. F. Njokanma, and T. A. Ogunlesi, "Do Working Children Have

Worse Academic Performance?," *Indian Journal of Pediatrics* 74, no. 10 (2007): 933–936; C. Dustmann, J. Micklewright, N. Rajah, and S. Smith, "Earning and Learning: Educational Policy and the Growth of Part-Time Work by Full-Time Pupils," *Fiscal Studies* 17, no. 1 (1996): 79–103; H. Akabayashi and G. Psacharopoulos, "The Trade-off between Child Labour and Human Capital Formation: A Tanzanian Case Study," *Journal of Development Economics* 35 (1999): 120–140; F. Blanco Allais, *Assessing the Gender Gap: Evidence from SIMPOC Surveys* (Geneva: Statistical Information and Monitoring Programme on Child Labour [SIMPOC], International Programme on the Elimination of Child Labour, International Labour Organization, 2009); B. Fuller, L. Dellagnelo, A. Strath, E. S. Barretto Bastos, M. Holanda Maia, K. Socorro Lopes de Matos, A. L. Portela, and S. Lerche Vieira, "How to Raise Children's Early Literacy? The Influence of Family, Teacher, and Classroom in Northeast Brazil," *Comparative Education Review* 43, no. 1 (1999): 1–35; J. H. Lillydahl, "Academic Achievement and Part-Time Employment of High School Students," *Journal of Economic Education* 21, no. 3 (1990): 307–316; R. D'Amico, "Does Working during High School Impair Academic Progress?," *Sociology of Education* 57, no. 3 (1984): 152–164; R. Assad, D. Levison, and N. Zibani, *The Effect of Child Work on Schooling: Evidence from Egypt*, Economic Research Forum Working Paper no. 0111 (Cairo: Economic Research Forum, revised 2005); R. Assad, D. Levison, and N. Zibani, "The Effect of Domestic Work on Girls' Schooling: Evidence from Egypt," *Feminist Economics* 16, no. 1 (2010): 79–128; H. Phoumin, "Human Capital and Hours Worked of Children in Cambodia: Empirical Evidence for Policy Implications," *Asian Economic Journal* 22, no. 1 (2008): 25–46.

6. Edmonds, "Defining Child Labour."

7. R. Jensen and R. Thornton, "Early Female Marriage in the Developing World," *Gender and Development* 11, no. 2 (2003): 9–19; B. Mensch, "The Transition to Marriage," in C. B. Lloyd, ed., *Growing Up Global: The Changing Transitions to Adulthood in Developing Countries*, Committee on Population, Board on Children, Youth, and Families, Division of Behavioral and Social Sciences and Education, National Research Council, and Institute of Medicine (Washington, D.C.: National Academies Press, 2005), 416–505; S. Jain and K. Kurz, "New Insights on Preventing Child Marriage: A Global Analysis of Factors and Programs" (report prepared by the International Center for Research on Women for the United States Agency for International Development, April 2007); C. B. Lloyd and B. S. Mensch, "Marriage and Childbirth as Factors in Dropping out of School: An Analysis of DHS Data from Sub-Saharan Africa," *Population Studies* 62, no. 1 (2008): 1–13; T. Tuwor and M.-A. Sossou, "Gender Discrimination and Education in West Africa: Strategies for Maintaining Girls in School," *International Journal of Inclusive Education* 12, no. 4 (2008): 363–379; E. Field and A. Ambrus, "Early Marriage, Age of Menarche, and Female Schooling Attainment in Bangladesh," *Journal of Political Economy* 166, no. 5 (2008): 881–930.

8. UNICEF, *Early Marriage: A Harmful Traditional Practice* (New York: UNICEF, 2005); Mensch, "Transition to Marriage"; Jain and Kurz, "New Insights on Preventing Child Marriage"; Jensen and Thornton, "Early Female Marriage in the Developing World."

9. M. Muleta and G. Williams, "Postcoital Injuries Treated at the Addis Ababa Fistula Hospital," *Lancet* 354, no. 9195 (1999): 2051–2052; K. G. Santhya,

N. Haberland, F. Ram, R. K. Sinha, and S. K. Mohanty, "Consent and Coercion: Examining Unwanted Sex among Married Young Women in India," *International Family Planning Perspectives* 33, no. 3 (2007): 124–132; D. F. Flake, "Individual, Family, and Community Risk Markers for Domestic Violence in Peru," *Violence against Women* 11, no. 3 (2005): 353–373; N. Gottschalk, "Uganda: Early Marriage as a Form of Sexual Violence," *Forced Migration Review* 27 (2007): 51–53; M. J. Hindin and A. O. Fatusi, "Adolescent Sexual and Reproductive Health in Developing Countries: An Overview of Trends and Interventions," *International Perspectives on Sexual and Reproductive Health* 35, no. 2 (2009): 58–62; P. Ebigbo, "Child Abuse in Africa: Nigeria as Focus," *International Journal of Early Childhood* 35, no. 1 (2003): 95–113; P. Ouis, "Honourable Traditions? Honour Violence, Early Marriage and Sexual Abuse of Teenage Girls in Lebanon, the Occupied Palestinian Territories and Yemen," *International Journal of Children's Rights* 17, no. 3 (2009): 445–474; UNICEF, *Early Marriage;* Jain and Kurz, "New Insights on Preventing Child Marriage"; S. Mathur, M. Greene, and A. Malhotra, *Too Young to Wed: The Lives, Rights, and Health of Young Married Girls* (Washington, D.C.: International Center for Research on Women, 2003); Jensen and Thornton, "Early Female Marriage in the Developing World."

10. UNICEF, *Early Marriage;* S. Singh and R. Samara, "Early Marriage among Women in Developing Countries," *International Family Planning Perspectives* 22, no. 4 (1996): 148–157; M. Ertem, G. Saka, A. Ceylan, and V. Deger, "The Factors Associated with Adolescent Marriages and Outcomes of Adolescent Pregnancies in Mardin Turkey," *Journal of Comparative Family Studies* 39, no. 2 (2008): 229–239; A. Raj, N. Saggurti, D. Balaiah, and J. G. Silverman, "Prevalence of Child Marriage and Its Effect on Fertility and Fertility-Control Outcomes of Young Women in India: A Cross-Sectional, Observational Study," *Lancet* 373, no. 9678 (2009): 1883–1889; Jain and Kurz, "New Insights on Preventing Child Marriage"; Mathur, Greene, and Malhotra, *Too Young to Wed;* K. A. Annan, *We the Children* (New York: UNICEF, 2001); S. L. Meyer, C. J. Ascher-Walsh, R. Norman, A. Idrissa, H. Herbert, O. Kimso, and J. Wilkinson, "Commonalities among Women Who Experienced Vesicovaginal Fistulae as a Result of Obstetric Trauma in Niger: Results from a Survey Given at the National Hospital Fistula Center, Niamey, Niger," *American Journal of Obstetrics and Gynecology* 197, no. 1 (2007): 90.e1–90.e4; G. S. Melah, A. A. Massa, U. R. Yahaya, M. Bukar, D. D. Kizaya, and A. U. El-Nafaty, "Risk Factors for Obstetric Fistulae in Northeastern Nigeria," *Journal of Obstetrics and Gynaecology* 27, no. 8 (2007): 819–823; A. Holme, M. Breen, and C. MacArthur, "Obstetric Fistulae: A Study of Women Managed at the Monze Mission Hospital, Zambia," *Bjog: An International Journal of Obstetrics and Gynaecology* 114, no. 8 (2007): 1010–1017; N. M. Nour, "Health Consequences of Child Marriage in Africa," *Emerging Infectious Diseases* 12, no. 11 (2006): 1644–1649; Hindin and Fatusi, "Adolescent Sexual and Reproductive Health in Developing Countries"; D. O. Onolemhemhem and C. C. Ekwempu, "An Investigation of Sociomedical Risk Factors Associated with Vaginal Fistula in Northern Nigeria," *Women and Health* 28, no. 3 (1999): 103–116; E. P. Gharoro and K. N. Agholor, "Aspects of Psychosocial Problems of Patients with Vesicovaginal Fistula," *Journal of Obstetrics and Gynaecology* 29, no. 7 (2009): 644–647.

11. A. George and J. Hancock, "Reducing Pediatric Burn Pain with Parent Participation," *Journal of Burn Care and Rehabilitation* 14 (1993): 104–107; P. A.

LaRosa Nash and J. M. Murphy, "An Approach to Pediatric Perioperative Care: Parent-Present Induction," *Nursing Clinics of North America* 32 (1997): 183–199; S. J. Palmer, "Care of Sick Children by Parents: A Meaningful Role," *Journal of Advanced Nursing* 18 (1993): 185–191; I. Kristensson-Hallström, G. Elander, and G. Malmfors, "Increased Parental Participation on a Paediatric Surgical Day-Care Unit," *Journal of Clinical Nursing* 6 (1997): 297–302; T. McGraw, "Preparing Children for the Operating Room: Psychological Issues," *Canadian Journal of Anaethesia* 41, no. 11 (1994): 1094–1103; J. Cleary, O. P. Gray, D. J. Hall, P. H. Rowlandson, C. P. Sainsbury, and M. M. Davies, "Parental Involvement in the Lives of Children in Hospitals," *Archives of Disease in Childhood* 61, no. 8 (1986): 779–787; M. W. Gauderer, J. L. Lorig, and D. W. Eastwood, "Is There a Place for Parents in the Operating Room?," *Journal of Pediatric Surgery* 24, no. 7 (1989): 705–706; R. S. Hannallah and J. K. Rosales, "Experience with Parents' Presence during Anesthesia Induction in Children," *Canadian Anesthetists Society Journal* 30, no. 3, pt. 1 (1983): 286–289; M. R. H. Taylor and P. O'Connor, "Resident Parents and Shorter Hospital Stay," *Archives of Disease in Childhood* 64, no. 2 (1989): 274–276; M. A. Schuster, P. J. Chung, and K. D. Vestal. "Children with Health Issues." *Future of Children* 21, no. 2 (2011): 91–116; P. Mahaffy, "The Effects of Hospitalization on Children Admitted for Tonsillectomy and Adenoidectomy," *Nursing Review* 14 (1965): 12–19; J. Robertson, *Young Children in Hospital* (London: Tavistock, 1970); C. L. Hanson, M. J. DeGuire, A. M. Schinkel, S. W. Henggeler, and G. A. Burghen, "Comparing Social Learning and Family Systems Correlates of Adaptation in Youths with IDDM," *Journal of Pediatric Psychology* 17, no. 5 (1992): 555–572; K. W. Hamlett, D. S. Pellegrini, and K. S. Katz, "Childhood Chronic Illness as a Family Stressor," *Journal of Pediatric Psychology* 17, no. 1 (1992): 33–47; A. M. LaGreca, W. F. Auslander, P. Greco, D. Spetter, E. B. Fisher, and J. V. Santiago, "I Get By with a Little Help from My Family and Friends: Adolescents' Support for Diabetes Care," *Journal of Pediatric Psychology* 20, no. 4 (1995): 449–476; B. J. Anderson, J. P. Miller, W. F. Auslander, and J. V. Santiago, "Family Characteristics of Diabetic Adolescents: Relationship to Metabolic Control," *Diabetes Care* 4, no. 6 (1981): 586–594; S. T. Hauser, A. M. Jacobson, P. Lavori, J. I. Wolfsdorf, R. D. Herskowitz, J. E. Milley, R. Bliss, D. Wertlieb, and J. Stein, "Adherence among Children and Adolescents with Insulin-Dependent Diabetes Mellitus over a Four-Year Longitudinal Follow-up: II. Immediate and Long-Term Linkages with the Family Milieu," *Journal of Pediatric Psychology* 15, no. 4 (1990): 527–542; M. M. Richards, M. J. Bowers, T. Lazicki, D. Krall, and A. K. Jacobs, "Caregiver Involvement in the Intensive Mental Health Program: Influence on Changes in Child Functioning," *Journal of Child and Family Studies* 17 (2008): 241–252; C. Wolman, M. D. Resnick, L. J. Harris, and R. W. Blum, "Emotional Well-Being among Adolescents with and without Chronic Conditions," *Adolescent Medicine* 15, no. 3 (1994): 199–204; A. Riddell, *Factors Influencing Educational Quality and Effectiveness in Developing Countries: A Review of Research* (Eschborn: German Development Cooperation [GTZ], 2008); A. Reynolds, "Comparing Measures of Parental Involvement and Their Effects on Academic Achievement," *Early Childhood Research Quarterly* 7, no. 3 (1992): 441–462; S. Christenson, T. Rounds, and D. Gorney, "Family Factors and Student Achievement: An Avenue to Increase Students' Success," *School Psychology Quarterly* 7 (1992): 178–206; D. Miller and M. Kelley, "Interventions for Improving Homework Performance: A Critical Review," *School Psychology Quarterly* 6 (1991): 174–185; M. M. Englund, B. Egeland, and W. A. Collins, "Exceptions to High School Dropout Predictions in a Low-Income Sample: Do Adults Make a Difference?," *Journal of Social Issues* 64, no. 1 (2008): 77–94; J. Fantuzzo, G. Davis, and M. Ginsburg, "Effects of Parental Involvement in Isolation or in Combination with Peer Tutoring on Student Self-Concept and Mathematics Achievement," *Journal of Educational Psychology* 87, no. 2 (1995): 272–281; C. Desforges and A. Abouchaar, "The Impact of Parental Involvement, Parental Support, and Family Education on Pupil Achievement and Adjustment: A Literature Review" (DFES Research Report 433, Department for Education and Skills, Nottingham, UK, 2003), available at http://publications.dcsf.gov.uk/eOrderingDownload/RR433.pdf (accessed 24 February 2009); A. Reynolds, "A Structural Model of First-Grade Outcomes for an Urban, Low Socioeconomic Status, Minority Population," *Journal of Educational Psychology* 81, no. 4 (1989): 594–603; A. Reynolds, "Early Schooling of Children at Risk," *American Educational Research Journal* 28, no. 2 (1991): 392–422; J. Griffith, "Relation of Parental Involvement, Empowerment, and School Traits to Student Academic Performance," *Journal of Educational Research* 90, no. 1 (1996): 33–41; National Center for Education Statistics, *Fathers' Involvement in Their Children's Schools*, NCES 98-091 (Washington, D.C.: U.S. Department of Education, 1997); H. Aturupane, P. Glewwe, and S. Wisniewski, "The Impact of School Quality, Socio-economic Factors and Child Health on Students' Academic Performance: Evidence from Sri Lankan Primary Schools," *Education Economics* (2011): 1–37; G. van der Werf, B. Creemers, and H. Guldemond, "Improving Parental Involvement in Primary Education in Indonesia: Implementation, Effects, and Costs," *School Effectiveness and School Improvement* 12, no. 4 (2001): 447–466; K. Callahan, J. Rademacher, and B. Hildreth, "The Effect of Parent Participation in Strategies to Improve the Homework Performance of Students Who Are at Risk," *Remedial and Special Education* 19, no. 3 (1998): 131–141; T. Keith, P. Keith, G. Troutman, P. Bickley, P. Trivette, and K. Singh, "Does Parental Involvement Affect Eighth-Grade Student Achievement? Structural Analysis of National Data," *School Psychology Review* 22 (1993): 474–476; P. Fehrmann, T. Keith, and T. Reimers, "Home Influences on School Learning: Direct and Indirect Effects of Parental Involvement on High School Grades," *Journal of Educational Research* 80, no. 6 (1987): 330–337; L. Feinstein and J. Symons, "Attainment in Secondary School," *Oxford Economic Papers* 51, no. 2 (1999): 300–321; Education Support Program, *Monitoring School Dropouts: Albania, Kazakhstan, Latvia, Mongolia, Slovakia, and Tajikistan* (Budapest: Open Society Institute, 2007).

12. For additional information on the relationship between work protections, unemployment rates, and economic competitiveness, see Chapter 5 of this book and J. Heymann and A. Earle, *Raising the Global Floor: Dismantling the Myth That We Can't Afford Good Working Conditions for Everyone* (Stanford, Calif.: Stanford University Press, 2010).

13. World Policy Analysis Centre, Education Database; UNESCO Institute for Statistics, "Public Expenditure on Education as % of GDP," 1999–2011 (most recent year available), available at http://stats.uis.unesco.org (accessed 20 June 2012); UNESCO Institute for Statistics, "Pupil-Teacher Ratio. Primary," 1999–2011 (most recent year available), available at http://stats.uis.unesco.org (accessed 20 June 2012); World Health Organization, *World Health Statistics 2011* (Geneva: WHO, 2011).

14. World Bank, "Poverty Headcount Ratio at $1.25 per day (PPP) (% of Population)," available at http://data.worldbank.org/indicator/SI.POV.DDAY (accessed 6 May 2011); UNICEF, "Chile: Statistics," available at http://www.unicef .org/infobycountry/chile_statistics.html#81 (accessed 11 May 2011); UNICEF, "Argentina: Statistics," available at http://www.unicef.org/infobycountry/argen tina_statistics.html#81 (accessed 11 May 2011).

15. UNESCO Institute for Statistics, "Gross Enrolment Ratio. Secondary. All Programmes. Total. (2009)," available at http://stats.uis.unesco.org/unesco /TableViewer/tableView.aspx (accessed 11 May 2011).

16. World Bank, "Mortality Rate, Infant (per 1,000 Live Births)," 2009, available at http://data.worldbank.org/ (accessed 11 May 2011); World Bank, "Mortality Rate, Under-5 (per 1,000)," 2009, available at http://data.worldbank.org/ (accessed 11 May 2011).

17. World Bank Education Data, available at http://databank.worldbank.org/ (accessed 6 May 2011); World Bank, *Sri Lanka: Country Summary of Higher Education*, available at http://siteresources.worldbank.org/EDUCATION/Resources/278200 -1121703274255/1439264-1193249163062/Sri_Lanka_CountrySummary.pdf (accessed 6 May 2011).

18. UNESCO Institute for Statistics and OECD, *Education Trends in Perspective* (Paris: UIS/OECD, 2002).

19. UNESCO, *EFA Global Monitoring Report 2009: Overcoming Inequality; Why Governance Matters* (Oxford: UNESCO, 2008).

20. Plan International, *Paying the Price: The Economic Cost of Failing to Educate Girls* (Surrey, U.K.: Plan International, 2008).

21. Organisation for Economic Co-operation and Development, *The High Cost of Low Educational Performance* (Paris: OECD Publishing, 2010).

22. In the United States, adults with higher educational attainment report better health than those with lower educational attainment. C. E. Ross and C. L. Wu, "The Links between Education and Health," *American Sociological Review* 60, no. 5 (1995): 719–745. A study of 22 European countries similarly found a powerful relationship between education and health. Men who had completed upper secondary or higher education were 3 times as likely as men with less education to report good health in Portugal, and more than 2 times as likely to do so in Hungary, Ireland, Luxembourg, and Poland. Women who had attained upper secondary or higher levels of education were more than 2.5 times as likely as women with less schooling to report good health in the Czech Republic and Hungary and more than 2 times as likely to do so in 8 additional countries. O. von dem Knesebeck and S. Geyer, "Emotional Support, Education and Self-Rated Health in 22 European Countries," *BMC Public Health* 7 (2007): 272–278. Even after variables such as childhood health, socioeconomic status, health insurance, and physical exercise are controlled for, more education is associated with better self-rated health and memory capacity among the elderly in Brazil. M. Ramos, "Impact of Socioeconomic Status on Brazilian Elderly Health," *Revista de Saude Publica* 41, no. 4 (2007): 616–624. Poor mental health, specifically depression, has been linked to low educational attainment in a number of U.S. and U.K. studies. L. Feinstein, R. Sabates, T. M. Anderson, A. Sorhaindo, and C. Hammond, "Measuring the Effects of Education on Health and Civic Engagement: 4. What Are the Effects on Health?," in *Measuring the Social Outcomes of Learning*

(Copenhagen: OECD, 2006), 171–363. In Belgium, the healthy life expectancy of men who have completed at least 3 years of postsecondary education is 15 years longer than that of their counterparts who completed only primary education. For women, this difference is 19 years. N. Bossuyt, S. Gadeyne, P. Deboosere, and H. Van Oyen, "Socio-economic Inequalities in Health Expectancy in Belgium," *Public Health* 118, no. 1 (2004): 3–10. In Switzerland, for each additional year of education obtained, mortality risk declined by over 7 percent for men and 6 percent for women, and in the United States, years of schooling have been linked to lower risk of mortality, greater life expectancy, and greater healthy life expectancy independently of other related factors. Feinstein et al., "Measuring the Effects of Education on Health and Civic Engagement"; E. M. Crimmins and Y. Saito, "Trends in Healthy Life Expectancy in the United States, 1970–1990: Gender, Racial, and Educational Differences," *Social Science and Medicine* 52, no. 11 (2001): 1629–1641; A. Lleras-Muney, "The Relationship between Education and Adult Mortality in the United States," *Review of Economic Studies* 72, no. 1 (2005): 189–221. Similar results have been documented in the United Kingdom, Austria, Bangladesh, Indonesia, the Netherlands, and the Republic of Korea. Feinstein et al., "Measuring the Effects of Education on Health and Civic Engagement"; G. Doblhammer, R. Rau, and J. Kytir, "Trends in Educational and Occupational Differentials in All-Cause Mortality in Austria between 1981/82 and 1991/92," *Wiener Klinische Wochenschrift* 117, nos. 13–14 (2005): 468–479; L. S. Hurt, C. Ronsmans, and S. Saha, "Effects of Education and Other Socioeconomic Factors on Middle Age Mortality in Rural Bangladesh," *Journal of Epidemiology and Community Health* 58, no. 4 (2004): 315–320; M. M. Hidajat, M. D. Hayward, and Y. Saito, "Indonesia's Social Capacity for Population Health: The Educational Gap in Active Life Expectancy," *Population Research and Policy Review* 26, no. 2 (2007): 219–234; W. Groot and H. M. van den Brink , "Measuring the Effects of Education on Health and Civic Engagement: 4a. What Does Education Do to Our Health?," in *Measuring the Social Outcomes of Learning* (Copenhagen: OECD, 2006), 355–363; Y.-H. Khang, J. W. Lynch, and G. A. Kaplan, "Health Inequalities in Korea: Age- and Sex-Specific Educational Differences in the 10 Leading Causes of Death," *International Journal of Epidemiology* 33, no. 2 (2004): 299–308.

23. In the OECD member countries, for example, men who did not complete secondary school are more than twice as likely to be unemployed as men who graduated with a secondary education, and similar results have been documented among women. OECD, *Education at a Glance 2008: OECD Indicators* (Paris: OECD, 2008). In low- and middle-income countries, there is a similar positive relationship between education and labor-market outcomes in unemployment and underemployment. UNESCO Institute for Statistics and Organisation for Economic Co-operation and Development, *Education Trends in Perspective— Analysis of the World Education Indicators* (Paris: UIS/OECD, 2005). Education can also address opportunity gaps between men and women. A study of 10 low- and middle-income countries showed that although the employment rates of men with no schooling and men with a primary-level education are approximately 40 percentage points higher than those of women with the same educational attainment, the gap is reduced to 28 percentage points between men and women with an upper secondary education and shrinks even further at the postsecondary level. UNESCO Institute for Statistics and Organisation for Economic

Co-operation and Development, *Financing Education: Investments and Returns* (Paris: UIS/OECD, 2002). Similar results have been documented in the OECD (OECD, *Education at a Glance 2008*). As well as leading to better employment outcomes, higher levels of education improve income in high- and low-income countries alike. O. Ashenfelter and A. B. Krueger, "Estimates of the Economic Return to Schooling from a New Sample of Twins," *American Economic Review* 84, no. 5 (1994): 1157–1173; O. Ashenfelter and C. Rouse, "Income, Schooling, and Ability: Evidence from a New Sample of Identical Twins," *Quarterly Journal of Economics* 113, no. 1 (1998): 253–284; UNESCO Institute for Statistics and OECD, *Financing Education;* E. A. Hanushek and L. Wößmann, *Education Quality and Economic Growth* (Washington, D.C.: World Bank, 2007); E. A. Jamison, D. T. Jamison, and E. A. Hanushek, "The Effects of Education Quality on Income Growth and Mortality Decline," *Economics of Education Review* 26, no. 6 (2007): 771–788.

24. UNICEF and World Health Organization, *Pneumonia: The Forgotten Killer of Children* (New York and Geneva: UNICEF and WHO, 2006).

25. World Health Organization and UNICEF, *World Report on Child Injury Prevention* (Geneva: World Health Organization, 2008).

26. "NGO Helps End Child Soldier Hire in Nepal," *Hindustan Times,* 16 December 2005; "Case Filed against Nepal's Child Soldier Recruitment Policy," *Hindustan Times,* 24 June 2005; "Supreme Court Bars Under-Age Recruitment in Nepal," *Xinhua News Agency,* 16 December 2005.

27. "Shi'i Family Law Needs to Abide by Constitution, Universal Values— Afghan Daily," *BBC Monitoring South Asia,* 10 April 2009; J. Boone, "'Worse than the Taliban'—New Law Rolls Back Rights for Afghan Women," *Guardian,* 31 March 2009; "Afghan Ministers, Rights Activists Oppose Women Rights Violations under New Law," *BBC Monitoring South Asia,* 9 April 2009; "Afghan Civil, Rights Organizations Call for Review of Law on Women," *BBC Monitoring South Asia,* 7 April 2009; T. Coghlan, "The Bravest Women in Kabul: Protesters March against Sex Slavery Law," *Times,* 16 April 2009; A. Gopal, "Afghanistan's Controversial Law Emboldens Women's Rights Activists," *Christian Science Monitor,* 16 April 2009; A. Hodge, "Karzai Risks Wrath of West over Shia Law," *Australian,* 19 August 2009; J. Page, "Karzai Approves 'Marital Rape' Law; West Split over Response to 'No Sex, No Food' Legislation," *Times,* 17 August 2009; R. Reid, "Speak Out for Women's Rights," *Canberra Times,* 20 August 2009.

28. L. Vanhala, "Twenty-five Years of Disability Equality? Interpreting Disability Rights in the Supreme Court of Canada," *Common Law World Review* 39 (2010): 27–47.

29. United Nations Summit, High-Level Plenary Meeting of the General Assembly, "Goal 1: Eradicate Extreme Poverty and Hunger," New York, 20–22 September 2010, available at http://www.un.org/millenniumgoals/pdf/MDG _FS_1_EN.pdf (accessed 20 June 2012).

30. Organisation for Economic Co-operation and Development, "Table 1: DAC Members' Net Official Development Assistance in 2009," in *Statistics on Resource Flows to Developing Countries,* available at http://www.oecd.org/document /9/0,3746,en_2649_34447_1893129_1_1_1,00.html (accessed 11 May 2011).

31. Polls show that Americans believe that the government spends about 20 percent of its budget on foreign aid; in reality, the figure is about 1 percent. W. R. Cline and J. Williamson, "Chapter 13: Fostering Development," in C. F. Berg-

sten, ed., *The United States and the World Economy* (Washington, D.C.: Institute for International Economics, 2005), 409–427.

32. MomsRising, "About MomsRising," available at http://www.momsrising.org /page/moms/aboutmomsrising (accessed 29 February 2012); A. H. Fine, *Momentum: Igniting Social Change in the Connected Age* (San Francisco: Jossey-Bass, 2006); K. Jesella, "Mom's Mad. And She's Organized," *New York Times*, February 22, 2007.

33. J. Heymann and M. Barrera, *Profit at the Bottom of the Ladder: Creating Value by Investing in Your Workforce* (Boston: Harvard Business Press, 2010).

34. Marginal-cost pricing refers to setting the price of a product as the additional cost of producing a unit of output, which is usually less than the average price, and also includes fixed costs of production. P. J. Hammer, "Differential Pricing of Essential AIDS Drugs: Markets, Politics and Public Health," *Journal of International Economic Law* 5, no. 4 (2002): 883–912; World Health Organization, "More Equitable Pricing for Essential Drugs: What Do We Mean and What Are the Issues?" (background paper for the WHO-WTO Secretariat workshop on differential pricing and financing of essential drugs, Hosbjor, Norway, 8–11 April 2001); P. Yadav, "Differential Pricing for Pharmaceuticals: Review of Current Knowledge, New Findings and Ideas for Action" (study conducted for the U.K. Department for International Development, August 2010).

Appendix 1

1. UNESCO's World Data on Education is available at http://www.ibe .unesco.org/en/services/online-materials/world-data-on-education.html (accessed 19 March 2012).

2. Country reports for the 48th International Conference on Education (Geneva, 25–28 November 2008) are available at http://www.ibe.unesco.org/en /ice/48th-ice-2008/national-reports.html (accessed 19 March 2012).

3. Planipolis is available at http://planipolis.iiep.unesco.org/basic_search .php (accessed 19 March 2012).

4. The Millennium Development Goals Reports are available at http://www .un.org/millenniumgoals/reports.shtml (accessed 15 June 2012). The Education for All Mid-Decade Assessment Reports are available through Planipolis.

5. Eurydice is available at http://eacea.ec.europa.eu/education/eurydice /index_en.php (accessed 19 March 2012).

6. World Bank, *Financing Higher Education in Africa* (Washington, D.C.: World Bank, 2010).

7. K. Tomasevski, *The State of the Right to Education Worldwide—Free or Fee: 2006 Global Report* (Copenhagen: UN Special Rapporteur on the Right to Education, 2006).

8. NATLEX is available at http://natlex.ilo.org (accessed 16 March 2012).

9. The Foreign Law Guide is available at http://www.foreignlawguide.com (accessed 19 March 2012).

10. The World Legal Information Institute is available at http://www.worldlii .org/catalog/215.html (accessed 19 March 2012).

11. The Global Legal Information Network is available at http://www.glin .gov/search.action (accessed 19 March 2012).

12. Lexadin is available at http://www.lexadin.nl/wlg/legis/nofr/legis.php (accessed 19 March 2012).

13. GlobaLex is available at http://www.nyulawglobal.com/globalex/index .html?open=FLR (accessed 19 March 2012).

14. The Pacific Islands Legal Information Institute is available at http://www .paclii.org (accessed 19 March 2012).

15. The Commonwealth Legal Information Institute is available at http://www .commonlii.org (accessed 19 March 2012).

16. International Labour Organization, "Recommendation 190: Recommendation Concerning the Prohibition and Immediate Action for the Elimination of the Worst Forms of Child Labour," available at http://www.ilo.org/public/en glish/standards/relm/ilc/ilc87/com-chir.htm (accessed 12 March 2012).

17. Reports to the Committee on the Rights of the Child are available at http://www2.ohchr.org/english/bodies/crc/sessions.htm. Reports to the Committee on the Elimination of Discrimination against Women are available at http://www.un.org/womenwatch/daw/cedaw/reports.htm (accessed 16 March 2012).

18. Lexadin is available at http://www.lexadin.nl/wlg/legis/nofr/legis.php (accessed 19 March 2012).

19. The Foreign Law Guide is available at http://www.foreignlawguide.com (accessed 19 March 2012).

20. The Emory Law Legal Profiles are available at http://www.law.emory.edu /ifl/legal (accessed 19 March 2012).

21. The *Guide pratique international de l'état civil* is available at http://www .ciecl.org/GuidePratique/index.htm (accessed 19 March 2012).

22. The Legislation of INTERPOL Member States on Sexual Offences against Children compendium of laws is available at https://www.interpol.int/Public/Chil dren/SexualAbuse/NationalLaws/Default.asp (accessed 16 March 2012).

23. NATLEX is available at http://natlex.ilo.org (accessed 16 March 2012).

24. The Doing Business Law Library is available at http://www.doingbusi ness.org/law-library (accessed 19 March 2012).

25. Lexadin is available at http://www.lexadin.nl/wlg/legis/nofr/legis.php (accessed 19 March 2012).

26. The World Legal Information Institute is available at http://www.worldlii .org/catalog/215.html (accessed 19 March 2012).

27. The Social Security Programs Throughout the World reports are available at http://www.ssa.gov/policy/docs/progdesc/ssptw (accessed 19 March 2012).

28. The Council of Europe Family Policy Database is available at http://www .coe.int/t/dg3/familypolicy/database/default_en.asp (accessed 16 March 2012).

29. The International Review of Leave Policies and Related Research is available at http://www.leavenetwork.org/ (accessed 16 March 2012).

30. The Maternity Protection Database and the Working Time Database are available at http://www.ilo.org/dyn/travail/travmain.home (accessed 16 March 2012).

31. The World Alliance for Breastfeeding Action's website is available at http://www.waba.org.my (accessed 16 March 2012).

32. UN Department of Economic and Social Affairs, *The World's Women 2005* (New York: United Nations, 2006) is available at http://unstats.un.org/unsd /demographic/products/indwm/wwpub.htm (accessed 16 March 2012).

33. When we were examining equal rights, we had access to all the world's constitutions. However, constitutional law, more than any other kind of law, comes alive through its interpretation in the courts. We were not able to examine case law around the world. The amount of information that would need to be analyzed and reviewed would dwarf that of any other set of policies and laws we undertook to gather. Although we did not have the resources to do this, it will be important to understand more fully the extent to which equal rights are protected in different countries. A consortium of constitutional lawyers from around the world could systematically achieve this.

34. NATLEX is available at http://natlex.ilo.org (accessed 16 March 2012).

35. The Social Security Programs Throughout the World reports are available at http://www.ssa.gov/policy/docs/progdesc/ssptw (accessed 19 March 2012).

36. The European Union's Mutual Information System on Social Protection is available at http://ec.europa.eu/social/main.jsp?catId=815&langId=en (accessed 15 June 2012).

37. The Mutual Information System on Social Protection of the Council of Europe is available at http://www.socialcohesion.coe.int/MISSCEO/ (accessed 15 June 2012).

38. The TRAVAIL database is available at http://www.ilo.org/dyn/travail/travmain.home (accessed 16 March 2012).

39. The U.S. Department of State's Human Rights Reports are available at http://www.state.gov/j/drl/rls/hrrpt (accessed 16 March 2012).

Acknowledgments

Every book has a story about how it came into being, and *Children's Chances* is no different. Its roots lie in an idea I had a decade ago to build a global data center that would examine laws and policies in every country around the world that shape the extent to which children and adults have equal opportunities; its fruition has been a remarkable team effort. With the generous support of the Canada Foundation for Innovation, the Canada Research Chairs program, the Canadian Institutes of Health Research, and McGill University, I have been extraordinarily fortunate to work with an exceptional team of dedicated researchers in creating the World Policy Analysis Centre, an initiative dedicated to increasing information on countries' ability to support population health, education, equity, and economic well-being. From its beginning, staff members working on the World Policy Analysis Centre have brought an extraordinary depth of commitment, constant questioning, and a yearning to get the answers as close to right as we could. The first phase of this initiative at Harvard was fundamentally shaped by Alison Earle, who helped me lead a team of talented young researchers in examining adult labor and family policies in 190 countries. This team included Stephanie Breslow, Aron Fischer, Francisco Flores, Lola Kassim, April Kuehnhoff, and Stephanie Simmons. At McGill, first Jeff Hayes and then Amy Raub and Ilona Vincent helped me lead a growing team of researchers who analyzed a far wider range of policies. The work carried out at the Institute for Health and Social Policy at McGill has greatly benefited from the indispensable work and analytical abilities of Efe Atabay, Kip Brown, Adèle Cassola, Nicolás De Guzmán Chorny, Danielle Foley, Amanda Grittner, Gabriella Kranz, Brittany Lambert, Adam Mahon, José Mauricio Mendoza, María Claudia Orjuela Laverde, and Ceyda Turan, as well as David Baumann, Samantha Berger, Ebony Bertorelli, Aneel Brar, Chelsea Clogg, Stephanie Coen, Chris Connolly, Mark Daku, Carrie Dickenson, Giulia El-Dardiry, Mehreen Farooq, Jad Itani, May-Ling Joa Ricart, Molly Krishtalka, Sophie MacIntyre, Erin Rogers, Anna Shea, and Tyler Wilson.

Several years into the project, I decided to dedicate time to shaping a book that cut across policy areas relevant to children. It was clear that to write this book, it would be critical to frame our new policy findings within the literature to date on the key issues affecting children globally and on policy effectiveness. Staff members—including Magda Barrera, Samantha Berger, Denise Maines, Gonzalo Moreno, and Parama Sigurdsen—did an exceptional job of filling in essential knowledge gaps. The work of students at McGill who carried out extensive global literature reviews was invaluable, including Aditya Badami, Elisheva Bouskila, Talia Bronstein, Zachary Burk, Brittany Carson, Jessica Drohan, Joshua Green, May-Ling Joa Ricart, Alexandra Lesnikowski, Xiaoyang Luo, Adele Meyer, Robert Pastore, Elizabeth Punnett, Niharika Singh, Lindsay Wright, and Andy Yu. Lipi Mishra reviewed the statistical details of many of the key studies.

I was extraordinarily lucky when I began work on this book to have Kristen McNeill join our team. Initially, Kristen focused on bringing together the literature for this project, but she grew interested in helping write the book. A gifted writer, intellectually probing, and combining remarkable persistence and patience in pursuing details, Kristen brought the benefit of an outsider's fresh eyes to the policy research. The book never would have happened in its current form without her and the opportunity we shared to write the book together, going back and forth many times over details, arguments, and global approaches.

This book was made possible not only by the foundations laid by the World Policy Analysis Centre team, but also by the contributions of institute team members to the book itself. Amy Raub created the maps and tables that are so integral to this work, and her thoughtful and analytic contributions shaped the data that were included and the way they are presented. Adèle Cassola, in addition to managing the development of the particularly complex Constitutions Database within the World Policy Analysis Centre, did an exceedingly detailed review of the text used in this book's tables and provided comments on the entire text. Denise Maines's attention to detail, capacity to prioritize and multitask, and efficient research skills were indispensable in the final stages of revising the book. None of us would have been able to do our jobs half as well if the Institute for Health and Social Policy had not been managed exceptionally effectively by Erin Bresnahan.

I presented the maps and findings in this book at a wide range of forums while I was writing it. These included, among others, a meeting of over 2,000 educators from over 100 countries, a meeting of 2,500 community organizers focused on equity, private- and public-sector leaders attending the World Economic Forum in Davos, meetings at UNICEF and UNESCO, and a series of academic meetings. I am deeply grateful for the time people spent at each meeting to offer suggestions and critiques. The work is far richer because of the input of youth themselves, adults in a wide range of fields who work with children and youth, and leaders in the public and private sectors who both shape the conditions children and their families face and benefit or lose from the results. Our community collaborations were enriched at every stage through the wisdom and energy of Jennifer Proudfoot.

To carry out this work, I needed to find time to write and carry out research while leading the institute. Mentors and colleagues gave immense support in the whether, why, and how of this both before I began to lead the institute and throughout my time here. I am deeply grateful for all the different kinds of support—intellectual, moral, and practical—I received during this work from Larry Aber, Paul Allison, Heather Munroe Blum, Harvey Fineberg, John Frank, Abe Fuks, Rose Goldstein, Clyde Hertzman, Rich Levin, Chris Manfredi, Tony Masi, Gilles Paradis, Arnold Steinberg, Denis Therien, Nico Trocme, and Paul Wise.

Families shape children's lives from infancy through youth and adulthood. This is as true for each of us as it is for the children in *Children's Chances*. From talking about public policy around the kitchen table before primary school began to being a lasting source of support, humor, and perspective, my parents and brother made this work possible from the start. From discussing the details of how research evidence can be effectively employed to address major problems to biking around the Island of Montreal, Tim has made this work better and life far richer in countless ways even with the schedule that the research and writing required. When it comes to learning about children, youth, and life, as for many parents, my own children have taught me many of the most important and unforgettable lessons; Ben and Jeremy, I hope we continue to learn together for many decades to come.

—JH

I became a part of *Children's Chances* very early in the writing phase but very late in the data phase. Coming into this project, I had a limited understanding of the enormous amount of data that the Institute for Health and Social Policy has put together. The learning curve that was necessary was made much more manageable by the leaders and members of the World Policy Analysis Centre, who were so generous with their time in explaining to me the intricacies of the databases they know so well and in answering the many questions that came up along the way. I once promised Amy that she would be acknowledged with a word for every map that was made in preparation for this book. However, that would involve writing an entire chapter's worth of text, which she deserves but which space does not permit. As managing coordinator of the World Policy Analysis Centre, Amy's deep engagement through hours of meetings with Jody and me and countless iterations of data presentation, as well as her endless patience for my never-ending questions, were truly extraordinary. Special thanks also to Adèle, Adam, Ilona, and Brittany, who, as well as managing individual databases, were deeply involved in the selection of the data included in this book. The amount of work put into the World Policy Analysis Centre by them and by Danielle, Efe, Nicolás, José, Kip, and Gabriella to meet the tight deadlines linked to this book's preparation was enormous, and their grace and good humour during this time were hugely appreciated. As well, the final stages of this book would never have been pulled off on time without Denise's amazing help with verifying a million details and finding the answers to dozens of questions.

I cannot thank Jody enough for giving me the opportunity to be involved in this incredibly rewarding project. Throughout this process, as well as the several years that I have been involved at the Institute for Health and Social Policy, she has always been an amazing teacher. Thanks also to the friends at work and elsewhere who keep me laughing and maintain my sanity (mostly) intact. Finally, a million thanks to my parents, who have been there for every chance taken in my childhood and adulthood, and whose brainstorming session over tea gave us the jump start we needed to give this book a name.

—KM

Index

Note: Page numbers followed by *f* and *t* indicate figures and tables.